HINDUTVA AS POLITICAL MONOTHEISM

ANUSTUP BASU

HINDUTVA
AS POLITICAL MONOTHEISM

DUKE UNIVERSITY PRESS   DURHAM AND LONDON   2020

© 2020 Duke University Press
All rights reserved
Text design by Aime C. Harrison
Cover design by Courtney Richardson
Typeset in Whitman and Knockout by Westchester Publishing Services

Library of Congress Cataloging-in-Publication Data
Names: Basu, Anustup, author.
Title: Hindutva as political monotheism / Anustup Basu.
Description: Durham : Duke University Press, 2020. | Includes bibliographical references and index.
Identifiers: LCCN 2019058225 (print) | LCCN 2019058226 (ebook) ISBN 9781478009887 (hardcover)
ISBN 9781478010944 (paperback)
ISBN 9781478012498 (ebook)
Subjects: LCSH: Hindutva—India. | Hinduism and politics—India. | Nationalism—Religious aspects—Hinduism. | Religion and politics—India.
Classification: LCC BL1215.P65 B367 2020 (print) | LCC BL1215.P65 (ebook) | DDC 294.5/1720954—dc23
LC record available at https:// lccn.loc.gov/2019058225
LC ebook record available at https:// lccn.loc.gov/2019058226

Cover art: Text from *Thoughts on Some Current Problems*, M. S. Golwaker, 1957

For Monu and Ritwik, with love

CONTENTS

Acknowledgments ix

Introduction 1

1 Questions Concerning the Hindu Political 11

2 The Hindu Nation as Organism 28

3 The Indian Monotheism 89

4 Hindutva 2.0 as Advertised Monotheism 150

Notes 209
Bibliography 251
Index 269

ACKNOWLEDGMENTS

For their help and advice, I would like to thank Pallavi Banerjee, Manisha Basu, Rashmi Bhatnagar, Moinak Biswas, Kalyan Kumar Das, Mohan J. Dutta, Ayan Gangyopadhyay, Pujita Guha, Istvan Keul, Bodhisattva Maity, Feisal G. Mohamed, Urvi Mukhopadhyay, Aswin Punathambekar, Michael Rothberg, Satadru Sen, Pratim Sengupta, Kirsten Strayer, Anastasia Ulanowicz, and the three anonymous reviewers of Duke University Press. I am indebted to Paul Bové, Aamir Mufti, Ronald A. T. Judy, Bruce Robbins, and other members of the *boundary 2* collective for providing the initial spark that resulted in the two essays that laid the groundwork for the larger project. Lauren Goodlad and Eleni Coundouriotis inspired another section that was published in *Journal of Human Rights*. I would like to thank audiences at UCLA, the University of Bergen, and the Center for Studies in Social Sciences, Kolkata, among other places, for their thoughtful responses to the talks that emerged from this study. Along with my colleagues in the English department, I am thankful to Susan Koshy and the Unit for Criticism at the University of Illinois for supporting this project. My graduate students over the years, especially Gautam Basu-Thakur, Debojoy Chanda, Reshmi Mukherjee, Debayudh Chatterjee, Ryan Sherwood, and participants of recently taught seminars, have stimulated my thinking. I am deeply thankful to Sandra Korn, editor at Duke University Press, for her patience and insightful advice.

Sibaji Bandyopadhyay's monumental scholarship and intellectual presence have been central, not just to the genesis of this book but to my life of the mind in itself. I remain eternally grateful to Marcia Landy, who, more than anyone else, taught me how to think about fascism.

I thank Manisha and Ritwik for all the love; Charlie, Ruger, and the dear departed Ozzie for being the leaders of the *Canis familiaris* front against authoritarian power.

INTRODUCTION

In the beginning of *Why I Am Not a Hindu*—a passionate and insightful "Sudra critique of Hindutva philosophy, culture, and political economy"—the intellectual and Dalitbahujan activist Kancha Ilaiah writes about a moment when he faced a vexing problem of identity. Born and raised in a small village in Telengana, Ilaiah hailed from the Kurumaa (shepherd) caste. It was only around 1990, when he was ending the fourth decade of his life, that he found himself in a new existential quandary. All of a sudden, the word *Hindutva* was being bandied around with fierce intensity, and the entire cultural machinery of the urban middle classes was insisting that he announce himself a Hindu. Refusing to do so would result in social castigation and a generally vitiated atmosphere. Ilaiah writes eloquently about why this was a nuisance:

> The question is, What do we, the lower Sudras and Ati-Sudras (whom I also call Dalitbahujans) have to do with Hindus or with Hindutva itself? I, indeed, not only I, but all of us, the Dalitbahujans of India, have never heard the word "Hindu," not as a word, nor as the name of a culture, nor as the name of a religion in our early childhood days. We heard about Turukoollu (Muslims), we heard about Kirastaanapoollu (Christians), we heard about Baapanoollu (Brahmins) and Koomatoollu (Baniyas) spoken of as people different from us. Among these four categories, the most different were the Baapanoollu and the Koomatoollu. There are at least some aspects of life common to us and the Turukoollu and the Kirastaanapoollu. We all eat meat, we all touch each other. With the Turukoollu we shared several other cultural relations. We both celebrated the Peerila festival. Many Turukoollu came with us to the fields. The only people with whom we had no relations, whatsoever, were the Baapanoollu and the Koomatoollu.[1]

Ilaiah's countermemory is a candid mapping of childhood instincts, familiarities, and identities. The "shock" of adulthood, for him, was being told that he had to now politically and culturally congregate with the Baapanoollu and the Koomatoollu and zealously distance himself from others. This was after some alienating school years in between, spent with Telugu textbooks that extolled unfamiliar Hindu gods like Vishnu or Durga, leaving out the ones he had grown up with: Pochamma who delivers from smallpox, Kattamaisamma who grants rain, or Potaraju who protects crops from thieves. It was thus an autobiographical journey that compressed profound historical questions of more than a century of nation and state thinking in the subcontinent, as well as its complex pendulations of identity. Ilaiah, from his own vantage point, felt that he was being coerced into joining a national majoritarian community that he, and people like him, never belonged to, in terms of piety or way of life. Later, he justifies the title of his book with a pithy and incisive sentence: "I was not born a Hindu for the simple reason that my parents did not know that they were Hindus."[2]

This powerful note of dissent points to the impasses in the way of what I will elaborate as a majoritarian quest for a modern Hindu political monotheism. If indeed the Dalitbahujans—an umbrella group in which Ilaiah includes the Scheduled Castes (SCs), Other Backward Castes (OBCs), and Scheduled Tribes (STs)—did not, in essence, consider themselves "Hindus," then the purported majoritarian specter of Hindutva would shrink to the sound and fury of a Savarna (upper caste) segment of the Baapanoollu and Koomatoollu that made up just about a quarter of the Indian population.[3] That too, with innumerable divisions among the Savarna groups themselves along the lines of class, culture, region, and language. The modern project of a Hindu political monotheism has been to induct the privileged and the pariah into a universal, congregational plane of Hindu identity. The question that Ilaiah, in effect, poses is whether the whole thing is simply a Brahminical minority's historical masquerade as a Hindu majority.

The book I present here is a long genealogy of Hindutva, culminating in a critical understanding of a mediatic and urban Hindu normative that has come into being in our times. It is not a presentist elaboration of what we are witnessing now, but a deep search of its historical origins. A good part of the recent story is, of course, quite well known. There has been the consolidation of a new techno-financial Hindu nationalist ideology with strong overseas connections over the last three decades, beginning, roughly in the early 1990s, with the globalization of the Indian economy, the rapid expansion of the electronic public sphere, and accelerated urbanization. The process gathered strength in the aftermath of the mass movement leading up to the destruction of Babri Masjid in 1992, periodic communal riots that gradually took the form of institutionalized genocide, the border war with Pakistan in 1999, an increasingly volatile Kashmir, intermittent events of cross-border terror, and a global swell of Islamophobic sentiments after 9/11. This unfolding scenario birthed a new, muscular Hindu chauvinism with growing pan-Indian populist traction. The new version is one that is for a good part more urbane, tech-finance friendly, and different from older agrarian-conservative models. The political rise of this Hindu right culminated in the ascension of the Hindu nationalist Bharatiya Janata Party (BJP) under Narendra Modi, when the party came to power in the Indian General Elections of 2014 with an overwhelming mandate.

But then, there is that other consideration: To what extent may this recent story of majoritarian insurrection in India be confined to the internal, long gestation of Hindutva, roughly from the 1920s? Or is it part of a wider planetary phenomenon, of people turning to default nativist positions, anti-immigrant sentiment, and xenophobia, prompted by a globalization of precarity, suspicion, and fear in the era of new media and finance capital? This book is a genealogy of Hindutva as political monotheism in relation to the colonial epistemological invention of "Hinduism," the broader arc of Indian modernity itself, and India's own constitutional revolution of 1950. At a secondary level, it ultimately aims to place the present Hindu ascension in a wider basin of global unrest, liberal crisis, and the rise of untimely chauvinisms like monarchism in Jair Bolsonaro's Brazil or neo-Ottomanism in Recep Tayyip Erdoğan's Turkey. That is, not to mention the first-world theaters: the return of a Jacksonist "Know Nothing" nativism in Donald Trump's United States, or the ominous spread of neo-Nazi politics in Austria and Germany.

Hindutva as Political Monotheism looks at the long genesis of Hindu political identity and nationalism through a hitherto underused but critically important prism. I begin by visiting the works of the Nazi jurist Carl Schmitt to draw out a tacit monotheistic imperative in European organic theories of religious and ethnocentric nationhood. Seen from that vantage point, the "oriental solution" would be that, in order for there to be a Hindu nation and a Hindu state, there had to be a Hindu monotheism. There had to be an axiomatic Church and a sense of Hindu laity that could then be parlayed into the political construction of a national *fraternité*. This was not just a question of affirming faith in one God (there have always been strong monistic currents in the Vedic tradition and many theistic ones in the devotional Bhakti movements), but a religiosity with a strong eschatology and providential destinying. The tendency to impart an Abrahamic cast to a vast, eclectic field of polytheistic, pantheistic, henotheistic, or atheistic forms of Indic piety can be traced as a consistent feature in the modern invention of the Hindu as a religious and eventually jealous political identity. In nationalistic discourse, it meant finding a pan-Indian congregational principle to subsume long-standing caste divisions, regional eccentricities, gender segregations, and practices of untouchability. In terms of political theology, it meant compacting a pantheon of 330 million gods into axiomatic Hindu icons like Rama or Krishna, absorbing errant, syncretic pieties, and picturing a singular Hindu telos. Finally the project had to make this Hindu template politically indistinguishable from an "Indian" one. The consummation, devoutly wished for, would then consolidate the nation as an organic unity, making the profane federalism of the Constitutional Republic obsolete. I trace the genesis and progression of this quest for a Hindu "political monotheism" as a literary and culturalist project during the nineteenth and twentieth centuries and eventually suggest that, in our times, it has been largely replaced by an advertised and informational Indian experience of urban normativity that some have called "Hindutva 2.0."

Chapter 1, "Questions Concerning the Hindu Political," connects Carl Schmitt's concept of political theology with some traditional notions of Hindu sovereignty and nationhood. I argue that the religious urge that defines the "political" for Schmitt—that "all significant concepts of the modern theory of the state are secularized theological concepts"—is necessarily an austere and monotheistic one.[4] In order to have a majoritarian "Hindu India"—one that is an organic and religious whole rather than a contractual federation—one would need an "Indian monotheism" that was normatively Hindu. This may be marked, within the parameters of Schmitt's organismic logic, as an imperative for any people who want to emerge as a political entity deserving and capable of sovereign assertion. In polytheistic and polyphonic cultures of the global South, this was actually a tacit condition that the framework of colonial modernity imposed when it came to engaging with the modern state, nation-thinking, and political representation. In the case of India, the imperative came with the Indological apparatus and its nineteenth-century geopolitical invention of "India" and its traditions, along with the demographic and juridical marking of a Hindu people. This question of compelling political monotheism, to this day, determines the revivalist strong state/strong economy Hindu model in the epoch of globalization. The invocation of Schmitt, apart from the prima facie fascist connection, is justified because, as I will demonstrate more fully, Hindutva as an ideology is almost entirely orientalist in its roots. Historically, as we know, the Hindu project has been a double-edged sword. On the one hand, it has birthed and generalized a puritan desire for a jealous majoritarian unity. On the other, it has faced considerable problems in its attempts to gather a multitude of faith traditions into a singular axiomatic of statist religiosity. I use the term *axiomatic* throughout this study as a singular religious passion that does not necessarily depend on theological consistency. The axiomatic, in this sense, is thus more of a techno-social regime of governmentality than simply a theologico-pastoral formation. I draw the idea for the most part from William Connolly's work on the American evangelical-capitalist resonance machine ("Cowboy Capitalism"): "An axiomatic . . . is a set of institutional knots with dense tangles and loose ends." It is not a static edifice of faith, but one that "twists and turns through time as it absorbs the shocks and additions created by previously exogenous forces." These exogenous forces include mutations in enemy axiomatics like Islam.[5]

In chapter 2, "The Hindu Nation as Organism," I point out some key bottlenecks in Hindu nation-thinking that followed the imperative of political monotheism, both in a Brahminical theocratic vein of imagining sacred territory, as well as in terms of a Hindu brand of ethnocultural nationalism. Here I talk about the twentieth-century discourse of Hindutva that, for the most part, operated with a set of Herderian pieties that never coalesced into a constitutive "whole" in terms of territory, identity, language, memory, and other crucial matters. Cultivating a unified Hindu theology for a monothematic religious passion and inventing a concomitant organismic nationhood were obviously very complicated missions in the essentially pluralistic civilizational complex of the subcontinent. It was perhaps because of this that Hindutva nationalism from the 1920s took a different route from earlier nineteenth-century regional reform organizations like the Brahmo Samaj or the Arya Samaj. The ideology of Hindutva sought a unifying ethnocultural consistency rather than a theological unity.[6] Such a development would be fine for the Schmittian model, which seeks a monotheme of religiosity rather than religion itself; and this persuasive principle could be based on race, culturalism, or ideology. The "political," as secular religiosity, had to simply present a captivating principle of martyrdom for a cause greater than the individual's own salvation. Similarly, in the discourse of Hindutva, there could be no artificial distinctions between religion, ideology, and culture; and, after a process of torrid political abstraction, there had to be only one "way of life" for the nation.

I examine the works of the philosopher Bimal Krishna Matilal (1935–1991) to glimpse the breathtaking range of Indic "little traditions" of faith, memory, and poesis that an axiomatic Hindu Tradition would seek to engulf or extinguish. The little traditions were and continue to be based on eccentric vernacular appropriations of the great epics, imaginaries clustering around local saints, deities, or pilgrimage spots, and often on a primary disavowal of a Brahminical cosmology based on the Vedas. It was this mélange of pieties that the purported Hindu political monotheism had to violently append to itself or abolish. While the Abrahamic religions themselves have had numerous heretical traditions, the difference in the case of the historical Hindu faith complex was that no presiding ontological framework or instituted church existed, at the end of the day, to demand filiation to a singular theistic principle. This was a void that twentieth-century Hindu nationalist missions hoped to fill.

Hindutva was consolidated with the coming into being of Hindu organizations like the Rashtriya Swayamsevak Sangh (RSS; National Volunteer Service), political parties like the Hindu Mahasabha and the Jan Sangh, and, eventually, ecumenical formations like the Vishwa Hindu Parishad (World Hindu Council) that looked to establish a ministry with clearly defined political, pedagogic, and pastoral missions.[7] I explore this project as a literary-cultural enterprise in the writings of Hindu right-wing ideologues like Vinayak Damodar Savarkar (1883–1966) and Madhav Sadashiv Golwalkar (1906–1973), visiting especially the points of bipolar tension: the squaring of a Hindu homogeneity with the hierarchies of caste; the utopian restoration of a greater India (Akhand Bharat) with the geopolitical realities of partition; Hindu mythology with Indian history; the particularities of faith with the universals of science; the "Aryan" inheritance of the North with the Dravidian identities of the South; axiomatic icons like Rama with millions of gods; or a desired Sanskritization of culture with myriad vernacular countercurrents. Within the purported "Tradition" itself, there were many subsurface tensions that had to be resolved or mystified at every step. The political quest here was for a unified and jealous religiosity, marking the many-armed, eclectic traditions of subcontinental Islam as a competing monotheism. This was an originary polarization that, in the fullness of time, would birth a nation or two.

This twentieth-century vision of a Hindu India may be better illuminated by wrapping it in a temporal double bind. It has to be viewed in the light of its discursive antecedents, in terms of the broader nineteenth-century Indological identification of "Hinduism" and the discourses of Hindu reform, Hindu anthropology, jurisprudence, and history. And then it also must be seen from the other end, in terms of millennial mutations in the era of information and globalization. I therefore go further back in time in chapter 3, "The Indian Monotheism." It elaborates the quest for an axiomatic Hindu "religion," a historical sense of being, and a matching template for nationalism, revision, modernity, and secularism as a wider literary-theological project in the nineteenth and early twentieth centuries. This axiomatic tended to assume the shape of a "monotheism" that was quintessentially Indian, as opposed to foreign imports like Islam or Christianity. Its early articulations followed the path of universal religion (or natural religion, as some of its Western interlocutors would say) and then gradually acquired jealous properties with the birth of nationalist discourses in the final quarter of the nineteenth century. Here I discuss the works of Raja Rammohun Roy (1774–1833), Bankimchandra Chattopadhyay (1838–1894), Sarvepalli Radhakrishnan (1888–1975), and M. K. Gandhi (1868–1948). The broader project was usually fronted by the abstraction of a neo-Vedantic monism—the Brahman as One—in relation to which the massive spread of Hindu polytheism, idolatry, and mythology had to be understood as allegorical approximations of a singular calling. This dispensation called for the elevation of the Bhagwad Gita as the Holy Book of the Hindu people, marked Manusmriti as Hindu Law, and cast figures like Rama or Krishna as Hindu ideals who offered greater prophetic revelations than Christ or the Buddha. The prime articulators of this modern Hinduism and of reform addressed the matter of caste variously: as scientific labor management, as original principle of communal and race harmony perverted by Islamic colonization, or as nonhereditary meritocracy. This overall enterprise came with a new time consciousness that challenged the temporal imaginary of progress postulated by a Calvinistic empire of capital.

I bookend this elaboration of a Hindu-normative Indian modernity, nationalism, and the secular with an introductory discussion of G. W. F. Hegel's 1827 reading of the Bhagwad Gita as theodicy, and with a concluding account of the powerful, foundational critique of Hinduism in the works of B. R. Ambedkar (1891–1956). The latter, especially, points to certain endemic features of contradiction and dissonance that haunt this quest for a uniform peopleness. Politically, such questions would continue to resonate over the decades and up to the present. From the vantage point of the Dalitbahujan, was the so-called Hinduism just a cover for Brahminism? Was the One of Advaita a warm universal, or was it cold, Sanskritic, and distant when it came to the vernacular masses? Was there such a thing called Hindu society, or was it just a confederation of castes that came together during communal riots? Could there actually be an axiomatic Hindu theology in the tradition of a Pauline Christianity, or do the scriptures, in the end, offer only a mélange of philosophical speculations inextricably mired in mythology and caste ethics? Did caste segregation and untouchability foreclose the possibility of a Hindu congregation and fraternité? Was a Hindu nation possible without a Hindu equity? My critical exploration of this nineteenth- and early twentieth-century tradition of moderate "reform" is not only intended to discover its secret commerce with the hardline Sangh Parivaar nationalism of a later moment, but also to understand the Savarna-normative nature of the secular Indian nationalist project itself.[8] That is, to see how an implicit principle of caste paternalism and tolerance informs the otherwise admirable Indian experiment in democracy and federalism.

I come to the present after these nonlinear excavations of a layered and weighted past. In the concluding chapter 4, "Hindutva 2.0 as Advertised Monotheism," I argue that, in recent decades, with the ushering-in of an informational world and networks of electronic urbanization, the literary-cultural project of Hindu nationalism has undergone fundamental transformations. Its defining themes and mythologies have been rendered spectral and auratic, no longer dependent on theological justification, literary elaboration, or historical apologies. This ecology comes with media protocols, ritual values, spectacle, and perception management; it involves instant, informational transfers between the past and the present, between science and dogma, and between the home and the world. "Hindutva 2.0," as it has been called, does not in essence seek long-pending, final resolutions for stories of becoming; nor does it present a unified worldview. Instead, it combines obscurantism with smart technophilia, the idea of financialization and progress with atavistic imaginations of time. It becomes an order of resonances rather than a closed book of the world, cutting across formations of mass culture and affect industries like Bollywood, consumerism, pop pieties, or yoga. It has its own modes of Disneyfication and a spectrum of industries from Vaastu, astrology, and herbal medicine to New Religious spiritualism and artful living. It includes Twitter and WhatsApp tribalisms that can create virtual congregations, bypassing caste strictures pertaining to custom, touch, food, and water. I call this new ecology of Hinduness an instance of "advertised modernization," with modernization characterized as a mutating scenario in which "modernity" does not trump "tradition," but in which the two shift to a different threshold of performance and mutual arrangement. "Advertised" is a conceptual shorthand for varied, multidirectional pulsations in an electrified public culture that deliver innocuous "take homes," "feel good" nostrums, and, in some cases, consumable fears without narrative obligation to truth or closure. In its exemplary forms, this urban and advertised sense of Hinduness is incipient and neurological; it is meant to be felt in the pith and marrow of being, between terror and the global sublime.

The ecology creates a metropolitan normal, by which a caste Hindu urban existence becomes the only form of life worth living in a world in which both desire and precarity are democratized. It does so by excluding Islam and other minorities by way of calibrated discriminations, from terror management to segregated details of lived life like culture, language, hygiene, breeding, aesthetics, proprietorship of women, or eating habits. This normal is the bedrock of affectations on which the increasingly strident, organized, right-wing assertions of our times anchor themselves. In other words, RSS-type forces work on such a plane to exert long-pending but decisive majoritarian effects on the polity. However, the plane itself is wider than them, and it tends to define the entire political spectrum itself in terms of soft and hard Hinduness. Among other things, this order, on the one hand, entails a final turn away from the welfare traditions of the Indian state after 1947 and the history of anticolonial nonalignment; on the other, it entails embracing a set of military-industrial alliances with a continuum of metropolitan power stretching from Washington to Tel Aviv.

This isn't to say that there was not a Brahminical bias in the workings of the Indian state and society before this time, but the present electronic version comes devoid of many caste, regional, and cultural accents that once stood in the way of a working politico-religious axiomatic. In recent decades this electronic Hinduness has increased its powers as a psychological parabasis for a majoritarian nation. I draw the term *parabasis* from Gayatri Spivak's work and from its classical meaning in Greek theater: the period of a performance in which the actors leave the stage and the chorus addresses the audience.[9] In other words, I am interested in the historical roots of a relatively recent voice of a wider urban consensus beyond usual suspects such as the ardent disciple of Golwalkar or the angry foot soldier of Modi. It comes from a plane of consistency—in terms of massified common sense, structures of feeling and perception—that seems to bind opponents together even as they disagree on matters like Kashmir, terrorism, corruption, development, or good governance. An insidious convergence of categories affiliated exclusively with a caste Hindu urban male existence seems to increasingly govern such democratic disputes. The idea of the parabasis as a choral unity, therefore, pertains to what Blanchot once called the silent "murmur" of discourse from which contending subjectivities erupt into being.[10] The feature that distinguishes this phenomenon from past forms pertains to the increasing metropolitan revision of regional eccentricities and the fervor for security and techno-financial growth. It is the possibility of a new, augmented dimension of the political in the Schmittian sense, an electronic Hindu political monotheism, if you will, surpassing the old impasses of print capitalism. In studying its long genesis, my objective is not to advance toward a prognostic reading of the present, since the owl of Minerva spreads its wings only with the falling of dusk. My purpose will instead be to explore, with some degree of speculation, the ground of the present.

1 QUESTIONS CONCERNING THE HINDU POLITICAL

Carl Schmitt and Political Monotheism

The relatively recent renaissance of hard-right thinkers of the state—such as Carl Schmitt, Leo Strauss, or Ivan Ilyin—can be, to a certain extent, explained by a general anxiety and introspection about the political legacy of liberalism. That is, a Rawlsian liberalism if you will, drawing a broad line from Locke to the American thinker, along with a parallel, more organic discourse of humanism from Hegel to his American neoliberal disciples like Francis Fukuyama. Including the latter—the formerly passionate and now slightly sober neocon—in that tradition might seem a bit provocative, but it also illustrates a broader problem in the horizon of Western universalism. If Fukuyama's historical monism has been frustrated, the recent wave of ethnocentric bigotry has also imperiled a notion of radical pluralism that Rawls deemed to be a permanent and desirable feature of modern democracies, not just a passing phase prior to assimilation.[1] In the old days, we would perhaps call Fukuyama's position center-right and Rawls's center-left. Not any longer, because a consensual middle ground, even in a dominant North Atlantic sense, can no longer be taken for granted. More than ever, the entire planetary scene has now become the crisis of a so-called centered paradigm of Bretton Woods governmentality that truly came into its own after the Cold War. This center has been muddled by strong currents of skepticism toward IMF/World Bank–style economism, especially after the 2008 crash, the rolling aftermath of the second Gulf War, renewed cultural and ideological wars, as well as by broader religious and ethnocentric assertions in general.[2] We have Lockean liberals and Burkian conservatives on both sides of the Atlantic trying to return to purer ideologies that were eclipsed by the "neoliberal turn," fostered first by the Thatcher–Reagan counterrevolution and then continued by the Clintonian DNC and Blairite Labour. To put it differently, finance capital seems to have decisively shifted its core operations to the right of the normative grounds of liberalism. It has displayed a greater tenacity to delink itself from liberal pieties and assemble forces with authoritarian and overtly plutocratic regimes. The wretched of the earth seem to be responding to that variously.

The malaise pertains to losing grip over temporal imaginations across the world. Liberalism is currently beset by a poverty of hegemonic language, not just in terms of being and becoming, but even when it comes to matters like sustainable development, rights, or climate change. The unease has been increased by protracted military adventures, the financial crisis, outsourcing, automation, increasing government debt, austerity, the eclipse of the welfare state, a destabilizing Middle East, and the Syrian and other refugee problems. Many Westerners, it would seem, have awakened to an intuitive understanding that the American empire, in contrast to those of the past, has birthed global institutions that can, in principle, survive and flourish without the active participation of or benefit for white Americans and their Anglo-Saxon cousins elsewhere. One can be the roadkill of the empire even while being at the junction of all roads in Rome, while possessing Roman entitlements and doing what Romans do. Our times are therefore marked by increasing threats of the mighty United States returning to its pre–World War I isolationism while Britain effects a temperamental, almost distracted exit from the European Union. Western Europe is beset with a range of unflinching nativisms, both of the *jus sanguinis* as well as *jus soli* varieties. Globally, the crisis has unfolded a scene in which authoritarian cultures may merge with the paraphernalia of financialization without cultural liberalization; or in which formally installed democracies may not automatically foster climates of political freedom and tolerance. Developing societies seemingly continue to embrace technology in the fast track without "science" as a holistic horizon of reason. They may adapt themselves to instruments of globalization without absorbing enlightenment values, or revel in information culture without a civil society.

Circumstances seem to have called for a rethink of the manner in which the Nazi jurist Carl Schmitt called the liberal bluff by denying its secular worldview an authentic ontology. All modern political concepts, Schmitt famously declared, were transposed theological ones. In other words, secular principles cannot stand on their own, basing themselves on universals pertaining to human nature, interest, or reason in lieu of God. Such principles can be secondary, almost decorative derivations of peace only after a primal holy war between good and evil has been settled. Schmitt therefore prioritizes a primordial piety over other matters, such as sentiment, memory, language, constructivism, or catastrophe, that bind people together. Alternatively, one could say that whatever factor—eventful, emotionalist, or cultural—assumes the shape of the political must be driven by a passionate religiosity beneath all concealments. The modern state, with all its artifice of reason, its separation of church and state, can be rendered possible only after this concept of the "political" has been settled.[3] Schmitt's Faustian wager pitches this concept as a mythic sublimation that precedes other working postulates of civic life like the Kantian *sensus communis* or the Rawlsian "overlapping consensus." The political is already the deep, the incipient, the replenishing. Its perpetuation is a quiet but alert one, for it must always have the potential to harden itself instantly to a stance of sovereign, law-exacting, or law-destroying violence when the exceptional scenario presents itself. The political is a reckoning of submerged warfare that is always ongoing underneath the dead calm of social existence. Social contracts, constitutions, or charters of rights hide this primal conflict but are unable to eliminate its subcutaneous and raw presence. Normal political processes, as a matter of fact, are a continuation of this war by other means. As a result, when the social accord is fixed in a manner mindful of this simmering intrigue between friends and enemies, the nation-state ceases to be an unstable amalgam of distributed sovereignties (the Weimar Republic, in Schmitt's times) and emerges in its singular essence. It does so until time erodes the political itself.

Chauvinisms, therefore, can subvert liberal democracies for two reasons. Either liberal constitutionalism has overlooked or ignored an incipient but fundamental question of friendship and enmity, or the principle of homogeneity and friendship that it proposed has itself been spoiled by pagan or heretical contaminations. Liberalism should therefore understand that the settlement of the friend–enemy question is an originary matter over which it has no command. It can institute itself formally only after that primordial question has been settled and by being always aware of the results. Hence, per Schmitt's logic, the Hegelian state could work not because it is an infallible architectonic of reason but because it is based on a Christological civic religiosity that excludes the Quakers, the Anabaptists, and the Jews.[4] The latter can certainly be given rights and be considered objects of toleration, but they can never be citizens in the "active" sense. This spectral country-in-essence is that which must be "taken back" from time to time, in extreme cases, from minorities, the bureaucratic government, or the legal and constitutional order itself. In other words, according to Schmitt, India can be a functional liberal democracy only after it is comfortably Hindu in an originary political sense, and the United States can return to a state of vanilla Rawlsian peace only after the country has been made WASP again.

I suggest a deeper study of the Schmittian notion of the political as a fundamentally monotheistic calling, not just a religious or theological one in a general, multicultural sense.[5] This is a mythopoetic automaton—unique and austere—that enables one to talk about the people and the state only after having categorically distinguished the believer from the infidel. The passion should be monotheistic or monothematic by secular transposition, because it has to be a singular impelling of devotion to the nation and the state. If we consider India as a modern postcolonial entity that has been historically bestowed with the apparatus of the nation-state, then the fiction of a "prepolitical" nation emerges. That is, a primordial picture of India before political models of the West were imprinted upon it. According to the Hindu right's vision of this prepolitical state, India was a (Hindu) civilizational conglomerate that had survived Islamic colonization precisely because the culture had largely managed to confine the state to mere military occupation. The Mughal regime, in that sense, was an "armed camp," as Perceval Spear once put it.[6] The state was not "political" in a constitutive sense; it had confined itself to tribute collection and was perhaps even what Karl August Wittfogel called the hydraulic-bureaucratic empire of oriental despotism.[7] This formation was generally compelled to leave diurnal Hindu life-worlds and communities alone and unconverted. Now, if that India is to be historically inducted into a modern politics of the nation-state, that is, if it is now to be constituted by politics rather than "have" politics, as Sunil Khilnani observed, and if that politics is to be covertly impelled by a monothematic religiosity, then it is the ardent belief of the Hindu patriot that the religious axiomatic should naturally be Hindu.[8] That said, it would logically follow that the nation can be achieved in its true essence only if the Hindu is allowed to settle very old scores with primal enemies.

This departure point is also where problems begin. Since we are talking about India, we have to refine the question of political monotheism in terms of creedal precision. In other words, there cannot really be an ontologically secure "Christian" or "Muslim" nation in and of itself—keeping in mind here Locke's perpetual heartburn with Papist intrigue despite his famed liberty of conscience, the Irish Question in Britain, or, in a completely different historical context, the relationship between Shia Iran and what was once Sunni-controlled Iraq.⁹ By that measure, a destinying project for Hindu India becomes an incredibly complicated proposition, given the common perception of the faith as a polytheistic religion featuring a pantheon of millions, with wide disparities in customs, rituals, and cosmologies of belief. Even a denominational grouping under the general canopy of Vedic Brahminism becomes a byzantine affair, with the caste system and the general syncretic presence of a breathtaking range of heterodox sects like the Aghoris, the Lingayats, the Kabirpanthis, or the Ravidasis.¹⁰ This is a formidable plurality we will look at in the next chapter. For the moment, let us mark the purported enemy.

The question of creed remains equally complex when we consider the history of Islam in the subcontinent and the role assigned to it as the competing monolith to an essentially Hindu India.¹¹ The majority of Muslims in the subcontinent have been Sunnis following the Hanafi school of jurisprudence, but then there have been the Shias, early Qarmatian groups and their remnants, the eclectic Sufi spread from Sind to Bengal, the Ahmadis who recognize a final prophet succeeding Muhammad, the Dawoodi Bohras, Khojas and other Ismailites, the Nawayaths of Konkan, the Mappilas of Malabar, the Kayam Khanis of Rajasthan, and dozens of orders that reside on a spectrum between Hindu and Muslim orthodoxies.¹² Historically, royalist Islam in India—from the Delhi Sultanate to the Mughal dynasty—has always been afflicted by tensions between the orthodoxy of a Sunni clergy establishment (Sharia) and the popular mysticism of the Sufis (Tariqa) or the radical disavowals of all earthly authorities by Ismailis or Qarmatians. With the advent of the Chishti, Suhrawardi, and Firdausi sects between the twelfth and fifteenth centuries, it was Sufism that emerged as the prime missionary force of Islam in the subcontinent. Later groups, like the Shattari, the Qadri, or the Naqshbandi, impelled by the pantheism of the Andalusian scholar and mystic Ibn Arabi (1165–1240), entered into rich syncretic and vernacular commerce with Hindu devotional sects. Active in the Punjab, they would contribute to an affective universe that would birth, among other things, the Indic monotheism of Sikhism.¹³ A. Azhar Moin's remarkable study has shown how the Mughal emperors, Akbar in particular, established a new form of sovereignty by styling themselves on the lines of Sufi saints. It was a form of kingship based on the charisma of holiness (*wilayat*) and a principle of tolerance (*zimmi*) rather than religious law (*sharia*) or holy war (*jihad*).¹⁴ In all, Imtiaz Ahmad has postulated three registers of Islamic practice in India. The first would be marked by traditional scriptural governance of a pan-Islamic kind; the second by local, customary deviations in religious behavior, including birth or death rituals or popular celebrations of Muharram; and the third would unfold to an eclectic cosmology including Muslim saints, Hindu gods, and a vast spectrum of beliefs pertaining to deliverance from disease, famine, misfortune, or malevolent spirits.[15]

For Schmitt, the unitary impelling of the political can of course have declared religious dimensions—as in Anglican England, Protestant Germany, or Catholic Spain—but more importantly, it must give rise to a monotheme of identity. The political must birth a concomitant religiosity that could be based on race, on ideological world view (like Russian Bolshevism in his time), or on ethnicities of various kinds. The citizen is, ultimately, an acolyte who requires an overt or covert ontotheology to worship the state and identify enemies. The Christian postulate of turning the other cheek, in that sense, applies only to members of a tolerant brotherhood and not to enemies like Saracens or Turks. Seen in this light, the Hindu nationalist phenomenon, as we shall see, exists between two conceptual poles: Hinduism as a denominational religion, and Hindutva as an ideology of cultural or ethnic nationalism that ostensibly is not reliant on a single faith but that reserves the sovereign right to arrange different Indian beliefs along a spectrum of normalcy and pathology.

I seek to bring the Schmittian diagram of sovereignty and the thought of an axiomatic Hindu nation into a critical relationship with a historical field of problems. The task is to lay out a constellation of themes, rather than to insist that the two are absolutely the same. But first, a couple of caveats. Why make Schmitt "travel" to this Indian context? Does his diagnosis supply us with some essential truths about the human condition or about the things that motivate humans to form stable nation-states? The answer to that would have to be no, since there are too many exceptions to the Schmittian rule, which—despite his passion for Hobbes and Machiavelli—relies too much on an organic model of national peopleness as an a priori assumption.[16] Schmitt himself would not be so hopeful about the stability or sovereign capacities of multicultural, large nation-state formations like Canada or India. Nevertheless, I find the Schmitt–Hindutva intersection interesting for three reasons. First of all, one can chart and detect a consistent monotheistic imperative working throughout the modern discursive invention of "Hinduism," even from its earliest inception in the second decade of the nineteenth century. Imparting an Abrahamic cast to a multitude of faiths was deemed essential for a proper denominational identity, political representation, and, in the fullness of time, nationalist imaginary. Second, as I have stated, the Hindu nationalist imagination itself is for the most part thoroughly orientalist and Eurocentric. Third, when this nationalism acquired an institutional form during the political mobilization of the 1920s and 1930s—around the time of Schmitt's writing and around the time of his Nazi turn—it was directly inspired by European fascism and a set of Herderian cultural-historical pieties. However, what makes Schmitt really pertinent is his idea of the jealous and monotheistic distinction between friend and enemy as the essence of the political. This has been at the core of Hindu nationalism's political project of a masculinist modernization of the traditional Hindu faiths and their flocks. The invention and focalization of jealousy has been essential to dispel the pluralism, otherworldliness, mysticism, and pacific nonviolence attributed to the religion by a nineteenth-century colonial religious anthropology.

Let us create a conceptual clearing by way of an elaboration of some Schmittian concepts pertinent to the project. While Schmitt's idea of Volk is organic, his conception of the state is not organic, as it had been for the romantics: it is instead much closer to a Hobbesian mechanical model. On the other hand, Schmitt's problem with the English political philosopher—despite Hobbes's understanding of sovereignty as a decisionist principle—is that Hobbes begins with the contract itself and not the primordial that comes before the contract and determines it.[17] This primordial is a settlement of the question of friend and enemy. It is primal in relation to the great themes of the European Enlightenment: aesthetics, reason, morality, or economic interest. It is also beyond the judgment of the individual, for one cannot have a private enemy (*inimicus*) in the political sense; the enemy is necessarily and already public (*hostis*). Some of the individual's best friends, therefore, may eminently be political enemies. The enemy is not determined by profit-based reasoning, for one can engage in lucrative trade with him. Similarly, he is not necessarily the morally evil or the aesthetically ugly, just as the friend is not always the virtuous and the beautiful.[18]

Schmitt was not the first to define the foe, but he certainly was one of the first major thinkers of the right to address enmity as a domestic concern rather than a matter confined to interstate relations. This becomes a matter of special import in a late modern era marked by the hardening of nation-state boundaries after the great wars and decolonization. There is an implicit understanding that informs classic Western social contract theory: the recalcitrant who refuses to accept the contract is free to leave the city or commonwealth for an "outside." This theme is found in the works as well as the political lives of Hobbes, Locke, and Rousseau.[19] Exile in that historical landscape was not necessarily a fatalistic or negative measure. It pertained to lines of flight to wider Europe and indeed, in terms of a stellar example, to the New World. In the late modern era, when the "frontier"—as a Eurocentric and essentially racist imaginary—is either closed or imperially monopolized, the domesticity of the enemy becomes acutely abject in character. Her humanity is then to be measured in terms of a nation-statist arbitration of her refugee status or immigration rights. Apart from Syrian refugees, the Rohingyas of Burma, or the left-liberals and Muslims in India who are often told to go to Pakistan, the abject domesticity of the enemy should remind us of Hannah Arendt's poignant observations about citizenship and human rights in the age of totalitarianism.[20] "Human rights," as a universal postulate, is Kantian in its spirit; however, it is only the particular nation-state that can guarantee its actual existence. The Nazi Final Solution to the European Jewish problem became a decision in Schmitt's exceptional times, during which the industrial extermination of the enemy was a rising option, while the possibilities for exodus had diminished severely.

The political is decided by a primal pathology prior to self-conscious peopleness; it therefore has to be an already-there organic unity. It cannot be associational or contractual precisely because it must express a singular and undivided will before reason and talk can proceed. Schmitt's political theology therefore necessarily defines the bearer of the political as a monotheistic congregation, jealous of any apostates, pagans, or heretics in its midst. It is the fervent religiosity that is important, not the religion itself, unless the religion acquires the capacity to invite sons to martyr themselves for a cause greater than their individual salvations.[21] In its elemental expressions, the political is a crusading mission. Within the domestic scene, the postulate assumes a particularly chilling form when Schmitt insists that the primary requirement for a working friend–enemy distinction is that an exterminating war should be a real possibility for both parties.[22] The state can be lean and mechanistic, but it has to respond to this sum of all fears at every step. The exception is the scenario in which the available juridical resources of the state are unable to meet that requirement and a secular miracle is needed to save it.[23] This miracle is a sovereign intervention—in its pure dictatorial and decisionist aspect—in the form of war against the enemy at home. It can also be a perpetual civil war as an index of relentless determination or purification.

These connected themes, of categorical jealousy to the point of exterminating violence and of the increasing military-industrial foreclosure of exile, make the refugee a central figure in contemporary fictions of sovereignty.[24] The specter of the concentration camp, in our occasion, haunts Trump's detention centers for Latino immigrants at the United States–Mexico border or the ones established for antihomosexual purges in Chechnya. It hovers around the National Register of Citizens (NRC) project that the present Hindu nationalist government in India has reactivated in the Indian northeastern state of Assam. According to early projections, this digital bureaucratic rationalization of a disproportionately poor and unlettered population threatens the residency and citizenship of four million people, predominantly Muslims. There is the looming danger of these people being reduced to an abject state of fatelessness if Bangladesh refuses to accept them.[25] The government has already promised in advance to mitigate any troubles of the non-Muslim population through the 2016 Citizenship Amendment Bill, which gives illegal immigrants from all religions except Islam an automatic pathway to citizenship, in blatant violation of the nondiscriminatory Article 15 of the Indian Constitution. The BJP, for its part, has promised a pan-Indian application of the NRC in its 2019 election manifesto, and Amit Shah, its president, has declared illegal immigrants to be "termites." The figure of the Muslim in contemporary India—imperiled by ghettoization, civic marginalization, a fearful culture of public lynchings, retailed acts of molestation and murder, systemic criminalization, and the prospect of an elemental stripping of citizenship rights—therefore reminds one of a chilling question that will resonate in various moments of this study. What will happen to the 200 million Indian Muslims if that long-cherished Sangh Parivaar dream of Hindu Rashtra actually comes to pass?

Peopleness, for Schmitt, is a metabolic phenomenon in the body politic prior to any juridical justification. That is also why such a people—in essence instinctive and infantile, in an Edenic state, and yet to bite the fruit of knowledge—needs a jealous God, around whom and around whose eventual secularization Schmitt constitutes his now famous description of sovereignty: The sovereign is he who decides on the exception.[26] The exception, in the sphere of the political, is paralogous to the miracle in theology because both God and the monarch who rules with divine right must intervene when people forget themselves from time to time in an endemic condition of sinfulness.[27] Primordial peopleness is thus to be distinguished from the historical predilections of an actual citizenry that might be confused, ill-informed, or prone to endless conversations and deferred decisions. The exception therefore cannot be made to conform to the performed laws and situational agreements of mortals. In crucial moments, the constitution itself can be put on hold, just as the originary covenant with the divine should trump all earthly social contracts of man. This provision becomes important because man-made law does not have absolute Mosaic status, and the secular constitution can only be a relativistic approximation of gospelic wisdom.[28]

It would be wrong to conclude that Schmitt is necessarily against the democratic state. For him, democracy can exist without parliamentarianism, just as parliamentarianism can exist without democracy. The dictatorial exception, in that vein, is not antithetical to otherwise equitable representational arrangements.[29] The primary condition here, once again, is that the concept of the state must presuppose the concept of the political. Following that, the state in its essence can be "a machine or an organism, a person or an institution, a society or a community, an enterprise or a beehive."[30] In formal terms, it can be almost anything, but with key qualifications. First, sovereignty must be distinguished from the state, and the state itself from the legal order. Second, the sovereign-state arrangement must have a provision for axiomatic transcendence, over and above parliamentary clamor, leading to what he calls the decision.

Schmitt's intellectual battle is therefore against a nineteenth-century liberal turn in Western jurisprudence and political philosophy after Hegel, by which the former transcendence of the state had been absorbed into the great administration of things. This was a century of immanence and neutralization, in which the bourgeoisie tied the state to economics and reformed the erstwhile sphere of the political as a zone of impersonal scientism, property, and trade devoid of risk. Most importantly, this hub of commercial activity had to be insulated from vainglorious military adventures of kings and nobility. In the realm of law, the great transformation ushered in a Weberian sociology of *ultima ratio* by which legal intelligence could be subject to regular calculation, bureaucratization, and a stable schema of juridical cognition. This age would eventually address the natural law question as well as the wane of a tradition of heroic republicanism by privileging a Montesquieu-style mixed constitutionalism, deferred decisions, and endless conversation in order to ensure freedom. By the time Schmitt was writing, liberalism had ushered in a secular age by replacing the Holy Alliance with the League of Nations.

Schmitt traces the historical roots of this transformation to the modern constitutional state of eighteenth-century deism, a secularized "theology and metaphysics that banished the miracle from the world" and created a machine that ran on itself.[31] The deistic "clockwork" equated the Newtonian lawfulness of nature with normative lawfulness; the metaphysics of Leibniz and Nicholas Malebranche became the theory that the will of the people was always good—and with the Jeffersonian revolution, the voice of the people became the voice of God.[32] Society itself was invited to dominate the state in moral and ethical terms. What was also forgotten is a key insight from Grotius: that law is not just reason; it is also desire inevitably understood in majoritarian terms.[33] The problem with organic theories of the state was that they made state and sovereignty coterminous with the people, when the people—an entity conjured from the immanence of life itself—lacked the capacity of decision. People lack this quality because they are by nature plural, and pluralism, in all forms, is detrimental to decision. Seen in that light, a political majoritarianism of the Hindu people would be impossible without a Hindu sovereignty distinguished from that very people, reputedly one comprised of many clamorous sects that are otherworldly, tolerant, and nonviolent.

For Schmitt, the liberal retirement from the political does not just involve a scientific foreclosure of miracles, but also a disavowal of dogma.[34] One such example would be the manner in which the anarchist assertions of the essentially good man, from Rousseau to Proudhon, dispense with original sin and sinfulness. Sin is absorbed into modern bourgeois therapeutic institutions, and the diminishment of hell is achieved with the twilight of atonement philosophy, especially its dimensions of justice and punishment. On the other hand, for Schmitt, it is a basic dogma-based understanding that a theologian cannot remain a theologian unless he believes that there are souls to be saved.[35] It would be fair to draw a logical continuation from that statement: in the age of profane secularism, the political cannot remain political unless one believes that there are enemies upon whom war must be waged, and who potentially must be exterminated. Liberal peace, in essence, means that there can actually be no liberal politics—only a liberal critique, or technobureaucratic transformation, of politics.

Schmitt, the enigmatic Catholic, will thus not allow God to be completely replaced by a universal fraternité of earthbound sons. In a sense there is a commonality between his desire to revive the political as theology and Kierkegaard's attempt to overcome an existence imposed by positive reason, or Nietzsche's quest for a new mythology. Yet the implicit figuration of "God" here is a provincial one, and not the Father of humankind. He remains the vital source of national jealousy, dogma, and damning enmity toward Lucifers on earth. He is a tribal God in that sense; his mystery reduced to instinctive and infantile feelings of enmity and friendship prior to the aesthetic, ethical, or interest-based judgments of man. Humanity is not a political category for Schmitt, since humankind, in and of itself, has no enemy, at least not on this planet.[36] The ideal nation-state can extend only to a certain part of the species, beyond which sovereignty is denuded by rising pluralities of language, culture, race, ethnicity, religion, and other factors. The dividing line between the essential people and the rest of mankind is the one at which the friend passes over to the enemy.

The "dictator" in Schmitt's work is important here to clarify two things: the figure must first be distinguished from that of the Asiatic despot, and then brought into a state of critical proximity with the sovereign ideal, as imagined by the Sangh Parivaar and, indeed, with the provision of "internal emergency" as articulated by the Indian Constitution. As an expression of the political, the dictator steps in to occupy and redress a point of rupture in the immanence of national life. It is here that one can locate Schmitt's kinship with, as well as differences from, Machiavellian republicanism. For both, it was always better (as it was in Rome) for the people to hold power, rather than the nobles of Sparta or the bourgeois financial and bureaucratic aristocracy in Schmitt's times. This is because people generally have less interest in abusing authority. They simply wish not to be dominated, while nobles, by nature, must dominate. Yet the dictator has to emerge from time to time, since, while the people are usually right in the particular, they often cannot come to a mutual agreement about the general, even in moments of danger. They are collectively strong but individually weak and cowardly.

Schmitt's conception of the dictator, however, comes with less insistence on republican virtue and temperance. Unlike Machiavelli, Schmitt was open to both types of dictatorship, that of the commissarial and that of the sovereign.[37] The first suspends the constitution in order to protect it at a moment of historical duress: it is precisely the type Machiavelli would recommend. The second does so in order to abrogate it and forge a new constitution through an authentic *pouvoir* constituent, that is, one that the dictator feels is more expressive of majoritarian will. Machiavelli would consider the latter a tyrannical subversion of institutions and customs. The cardinal rule in determining the exception, for Schmitt, is that the nature of the exceptional cannot be anticipated in advance, even with the collective wisdom of the constitution and traditional institutions. Consequently, the powers of dictatorship may not be specified and bound by the normative, especially in moments of terror and elemental unraveling: "Every norm (*normatio*) presupposes a normal situation, and no norm can be valid in an entirely abnormal situation."[38] Yet the authentic dictator must perform in the interests of what the political, in essence, is. His rule cannot be arbitrary, like that of a despot. As an expression of sovereign power, he must reside in the interval between *sein* (normativity or law) and *sollen* (facticity or obligation). He must abide by a people's sense of right and their innate desires, from which point laws can either be discarded or rendered afresh; otherwise, the exception does not qualify as a sovereign one. It becomes the catastrophic idiosyncrasy of an individual, like the fabled madness of King George. The figure of the dictator must be a precise manifestation of the will underlying the life of law itself, a will hiding behind the formal norms and representational pieties of democratic republics. He has to emerge intermittently and rise above the clamor of the Sanhedrin to make the ultimate decision without washing his hands: Is it to be Christ or Barabbas?

Hindu Nationalism and the Monotheistic Imperative

The purpose of this brief excursion has not been to access the entirety of Schmitt's thinking, with all its various aspects, remarkable complexity, and tribal limitations. For instance, in an enlightening recent essay, Feisal Mohamed has pointed out that while Schmitt's idealism necessarily posits the dictator as a reluctant miracle-worker, he has very little to say about the vastly more common situation in which an emergency is manufactured in order to wrest dictatorial powers from a state apparatus.[39] In this book, Schmitt functions as a ruse to isolate a few illiberal (fascist) perspectives—on the modern state, secularism, political theology, and sovereignty—that are pertinent not just to a contemporary specter of Hindu India, but also to exceptional moments in the career of the Indian state. I have no interest in an instrumental reading of India in Schmittian terms, since, due to entirely historical reasons, authoritarianism in India has taken a number of different forms in terms of culture, masculinity, and frameworks of cognition, metaphysics, and desire. It has done so, most importantly, in terms of its evolving relationships with monopoly and neoliberal incarnations of capital and empire. Such differences will become prominent in the elaborations of Hindutva ideology that follow.

It has been argued that it would be inaccurate to read Hindu right-wing nationalist mobilization in terms of European Nazi or Fascist cults.[40] Exact parallels to the Indian situation can be found in neither the assemblage of capitalists, petit bourgeois, and the landlord class that impelled Mussolini's movement in an Italy beset by the agrarian question, nor, by contrast, the urban template of nationalist socialism that characterized Hitler's much more industrial Germany. Nevertheless, the summoning of a monotheistic Schmitt here is intended to create a conceptual diagram and vocabulary that is yet of relevance to the Indian context. It is not to impose a total explanatory model. The invocation is a sparse one, to examine right-wing Hindu nationalism in relation to three important themes pertinent to nation-thinking and sovereignty: the modern understanding of religion, the romance of the past, and the concomitant monotheistic imperative of political theology. The sparseness, in this sense, also derives from staying clear of that other can of worms: the extent to which the bureaucratic militarism of Nazism itself in Hitler's Germany eventually satisfied Schmitt's political romanticism or, for that matter, Martin Heidegger's agrarian conservatism.

I want to bring the historical specter of European fascism into a contiguous relationship with the absolutist temptations and their liberal disavowals within the broader picture of Indian nationalism. That is, the ways in which fascism, in conjunction with indigenous models in a deeply hierarchical society, was always an internal postulate of modernity and the state question in India. It was a working postulate alongside other European ones like socialism, democracy, secularism, or Westminster parliamentarism. In recent times, Benjamin Zachariah has explored this question in relation to a broader Indian zeitgeist, beyond the usual suspects of Hindutva like Savarkar or Golwalkar, discovering wider resonances across the political spectrum and in disparate figures such as Benoy Kumar Sarkar, hero and ideologue of the Bengal Swadeshi Movement, the Congressional socialist Syed Mahmud, or Sir M. Visvesvaraya, engineer technocrat and Dewan of the princely state of Mysore.[41] Fascism was one inspiration within a wider authoritarian spectrum of aristocratic and feudal traditions, in a nation historically birthed out of territories directly ruled by the Raj as well as more than 650 princely states. The temptation for strong fathers was, early on, prompted by admiration for Hitler's Germany and Mussolini's Italy, both of which stood up to the modern imperial powers of Western Europe. In different ways, the list also included Ataturk's Turkey and, if we go further back in time, nationalists like Mazzini and Garibaldi. Despite the looming presence of Gandhi, the desire for a leader who cultivates a masculine and martial self, one who cures dissipation and unites with an iron hand, remained consistent during the emergence, partition, and republican transformation of the nation itself as idea and as raucous political phenomenon. As Zachariah points out, in the 1920s and 1930s, "fascism" proper could only be located in "fuzzy" terms, in broader Indian introspections about militarism, national character, labor discipline, mass mobilization, eugenics, Aryanism, pleasures of new homosocial congregations, and the alluring prospects of modern social engineering.

Hard Hindutva apart, the authoritarian question would resonate in Gandhi's ambivalence toward Mussolini, in the secular nationalist Subhash Chandra Bose's (1897–1945) desire for an Indian synthesis of fascism and socialism, and in the mainstream Indian left's failure to come to terms with Stalinism.[42] The impulse would mark the complicated legacies of the Indian Emergency, the Indian state's gross militarization and human rights violations in Kashmir, areas in the northeast, and various tribal belts, the dynastic rules of the Indian National Congress and other parties, and the currently alarming fact that the idea of military rule is quite popular among Indian millennials.[43] Hitler's *Mein Kampf* remains a bestseller in modern India, potent enough to rival Dan Brown's *Da Vinci Code*.[44] It must also be remembered that, well before the rise of contemporary political Hindutva in the late 1980s, sovereign "exception" had been a regular feature in the workings of the republic. In the years of high Nehruvianism between 1947 and 1966, president's rule had been invoked ten times. After the death of Nehru (1888–1964) and during the gradual unraveling of the consensus he represented, between 1967 and 1986, the law was activated seventy times.[45] In the career of the Indian state, it has been a matter of periodic introspection—by Dravidians in the 1950s, Khalistanis in the 1970s and 1980s, tribal populations everywhere, and marginal peoples in the northeastern states and in Kashmir—whether, and to what extent, is the Indian union always secured through centrifugal measures of internal colonization carried out by the Hindi-Hindu heartland.

Can there actually be a Hindu "monotheism" of the political kind? If that is to be a core, exacting definition of peopleness, what would happen to the immense pluralities of subcontinental life? How would minorities within the Hindu denomination be placed along the friend–enemy spectrum? The armature of Hindu nationalism on current display includes both the desire to be a part of the global metropolitan order *and* increasing nativist repulsions against new urbanism and corporate capitalism. Can these dualities be resolved into a singular axiomatic? That apart, in Schmittian terms, a Hindu sovereign takeover, unless it followed a bloody insurrectionary path driven by Cromwellian hauteur, would look like the following: a leader assuming premiership through the parliamentary process, appropriating dictatorial powers by invoking Part XVIII of the Indian Constitution, and then abrogating the constitution itself along with the given parliamentary dispensation. The dictator would subsequently be able to commission the drafting of a new constitution and redress the state structure and legal order in line with an organic sense of right coming from the Hindu people. Indian versions of such ideas and concomitant fears have been voiced in the past. Is this still part of the agenda, at least for Sangh Parivaar purists even if not for parliamentary pragmatists?

The partial or total abandonment of the Indian Constitution has been a persistent theme of unremitted desire in Hindu right-wing discourses.[46] It has been stated repeatedly that the Anglophone revolution of 1950 created a democratic republic that is alien to the structure of Hindu feelings and principles, which are apparently one with the being of Bharat, the vernacular nation ignored by Nehruvian fathers. Under the stewardship of B. R. Ambedkar, the design of the constitutional state and the separation of powers was clearly prompted by the Madisonian caution of Federalist Papers 9 and 10 regarding the threat of a majoritarian insurrection against its own democratic political system. This is exactly where the general Sangh understanding of democracy departs from the parliamentary spirit of the Indian Constitution. In Hindutva ideology, democratic rule is indistinguishable from majoritarian rule. Hindu national power, accordingly, must not be dissipated along regional or linguistic lines; India must therefore have a unified state rather than a federal one. Instead of having executive power vested in the office of the prime minister, besieged by the clamor of parliament and the cabinet, it should be gathered in the presidency. "Democracy" as such, should not be based on individual citizenship but on an organic corporatism of (caste) communities tied together by love, trust, duty, and kinship in accordance with an abiding Indian tradition. The axiomatic state should rise immanently, from a national bedrock of autonomous village communities where mass contractual representation in terms of raw numbers and individual choice may be tempered by a naturalized upper-caste paternalism. The state should be centralizing, but minimally intrusive into the normative culture of the everyday, which, by default, would be Hindu. In an ideal scenario, the president with authoritarian powers should be guided spiritually by a council of sages operating as the Raj Guru (the Brahmin advisor to the king).[47]

In the wider Sangh Parivaar, one can detect a consistent desire to overwrite the democratic arrangement, divest it of any liberal ontological bearing, and make it subservient to a core, Brahminical stewardship.[48] The Marg Darshak Mandal (Council of Path Finders) of the Vishwa Hindu Parishad (VHP; World Hindu Council) is an illustrative institution in this context. Manjari Katju has pointed out that ever since the mid-1980s, the Mandal has been increasingly defined as a College of Holy Men, an extraparliamentary institution of pastoral power for the world itself, not just India.[49] It is this assembly of god-men—now imagined along the lines of an ecumenical council with papal infallibility—that must incarnate the revived authority of the Raj Guru. It must be vested with the power to authenticate the works of the democratic state as well as the laity of citizens. The formal paraphernalia of secular polity would thereby become instrumental in relation to a Hindu theocratic wisdom with a sovereign monopoly over interpretive and name-giving rights. The key Schmittian question, however, in the light of all these historical aspirations and undertakings, would be whether, in terms of an original majoritarian essence, the "Hindu" identity qualifies as the political, or whether it has always remained a conglomerate of castes and regions, never quite animated, in a pan-Indian sense, by a singular jealous passion. If the identity itself is to be spiritually presided over by a Savarna elite that represents barely a quarter of the population, then to what extent and in which ways does the question of homogeneity become complicated? This, more or less, is the broad line of inquiry that I seek to pursue for the rest of the book.

2 THE HINDU NATION AS ORGANISM

Fascism and the Historical Roots of Hindutva

It would be fair to say that Schmitt's general prognosis—of the long, nineteenth-century liberal honeymoon of the West coming to an end—was wildly exaggerated. He was wrong about the stability of associational states and could not anticipate that *Volkerbund* organizations like the UN would actually foster a workable postwar peace—the specter of nuclear annihilation and the Cold War notwithstanding. This was admittedly a Rawlsian peace rather than a Kantian one, tensely mediated not just by the NATO or the Soviet Bloc but also by brave new cooperative forms like the Non-Aligned Movement after the Bandung Conference of 1955. It could also be justifiably argued that India as a free democratic nation after 1947 could not have been imagined along Schmittian lines; the political form had to be associational and had to accommodate immense pluralisms. The Constitution of India that emerged after heated debates within the constituent assembly was one that has been broadly identified as "Nehruvian," mixing liberal democracy and French republicanism with a Fabian socialist impulse. The polity that the scenario birthed after 1950, when Nehruvianism gradually took a bureaucratic form rather than one of populist mobilization, was closer to the "passive revolution" of Italy during the Resorgimento rather than that of France under the Jacobins.[1] For Schmitt, and indeed for the Hindu right, the whole thing would make a disabling, pluralistic clamor without a clear moral center providing for the sovereign decision. India, in that sense, would always be in a state of catastrophic balance or chaotic dissipation.

In terms of beginnings, it would be quite easy to place the writings of the Nazi jurist and the genesis of organized Hindu nationalism against a common historical backdrop. The major discursive and institutional affinities between Hindutva and European-style fascism are well known to students of Indian history. Both V. D. Savarkar, original Hindutva ideologue and president of the Hindu Mahasabha party, and M. S. Golwalkar, the second Sarsangchalak (supreme leader) of the RSS, had consistent links with the hard-right in Italy and Germany. Savarkar would give a series of speeches in the late 1930s, defending the Reich and its anti-Semitic policies, which were covered in the Nazi daily *Völkischer Beobachter*. The newspapers *Kesari* and *Mahratta* in turn published features on the rise of fascism and the imminent collapse of democratic societies. Balakrishna Shivram Moonje (1872–1948), another leader of the Hindu Mahasabha, visited Rome in 1931 and was deeply impressed by the martial order of youth organizations like the Balilla and Avanguardisti. The experience would prompt him to start the Nasik-based Bhonsala Military School in 1937 in order to form a Hindu nationalist youth militia.[2]

In this overall context, Schmitt's concept of the political and his idea of sovereignty as power held in reserve may be compared with a key, much-cited postulate in Savarkar's 1923 pamphlet, *Hindutva: Who Is a Hindu?*:

> The life of a nation is the life of that portion of its citizens whose interests and history and aspirations are most closely bound up with the land and who thus provide the real foundation to the structure of their national state. . . . So with the Hindus, they being the people whose past, present, and future are most closely bound with the soil of Hindustan as Pitrbhu [Fatherland], as Punyabhu [Holy Land], they constitute the foundation, the bedrock, the reserved forces of the Indian State.[3]

The idea of reserved forces refers to the pool of national energy that, for both these ideologues, may be weaponized in an instant when it came to primal wars between essential selves and essential enemies. The "bedrock" is one on which sacrifice and martyrdom could be demanded for a purpose greater than one's redemption. The thought of an axiomatic political religiosity, in this context, is important for Savarkar: "The leaders of our race should have realized what an immense amount of strength could be derived if but the new national state was backed up by a Church as intensely national."[4] Then of course, we have that other, much-cited passage from Golwalkar's 1939 tract *We, or Our Nationhood Defined*. Here, after a categorical fixing of nationalism as substantiated race pride, the RSS supremo praises the resurgent Germanic zeitgeist of the 1930s as an expression of Nazi virtue. When that revived spirit administered a "purging" of Jews in order to "keep up" the purity of race and culture, it was, for Golwalkar, a manifestation of "race pride at its highest." It was a "good lesson" that Hindustan could learn from and profit by.[5] This moment was an illustrative one in Golwalkar's overall effort to distinguish pure nationhood from a disabling "democratic" conception, as a "haphazard bundle of friend and foe, master and thief."[6]

It was not one-way traffic in terms of ideology, mythological exotica, or rituals of power. Impulses toward Indological mysticism, occult thinking, and Aryan primordialism were vital to European fascism. It involved figures like Heinrich Himmler, Walther Wüst, or Jakob Wilhelm Hauer in Germany, and Houston Stewart Chamberlain or the Italian philosopher Julius Evola in greater Europe. This was a radical turn in the general field of German Indology that had earlier inflected the thought of Herder, Schopenhauer, Humboldt, or Nietzsche; it had now entered into a combustive blend with the anti-Semitism and racism of an Arthur de Gobineau or a Richard Wagner. This wide discursive terrain echoed several themes: the Hindu caste system as model for the rule of the Übermensch, the Kshatriya code of honor and fierce battle-readiness, the adoption of the Swastika as emblem of regeneration, the comparison of Jews and Romani people with the Chandalas of yore, and the figure of the Chakravartin as Indo-Aryan world conqueror.[7]

Hindutva, as a political mobilization of right-wing nationalist feelings, did not merely adopt select structural fixtures, a grossly orientalist vision, and providential Aryan enthusiasms from the West. The general concept of nationhood in this terrain was aligned with a German tradition of organismic thinking that came into being in the latter half of the eighteenth and the early nineteenth centuries. It involved idealizing a nation and its vital expressions in the form of *Gestaltung* (a creative self-fashioning) and *Kulturpolitik* (culture as politics of self-determination and evolution). As Pheng Cheah, in recent times, has shown, the organismic nation was marked by a modern understanding of epigenesis that had departed from its original moorings in neo-Aristotelian biology and was thus different from a Cartesian model of preformationism.[8] The latter was a mechanistic idea that had dominated Western political philosophies since Hobbes. The Hobbesian state was an automaton that came into being with the social contract; it had to be held together by despotic benevolence and spiritually charged from without.[9] In Cartesian terms, this was a body with organs that drew vitality and purposiveness from the soul. Without the animation of the soul, the organs themselves were no different from saws, hammers, or axes. This system of efficient causes presumed a first cause, a preformative germ of essence, or a divine inspiration that came from a Godly source outside it. In contrast, the organismic model was marked by an autochthonous *Bildungstreib*, that is, a formative drive immanent to the body and responsible for its diurnal regeneration. The organismic nation was, accordingly, a self-mutating entity that grew and adjusted to historical climates in line with a telos intrinsic to its own nature. Its morphogenesis did not depend on an external creator and its whole was greater than the sum of its parts. The life of such a nation was aleatory; it was marked by a purposive but nontechnical causality. Being touched by and belonging to such *Volksgeist* was waiting for momentous transcendence—a Kantian freedom from finitude and death.

Speaking of Schmitt in passing here, Cheah correctly infers that his notion of the state is more preformative than epigenetic.[10] However, as I have stated, the Nazi jurist's notion of the political, as the compelling national monotheme that precedes the artifice of government, is organic in expression. This is necessarily so because Schmitt is avowedly opposed to pluralistic and associational theories of peopleness. I have serious points of contention with Cheah's overall project, but for the present I accept his genealogy of the organismic and maintain that Hindu nationalism borrowed some of its prominent themes. That discussion itself must be prefaced by an important caveat: the organismic cast of Hindu society is a modern invention; it, or anything similar, is not found in the scriptures. It does not feature in the Dharmasastras. It is not assumed in the vivid picture of the totalitarian welfare state that we see in Kautilya's Arthasastra, composed and elaborated probably between second century BCE and third century CE.[11] This caveat in itself pertains to an important question that needs to be foregrounded early on: Can a caste society be imagined in terms of organic homogeneity? Can the Hindu nation, as organismic postulate, be squared with the pictures of the past, with the very antiquity it claims for itself? Allow me to introduce an illustrative parenthesis here.

Kautilya's ideal kingdom does not take an organic Volk for granted; the state here is an artifice of a relayed administration of intoxicants and poisons, intricate networks of espionage and policing, a monopoly of marketable illusions, and an ongoing royalist conspiracy dedicated to the balancing of power between important personages and interest groups. It works through calibrated measures of trust and suspicion, the enticements of lucre and women (including, in extreme cases, the queen herself), and an always-alert mechanism for entrapments and assassinations.¹² Kautilya's universe runs on the naturalist principle of Matsyanyaya (the big fish eat the small); here the violence of the natural world always remains in the heart of the city. The artifice of the state and society must be invented precisely to tame the interacting forces of a wild nature to a state of catastrophic balance. The otherwise natural tendency of Matsyanyaya must be repressed in order to protect the weak. The Arthasastra therefore unfurls a legal system that is not overdetermined by familial law, as in the case of Rome that Hegel noted with displeasure. The crown prince and other sons of the king are to be treated as potential parricides and be subject to relentless scrutiny and measures of disempowerment.¹³ They are to be paid less than the priest, the commander of the army, and an entire stratum of high officials. The Varna (caste) system has to be rigorously maintained in the kingdom. Nature qua nature can exist only as geostrategic buffer areas in a complex map of foreign policy. That apart, nature has to be rendered absolutely decorative within the auspices of statecraft. The forest reserved for the king's sport has to be cordoned off with ditches, leaving only one entrance. It has to be artificially implanted with delicious fruit trees and thornless bushes. A lake has to be populated with harmless creatures and elephants and bison. Beasts of prey like tigers have to be deprived of their claws and teeth.¹⁴

In contrast, the modern notions of an abiding Hindu national essence purportedly stretching back to thousands of years in the past, like those of Golwalkar or Deen Dayal Upadhyay (1916–1968), follow organismic lines, albeit with a cosmic bent that makes matters somewhat confusing.¹⁵ That is, they insist on terrestrial homogeneity as well as cosmogonic inequity. The national body is a composite anthropomorphic entity—the Virat Purusa (the cosmic Man)—in these texts. It is naturally hierarchical but animated by a primordial harmony like that which exists between organs. It works neither by equity contracts, nor by Kautilya's totalitarian strategy. With the promised revival of Hindu virtue, this nation, in its perfection, will be marked by a balanced metabolism of a natural caste patrimony and a principled docility of the lower orders. Citizenship shall be defined by selfless service and sacrifice, not by individual rights and interests. The state here can only be an organic expression of an originary Brahminical peace; it may not be a profane artifice to ward off a natural state of (caste) war.

The essential caste imagination that marks the Hindu nation forecloses the idea of fraternité as the uniform brotherhood of liberated sons. The picture therefore requires a secret theodicy to square the inequities of profane life with the vision of a common transcendence. It needs a singular theistic "Tradition" and an antiquity as parallel inventions to complement the modern invention of the nation itself. That is, it needs a Tradition that brings with it a profound weight of time that is greater than lived *Kultur* or enshrined national history. Such a Tradition is necessary for the One Hindu Nation to claim a cosmology rather than simply a world of caste inequalities. It must be able to appeal to a memory greater than mere textual or historical remembrance. "Tradition," in this special sense, is akin to the great "unsaid" of the Abrahamic traditions. It is truth not explicit in the Bible, law that is not formalized in the Torah, or prophetic exemplum not recorded in the Koran. Tradition in the uppercase comes into being when all small "traditional" or customary reckonings of the "great unsaid" are subjugated under one oracular authority. In the case of the Hindus who have only lately tried to emerge as a people of the Book, Tradition is that which affirms the great organic harmony even while announcing that it has, in essence, lost its voice in the age of profane dissipation. The nationalist cosmology can therefore become "Traditional" in the uppercase only after a sovereign extraction from a vast body of minoritarian cultures of faith, imagination, memory, ethics, and storytelling; it must be of a time beyond time, not of this earthbound temporal order of inequities and unhappiness. Tradition as such can be voiced in its pure essence only through Sanskrit, the language of the gods, and not in the lived, immanent vernaculars equivalent to Fichte's German language.[16] As we shall see, it essentially becomes a colonial imperative for self-determination, by subsuming little but vital streams of vulgar eloquence.[17] It claims a hoary antiquity, but its genesis and perpetuation are locked in the temporal and cognitive trappings of the very modernity that it imagines as its intimate enemy. "Tradition," as such, can birth itself only within a framework of Indological Sanskritization.

But then, aren't we all, as legatees of the colonial intervention, working within the epistemological framework of the modern? Are not all archives tainted? Aamir Mufti has staged this question of enframing with illuminating difference as a condition of Fanonian suffering in the phenomenology of colonial conquest. The restoration of aura to a national tradition or a past should come with an inevitable melancholy and sense of insufficient mourning. This struggle should also mark Anglophone critiques of Indian social and historical realities, including this one. It should be motivated by a critical consciousness of the irony and agon of usurpation, in being inevitably compelled to mobilize a colonial apparatus to create and identify vernacular objects, as well as their frameworks of study. This mode of thinking must self-consciously retract at every step from the feverish empirical apparatus of what Sara Suleri calls the Indian sublime.[18] That is, among other things, from an anxious modern desire to positively "read" the subcontinent from old orientalist dispatches. For instance, one needs to regularly invoke (and I will) the counternova of a great Indian pluralism of little traditions to challenge the spectral image of a monolingual Tradition that Hindutva brandishes at every step. However, that invocation itself must be accompanied by the consciousness that these little cosmologies—as we see them, as we honor them and marshal them—are not authentic ones unsullied by the invasions of the colonial modern. Such invocations merely gesture toward a lost excess beyond the excessive taxonomies of modernity. There is no pristine truth of pluralism either, one that is categorically outside the modern logic of what Mufti calls nation-thinking.

Mufti's postulation of a double consciousness and acknowledgement of rupture in the historical constitution of the self is a crucial matter of difference when it comes to Schmitt's Europe and the colonial/postcolonial dispensation. It is this critical admission of irony and amnesiac mourning—an understanding of the bygone as necessary fiction with a phantom aspect—that is absent in Hindutva discourses. Imaginative reconstructions of the past, in that spirit of irony and mourning, would be essential narratives for remembering that beings are irreparably partitioned. They would set historical tasks for the future by first recognizing the self as a product of historical destitution, with a memory "blocked" by colonial culture and epistemology. In the course of his magnificent elaboration, Mufti invokes a poignant observation by G. N. Devy: "In India . . . modern critical consciousness is confronted by the mid-nineteenth century as a sort of cutoff point, "incapable of tracing [its] tradition backwards" beyond that moment. It is a profoundly significant perception, one that helps illuminate the aporia of a range of disciplines in the humanities, as of literary production itself."[19]

The coarse positivism of Hindu nationalist dogma—of Sanatan Dharma as the eternal religion of the nation or Parampara as Tradition—abnegates such critical dwellings. With the never-ending construction of this pan-Indian edifice, the situated, meat-eating Shakta of Bengal is invited into a Hindu national fold with the vegetarian Vaishnavite of Tamil Nadu, just as the eclectic Bohras of Gujarat or the Mevs near Delhi are consigned to a monolithic "Islam." Yet there is no authentic discursive paraphernalia of the self, no unblemished framework of reckoning to affirm such a Hinduness or Muslimness in terms of original essence or perpetuation. Becoming Hindu or becoming Muslim in both cases—by way of narration, remembrance of ancestral pasts, or convergences of affectations and piety—are processes already locked into a colonial cognitive apparatus of religious psychology and anthropology. As a result, this Hindu mind can only make instant, schizophrenic journeys between now and then in order to bring about violent compressions in temporal imaginations. It must jet between Vedic mathematics and modern technology, between Ganesha and organ transplants, or between the Mahabharata and nuclear weapons.[20] It must necessarily read Indian history, unwittingly, according to orientalist frameworks and temporal imaginations set by James Mill's *History of British India* (1817). In the realm of popular culture, it can compose all entities, factual or fictional—from the city of Mohenjodaro to Queen Padmavati—into essentially nineteenth-century mythic creations of Bollywood. As a countermove, let us, in Mufti's critical spirit, gesture toward the immense richness of a kaleidoscope of minoritarian "traditions," in the lowercase, that a monotheistic ideal of Dharma and Parampara must violate, impoverish, and then conquer in order to achieve the organic nation with a singular Hindu destination.

The Dharma of the Gods: The Question of Theism and Traditions of Storytelling in the Works of Bimal Krishna Matilal

In the times of the Rg Veda (circa 1500 BCE), the gods in the pantheon were often what Surendranath Dasgupta calls "hypostatic powers of nature."[21] These divine forces became anthropomorphic personifications much later. Dasgupta, in his elaboration, divides the Hindu deities into three major groups: terrestrial, atmospheric, and celestial. Early in the Vedic age, they seemed to function in a manner Max Müller described as henotheism or kathenotheism—"a belief in single gods, each in turn standing out as the highest."[22] All deities can thus, situationally, assume the highest power: it is Agni who is paramount when the desire is for fire and Varuna when it is water. There is a hierarchy among gods and offices but no Zeus-like figure to dominate the pantheon. Dasgupta notes an eventual drift toward monotheism in the Vedic compendium, reaching the first clear articulation of the concept of Brahman in the Satapatha Brahmana.[23] This supreme power is then abstracted from Vedic ritualism and given a metaphysical grounding in the Upanishads.[24] The Brahman becomes the cosmic principle, while its evolute, the Atman, becomes the inner essence of man. In sum, Dasgupta notes three streams of thought in the ancient Indic tradition: one in which the Atman or Brahman becomes the only reality, with everything else as unreal evolutes of a consummate illusion; one in which a pantheistic creed identifies the Brahman with the universe; and one in which a theistic impulse tends to imagine Brahman as the "Lord Controller" of creation.[25]

The intricacies of this theophilosophical terrain are beyond this project. We can only flag certain questions that will remain pertinent when it comes to a modernist desire to invent a "Hinduism" in the Abrahamic cast. Among the classical systems of Indian philosophy that clustered around or against the Vedic compendium in the later centuries, Jaimini's Mimamsaka (logic), the materialist Carvaka, the Buddhists, and the Jains all deny the existence of Isvara (God), as either progenitor or supervisor. Samkhya (ennumerism) declares that the principle of Prakrti (material nature) and its inherent telos is sufficient for cosmology. It is only later in this dualistic tradition that a god is proposed. Patanjali's Yogasutra does posit an intelligent being as personal Isvara, albeit one that does not create the Prakrti. He merely balances its components and gives them a dynamic rendering to ensure an efficient distribution of Karma. This God is not the progenitor of the universe but the telos of yogic practices. Kanada's Nyaya-Vaisesika involves belief in a creator deity, but one who does not fabricate the universe ex nihilo; he does so out of preexisting atoms, by fiat and by his will, like a potter molds clay. In Sankara's nondualistic Vedanta, the singular Brahman is to be distinguished from both the phenomenal Jiva (individual being) and the phenomenal Isvara (God). The latter, in some streams of Vedantic thought, is produced as a reflection of the cosmic consciousness in an otherwise abiding Maya, or illusion of the world. He is, undoubtedly the thought of the good and the powerful, but one of illusory imaginings and subservience to the Ultimate Being.[26]

This does not mean that major and minor theistic impulses did not materialize within this broader tradition in the later centuries, especially in contention with the Bhakti-Puranic cults, Islam, and Christianity in South India.[27] Within the Vedic order, broadly speaking, this would mean the unification between the Jnana Marga (path of knowledge) of the Upanishads with the Karma Marga (path of works) of Vedic ritualism, while also responding to radical Buddhist momentariness (kshanavada) and Jaina relativism. The stellar axiomatic in this terrain would undoubtedly be the figuration and discourse of the Krishna of the Mahabharata—especially in the Bhagwad Gita portion. Yet as Bimal Krishna Matilal (1935–1991) points out in his explorations of the theistic question, elsewhere in the Mahabharata Krishna declares repeatedly that he is not all-powerful, despite his contrary statements in the Gita. He admits to the sage Uttanka in the desert in the Ashwamedhika Parvan that he was helpless in trying to stop the apocalyptic war.[28] Neither his might nor his intelligence could change the course of destiny because, paradoxically, while in human form Krishna was bound by human finitude. He thus exonerates himself from responsibility without abdicating his claim to be the One who is the soul of all things manifest and nonmanifest, the eternal god of gods, identical to all Vedas, and the origin and destruction of all things.

Krishna is Kala, or Time itself.[29] Yet, in his mortal frame, he is subject to the sovereignty of Time. There are enough reasons to think that Krishna is an earthbound expression of Kala rather than Kala being a holistic and punctual cosmic manifestation of Krishna. The Great War that is won by his strategic ministrations results in the devastation of an entire civilizational order: millions perish, only a handful survive, and the Pandavas inherit a kingdom of widows, the elderly, and the orphaned. Matilal points out that this Dharmayuddha (War of Dharma) could never be accounted for along the conceptual lines of "just war," in the Christian tradition since Augustine. This is because God is never clearly on one side of this catastrophe without redemption (EE, 94–95). In the beginning, Krishna offers himself as advisor and charioteer to one side and his Yadava army to the other. It is Duryodhana who makes the incorrect choice by opting for the army instead of the man himself. Once the cataclysmic war is over, Krishna is cursed by Gandhari, the mother of the slain Kauravas, for his failure to prevent it; as a result, he meets a rather ignominious death at the hands of a lowly deer hunter, and his Yadava clan, along with the city of Dwarka itself, is also destroyed.[30]

Matilal illustrates the sovereignty of Time with the example of Vishnu's avatar in the Ramayana as well. Toward the end of the Valmiki Ramayana, Time (Kala) comes to meet Rama disguised as a sage. He lays down the condition that Rama must kill any person who enters the room and disturbs their conversation. Rama's dutiful brother Laxmana is thus asked to guard the entrance. At that hour the mighty and temperamental sage Durvasa arrives and demands an audience with Rama, landing the doorkeeper in a quandary. Laxmana knows that the irate sage will curse the entire royal family if his wishes are not met. He is thus forced to violate his instructions and enter the consultation chamber. Later, when Rama meditates about his course of duty in such circumstances—whether to kill his innocent brother or break his vow—another great sage advises him to exile Laxmana: "Abandon him, (for) Kala, 'Time,' is all powerful, do not fail to keep your promise. For when a promise is not kept, Dharma is destroyed."[31] Rama is therefore told that even he cannot render time anthropological. Time is of cosmic thickness and inscrutability; it is neither natural nor subservient to human calculation.

Time as Kala creates and destroys without offering humans any proper narrative of paradise, fall, and redemption. It does so in a manner seemingly indifferent to the question of human benevolence; no desire touches it, and it submits to no systemic theory of causation.[32] In such a scenario, the Hindu national organism could be imbued with a monistic destinying in limited ways—though perhaps only with a weak eschatology and a vague notion of providence. The question of origin and destination is shrouded by positive ignorance (*bhavarupa avidya*), a theme that consistently runs through many traditions of ancient and modern Indian thought. Consider, for instance, Bhagwad Gita 2.28: "Invisible before birth are all beings and after death invisible again. They are seen between two unseens. Why in this truth find sorrow?" From the perspective of an Abrahamic religiosity, what would also remain a perpetual problem in Hinduism was the matter of addressing the origination of evil in the world.[33] In this light, one of the necessary tasks in instituting a Hindu monotheism would be to furnish a discourse similar to that of the Lutheran nominalist theology of *via moderna* that would insist on the omnipotence of the almighty and affirm faith in a singular teleology.[34]

Further, there is the difficulty of extracting a consistent moral philosophy from the Vedas, the Sutras, the Upanishads, or the Dharmasastras. Aesthetic theories of Rasa, especially in later thinkers like Anandavardhana (9th century) and Abhinavagupta (late 10th century) are tied to a performative of Bhakti religiosity toward a personalized god. Yet in this tradition, too, the question of bliss is always prioritized over that of morality. Matilal points out that over the last two millennia, scriptural traditions of South Asia have involved themselves with logic and epistemology, religious duties and rituals, metaphysics and soteriology. But they have hardly ever furnished a constitutive moral worldview. The Dharmasastras by Manu, Apastamba, Gautama, or Vashishtha—all written between the first and third centuries of the first millennium CE—speak only about social ethics and catalogue virtues, vices, and obligations accordingly, without introducing a moral dimension into the picture. On the other hand, despite emanating from divine wisdom, some Vedic rituals like *syena* or *abhichara* were distinctly designed to harm others. It was understood in commentaries that it was "immoral" to perform them. Dharma had its roots in the Vedas, but not everything in the Vedas was not Dharma.[35]

That apart, Dharma, strictly speaking, was not a comprehensive term. It was only one of the three major objectives in life, the other two being Artha (wealth) and Kama (desire, libidinal or otherwise).[36] Potentially, therefore, the spheres of material flourishing or sexual chastisement could be isolated from the realm of Dharmic considerations. Vatsayana, for instance, begins his famous Kamasutra by declaring that while Manu had taken care of the commandments of Dharma and Brihaspati those of Artha, he, Vatsayana, aimed to abstract the rules of Kama from a larger work in a thousand chapters by Nandi, the follower of Shiva.[37] He does acknowledge a hierarchy among the three postulates but in terms of an almost mathematical calibration, not a categorical one. All actions should satisfy the needs of Dharma, Kama, and Artha together, or at least one of them without being at the expense of the other two.[38] Yet while explicitly forbidding sex with women from higher castes or women who have been "previously enjoyed by others," Vatsayana, in part 1, chapter 5 of his treatise, provides a generous list of exceptions with matter-of-fact nonchalance: a higher-caste woman who has had sex with multiple men; a twice-married woman; the wife of a powerful friend of one's enemy; a woman with a rich husband who can be killed and his property usurped; a woman who controls the woman one covets; a woman useful to destroy the king; and so on.[39] Following that, he devotes all of part 5 to ways in which one can seduce the wives of others while protecting one's own. The ethics of sexual politics—devoted to matters of caste purity, honor, and property—does not furnish a moral governance of Kama.

It was this overall absence of a consistent moral philosophy, understood in Western Christological terms, that prompted Max Weber to conclude that there was no concept of morality in Sanskrit, only strict determinations of private and public virtues and general prohibitions.[40] This conclusion emerged from a general, orientalist judgment of Asiatic sultanisms and religious cultures as formations never nourished by a *theologia revelata*. In them, Hindu jurisprudence is seen to be restricted to the science of the law and essentially divorced from philosophy, moral or otherwise. Unlike Thomas Aquinas, the writers of the Dharmasastras would not attempt to justify their edicts in a tribunal of philosophy. In this order of things, a precept might be theologically sound but philosophically false, and vice versa. As a result, that other Nietzschean possibility of enlightenment secularization—saving Biblical morality by abandoning Biblical theology—does not arise.

Matilal rightly calls Weber's conclusion that of a "shallow critic" mired in an orientalist worldview (EE, 23). Ancient Indians discussed morality all the time, but they did so in the form of narrative instantiation—exemplary or grotesque—in epics, fables, or folklore. Such forms of elaboration involved situational tales in which Dharma itself was perpetually afflicted by questions of temporality, chance, self-consciousness, or agency. The task for Matilal, in that vein, is to abstract Dharma as a theory of rational behavior based on moral virtues and their complex applications in the world. Was Rama following the path of righteousness in killing the monkey king Valin—treacherously, in a manner that does not befit a Kshatriya Prince—in the fourth book of the Ramayana? Was he right in beheading the Sudra ascetic Shambuka in the seventh book for performing penances reserved for Brahmins? Was Krishna right in goading Arjuna to kill Karna in the Mahabharata while the latter was unarmed, helplessly trying to extract his chariot wheel struck in the mud? Was he being Dharmic in advising the Pandava prince Bhima to literally "hit below the belt" and kill Duryodhana in the climactic mace fight of the Great War?[41]

According to Matilal, if the great Indian epic tradition yields a moral lesson, it is that the concept of Dharma is illusive and perpetually riddled with ambiguity. *Dharmasya tattvam nihitam guhayam*: "The truth of Dharma lies in the dark cave" (EE, 33). What these traditions in the lowercase yield is a gargantuan, pluralistic body of storytelling down the ages. From the Sanskrit work of Valmiki (circa 1st century CE) to the Tamil Ramayana of Kambar (12th century), the Bengali rendition of Krttivasa (15th century), the Awadhi Ramcharitmanas of Tulsidas (16th century), and beyond, the story of the prince of Ayodhya is a complex unfolding of counteracting rationales and Dharmic perspectives. In some versions, a mortally wounded Valin could chastise Rama for breaking the warrior code and killing him from behind. In others Rama could try to exonerate himself by arguing that the act was in the family interest (*kula dharma*) since he had to slay Valin to solicit the help of his rival brother Sugriva in defeating Ravana and saving Sita. He could declare imperiously that since Valin was a mere monkey that could be hunted, the Kshatriya norms of just battle did not apply in his case. Conversely, Rama could be reminded that he had no personal enmity with Valin; as a matter of fact, he could have asked for the latter's support in the war against Ravana, since Valin was a great warrior who had defeated Ravana in the past. Rama could be told that naturalistic laws of hunting and devouring were not applicable here since humans do not consume monkey meat. Matilal points out that in an otherwise Bhakti rendition of the story by Krttivasa—in which Rama is accorded divine status as an avatar of Vishnu—the poet laments his act as a "grave error." In Tulsidas, an embarrassed Rama offers to bring Valin back to life. However, here Valin himself is revealed to be a devotee of Rama; he chooses to die watching the face of his Lord.[42]

The extraction of a singular moral compendium and epic memory gets infinitely complicated in many diverse acts of telling and instantiating. These narrations range between imperial Brahminical-Sanskritic claims and radical, vernacular counterflows among the vulgate. They feature not only the epics and their variants, but also folktales, lore traditions, and fables. A. K. Ramanujan, in the course of his magnificent work on the traditions, has pointed out that Indic folklore streams—distinguished from the epics as well as the Puranas—are rarely guided by Brahminical Karma ideology. Here the gods smell, sweat, or sneeze; the goddesses menstruate. Local gods are married to more famous gods of the pantheon and lowly mortals rise to divine status.[43] The "traditions" as such—both written and oral, performed and remembered, socially theatricalized and internally felt—have always been voluptuous in form and dissemination. They have been marked by conflicting lines of interest, historicity, identity, language, and perspective. In this wider sense, traditions in the lowercase include folk Ramayanas told from a southern perspective sympathetic to Ravana, or from the point of view of the wronged Sita. They feature Sramana denunciations of Krishna as well as Jaina appropriations of Rama as one of their ilk of ahimsa who allows Laxmana to slay Ravana, or the Buddhist Dasaratha Jataka, in which Rama and Sita are like brother and sister. Such an itinerary would recognize the Adbhuta Ramayana, in which it is Sita who finally kills Ravana, as well as a Santhal version in which she is seduced by both Ravana and Laxmana, and acknowledge inevitable Vaishna-versus-Shaiva tensions built into these hundreds of renderings.[44]

Perhaps it was this difficulty—of extracting a consistent moral philosophy from the scriptural and epic sources, or of deriving them from any paramount authority—that led Hegel to conclude that Indian religion was inseparable from Indian mythology. Meanwhile, it is this immense historical babble of poiesis, imagination, and remembrance that the powers of Hindutva wish to extinguish. Such a destruction would be essential to fix the state of the Hindu as necessarily Brahminical and resolutely monolingual. In Hindutva ideology, variety and osmosis between dynamic traditions must be replaced by a manufactured and jealous "Epic of Tradition," especially in the context of the modern culture industry, in order to institute a masculine, Savarna national morality robbed of all errant and queering energies. Dilemmas and ambiguities must be replaced by representational pieties and an urban Hindu common sense in the age of the modern.

However, moral questions apart, there was also the modern issue of squaring an esoteric Tradition with the materialist and acquisitive principles of capital. From a European perspective, for an active national ethos to emerge there had to be a Hindu equivalent of Weber's Protestant ethic, at home with the world and the works of the profane.[45] The problem here was with a central common soteriological impulse informing the Indic faiths, both the Brahminical as well as the Sramana orders (except for the Carvakas). It was the notion of universal sorrow (*sarva dukham*). This leads to the paradigmatic notions of nonaction and nonviolence that feature in the Karma theory of the Vedic schools as well as Jainism and Buddhism. As Matilal observes, the thought of abiding sorrow can lead one toward renunciation (*akarma*), an otherworldly withdrawal from complex moral conundrums that the tasks and facts of life will inevitably bring (EE, 125–26). Human insufficiencies of intellect and training, or situational complexities, will always increase the ledger of Karmic lesions on the soul that will have to be carried on to the next life. A turn away from action and engagement was therefore always an option, since Moksha was the desired freedom from Samsara (metempsychosis)—this relentless embroilment in the world of dross, birth after birth. The objective was not to essentially take sides in a relentless earthly battle between good and evil, but to transcend that apparent dualism altogether—for one's own soul, not necessarily to please any theistic god. Within this broad picture of sorrow and deliverance, the Indic traditions supplied a variety of soteriologies: salvation through constant devotion and service to God (Vaishnava); complete dissolution of the ego in the absolute of Brahman (Vedanta); eternal bliss through antinomian ecstasies (Shaiva, Tantra); eternal return to the Divine Mother (Shakta); grasping of the void in a state of tranquility (Yoga); materialist denial of all metaphysics and afterlife (Lokayata); or total surrender to Niyoti as a sovereign fate (rather than a creator God or Karma) that determines the eventual release of souls (Ajivika).[46] The point, however, was whether any of these offered any significant civilizational motivation for the gathering of surplus.

Modern readings of the Bhagwad Gita, especially nationalistic ones, suggest that Krishna propounded the theory of desireless action (*nishkamavrata*) to temper this general stance of withdrawal from the sensory or the materialistic. However, it could also be argued that in elaborating a worldview attested by his own cosmic authority, Krishna had a practical motive. On the eve of battle, he had to stop a melancholic Arjuna from laying down his arms and abandoning the Kshatriya code.[47] Krishna's idea of Karmayoga in the Gita was directed, in the immediate sense, to the positive affirmation of warrior duties. It was fine to perform the tasks of the world, but with a profound sense of detachment, without any craving for the fruits of action. The question of Karma therefore becomes subsumed into that of Swadharma (innate nature), but without the ego. In the case of Arjuna, Swadharma would be an instrumentalization of the warrior self in the task of killing grandsires, uncles, friends, teachers, and cousins. The killing itself was a chronicle already foretold in the three orders of time, willed by Krishna himself as Kala. Yet, as we will later see in greater detail, this instrumentalization of the self, according to the dictation of Dharma as theodicy, cannot be easily merged with modern ideas of freedom, interest, and self-determination.

The final, and undeniably the most important roadblock in the pathway of universal Dharma—at ease with modernity and capitalism—pertains to the question of caste. Within the "Tradition" debate, there are two meanings that may be assigned to *caste* as a signifier. According to a dominant narrative of Hindu revivalism, an original, merit-based, fourfold Varna system was dissipated into thousands of hereditary Jatis (mixed-caste, racial, linguistic-regional, or occupational identities) in the age of the profane. Ideologues of Hindu reform in general, possibly since Dayanand Saraswati's *Satyarth Prakash* (1875), have insisted on this distinction. According to that logic, caste—as regular Jati discrimination, untouchability, and local hierarchical compartmentalization of rights and duties—is a modern perversion largely brought upon by Muslim rule. The Vedic form of the Hindu society was based on a modern spirit of scientific management, division of labor, or even communism, in some accounts, but along the lines of an organic achievement, not a contractual one.[48] In the hoary days of Hindu antiquity, Varna determination was independent of birth.[49]

One can certainly say, as Matilal does, that there was unease about the idea of Varna by birth within the complex of Hindu traditions themselves. This questioning is present in Yudhisthira's conversation with King Nahusa in the Vana Parvan of the Mahabharata, or the famous story of Satyakama Jabala in the Chandogya Upanishad.[50] In the great epics themselves, there are numerous instances when people of humble, illegitimate, or mixed birth—Ekalavya, Vidura, Karna, Ghatotkacha, or Yuyutsu in the Mahabharata, or Guhan or Shabari in the Ramayana—accomplish significant feats and achieve recognition. Shiva of the Trinity—the original untouchable and slayer of Brahmins in many legends—appears in the Mahabharata as the lowly mountain-dweller Kirata. Vyasa, the legendary compiler of the Mahabharata, is himself the son of a fisherwoman. Valmiki, the composer of the Ramayana, is traditionally believed to be a Dalit. Aside from Sramana orders that are today recognized as separate religions, there were formations like Vamacara (left-handed) Tantra within the folds of "Hinduism" itself that, apart from dwelling in ecstasies involving blood, meat, alcohol, and ritualistic sex, were based on a fundamental disavowal of Varna as destiny.[51] In later centuries, the many currents of Bhakti devotion—cutting across Vaishnava, Shaiva, Shakta, and Nirguna universes[52]—would bestow not just inclusion, but saintliness on Kannappan the hunter, Ravidas the leather worker, Sena the barber, Mira the woman, or Kabir the weaver.

In that case, how does one abstract a single and unadulterated theory of Varna as a theological principle? That is, a principle that derives not from human speculations but from God himself? It is argued that the Krishna of the Bhagwad Gita (specifically, 4.13 and 18.41–47) calls for a fourfold Varna division based on *gunas* (inherent qualities of an individual) and actions. Yet it is often not clear whether he means this as an absolute rule of free individual expression and recognition of the same, or as a sociology of expectations and stigmas dictated by birth and clan identity. Even if one were to assume that, in such a schema, a sinful Brahmin may lose his status while a meritorious Sudra may rise in station, it does not negate the reality that one is born into a Varna and immediately assigned a set of duties and strictures accordingly. Twice in the course of his exhortation (3.35 and 18.47), Krishna declares that it is better to perform one's own duties imperfectly than to do the tasks of others with great excellence. He does so in order to compel Arjuna to give up his mental flirtations with asceticism. Arjuna needed to give full expression to his innate warrior self, to the point of killing or being killed, even if, with a sudden meditative turn, he could hypothetically perform the task of philosophizing better than others. The question of Swadharma (determination of one's own nature) is therefore removed—at least in this case—from the individual's own resolve. War is dictated by Arjuna's clan responsibilities, namely, protecting his house from the degeneration that would automatically happen with the dereliction of the Kshatriya code (1.39–1.41). In terms of the general movement of the Gita, it would seem that the warrior aspect of Arjuna is fixed by fate, or by Krishna himself as the incarnate will of the three orders of time.

The Hindutva insistence on original Varna as recognition of merit over birth, cannot be extracted as a consistent principle from scriptures and treatises on law, or from events and didactic passages in the epics. Nor can merit be established as an operational schema in a sociology of caste institutions, or a historical ethnology of Jati formations and their lineage-based privileges or obligations. Moments of textual ambiguity are waylaid by many other instances such as the one Sheldon Pollock points out in Jaimini's Mimansasutra, where the principled exclusion of the Sudra (*apasudradhikarana*) from the domain of Sanskrit studentship (*upanayana*) is a matter already settled in Dharma, along the lines of a "theodicy of privilege." The conclusion, in the general Mimansa tradition, is that the "restriction is ultimately self-validating since we cannot explain it otherwise."[53] It is a great unknowing of the ways of the gods that dictate that the untouchable may not have access to the language of the gods.

There is another note of complication when it comes to a nostalgia for the "original" Varna system. Matilal points out that, in the Vedic texts, the birth of Varna is a cosmic phenomenon, as it appears in the famous Purusa Sukta (hymn 10.90) of the Rg Veda. It involves the issuing forth of the four types from the cosmic body (Purusa): the Brahmins from the mouth, the Kshatriyas from the arms, the Vaishyas from the thighs, and the Sudras from the feet. On earth, this system sublimates an ideal anthropomorphic social order in which the divisions work accordingly: the Brahmins perform the priestly and intellectual functions; the Kshatriyas rule and wage war; the Vaishyas trade; and the Sudras serve the others without complaint. However, unlike later, first-millennium texts like the Bhagwad Gita or Manusmriti, the Vedic postulate of Varna has nothing to do with what would later surface as the doctrine of Karma. That is, Karma as action with moral and ethical consequences and accruements of positive or negative traces (*karmaphalahetu*) from one birth to the next. The meaning of Karma in early Vedic literature is largely restricted to ritual acts, and the determination of caste takes place in accordance with Rta, the principle of cosmic regularity, balance, and order. Among the Upanishads, the Svetasvatara and Chandogya provide a glimpse of Karma in its later conceptual sense, but only as one among several determining factors such as nature, chance, destiny, matter, and time (EE, 429–30).

With the entry of Karma proper into the picture, the concept of Dharma largely replaces that of the Rta. It is now human agency—good or bad works and moral choices in past lives—that determines caste in a given birth, but as per a temporal schema of justice that transcends human finitudes of life and death. This transformation was clearly in response to Sramana orders like Buddhism and Jainism. It is assumed in this scenario that being born into the house of a Sudra is punishment for past sins that naturally remain unseen (*adrstya*) in the phenomenal world. While accepting humans as technically free agents who create their own misery, Karma theory also forecloses anything similar to Christian grace. Matilal notes that later Karma, in assemblage with the Ajivika notion of Niyoti (fate), makes the institution of Varna the expression of an inscrutable will that engineers a moral government of the universe down to the minutest atom.[54] With the Karma-Niyoti compact, Varna becomes a cosmic theodicy throughout a number of different ethical universes imagined in the "Tradition," from Sankara (8th century CE) to Madhava (13th century) and beyond.[55] Questions of justice and equity therefore cannot be of this world and of the lived time of humans, since it might take several cycles of life to ascend from a Sudra to a Brahmin. Technically, therefore, Varna does not allow social mobility for the individual unless dictated by exceptional turns of fate that raise the political power and riches of the Jati itself. It could thus be said that Karma is the principle of regulation here, while Niyoti may account for the exception. The former makes the destination of the soul an individual question; the latter already prepares a sociology of duties based on the caste one is born in. From the vantage point of the modern, caste in a wider sense forecloses the possibility of an organic Hindu corporate body of equitable metabolisms. Since individuals, in a fundamental sense, are of uneven Karmic naissance, it is difficult to achieve a modern balance between cosmically determined inequities, on one hand, and an abstract equality of law, representation, and rights, on the other. It is also difficult to imagine a uniformly congregated Hindu people, when it is understood that one body can pollute the other in Karmic terms.

In Weber's eyes, Karma rationalizes Varna, giving birth to what he famously called "the most consistent theodicy ever produced."[56] For Dumont, writing half a century later, the Karma–Varna assemblage not only created inequality as a social reality, but accorded it positive theological value.[57] Matilal objects to these magisterial conclusions; for him, the traditions had always been self-conscious, and there was no universally presiding theodicy. The Karma–Varna assemblage itself came into being in the Bhagwad Gita or in the Manusmriti in response to and amid eight centuries of Buddhist and Jaina dominance over Indian religious thinking, metaphysics, and aesthetics. It gave Varna a footing in the overall dispensation of Dharma but hardly a stability.[58] The question of Jati and Varna was always complicated by competing reckonings of tradition that were artisanal, ecological, and based on everyday customs and pieties. This pluralism would always threaten a perfect Hindu bureaucratic rationalization of the polity, the imposition of a national form over regions, and the submission of all powers of thinking to the modern state. In their own claims to the past, these minoritarian pictures point to a modern problem, not only in relation to the idea of a monotheistic flock understood in Abrahamic terms, but also apropos the Western anthropological category of religion itself. As Matilal put it, "The social reality [called] religion did not exist in ancient or classical India"—at least in a core, etymological root sense of the word, as *reliq*, or that which binds and relegates.[59] "Religion" in this sense, as Talal Asad has shown, was constructed as an anthropological category within the parameters of European secular introspection and the modern expansion of empire.[60]

The Hindu Nation as Organism: Problems and Pieties

In Hindu nationalist discourse, the return to a glorious Vedic dawn is a matter of total recall that requires no evolutionary or dialectical engagement with history. The return cannot be proposed in the chronometric order of the modern, one with determined pasts and limited futural possibilities. Instead, the unhappy sides of history, and the modern delirium of the signifier itself, have to be jettisoned, and then select spectaculars of the past have to be inducted into a primal origin myth and deep time. Here I want to trace Hindutva as statist desire—primarily via the works of Madhav Golwalkar—in critical proximity to the question of political monotheism.[61] In the process, we can mark the violence this Hindu axiomatic promises to inflict on the picture of pluralism we have drawn from Matilal and, at the same time, illustrate the historical imbroglio of a project that wants to narrate an organismic Ram Rajya (Kingdom of Rama) into being. That is, one that can cut across warring imaginations surrounding the epic itself and unite descendants of the vanquished well as the victorious.

In Golwalkar's 1939 pamphlet *We, or Our Nationhood Defined*, this desire took the shape of an organic union of the pentagonal ideas of territory, race, religion, culture, and language. This represented an unimpeachable integrity; if even one of these constitutive principles were absent, according to Golwalkar, the nation would arrive stillborn, despite the renewal of Hindu hearts. Such high organicist principles, which undergird RSS-brand Hindutva, have been resilient, even after the altered geopolitical realities of partition. They also point to certain old conundrums of the Hindu right and to the breathtaking ambitions of its project when understood in its full form.

Golwalkar's pentagonal unity is what Schmitt would call the desired political; it is one that is anterior to state or law and, once awakened, promises to eviscerate politics in the normal sense. We can call these a set of "Herderian" pieties, pertaining to some prominent themes of nationhood, Volk, patriotism, virtue, religion, language, and aesthetics in the organicist imagination. I use this conceptual shorthand with due apologies to Johann Gottfried Herder, since Golwalkar's text does not otherwise nearly emulate the German thinker's complexity of thought and cosmopolitan vision. In Golwalkar, such pieties supposedly point to a set of existential commitments above the fray of ordinary interests and representations. In a large country with innumerable cultures and languages, they function as a loose ensemble of idealist postulates without arranging themselves into a realistic narrative with clearly defined means and ends. They are weaponized in an instant in regular Hindutva politics; yet they are also the points of agony and heartburn in the quest for a phantasmal, but total Hindu India. Let us now glimpse at some of these pieties.

TIME AND ORIGINS

The Hindu nationalist idealization of the nation as singular Samaj (society) takes the shape of an organismic Varna harmony rather than a contractual social order. However, there is also the inevitable pressure to locate that Varna arrangement in time. When did it flourish perfectly, and when did it begin to decay? Why, for instance, is there no mention of Varna in the edicts of Ashoka the Great (3rd century BCE)? It is an almost inescapable imperative of modern skepticism and epistemology that if one proposes such ideal origins as truth, that origin itself must be located in a temporal order of history diseased by disenchantment and emptiness. This is where the project of Hindu revival becomes infinitely more complicated than, say, a Benedictine Christian resurgence after the dark ages. As a project of memory and reconstitution, it becomes breathtakingly more ambitious than reviving the Athens of Pericles, the Caliphate of Harun al Rashid, or, as in the case of the fascists, much more grueling than Mussolini's attempt to salvage the Circus Maximus and the Rome of Augustus. A total Hindu reclamation of India as space restored to sacredness would be more daunting than the Zionist reclamation of the land of the Hebrews that Golwalkar was witnessing with deep skepticism in 1939. The period of Vedic naissance, its glorious flourishing and its protracted twilight—preceding a millennium of Buddhist dominance, eight centuries of Islamic rule, and then two hundred years of British colonialism—

has to be pushed back deeper into the wombs of time. For Golwalkar, the decadence began with the rise of emasculating Sramana sects around 500 BCE and then gathered pace with the invasion of the Muslims. For a figure like Dayanand Saraswati (1824–1883), on the other hand, the rot had already set in a thousand years before the Great War of the Mahabharata itself.[62] The point of origin is thus perpetually evanescent, receding beyond the historical, archaeological, or genetic apparatuses of the modern. This backtracking begins with the question of the antiquity of the Vedas, the great epics, and other sacred literature; it continues with various questions about the birth of Rama, the historicity of the Kurukshetra War, or the purported "Saraswati civilization," now more than nine thousand years old.[63]

Golwalkar had declared in 1939 that the Vedas came into being in "times of the dim past, into the mysteries of which history dare not venture."[64] The Mahabharata was more than 5,000 years old in his reckoning, and the Hindus had occupied the land for eight to ten millennia before any "foreign" race set foot on the subcontinent. Time, in the terms of the Aryan naissance, is geological. Golwalkar explains Bal Gangadhar Tilak's (1856–1920) thesis that the race originated from the North Pole by declaring that the North Pole itself was at that time in India, where Bihar and Orissa are presently situated.[65] This postulate of deep origins draws from the nineteenth-century climate of romantic orientalism, neo-Platonism, and a general swarm of antinomian energies that touched Nietzsche and inspired theosophists like Madame Blavatsky (1831–1891). The world itself was Hindu, in the beginning, and the Aryans were the root race with a universal monotheme. It was the Aryans, Blavatsky had declared, who had gone to Egypt and built the Sphinx and the pyramids.[66] Her antinomian assertion was situated within a greater tradition that included now relatively obscure works like Edward Pococke's *India in Greece* (1856) or James Francis Hewitt's two-volume *Primitive Traditional History* (1907).[67] The vision of Aryan/Hindu colonization of the world was carried forward in Arya Samaj discourse, from Saraswati's *Satyarth Prakash* (1875) to Har Bilas Sarda's *The Hindu Superiority* (1906) and beyond. This overarching nineteenth-century imagination of an Aryan genesis—with the known civilizational world itself figured as remnants of that original diaspora—was similar to the idea of the *vagina nationum* in Tacitus, transmitted via Teutonic migration myths that were summoned repeatedly in the modern era to shape protonational imaginaries after the peace of Westphalia.[68]

In 1940, a year after Golwalkar completed *We, or Our Nationhood Defined*, Chaman Lal published *Hindu America: Revealing the Story of the Romance of the Surya Vanshi Hindus and Depicting the Imprints of Hindu Culture on the Two Americas.*[69] Deploying a rather fantastic visual anthropology involving totems and practices, architecture, craniology, and fertility rituals, Lal argued that Suryavanshi Rajputs had migrated to the New World continents more than ten thousand years ago. America was the Patala Desa mentioned in the Vishnu Puran and was the home of Ulupi, one of Arjuna's wives in the Mahabharata. Such Rajput voyages were conducted independently or through already-present Hindu outposts in Japan and East Asia. The Suryavanshis birthed the race of the Sun God, and it was their Inca progeny who had produced the perfect communist society based upon the Varna system. It was, however, only one of many colonial outposts of the ancient Hindus in a planetary continuum that stretched from Peru to Rome, Egypt, Hyperborea, Greece, and beyond.

Lal's thesis was not novel. It was the mirror image of a common origin thesis formulated in the moment of inception of Indological philology itself, when William Jones (1746–1794) wrote: "It is remarkable that the Peruvians, whose Incas boasted of the same descent, styled their greatest festival Ramasitoa; whence we may suppose, that South Asia was peopled by the same race, who imported into the farthest parts of Asia the rites and fabulous history of Rama."[70] The important point in Lal's case is not about human movements across continental distances and oceans in the Neolithic age. It is about the belief that such journeys were made by Hindus already constituted in a cultural and civilizational sense, secure in a single firmament of faith, and governed by eternal laws and institutions. The Aryan was perennial. He could not be imagined in a state of savagery. According to Lal, the Neolithic Rajputs gave Latin America the enlightenment of the Gurukuls and the wisdom of the Panchayats. The primitive Mexicans worshipped Indra, and Ganesha morphed into the Mayan rain deity Chaac. This was a picture of profound inception that could be linked punctually, across the millennia and across the seas, to an unfolding Hindu remembrance and promise of return. A destinying arc had to be completed with the maturation of world history itself. "The fire of sacrifice (*yagna*) that was kindled by our forefathers in Patal Desha (America) is still burning in the hearts of many million Americans and the day is not far off when a free India will reclaim America to her cultural fold."[71]

Lal's text does not represent Hindu chauvinism in the generic sense. It has a cosmopolitan flavor to it and was blessed by an impressive array of nationalist leaders at the time of its publication in 1940. The book comes with forewords and letters of endorsement from Dr. Rajendra Prasad and Sarvepalli Radhakrishnan—who would become the first and second presidents of India—and from the poet and freedom fighter Sarojini Naidu, the educationist Pandit Madan Mohan Malaviya, and the Indian theosophist Bhagwan Das. The project was understood to be very much within a mainstream Indian nationalist imagination and its desire for remittance and recognition from a history written by victors. This tendency assumes a sharper form in Hindutva discourse, where historical time had to be transcended to redeem a glorious past because history itself was a tale of privation. It accorded—in linear, disenchanted time—a merciless account of great oblivion, defeat, dispersal, and subjugation. History was not simply about the invasion and tyranny of Muslim and Christian foreigners, but also of a progressive loss of true Savarna virtues. It was full of trickery, deceit, and tragic betrayals. History, in essence, has been a liberal-Marxist plot in the RSS imagination; it must be broached only to invite a turn away from it and its temporal entrapments, to gather a sense of pride and identity in the very event of its refutation.[72]

The image of time we see in Chaman Lal's text draws from a general impulse of theological and eschatological thinking in the Hindu canon. Time, or Kala, here is a massive, cosmogonic compass that is beyond immediate existence or memory. It has a slow but looming appetite; it begets only to engulf and destroy. It stretches from the smallest unit of humanly controllable instant, such as the blinking of an eye, to the infinite temporality of the Brahman, crossing the time spans of the forefathers (*pitrs*) and gods (*devas*) on the way.[73] Manu's Dharmasastra, the Vana Parvan of the Mahabharata, and other texts of early Vedic literature speak of the four Yugas or ages: Krta (or Satya), Treta, Dwapara, and Kali, the present age of the profane. In these texts, the completion of the four epochs, a Mahayuga, takes 12,000 earthly years and a thousand of these is equivalent to one night and day of Brahman. In the later Puranic texts, these years are treated as divine ones; their numbers had to be multiplied by 365 for them to be commensurate to human measures of time. As a result, Kali, the smallest and the most degenerate of the ages, assumes a gargantuan span of 432,000 years.[74]

These are figurations of deep time and do not have to be taken literally in terms of quantifiable numbers.[75] They pertain to an art of rhetorical exaggeration that is central to epic concepts of antiquity. They can be understood as pure magnitudes to invoke fear, shame, or reverence, like the unreal armies of the Mahabharata. One does not therefore have to conclude that the Vishnu Puran gives us a positive temporal schema by which the exploits of Rama in the Treta age and the historicity of his birthplace actually shift to a million years or more from our contemporary moment. Yet what the Puranic imagination does is create a breathtaking existential distance between humans of the present and the Dharmic exemplum. It is beyond question that the order of the now is that of the Kali, in which the progressive decline of righteousness has turned the world upside down, and Mlechchas and lower-caste kings rule the world. It is also true that a grand cosmological churning, not apparent in humdrum existence, will restore the true order. Inhabiting such a system is like living on the earth, which curves at every point to its vast planetary roundness while the ground beneath our feet appears flat. This also means that time reckoning in the ancient Indian context could be both cyclical in a cosmic sense and linear in the punctual here and now. The banality and confusion in Golwalkar-style Hindutva thinking lies in making the two identical, and then vectorizing the whole thing in the service of a statist mythography. This in itself often yields a strange picture in which cosmology is made terrestrial and a human world governed by natural laws is abnegated. The sky, meanwhile, remains the heavens without something like a Pascalian fear of infinite space. A total merger of cosmology and geography eviscerates historical consciousness and seeks to reenchant the world, dispelling or colonizing secular scientific thought.

An apparent duality of temporal imaginations, however, poses a question about the valence of human action, both individual and collective. This time consciousness presents a too-distant and therefore a too-feeble eschatology when it comes to finite human destinying. What can we, as mere mortals, do for the resuscitation of true order in time? That is, if we believe that the cyclic order is cosmologically determined, too massive to be affected by our meager contributions, and will proceed anyway? If one has to return to a point when humanity itself was Hindu, how long would it take Indians to spiritually reclaim their lost tribes in the Americas? There are quite a few existential quandaries and points of tension here. These do not just give birth to agon and circumspection. They also affect a new masculinist Hinduism with anxieties relating to that other traditional self-image—that of a disabling otherworldliness and nonviolent fatalism. In order to be the Hindu sovereign, one has to exercise active command over imaginations of time in the world, and, like Guy Debord's Napoleonic figure, monarchically direct the energy of memories.[76]

History becomes a singular story of a progressive decline in purity, and a catastrophic accrual of wreckage and pollutants. This is precisely why the thought of metric time is itself a thought of rupture. In an ideal sense, the loss of original essence cannot be located as an event in a temporal series. Rather, the rupture itself is the inauguration of historical time, like the union of Cronos and Clio, or the separation of the two from Aeon in the Greek world. History begins the instantaneous degeneration toward Kali. In that ideal sense, therefore, it is pointless to assign historical dates to the compilation of the Vedas, for the Vedas were always composed at a time prior to time. In the Samkhya creation story narrated by Manu—cited in the Rg Veda itself (10.129) and in agreement with the one in the Santi Parvan of the Mahabharata—the Vedas were "milked from the fire, the wind, and the sun."[77] It is only after this event that the great one (Paramatman), or the first cause, "emitted time and the divisions of time, the constellations and planets, rivers, oceans, mountains, rough ground and smooth ground." Thus began time, and it was in the beginning of time itself that Purusa, the primordial man, created the four Varnas (*Manu*, 1.31).

The idea of deep time and deep recall must envelop the present, much like the event the Greeks called *kairosis*. It must curve into the finite, here-and-now fragmentation of auspicious and inauspicious moments (*rahukala*). Deep time must wrap around historical consciousness in order to absolve or condemn it. What is at stake here is the consciousness of being perpetually somewhere on the cusp of these mammoth measures, living closer to eternity than to secular time, and waiting for a rebirth of the righteous Krta in a single stroke. We could, here, think of a beautiful folk illustration, from A. K. Ramanujan, depicting the reverse scenario, the instant arrival of the age of dross:

> A story is told about two men coming to Yudhisthira with a case. One had bought the other's land, and soon after found a crock of gold in it. He wanted to return it to the original owner of the land, who was arguing that it really belonged to the man who had now bought it. They had come to Yudhisthira to settle their virtuous dispute. Just then Yudhisthira was called away . . . for a while. When he came back the two gentlemen were quarreling furiously, but each was claiming the treasure for himself this time! Yudhisthira realized at once that the age had changed and *kaliyuga* had begun.[78]

The task of Sangh Parivaar–style historicism, trapped as it is in a colonial framework deriving from James Mill, is to reduce such temporal imaginations into coarse positivisms of rise and fall. There are, of course, periods of golden flourishing or lucid intervals in history, frequently broached by the Hindu right—ancient India's Gupta Empire, the Vijayanagar of the south between the twelfth and fourteenth centuries, or the solitary exploits of Rana Pratap or Shivaji.[79] These events often become strange figurations—undeniably historical, but no longer temporal. It is his elevation from a temporal order of history that has lately allowed Rana Pratap to "win" the Battle of Haldighati in 1576.[80]

These invocations are also inevitably touched by the unhappiness of historical complexity, evanescence, and dissipation. History, as it is, does not yield a Hindu version of what Foucault once called a Jupiterian history purposed by sovereignty. The Vaishnavite Guptas ruled an empire between the fourth and sixth centuries CE that was dominated by Buddhist and Jain currents of thought. It was preceded by eras of Sudra kings (the Nanda and Mayurya dynasties), Buddhist monarchs (Asoka), and Brahmin ones (the Sungas). India, during this era, absorbed perpetual winds of change blowing from the Achaemenid and Seleucid empires, Indo-Greeks under a figure like Menander, and from Bactrian, Scythian, or Parthian nomads in the Eurasian steppe. The Gupta Empire itself was progressively denuded and eventually destroyed by periodic attacks from the Alchon Huns from central Asia. Hindu nationalist accounts also gloss over the fact that political power in the Indic context was seldom concentrated in the form of a despotic state. Rather, much of it was distributed immanently in local caste, tribe, or mercantile networks, and in clan-based confederacies (*gana sangha*) rather than kingdoms.[81] Culture and intellection were always inflected by Greek, Arabic, or Chinese philosophy, art, mathematics, medicine, architecture, and astronomy. The massive history of trade with the world at large before and after the Gupta era—from China to western and central Asia, up to the Caspian and Black Seas; the Roman Empire; Egypt and the eastern Mediterranean world; East Africa and the Ethiopian-Byzantine circuit; and then Thailand, Cambodia, or the Golden isles of the east—should all challenge the myth of a pristine civilizational genesis, secure in its endosmosis. Such a complex scene would include the early flourishing of Buddhism and Jainism between 200 BCE and 300 CE, the eventual induction of Syrian Christianity into the picture via the legend of Saint Thomas, followed by the Nestorians and then Islam via traders from Arabia.[82] Legends also trace a Jewish presence along the Malabar coast back to the destruction of the Second Temple in 70 CE.

The Gupta epoch, despite its glorious achievements, strictly speaking, cannot be included in that primordial time Golwalkar invokes when he says that Hindus ruled the land for ten thousand years before a "foreigner" ever set foot on the subcontinent. His statement is a rhetorical flourish, an imperious "wiping" of timelines, a gross invocation of deep time to negate the metric imprints of history. There is therefore also an abiding note of pathos in Hindu nationalist discourses even as they celebrate the Guptas, or monumentalize Shivaji. For such moments too fall within an otherwise relentless process of caste clamor, deterioration, Buddhist dominance, Islamic rule, and temple destruction.[83] "We want a 'Man' with a capital 'M,'" Golwalkar wrote in 1957, "We want a virile, masculine man. Now our people are feminine men."[84] The emasculated ones, as he saw it a decade after independence, were building an India in the image of Gandhi, that pacific and androgynous father of the nation. Golwalkar's construct of the masculine Hindu too is, in many ways, the mirror image of the "manly Englishman" conjured up by the Raj after the Mutiny of 1857 and the Morant Bay uprising in Jamaica in 1860.[85] This dualist attitude toward the monumental or antiquarian equipage of history is precisely why absolute denial is interspersed by neurotic approximation: the Hindu "historian" P. N. Oak's oeuvre claims the Taj Mahal, the Qutub Minar, and even the Kabah in Mecca for the Hindus. In his work, the time of Hindu origins curves into secular time and frameworks of historical cognition to annex Westminster Abbey as a Shiva temple; ancient Italy as Hindu land, or the Pope himself as Hindu priest.[86]

There could, however, be another way of looking at the annals of modern Hindu nation thinking and reconnaissances of the past. Michel Foucault has suggested that the function of such discourses of origins and mythic time may not actually be to record the past, but to speak of right in relation to power. He invokes a Frankish legend that was in currency from the beginning of the middle ages up to the Renaissance. It held that the French were descended from the Franks, who in turn come from Trojan stock. They had left Troy under Priam's son King Francis and had eventually found their homeland in France after sojourns on the banks of the Danube and the Rhine. Yet, as Foucault points out, this invocation of fantastical origins is not actually a call for a return to Troy or to revive a Trojan heritage. What it does is set up a story of France by a double elision, both of the stories of Gaul and of imperial Rome that had colonized Gaul. In casting both the French and the Romans as refugees from Troy, it appeals to a principle of equity and just inheritance. With the eclipse of "elder brother" Rome, the younger brother becomes the heir "by virtue of the rights of peoples." France therefore becomes a legatee to the empire; the rights and power of the King of France become akin to those of the Roman emperor.[87] Similarly, in the course of an insightful reading of

Hobbes, Foucault suggests that the periodic recall of the Old Saxon state—a perfect combination of Moses, Athens, and Sparta—served to establish the rights of the ones vanquished by William the Conqueror. It was part of a "settling" of Englishness through movements of war and peace, Norman overlordship and Saxon rebellion.

At the heart of such mobilizations of myth and affectation in Europe was thus a question of equity. It involved the production of uniformity and, in time, a republican enthusiasm by the slow maturation of parity between the races, remittance of debts between the historically victorious and the defeated, and between the dominant and the dominated. There has been no paucity of such strategic use of myth and other primordial summons in the Indic context. Drawing up fictitious caste histories along with ceremonials and abjuration of meat and alcohol have been standard procedures for caste ascendancy, especially from the late eighteenth century onward. The fabrication of competing imaginations of time, desire, and becoming have been primary features of Sramana, Bhakti, and Lokayata departures from the Vedic-Brahminical fold.

The Hindutva invocations of primordial origins are, however, of a different nature. They invoke a mythic past, defined essentially in terms of Varna, in order to redeem it in the form of Jati revenge against Islam, not Jati parity within Hinduism. That is, with the idea of Jati itself introducing a vernacular complexity into the question—since the word means race, religion, linguistic group, and gender, as well as caste, in North Indian languages. The axial myth of the nation, among other things, must be there to picture one Jati and one revenge by foreclosing the emergence of countermemories and competing fictions of Jati identity. That is also precisely the reason why such memorializations expose the Hindu project itself to questions, such as whether one can imagine a monothematic Hindu justice beyond the caste system and the naturalized subjugation of women. Is an equitable historical settlement between the Hindus and Muslims also an equitable settlement between the Hindu castes? Is there not a profound debt of the bygone—involving inequity and the righteous rage of the lowly Sudra, the outcast, the woman, or the enslaved—to be settled within the purported Hindu fold itself?

This was a question of the past that Nehru saw in Bergsonian terms: "The piling up of the past upon the past goes on without relaxation," says Bergson in his *Creative Evolution*. "In reality the past is preserved by itself, automatically. In its entirety, probably, it follows us at every instant. . . . Doubtless we think with only a small part of our past, but it is with our entire past, including the original bent of our soul, that we desire, will, and act."[88]

The debts of the ages were clearly too profound. Nehru wrote his *Discovery*, as he himself said, to rid himself of the weight and furniture of the bygone, and perhaps to rationalize the present and align it with a future that appeared dark to him during his internment at the Ahmednagar Fort in the autumn of 1944. He realized that, in an ideal sense, a new constitutional revolution and a democratic republicanism would be possible only when Indian lives ceased to be "encumbered with the dead wood of this past."[89] One had to break with it. Old as India was, she had to grow young again. In stark contrast to Golwalkar and his brethren, Nehru, their archenemy and the architect of modern India, saw both Vedic revivalism and Islamic theocracy as anachronisms, since "there [was] only one way traffic in time."[90] His republicanism thus came with not just a radically new social contract, but also a new covenant of time and memory, one with promises of parity and without primordial imperatives of revenge.

RACE AND LAW

One could say that, after the immaculate conception of the Vedas, sovereignty began with the slight ripening of time itself. Let us consider another origin story, this time about the birth of Aryan kingship. In the Santi Parvan of the Mahabharata, the old Kuru patriarch Bhishma tells his Pandava grandnephew Yudhisthira about the birth of human sovereignty. In the beginning, when Dharma prevailed in the hearts of men, there was no need for kings—much as in the Israel depicted in Judges 17:6 of the Bible. However, error inevitably crept in, perceptions became clouded, and virtue began to decline in the state of nature. Men became overcome with avarice and anger; they forgot to offer libations to the gods. The Vedas disappeared and with them the sway of righteousness. At that hour, Brahma invented the institution of kingship by composing a treatise of a hundred thousand chapters. The maintenance of Dharma and the regulation of vice therefore became the preserve of the royal office. Lord Vishnu, at the behest of the gods, then conceived the first monarch. This was not an easy process, however, for a monstrous other was born with the first Aryan king.

Vishnu first gave birth to Virajas by the fiat of his will. However, Virajas himself and also the first few of his descendants were inclined toward renunciation rather than kingship. The seventh man in this line was the wicked Vena, and the Rishis (sages) who were true utterers of the Vedas slew him. Chanting mantras, they pierced the right thigh of Vena. Thereupon emerged a short-limbed person, resembling a burnt tree, with blood-red eyes and black hair: this entity became the progenitor of the Nishadhas (hunters), the wicked tribes that live in hills and forests, and others called the Mlechchas (barbarians), residing in the Vindya Mountains. Subsequently, the Rishis pierced the right arm of Vena, from which sprung Prithu, eighth in descent from Vishnu and the first king who was well versed in warfare and the Vedas.

The birth of the Nishadha and his immediate exile to a categorical "outside" in the south therefore happened just prior to the advent of the first Arya king.[91] Now if we "historicize" this myth, it would be inaccurate and simplistic to account for this primal difference between the two immaculately conceived brothers—the fair Aryan one and the dark, Dravidian entity—only in terms of a biological conception of race. Historically, so-called Indo-European speakers were a linguistic group, not a race. The figure of the Arya would not derive from a single ethnic identity but from a Sanskrit speaking one complemented by markers of prestige, disciplined endosmosis, and access to Vedic knowledge and customs.[92] However, when the thought of an ideal Varna system enters the order of Hindu nationalism, it is marked, among other things, by a modern racial imagination. The Aryans were not a "race" in a contemporary biopolitical sense, but they became one from the mid-nineteenth century within the auspices of a certain form of orientalist Indology and its legatee in modern Hindutva.[93] They became so within the auspices of a wider epistemological turn, in which a xenological scientism of race after Darwin—including Social Darwinism, or craniology and phrenology—replaced religion, culture, or civilization as the index of colonial difference.[94] Lighter skin pigmentation, especially in North India, may be traced back to a multitude of "foreign" sources in time: Indo-Greeks, Arabs, Bactrians, Turks, Mongoloids, Huns, Parthians, and Europeans. Yet, a primary imagination of caste purity, endosmosis, and the "out of India" theory of Aryan naissance distills this mix into the political phenomenology of an indigenous and masterly race identity. Consider, for instance, this passage from the *Satyarth Prakash* (1875) by Dayanand Saraswati, the founder of the Arya Samaj: "Manu also corroborates our position. He says, 'The countries other than Aryavarta are called Dasyus and Mlechcha countries (*Manu* 10.45, 2.23).' The people living in the northeast, north, northwest were called Raakshasas. You can still see that the description of Raakshasas given therein tallies with the ugly appearance of the negroes of today."[95]

The pure specter of the Arya precedes the detritus of history; that is, the degeneration, the meekness, and femininity ascribed to the historical Hindu, now swarthy under the tropical sun. The Arya therefore transcends all tribunals of justice or memory; he is a figure lodged tenuously between a natural aristocracy and a barbarian democracy. His temporality is a double bind of time wrapped around the substance of history; it is that which was before history began and that which will once again be when history is over. This race thinking takes many shapes and forms, from a notorious Indian social predilection for fairer skin to eugenics-based ideas of innate caste merit or pathology. But if the ancient Dharmic model is to be reinvented as a lean, seamless, modern nation-state culture, what would then happen to the principle of absolutist exclusion that separates the kingdom of the Arya from the wild abode of the Nishadha? This original distinction—based on race imaginations esoteric or biological—has resonated through intricate histories of assimilation, annexation, inventions of fictitious pasts, and transfer of identities.[96]

When the phantom aspects of nobility and absolute bestiality are distributed among modern race configurations, the spectral Aryan presumes the dark matter of the Nishadha. History becomes a long story of miscegenation, that of the Nishadha coming down from the mountains and of Arya descendants traveling south of the Vindhyas. The Hindu nationalist nostalgia for pure race origins is perpetually haunted by a secret schizophrenic realization that an absolute return to that racial state of the Arya is not possible. All Indians are thus Aryas and Nishadhas at once, albeit in differential measures. This is an ontological calibration—aesthetic, religious, and political—that works in multiple registers of Savarna common sense. The name of the caste is preserved by patrilineal perpetuation; yet it is the aspect of race—growing darker from the city to the forests and hills, or from north to south—that is a reminder of a primal purity or fallenness. Caste politics aside, the work of this race thinking becomes visible in present-day turmoil over tribal rights in India and metropolitan attacks on Schedules 5 and 6 of the Constitution, which guarantee these rights.

The idea of race here is not entirely identical to European biologism. Rather, it is an assemblage of themes: a cosmological Varna purity in conjunction with a post-Darwinian science of race and the antinomian invention of the Aryan people. But where does the city end and the forest begin in a Hindu democracy? Second, in an ideal scenario of revival, can the diagram of Varna society be extended to cover national territory and all its races? The importance of such questions lies in the fact that political monotheism and the issue of purity have been, in modern history, generally inextricable from the question of race. In India this has been evident in the absolute identification of the Muslim with a Turko-Arab pathology. In Israel it has been clear in the predicament of nonwhite Jews, apart from Palestinians. These and other contemporary phenomena in the world point to that still ominous observation made by W. E. B. Du Bois about the essence of modern politics being centered upon the problem of the color line. It also brings us to a third question: To what extent is the idea of Varna society amenable to that multicultural thing called assimilation, in both a synchronic and diachronic sense?

A design of the perfect Varna society can be drawn up from the work of Manu, who, according to Golwalkar, is the first and finest lawgiver in human history.[97] This is an ideal text to visit in this regard because it has been upheld by the modern episteme as the key compendium of Hindu law, and championed by the Hindu right as the proper picture of Hindu society and counterpoint to the Indian constitutional revolution. Manusmriti recommends a system in which the Brahmins remain free of avarice and focus on Vedic rituals to please the gods. The Kshatriyas become the protector class, as kings and warriors who uphold the righteous order. The Vaishyas engage in trade, and the lowly Sudras serve the other three classes without complaint (*Manu*, 1.88–91). Varna is a cosmic regime that is to be maintained by a regulation of energy flows—the elemental *sattva* (spirituality), *rajas* (virility), and *tamas* (torpor)—in human social expressions. Laws and regulations should thus pertain to maintaining purity, preventing pollution, observing penances and rituals, and practicing endogamy. Individual stations in life are determined by the Karmic consequences of previous lives and by the different ratios of the three elements in the self. The social and natural orders themselves are dependent on a Brahminical ministration of cosmic force fields through sacrifices and supplications to the gods.[98] Meanwhile, at the other end of the spectrum, the Sudra—in whom tamas is predominant—can absolve himself of his bestial state in the next birth or two through good works in the present. His name itself should breed disgust (2.31), but in advanced years he may be respected and recognized as an elder in the tenth decade of his life (2.137).

The notable point here is that Varna society in Manu forecloses the concept of laity as a spatial impossibility. This Aryan world systematizes a calibrated distancing of the self from the racial, the heretical, or the mongrel other. It requires a categorical separation of the *janapada* (kingdom or realm) from the jungle, and the priestly and royalist heart of things from the rest of society. Manusmriti is indeed a normative test. However, a good portion of it is also a manual on statecraft and the Dharmic management of inevitable racial mixing between pure bodies and polluted ones. The scholars Wendy Doniger and Brian Smith have connected this form to a general template of the Indian treatise after Panini, in which the wise author states one profound rule and then the rest of the text goes on to enumerate a series of increasingly specific exceptions, escape clauses, and concessions.[99] Manu, likewise, provides an exhaustive taxonomy of inevitable violations and then specifies ways to mitigate the resulting Karmic and biogenetic lesions on the corporate body of Aryan society. Once he gets into the realm of exceptions, outliers, and mixed entities, the strictures and typologies proliferate wildly. In this domain, there are the heretics (*pasandas*), the outcasts (*apasadas*), the outlaws or believers in different gods (*vratyas*), the atheists (*nastikas*), and the multitudinous offspring of *pratiloma* (against-the-grain) unions. These latter unfortunates range from the hunter (Nishadha), born of a Brahmin father and a Sudra woman, the charioteer (Suta) born of a Kshatriya father and a Brahmin mother, down to the poet or panegyrist (Magadha) fathered by a commoner in a royal or priestly womb. The outsider is not just created by race and miscegenation, but also by ideologies, apostasies, physical disabilities, and sheer eccentricities.

"Excluded, defective men, going 'against the grain,' produce still more excluded, defective classes, fifteen of them," Manu declares in the tenth book (10.31). These relationally tainted bodies are assigned to a range of professions and habitats that are distanced from the sacrificial fire, the king's throne, and the kitchen in a graduated manner. From the carpenter to the pugilist, the boatman, the dancer, the sugarcane boiler, the mountaineer, precipice dweller, or, indeed, the southerner (Dravida), these figures constitute a thickness of lived life. They supply creative and utilitarian energies that are essential for any functional society. But in the interests of a cosmic balance of forces, the mixed castes must be distributed in space in terms of purity and pollution, tactile, auditory, optical, or olfactory access, and rights of insemination. They must also be subject to discriminatory laws of movement and habitation. Some necessarily had to be itinerant bodies able to pass through without residential rights. Others could occupy only servant quarters, precincts of the market, or cremation grounds (10.12–56). Finally, untouchables like the fierce ones (Chandalas), the dog-cookers (Svapaca), and aliens (Dasyus) had to be totally ostracized from town and village.[100]

Manu's Aryan world is not one that seeks a territorial continuum with the other, or even an imperial extension into the space of the other. It insists on a regressive calibration of the entire space—on a scale of diminishing sacredness—from the civic order to the state of nature. It manages inevitable traffic between spheres through measures of punishment and penance, inclusion and absolutist exile. In the same spirit, Manu advises Brahmins against staying in lands populated by heretics or ruled by Sudras (4.61). His endogamous world must simply be a secure area for the Vedantin to partake in sacrifices and offerings to gods, guests, dependents, and ancestors, with the entire social order below this class designed as a support system. Within its auspices, race does have a bio-ontological component to it—the tamasic constitution of the lower-born imparts a dark complexion to their bodies—but one that works within a larger theodicy of unerring Karmic essences. Even if a man hailing from lowly stock looks like an Aryan, he is bound to reveal his nature ultimately (10.57). Similarly, ghastly appearances caused by leucoderma or leprosy are no more or less Karmic than the lowliness of the Sudra or the bestiality of the Chandala (3.92). The Vedantin should avoid a Chandala for the same reasons he should avoid a family with hairy bodies (3.7).

In contrast to the cautious cartography of the sacred in Manusmriti, one could invoke a utopian scene in Valmiki's Ayodhya, the capital of the kingdom of Koshala, ruled by Rama's father Dasaratha. This city was the result of deep Dharmic maturation; it had been ruled uninterrupted by Sagara and his sixty thousand virtuous descendants. Prosperity was universal and the magnificently built Ayodhya was totally free of thieves, atheists, or revolutionaries. It was inhabited by men of noble birth, well versed in the Vedas. Yet the reason why this picture of a perfect moral order could be rendered complete was because Ayodhya was entirely bereft of mixed castes.[101] It was thus an absolute Varna sexual discipline that had birthed a harmonious peace, only to be broken later by the conflict and miscegenation of Kali Yuga. This mythical scene in Ayodhya, as we know, occupies the core of Hindutva historicism, which, extrapolating from Foucault, is based on the denial of the relationship between caste war and history. No matter how far back one goes, profane historical knowledge does not present nature, right, order, or peace for Hindutva. Hindutva's historicism is therefore founded on an idealism that knowledge and truth belong to the order of Brahminical peace; that they cannot belong to the side of violence, miscegenation, and relentless caste war.[102]

Manu's social harmony is the expression of a cosmic schema by which Karmic pollutants cannot be allowed to pile up high enough to upset the order of things, leading to famine and other catastrophes. It is the Brahmin that has to purify, balance, and restore through ritualistic damage control.

However, even this principle cannot be an earthly universal, since realist and pragmatic concessions must be made at every step, depending on the law and custom of each region. This makes the cosmological imagination itself situational.[103] A king should ordain as law "whatever may be the usual custom of good, religious twice-born men, if it does not conflict with (the customs of) countries, families, and castes" (*Manu*, 8.46). The paramount status and severity of law is always mitigated by exceptional circumstances (*apada*) in which case they can be broken with unhappiness and the hope that the transgression will be never repeated. In adversity (*anaya*), distress (*arti*), or near starvation (*ksudha*), a father may kill his son, or a priest may eat the meat of dogs (10.101–8).[104]

It is assumed that the state of Dharma depends on the power of custom, benedictions or calamities brought forth by time, and the relative distribution of Vedantins, dutiful Kshatriyas, atheists, or untouchable Nishadhas in a given time and space. Here there are no universal laws under a single creator God. Manu's text, too, is a treatise on lawfulness, not the law itself. The man who has killed a priest therefore may either live in the forest for twelve years to purify himself, throw himself headlong into blazing fire, or walk a thousand miles reciting one of the Vedas (11.73–76). These are not normative choices of equal preference; it is understood that they depend on the state of Brahmin hegemony in the region. This provisional condition makes the Dharmic question itself acutely local in Manusmriti. The idea of Punya Bhu as sacred realm that can be derived from the text is, by default, an exclusive area dominated by Aryan Brahmins and Kshatriyas. It cannot undergo a modern extension to cover the terrestrial nation, since a homogenization of space would destroy the notion of the sacred itself. Manu, taken literally, imagines an apartheid domain of graduated internal striations as well an absolutist outside. His theodicy does not envision a dialectic between the law of the state as universal and that of the family as particular. Both are regional and situational. The man of caste in Manu is thus quite unlike the tragic pagan in Hegel who is always rendered criminal by either the law of the state or that of the family.

Extending Manuvaad (the modern ideology derived from Manusmriti) to the rationality of the territorial nation-state is a contradiction in terms, since Manu, in essence, forecloses civic religiosity. For him, to be moral is inevitably to particularize and contextually nominate. A. K. Ramanujan has pointed out that it is precisely in this sense that the modern Indian constitution overthrows Manu by ushering in a context-free jurisprudence of the law of the land, one that trumps regional particularities of custom. The temporal imagination of the modern follows the Great Indian Railway timetable; the manic city irreverently absorbs caste bodies into the crowd, and Ragas, now freed from a cosmology of auspiciousness, may be heard any time of the day.[105] Yet Manuvaad, as a modern metaphysics of Hindutva, comes into being as an agonistic duality between experience and the signifier. This metaphysics insists on a permanent rereading, a neospiritual affirmation of a mysterious patrimonial essence in Manu that is always missed by moderns who suggest that he is a father who is not ready to embrace all sons. In a general state of fallenness of language, all democratic readings of the high Hindu word in Manu are necessarily misreadings of Manu. The thought of this lost, now unapparent heart of things actually frees the Sangh Parivaar to conduct exercises of Manuvaadi chauvinism on multiple registers of Jati as perverted Varna: religion, caste, ethnicity, race, culture, language, and gender. The substance of the Manuvaadi axiomatic becomes the violence dispensed to construct it as an organismic whole. The specter of a Hindu Rashtra grows ominous not at the point when the Dharmasastra is formalized as letter of the law at the expense of the present Indian constitution. It becomes so much earlier, when the "spirit" of Manusmriti is revived as singular principle for a national life of customs.

TERRITORY, IMAGINATIVE GEOGRAPHY, IDENTITY

In the early summer of 2017, Tarun Vijay, the BJP leader, courted controversy by telling Al Jazeera television that "Indians," categorically speaking, could not be racist because they had lived with dark-skinned compatriots in South India for centuries. Vijay's comments came in the wake of attacks on African students in the Greater Noida region. These alien black men were suspected by the Hindu mob of vices like sexual debauchery, drug use, and even cannibalism. Apart from situating itself in a wider basin of memory and instinct that recalled the worst racial stereotypes of colonial discourse, Vijay's statement, in a single stroke, racially distinguished a heartland Savarna self of "India" from people south of the Vindhyas. This imaginative geography has a long history.

As primal figurations of an essentially nineteenth-century race imaginary, the Arya belonged to the north, while his terrible other, the Nishadha, was banished to the south. The former would claim Sanskrit as his domain of privilege, while the latter would always have his tongue deemed barbaric in comparison. Within the auspices of a modern Hindu Raj, the descendants of the two had to come together in time to form a uniform national flock. In order to do that, barriers of caste had to be negotiated and spatial imaginaries on either side of the Vindhyas had to be conjoined. The normative invitation of Hindu nationalism is for all to participate in a common Aryan ancestry of the spiritual as well as the biological kind, but with differential claims with regard to purity, prestige, and distance from an imagined civilizational center. The historical tensions inherent in this pan-Indian project are well known. This was a culture/race/language question that animated not just Dravidian nationalism, but also decidedly influenced the high Hindu vantage point of C. Rajagopalchari (1878–1972), the last governor-general of India, who told B. R. Ambedkar, chairman of the Constitutional Drafting Committee, that a natural Indian arrangement should have two federations, one for the north and the other for the south.[106]

According to Manu, the country that the gods made between the two divine rivers, the Sarasvati and Drsadvati, was the Brahmavarta, the land of the Vedas (*Manu*, 2.17). This was the land of the good people, where priestly control reigned supreme. Next, the stretch between the Himalayas and the Vindhya mountains—to the east of Vinasana, where the Sarasvati disappeared, and to the west of Pragya, or present-day Allahabad—was the middle country of Aryavarta, the abode of the Aryans. This land, where the black antelope ranged in a natural manner, was the land of sacrifices. Beyond it was the domain of the barbarians or Mlechchas devoid of Sanskrit. Manu advises that the twice-born must make every effort to settle in the sacred lands. However, a Sudra starved of livelihood could live anywhere (2.21–2.24). The territorial distinction, therefore, was based on an ontological principle of purity, not on considerations of politics, commerce, or war.

We see such North–South divisions in other texts too. Baudhayana, in his Dharmasutra, lists five characteristics peculiar to the people of the South: "eating in the company of an uninitiated person, eating in the company of one's wife, eating stale food, and marrying the daughter of the mother's brother or the father's sister." He also provides a similar list of matters peculiar to the North: "selling wool, drinking rum, trafficking in animals with teeth in both jaws, making a living as a soldier, and travelling by sea" (Dharmasutra 1.2.4).[107] The crucial matter here is that defilement occurs only if any of the practices are performed in geographically inappropriate locations, under improper regional jurisdictions. Baudhayana offers a cartography of the land of the Aryas similar to that of Manu, with the land between the Ganga and Yamuna rivers taking center stage and the southern and eastern extremities marked by the disappearing river Sarasvati and the ranging ground of the black antelope (1.2.9–10). He calibrates border areas, like Avanti in the south (present-day Malwa) or Magadha and Anga in the east (present-day southern Bihar), in terms of diminishing holiness and mixed blood (1.2.13). Beyond that, if one ventures toward Vanga (Bengal) in the east, or Kalinga (Orissa) in the southeast, he commits a sin through his feet and must perform sacrifices to absolve himself.

I am not suggesting that this North–South division was absolute in ancient literature, especially after the first century CE. There were certainly other subcontinental geographies stretching from the Eurasian steppes, Bactria, Tibet, and Burma down to Ceylon that mark a tension between the story of "Arya" naissance and an irresistibly Asiatic India. We see this in the Mahabharata, for instance, especially at the beginning of the Bhishma Parvan (book 6) when Sanjaya, blessed with telescopic powers, describes the known world to Dhritarashtra, the blind king of the Kuru clan. This description however does not aid the cause of Hindu nationalist chauvinism. According to Sanjaya, Bharatvarsha is the least sacred of seven lands on earth, situated at the southern end of a scale of ascending holiness as one travels north, with the northernmost Airavatvarsha being the holiest.[108] Kautilya, in the Arthasastra, describes the land as extending from the highest peaks of the Himalayas to the sea a thousand *yojanas* away toward the south.[109] There are other passages in Kalidasa's Meghduta (5th century CE), the Vishnu Purana, and Buddhist and Jain tracts that foreground an expansive imaginary of a landmass bordered by mountains in the north and the sea in the south, combining cosmography with cartography. These texts extended sacred space by weaving onto each other, unfolding a rich, pluralist tapestry. Tamil traveled north and Sanskrit culture undeniably inflected the south. Sangam literature venerated the Vedic sage Agastya as the one who lowered the Vindhya Mountains and settled in the south. There were wider cognitive mappings based on trade routes, conquests, pilgrimage networks, or theological institutions like the four Mathas established by Adi Sankara in the eighth century.[110] However, such wider mappings did not foster a geopolitical whole in the modern sense of terrestrial sovereignty; nor did they diminish the ontological pull of the Brahmavarta. Holy places, tied to local cosmologies of piety, could exist without immediate reference to state power or a continuum of habitat, culture, or identity. A distribution of the sacred could prevail without a great political smoothening of space in terms of proto-national peopleness. Manu Goswami points out that it was only toward the end of the nineteenth century—in a new dispensation of commerce, communications, and bureaucratic technologization of life—that "Hindustan" ceased to refer to the Indo-Gangetic plain and became equated with the area ruled by the Raj.[111] This was a paradigm shift, from an older sovereignty over peoples to one over space.

In Hindu nationalist discourses, such diverse reckonings of time and space are violently appended onto a perennialist continuum of "national" peopleness and territorial integrity. The compression itself is marked by a naturalized Aryan race hegemony of the north, and a valorization of the Vedic-Sanskritic order over the Bhakti vernacularisms of the south, which came with strong Jain and Buddhist imprints. The great texts themselves were arrested and enframed by an invented, authoritative Tradition and denied long-standing vitalities of mutation and change. This literary colonization of massive and myriad oral worlds created a dynastic lineage, much in the tradition of Western philology. The Brahmanas had to come before the Upanishads, the Ramayana had to be older than the Mahabharata, and the many Ramayanas and the many Mahabharatas had to be compressed into master texts. This entailed a process in which the Ramayana of Tulsidas (16th century), for example, had to be accorded a natural privilege over that of the Tamil Kambar (13th century) or the Bengali Krttivasa (15th century).

In terms of modern editorial redactions of epic traditions, the case of the standard edition of the Mahabharata by the scholars of the Bhandarkar Research Institute between 1925 and 1966 is an illuminating example.[112] It was a mammoth undertaking, involving, initially, 1,259 collected manuscripts, out of which about 800 were collated and gathered under northern and southern recensions. The project followed the Lachmann philological method, familiar in studies of European antiquity, in the construction of a lost original based on the principle of *lectio difficilior potior*.[113] It was a decidedly civilizational and national quest, but one in which Sanskrit texts (assumed to be between 500 BCE and 400 CE) would enjoy an originary privilege over southern ones—in Grantha (Tamil), Telugu, or Malayalam—from the first century CE and after. The Oriental Institute in Baroda produced a similar critical edition of the Ramayana between 1960 and 1975, eliminating a whole quarter of the southern recension.[114]

Hindutva has to refute the Aryan invasion and Aryan migration theories for it to have a moral center, especially in relation to the Dravidian question. In fact, it has to peddle the isomorphic "out of India" myth with dogged resolve, against all apparent evidence, to claim the pure indigenous birth of an Aryan "race." It cannot be admitted that Vedic-Brahminical culture was itself a foreign colonial imposition and that its racist remnants survive to this day. Golwalkar unsurprisingly refutes the Aryan controversy as a British plot; he dismisses contemporary Periyarite rumblings about the secular Tirukkural being the authentic scripture of the South as opposed to the Vedas, and denounces the Dravidian nationalism of his time as misplaced separatism.[115] It was necessary to distinguish a taller and fairer Aryan stock from the descendants of proto-Australoid or Mongolian lines. However, that difference itself had to be virtualized and pushed back deep in time, prior to territorial imaginations of North and South: "Whatever diversity of race we may have had in this country to begin with was obliterated long ago by time and processes of history" (BOT, 115). Any commerce of violence or love between Aryans and the lesser races like the Dravidians or Mongoloids must therefore be reckoned with in terms of just paternalism and landlocked endosmosis. It was an organic theater internal to a "people" predating history. By the time we enter history, time has already healed all wounds of a founding violence and the Arya is merely a marker of nobility, a sign of (Savarna) culture.[116] This was true even in the Treta Yuga, when the events depicted in the Ramayana supposedly took place. A singular Hindu suzerainty over the entire cultural landscape of the subcontinent can be asserted only by a disavowal of the epic traditions and folklores of the South that read the story of Rama and Ravana as that of an Aryan invasion:

> It is being made out today that the struggle between Rama and Ravana was the one between Arya and Dravida. How ludicrous! Ravana himself was a great Sanskrit scholar and a devotee of Shiva. He is even reported to have set the Sama-Veda to music. His father Vaishrava was a Brahmin and so was his grandfather Pulastya. *If anything, Ravana was oppressing the South and Rama only liberated the Southern people from his oppression!* (BOT, 115–16, emphasis added)

This passage is a perfect example of the Golwalkar style, which mobilizes a repertoire of flawed history, myth, and the anecdotal with a weaponized caste Hindu common sense. In the first move, he skirts the biological question of race with the assumed compact between Varna and Vedic scholarship. Ravana cannot be Dravidian because he is a Brahmin. The Brahmin of the south can emerge only when all racial differences have already been obliterated, since the Dravidian was originally not allowed into the Aryan-Brahmin Vedic order. As marker of nobility, "Brahmin" rises above the Aryan-Dravidian divide and uproots the king of Lanka from his flock in the south. He was not of them, but their oppressor. When Rama defeats Ravana, he "liberates" the "Southern people," now immediately distinguished once again from the tyrant as well as the savior. The "Southern people" return to occupy the space vacated by the "Dravidian"—as sunken term—since, at that point, they are neither of the victor nor the vanquished.

In Golwalkar, and in most instances of Sangh Parivaar discourse, the Aryan operates as a mythic prefiguration of the Hindu. His pristine form and actions are to be located before the tumult of history, and thus he may not be produced in its tribunals of judgment. As a result, the Aryan can already authorize and Brahminize, can establish ontological markers of privilege, before a profane, crossbreeding democratization of Hindu identity. This imaginary, of a racial ontogenesis of privilege in patrilineal terms, is difficult to erase from stories of masters as well as slaves. Manu, for instance, declares that someone born from an Aryan father to a non-Aryan woman may become Aryan by acquiring qualities—but not one born from the union of a non-Aryan man and an Aryan woman (*Manu*, 10.67). The Brahminical Aryan is therefore the only legitimate original father; he is the one whose insemination births the Hindu in both the north and the south at an hour that predates memory. History itself can only be a feeble tracing of that font of meaning and naissance. On December 17, 1960, while addressing the students of the Gujarat School of Social Sciences, Golwalkar provided a graphic illustration:

> But our forbears were not fools. They had the capacity to think independently. Not even a fraction of the courage they showed in making experiments is to be seen today. Let us take only one instance. Today experiments in crossbreeding are made only on animals. But the courage to make such experiments on human beings is not shown even by the so-called modern scientists of today. If some human crossbreeding is seen today it is the result not of scientific experiments but of carnal lust. Now let us see the experiments our ancestors made in this sphere. In an effort to better the human species through crossbreeding the Namboodri Brahmanas of the north were settled in Kerala and a rule was laid down that the eldest son of a Namboodri family should marry only the daughter of the Vaishya, Kshatriya, or Sudra communities of Kerala. Another still more outrageous rule was that the first offspring of a married woman of any class must be fathered by a Namboodri Brahman and then she could beget children by her husband. Today this experiment will be called adultery but it was not so, as it was limited, [sic] to the first child.[117]

All primal fathers of "India" therefore become Aryans and the Aryan himself becomes the cipher of Brahminical authority. Rama's deliverance of the "Southern people" from Ravana presumably came after the original event of insemination that had to be spiritually distinguished from the base dynamics of human lust as well as the moral sociologies of the marriage institution. The Southern people were Aryan progeny once removed: the outcome of a "scientific experimentation" before the history of science or the birth of ethical distinctions between man and beast. This ruse of Hindu sovereignty is entirely modern in its tactics, and quite a few Western parallels can be invoked to understand how, within this template, racial fictions and histories of conquest are mobilized to settle immediate questions of equity and public rights. The conquered Algerians, for instance, were taught to look up to "our ancestors, the Gauls"; or, as Derrida pointed out, up until 1980 an official lie was upheld about white migration in South Africa preceding black migration.[118]

On the other hand, people of the south themselves forged modern paleo-geographic myths to reverse the Aryan scene. Sumathi Ramaswamy speaks of imaginative "place making" in the annals of Dravidian self-determination, in which the lost continent of Lemuria becomes the originary homeland for modern Tamils.[119] Hypothesized initially in the theosophist Helena Blavatsky's *Isis Unveiled* and then systematized in her 1888 magnum opus *The Secret Doctrine*, Lemuria was said to have been a landmass south of Asia, stretching from India to Tasmania. It is sometimes conflated with and sometimes distinguished from Plato's Atlantis. In the subsequent body of theosophical writings, including W. Scott-Eliot's *The Lost Lemuria* (1904), the land was the home of the "third root race." Man attained humanity and consciousness midway through the Lemurian cycle, 18 million years ago, when the fourth of the sub-races came into being.[120] It was from the late 1890s that this colonial theory was critically and cautiously appended to legends of primeval Tamil origins, connecting it to flood myths and other classical literary tropes. The man from South India was thus the descendant of the singular antediluvian race, and the first language spoken by humanity was Tamil. Civilization had traveled north—including to the scene of the birth of both Sanskrit and Arya—and not the other way around.[121]

On the other hand, the purported scene of Aryan birth—and the spread of concentric circles of diminishing holiness—has been difficult to efface from the Hindu nationalist cultural unconscious. The expanse of the Brahminical sacred was an organic whole of Bharat (India); it therefore had to be Akhand (undivided). The Hindu Aryan claim was a primal one; it could not be challenged either by Pakistan or by competing regional nationalisms in the south and elsewhere. The idea of Akhand Bharat is therefore as much a disavowal of the historical event of Partition as it is of the federal structure of the Indian union.[122] For Golwalkar, the subcontinent was a space divinely given to the Hindus since times without beginning (*anadi*). It was marked by natural barriers on all sides, in the form of mighty mountains in the north and seas in the south. The people of Bharat knew that they were one nation before the Europeans learned how to roast meat.

However, the Aryan scene is not, in the final instance, determined by natural boundaries. It is constituted by postulates of a spiritual geography pertaining to Dharma, nativity (*matrubhoomi*), works (*karmabhoomi*), salvation (*mokshabhoomi*), and the haunts of the gods (*devabhoomi*). These actually make Akhand Bharat an immensely amorphous and mobile figuration, capable of exerting civilizational patrimony over neighbors. Iran in the west was Aryan, according to Golwalkar, as was Sri Lanka in the south or Burma in the east. However, the Aryan movement in either direction had to be centrifugal from the primeval center of Brahmavarta. That explained how the Avesta of the Persians had to be understood as an lesser approximation of the Rg Veda, or how the "westward" travel of the Indo-European family to Sumer, central Asia, Anatolia, and eventually to Europe led to the founding of progressively inferior civilizations in terms of spiritual qualities. Golwalkar's model is thus an austere mirror image of the Aryan Invasion theory, and analogous to the Latinate dispersal of romance languages across Europe in the age of imperial Rome.[123] Places in the mental geography that we find in his text are marked only by the sovereign name-giving powers of Sanskrit: Upaganastan (Afghanistan), Trivishtap (Tibet), or Sringapura (Singapore) (BOT, 80–83). From this epicenter of the sacred, a "far-flung empire of the spirit" had also fanned out to claim the world itself—the Americas before Columbus, Cambodia or Japan in the east, or Siberia and Mongolia in the north (BOT, 9).

Akhand Bharat represents the fundamental imagination of Aryan nationhood maximized to the point of utopia. It signifies triumphalism about a hoary past as well as a profound pathos in relation to the geopolitics of the present. Writing roughly fifteen years after the partition and in between the wars with China and Pakistan in the 1960s, Golwalkar laments:

> How many of us feel the insult that we are denied access to our holy Kailas and Manasarovar, that we have no chance even to take a dip in the sacred Sindhu, which gave us the name Hindu and Hindustan? Takshashila, once

the world-center for the diffusion of Hindu thought, is no more with us. Mulasthan (Multan), which witnessed the incarnation of the terrible Narasimha for the protection of Prahlad from the demon Hiranyakashipu, is once again under the heels of a demonic domination. Do all these memories burn in our veins? (BOT, 95)

Reinvigorated Hindu sons cannot tolerate the vivisection of the motherland. Golwalkar clearly expresses his revanchist desires to that end: "If Partition is a settled fact, then we are here to unsettle it" (BOT, 93). The apparatus of history itself, and the prism of geopolitical perception it provides, is a profane externality. Its "oppressive weight" cannot be allowed to deaden the conscience of a brotherhood readied for martyrdom. "Embers of ancient devotion" must produce a "holy conflagration" to consume all aggressions of the past and Bharat Mata (Mother India) must be reinstated "in her pristine undivided form" (BOT, 93). To re-create Akhand Bharat, the holy conflagration must consume not just Afghanistan and Pakistan in the west or Bangladesh and Myanmar in the east, but also a part of Tibet where Mansarovar is situated. India, according to Golwalkar, should never have agreed to the cease-fire in the border skirmish with China in 1962 (BOT, 270–73); in 1965, Indian soldiers should have been allowed not only to liberate all of Kashmir, but to march on to Lahore, Rawalpindi, and Karachi, destroying not just the military potential of Pakistan but an entire Islamic horde from Turkey to Iran (BOT, 304–5).

It is perhaps the division of the primal scene of Vedic naissance in the northwest—the Brahmavarta—that is more intolerable than anything else. It would be fair to say that, for the Hindu right, the partition in the west has been a matter of greater heartburn than the division of Bengal in the east. This feeling has resonated repeatedly in Hindu nationalist discourses up to the present in the form of an unfinished project of territorial integration, one necessary to secure a bulwark against an extended sea of Islam. In 2015, for instance, the VHP leader Pravin Togadia urged Hindus to have more than two children each, not just to dominate Indian minorities, but also to ensure that one day the tricolor flies over Kandahar, Lahore, and Dhaka.[124] This fantasy wavers between German racist-imperialist ideas of *Lebensraum* and the eternal hope that modern Pakistanis and others will eventually respond to the primal call of Hinduness. In a 2015 interview given to Al Jazeera television, the BJP national secretary Ram Madhav explained Prime Minister Narendra Modi's surprise halt in Lahore to greet his Pakistani counterpart Nawaz

Sharif on his birthday as a gesture in the direction of reconstituting Akhand Bharat in time through "popular goodwill."[125]

An important caveat is necessary here. I am not suggesting that a reunification of nations in South Asia is not a desirable idea in any shape or form, or that the Hindu right has a monopoly over that realm of ideas, memories, and affectations. What distinguishes the Hindutva fantasy of Akhand Bharat is the imperial desire to extend a core, Hindi-speaking North Indian Brahminical dominance over a formidable territorial expanse. In current geopolitical circumstances, this project can only be an infinitely deferred dream at best, and an apocalyptic nuclear death drive at worst. Yet this vision of utopian restoration sets up a gravitational field for signs and affects. It creates a powerful theme of usurpation and loss that, at the end of the day, determines lines of filiation as well as hatred. Pakistan is at once a territory abstracted, amputated, alien-occupied, and distributed. It designates not just an enemy beyond the Radcliffe Line, but also a thousand "mini-Pakistans" as ghettos of rot and impurity within the Indian body politic (BOT, 174–76). One inevitably needs Pakistan—as a perpetual source of fear without catharsis—to complete the Church of political Hinduism that is always under construction.

Hindutva nationalism is thus resolutely terrestrial in its imagination. It envisions its flock in terms of an insular endosmosis down the ages. The primary fear of a loss of Varna purity, and a traditionalist stricture against crossing the dark waters, foreclosed adventurism in the past, even though the modern Hindu nationalist envied Islamic or Christian empires. In this context, I would like to highlight a neglected feature of V. D. Savarkar's otherwise much-discussed thesis in *Hindutva*. In this text, the normative condition for Hinduness famously becomes a convergence of the land of birth, the land of works, and the land considered holy. Muslims, Christians, and communists are perpetual outsiders even if they pass the tests of blood and soil, since their cultures and ideologies make them beholden to alien destinations like Mecca, the Vatican, or Moscow. Meanwhile, there is a progressive series when it comes to national belonging: the Brahminical Sanatan Dharma is only a small part of Hinduism, and Hinduism itself is only a small part of Hindutva. Hinduism may well develop into a world religion like Buddhism, but since Hindutva is a postulate of sovereignty, it may not, in an ontological sense, travel beyond the motherland (*matribhu*) and holy land (*punyabhu*). It may travel only as culture. One does not have to reside in the territory of India to be a Hindu, but it is a determination of Hindutva that Hindus and their descendants anywhere must affirm India as ancestral land. It was in this sense that the geographical limits of Hinduism were the limits of the earth, while India was the limit for any worldly entity from without that was not the subject of Hindutva. The Hindu, therefore, was marked in terms of his cosmopolitan privilege at home and a cosmopolitan imperative abroad. One must necessarily be an outward-looking Hindu while residing anywhere outside of India, since it was to India that one had to look as the land of ancestors and as a civilizational font of being. Conversely, the Muslim, the Christian, or the communist in India could not extend their imaginative cosmos to Karbala, to Golgotha, or to the workers of the world. Their existence depended on being in the prison house of Hindutva as territorialized national ethics, and on their scrupulous discarding of any cosmopolitan vision.

Savarkar, in effect, postulates this as an originary covenant of the Aryan Hindu. It is based on a strange insistence that the "Aryans" categorically diverged from their cognate peoples, like the Persians, when they entered the subcontinent (Savarkar, unlike Golwalkar, subscribed to the Aryan migration theories). There was some magic in the land itself, albeit one that touched only the incoming Aryans and not the original inhabitants. The moment that the primal Aryan patriarchs crossed the Indus, "they ceased to belong to the people they had definitely left behind and laid the foundation of a new nation."[126] Savarkar declares that it may not be assumed that the indigenous peoples of the subcontinent—the non-Aryan Panees, the Dasas, or the Vratyas—contributed to the charter of the Vedic religion.[127] The Aryans alone did this, while the others either submitted to Vedism in time or flirted with a variety of heterodoxies. It was thus between the principled oblivion of their own Persian pasts and the absolute barbarism of the other that the Aryans instituted the primeval faith, foreclosing the possibility of what might be called a kind of creolization. The Vedas were immaculately born in the land of the Vedas once the race capable of writing the Vedas arrived there. It was from that moment that a proper indwelling in Hindusthan entailed a total submission of all questions of ontology, all predicates of imagination and memory, to the Aryan holiness of the land itself. The Hindu could, as in modern times, live elsewhere but could not seek the sacred elsewhere.

This was an austere convergence between identity and territory that perhaps Schmitt would have admired as an ideal ground for the political. That is, unlike in his case, where his German ancestry could be at odds with the extended geography of his Catholic faith, here the Hindu was a Hindu precisely because he was rooted in sacred ground. Once inside the subcontinent, anyone who does not subscribe to the being of Hindutva is the enemy. What would then be the fates of the Muslims, the Christians, and the communists in Akhand Bharat? Historically, the Hindu right has prescribed and practiced a set of solutions that are easily identifiable. The extreme one is, of course, in line with the Nazi extermination of the Jews, which a youthful Golwalkar enthusiastically endorsed in the undivided India of 1939. But relatively moderate measures have also been proposed by him and others. To begin with, in Akhand Bharat, the credo that must be discarded is what Golwalkar disdainfully calls a cosmopolitan "serai theory" of territorial nationalism.[128] Unlike a roadside inn where all are welcome, the matter of belonging to a nation has to be determined by a perpetual test of patriotism. People declared cultural aliens have to induct themselves into a mainstream mental pattern of the nation. This return to the fold entails a scrupulous submission to an ancestral Hindu way of life in attire, speech, customs, marriage ceremonies, and funeral rites.[129] Islam or the teachings of Jesus of Nazareth could remain personal (*vyakti*) devotional preferences only if thoroughly redacted from the public religiosity of the nation (Rashtra Dharma). Such a public religiosity, in turn, would not recognize any division between its own Hindu church and the state. Moreover, this theocratic order would categorically define Indian Islam and Indian Christianity as historical remnants of slavery and conquest. The Muslim, in such a scenario, had to choose between a deep recall of Karmic debts to Hindu ancestors and the perpetuation of an acquired, historical pathology of foreignness. Such imperatives, according to Golwalkar, would constitute a mode of just assimilation (*parakrama-vad*), one similar to that by which Huns and Shakas had once become Rajputs. That is, as opposed to the contractualism (*sankuchita-vad*) or the Hindu surrender to alien conquerors (*sharanagati-vad*) that characterized a different and despicable past (BOT, 128–33).

True Hinduness, for Golwalkar, is an innate principle, prior not just to known history but also to psychobiography and communal identity. For the Indian Muslim or Christian awaiting reconversion, it is therefore a matter of responding to amniotic memories and a national Swadharma that already exists in the core of being. Golwalkar explains that Hindus are unlike other people, who arrive in this world in a state of nakedness:

> [A Hindu] gets his first samskar [rite of passage] when he is still in the mother's womb, and the last when he is consigned to the flames. There are sixteen samskaras in the Hindu that make him what he is. In fact, we

are Hindus even before we emerge from the womb of the mother. (BOT, 118–19)

The declared other—the Indian Muslim, Christian, or communist—must therefore conform to a public religiosity of Hindutva in order to honor such a primal insemination—both Karmic and biological—by original Aryan fathers. In relation to this primal debt, everything else can only be mere ornaments of a great forgetting precipitated by the forces of history. It is only after birth, through the external formalisms of baptism or circumcision, that a Christian becomes a Christian or a Muslim a Muslim. This is also the precise reason why, in the Hindu nationalist universe, returning to the fold is not exactly an act of "reconversion," since one cannot convert "out" of Hinduness in the first place.[130] What can be performed instead is a conscientious task of purification and a return to the home that was always present.

Golwalkar's and Savarkar's Akhand Bharat is a thoroughly orientalist and jealously insular construct. It represents a stark counterpoint to that powerful, alternate imagining of India in Nehru, which is marked by an Asiatic worldliness of vision. Nehru's Indian civilization was, at every step, inflected by Pehlavi culture, Tibetan or Chinese Buddhism, trade, instruments, and ideas from as far as the eastern Mediterranean or northeastern Africa. Image worship, according to Nehru, probably came from Greece, which was much more Asiatic than European, and Sufism—in its Indian alignment—was a distinctly neo-Platonic impulse. During its decline after the Gupta Empire, India made the error of failing to learn from Harun al Rashid's Baghdad, even though the Arabs had learned from India in the past.[131] It was the British, in Nehru's estimation, that first isolated India from a broader Asiatic and worldly civilizational process.[132] Both Savarkar and Golwalkar, we may add, were scrupulously following the same path.

LANGUAGE, COUNTERMEMORY, AND CULTURE

In Hindu nationalist politics, it is necessary to have what I call an ongoing "Epic of Tradition" in the realm of mass culture and publicity. This Epic is a regime of permitted visibilities and statements. It is there to translate the plenitude of customs, practices, and novelties into a singular paradigm of civic religiosity. It has to aesthetically and ethically inform the details of lived life and arrange them in a spectrum of normalcy in a Hindu ethnoscape. The Epic of Tradition must clear the jungle of histories to create one memory and the thought of one oblivion that needs to be superseded. It must declare an absolute Hindu presentism to conquer the past as well as the future, encumbering all stretches and varieties of remembrance. This axial memory must be solidified as a promised deliverance and a promised revenge in the form of divine figurations like Rama Purushottam, now exalted as national symbols. A particular version of the story of Rama, cleared of all folk contaminations, must become the national Gospel, so to speak, and consign all lesser gods to gnostic or pagan status. This would be a nationalist abstraction of the Indian universal: all stories becoming the story of the Ramayana; or, as A. K. Ramanujan once put it, the known world itself becoming leftovers of Vyasa.[133] National Culture, as ongoing Epic of Tradition, must impart a gravitational thrust to all narratives. It must announce that the only stories worth telling are those that can be told in front of select idols and the majoritarian nation in order to sacralize them. The Tradition, must—at all levels of discourse, desire, and solicitation—be the factor of decision.

According to dominant Shakta sources—the Markandeya Purana, for instance—Mahisasura was a demonic entity, a hybrid of a Tamasic Asura and the water buffalo.[134] Blessed with a boon from Brahma earned after severe penances, Mahisasura defeated the gods who then supplicated the great Trinity for deliverance. Brahma, Vishnu, and Siva pooled their powers to create the goddess Durga, who subsequently slew Mahisasura to fulfill an original prophecy that he would meet his end at the hands of a woman. It is a well-known story celebrated every autumn during Durga festivities in different corners of India. In the spring of 2016, however, the national news spotlight fell on a radically different version of the legend. While recounting the many sins of left-wing students in the Jawaharlal Nehru University, Smriti Irani, the Human Resources Minister in the Narendra Modi government, railed about a decidedly "antinational" perversion of the Durga and Mahisasura story. In a parliamentary speech, she read significant portions from a pamphlet distributed by SC (Scheduled Castes), ST (Scheduled Tribes), and other minority students of JNU. The students, observing the "Mahisasura Martyrdom Day," condemned Durga Puja as a racist festival in which twice-born Hindu groups celebrate the deceitful murder of a king of the dark-skinned indigenous tribes. According to this version of the legend, Durga was a fair-skinned prostitute the Aryans had sent to lure Mahisasura into marriage. She had then treacherously killed the Asura king in his sleep after nine nights of conjugal bliss.[135]

Irani condemned the publication as self-evident blasphemy, intended to hurt Hindu and national sentiments. However, scholars and journalists subsequently clarified that this "depraved mentality" had in fact emerged from a long-standing tradition among the tribal populations of several east-central provinces like Chhattisgarh, Jharkhand, Bihar, and West Bengal. Notable among them were the Asurs, a tribe of about 10,000 members with a language listed as "definitely endangered" by UNESCO. For the Asurs, the tragic figure of Mahisasura has always been that of a bulwark against the Aryan invaders; his day of passing has been an occasion for mourning. The particular controversy was one among many similar cases of dissonant imaginaries clustering around the same legendary figures and events. The minoritarian ones challenge Brahminical certitudes, pose countermemories, and effect local displacements of dominant narratives.[136] The modern Epic of Tradition in turn seeks to eliminate or colonize them.

Such battles of being and remembrance present an abiding dialectic within "Hinduism," between the Vedic model of rituals and sacrifices under Brahminical ministrations, and a Puranic one comprising local stories, idol worship, vernacular saints, pilgrimage sites, animism, hylozoism, and fertility rituals. The modern quest for an "Indian monotheism," has largely been about resolving the contradictions of the former, and, in time, erasing, controlling, or diminishing the voluptuousness of the latter. The Puranic imagination has quite often been a matter of suspicion and unhappy consciousness for the Hindu nationalist. It has often been looked upon as a channel for lusty and wayward travels of memory and desire, and as a repository of superstition and false belief. The Puranic therefore had to be enframed and revised via a religious anthropology of the modern. The question of the supernatural here can be brought into a state of proximity with the Schmittian postulate that the "exception" stands in for the miracle in the age of the secular. The sovereign, in that vein, is also the one who superstitiously decides on the superstitious and magically proclaims that there can be no magic. The accompanying monotheistic imperative here is that unlike the bickering gods of Homeric skies, there should be a single font and administration of the miraculous. Superstition, in this sense, is heretical and capricious not because it affirms unrealistic beliefs, but because it competes with the axiomatic magic of the state and its Brahminical monopoly over faith, realism, and improvisation. The iconoclastic disavowal and perversion of Durga is an example of such insurrections of countermemory coming from the forests and hills.

The modern problem of securing a Brahminical monopoly over myth becomes clearer when placed against the vast historical relief of relentless tribal assertions against the colonial state and the indigenous elite throughout the nineteenth century and the first few decades of the twentieth. Sumit Sarkar has pointed out that these uprisings, driven by the miraculous, were more frequent and more violent than those of any other Indian community under colonial yoke, including the peasantry. In 1868, for instance, the Naikda forest tribe in Gujarat attacked police stations to establish a Dharma Raj. A miracle worker called Sambhudan led the Kacha Nagas of Chachar in 1882, claiming to have made his followers immune to bullets. The year 1886 witnessed the uprising of Rama Dandu (Rama's army) in the Chodavaram area. In 1900, a Konda Dora named Korra Mallaya commanded thousands by declaring himself a reincarnation of one of the Pandava brothers and his infant son the reborn Lord Krishna himself.[137] Sarkar states that a frequent motivating factor in these insurrections was a Christian millenarian impulse imbibed from Lutheran, Anglican, and Catholic missions. This was perhaps most famously on display in the Ulgulan (Great Tumult) by the Mundas of the Chota Nagpur area in 1899–1900. It was led by the sharecropper Birsa Munda (1874–1900), who had received some missionary as well as Vaishnavite education. Having seen the vision of a supreme God, Birsa had declared himself a prophet with miraculous powers. About a quarter of a century later, hearing perhaps the distant thunder of the First World War, the Oraons of Chota Nagpur commenced a radical movement impelled by a millennial vision centered around the imminent arrival of a messianic figure variously addressed as "Birsa" or a German "Kaiser Baba."[138] The existential lure of a providential transcendence and an eschatology of promised deliverance from centuries of fatalism and inertia of feudal caste arrangements were often prominent in such suicidal undertakings. It was, evidently, an impelling that the traditional Hindu cosmologies lacked and prohibited.[139]

Compacts between subaltern insurrectionary energies and the many-armed flows of the Puranic present one of the greatest obstacles in the way of constructing a Hindutva axiomatic as political theology—or in other words, the monopolistic determination of the excluded and the foe when it comes to a core national imaginary.[140] This purported imaginary is in itself a mix of orientalist romanticism, a selective, often shamefaced approximation of scriptural and mythic material; and a sexual morality of colonial-Victorian inheritance. It can thus approach the hills, rivers, and forests only with Nietzschean ill-health and suspicion. The Puranic, on the other hand, is an extension as well as an invagination of the substance of memory—a wrapping of the self around the other. It is also the method by which the lapsed, the untouchable, or the demonic forest dweller has been traditionally subsumed into caste society. From the beginning of the second millennium, Puranic modes had threatened to sideline Vedic Brahminism as esoteric and inconsequential to everyday life and to marginalize once-powerful Sramana orders that came with strict insistence on renunciation. The Puranic had created Kali as a sublimation of hundreds of village goddesses across the subcontinent.[141] It had valorized the cult of Radha over Krishna, transformed the warrior-dialectician Krishna of the Mahabharata into the fornicating god of the Vrindavanas, and had invented obscure avatarisms of Mohammad and Jesus in regional "Hindu" lifeworlds. The Puranic is therefore a pure multiplicity. It is neither good nor bad, but a stratum of novelizing energies and vectors of remembrance. It consolidates pieties, gathers lessons of experience, and releases the powers of disenchantment. It is animated by engines of conservation, instruments of power, as well as by forces of radical dissipation. The Puranic, in the fullness of time, invites compromises like the Varaha (boar) incarnation of Vishnu that probably emerged in central India as one of many such totemic compacts between tribal cults and Brahminical sects.[142]

At the other end of the spectrum, there is a figure—a strange counterpart to the demonic Mahisasura—who frustrates that other important task of Hindutva, the monopolistic determination of Tradition itself; that is, Tradition as a vernacular axiomatic that can be mobilized aggressively against a liberal Anglophone state structure. This second figure would be that of Gandhi, the nonviolent Mahatma armed with a unique vision of nationalism that he took to village and country. It was through him that the ideology had acquired a pan-Indian mass base, with its own language, moral economies, and metafictions. This was done by way of the ritualistic and the customary (prayer and fasting), artisanal imaginations (the spinning loom and *khadi*), and grand symbolic gestures like the Salt March of 1930.[143] The looming shadow of the Mahatma continues to inform the Indian political imagination to this day, setting up a plane of discursive translations and affectional transfers between the Anglophone state and the vernacular masses.[144] All political formations and ideologies, including the Nehruvian wing of the Indian National Congress as well as the communists, in various ways, have had to contend with this national mythopoiesis founded on a novel mode of civil disobedience and a primary disavowal of industrial modernity.[145]

The Gandhian ideology has therefore been a matter of persistent heartburn for the Sangh Parivaar. If there could be a quintessentially Indian, vernacular critique of Western modernity, it was Gandhi who owned it. It was he who had established a moral and civilizational bulwark against colonial rule based on his unique inflection of concepts like Swaraj (self-rule), Satyagraha (civil disobedience), and *ahimsa* (nonviolence).[146] Gandhi had set up powerful channels of exchange between custom, righteousness, and law in a new register of political self-determination. In the process, the androgynous and pacific saint seemed always to disrupt masculinist neo-Brahminical attempts to conquer icons and memories or to absorb folklore into a jealous caste Hindu common sense. The Mahatma's invocations of Rama were devoid of Kshatriya vitriol; his Raghupati Raghava was perhaps closer to the Balabhadra of Vimalsuri's Jaina tradition than he was to the militant incarnation beloved by Golwalkar and his disciples.[147] His Ram Rajya was also the Islamic Khudai Raj and the Kingdom of God.[148] Gandhi forged a compelling vision of the traditional, combining select scriptures with the romanticism of a Carlyle or Ruskin, the agrarian conservatism of a Tolstoy, and an American-style transcendentalism. The formerly suit-clad, London-trained barrister was introduced to the Bhagwad Gita not through Sanskrit or even vernacular Indian sources, but by way of the theosophist translation in *The Song Celestial* by Sir Edwin Arnold. This text would remain central to his eventual transformation into the khadi-wearing ascetic. For Gandhi, the Gita was not a book of war. It was a primer for Abhyasa (single-minded devotion), Vairagya (indifference to all other interests in life), and a cure for all forms of egotism.[149] This reading followed the lines of natural religion: Arjuna's battle was a primal act of noncooperation between good and evil, ontologically indistinguishable, at the end, from the struggle between Ormuzd and Ahriman in the Avesta, between Jesus and the Pharisees and Sadducees in the New Testament, or Mohammad and Mecca in the Islamic scriptures.[150] Gandhi, revealing an almost Narodnik side, would also declare, among other things, that Lord Krishna preaches socialism in the Gita, or at least propounds an altruistic trusteeship of wealth.[151] It was thus, all in all, a compelling "Hindu" moralism of secret cosmopolitan deliberations. This moralism was exactly opposite to what we have mapped as the desire for Hindu sovereign assertion in the Schmittian vein, for Gandhi would say, "In the language of the Gita I want to live at peace with both friend and foe."[152]

The project of a modern Hindu monotheism is therefore compelled to situate itself in a historical field of problems between the eccentric tribal in the forest and Gandhi the father of the nation. The Hindu patriot knows that in such an elemental scene bookended by Mahisasura and the Mahatma, he may banish the Asur prodigal but not assume Gandhi's mantle of the nation's *Bapu* (father). The masculinist Hindutva ideologue is therefore forced, to a large extent, to address the nation in that same Gandhian plane of the vernacular that features the untouchable as *Harijan* (child of Vishnu/Krishna) and is animated by concepts like *Swadeshi* or *Ahimsa* (nonviolence). It is Gandhi the father who still retains paramount name-giving rights, and the authority to donate sense to the world. He ties the notion of Swadharma to his greater picture of the nation as artisanal, agrarian, and pacific, making it difficult for the emergence of a jealous and militant Hindu nationalist ethics of the self. Gandhi does not recognize Swabhimaan (selfhood) as Hindu ego. In the eyes of the Hindu nationalist, another major fault of Bapu has been to nominate Nehru as his successor—and to permit Nehruvianism as state ideology—instead of authorizing the Hindu wing of the Congress Party led by Sardar Vallabhbhai Patel (1875–1950). Patel has recently emerged in the Hindutva revisionist project as the figurehead representing a missed opportunity in history, one in which the Gandhian patrimony could have been bestowed on him and the Hindu cause at large. That apart, the present-day Hindutva battle against Gandhi in relation to memory, being, and civilizational ethos centers upon the primal event, guilt, and disavowal of parricide. There have been numerous efforts in recent decades to sacralize the murder of Gandhi itself, and to politically rehabilitate the 'former' RSS man and Hindu zealot Nathuram Godse (1910–1949), who bowed and touched the feet of the Mahatma before shooting him down.[153]

For Hindutva, the spirit of Gandhi must not be allowed to name Godse as killer, to designate his own assassination as sacrifice, and to mark the event itself as a moral abomination. Just as, at the other end of the spectrum, the descendants of Mahisasura must not be permitted to imagine and commemorate the Asura king as bulwark against colonial invasion. It is in this sense that the killings of Demon King and the Father of the Nation become strange mirror images of one another. This is a crisis that perpetually interrupts the task of claiming the nation in terms of a politics of morality and commanding the vernacular babel. It is—in the no man's land that lies between the Asura and the Mahatma—a crisis of Sanskritization.[154] Both the cosmopolitan vernacular of Gandhi and the jungle legend of the king of demons variously present roadblocks in the way of inventing an apex linguistic-cultural civilization that is, in a total sense, Sanskritic. This invention is an imperative for a North Indian caste Hindu sovereignty, even though there are proto-Dravidian (and Munda) linguistic marks in the Rg Veda itself; even though the master text itself was not composed in what is known today as Sanskrit; and despite the fact that, to this day, India is home to languages belonging to five philological groups, including Tibeto-Burman, Austro-Asiatic, and a panoply of tribal tongues.

As we have noted, an ongoing Sanskritic invention of Tradition, for more than two centuries now, has largely followed an Indological model of a Latinate dispersal of Romance languages in Europe after the twilight of the Holy Roman Empire. It begins with the primary disavowal of Persian—as an original claimant to the status of "Aryan" language—and of the formidable corpus of Buddhist literature in Pali. The disavowal of course, gathers special strength when it comes to the indelible Islamic imprints on Indian culture. It proceeds, as we have seen, with the assertion that Sanskrit, immaculately conceived in India, moved westward and southward and created the Avesta or the Tirukkural as secondary approximations of Vedic wisdom. Sanskrit is also understood as having birthed and categorically exhausted the entire gamut of vernacular imaginations and their capacities of creolization. In other words, worldly excesses in vernacular linguistic universes that are beyond Sanskritic limits and origins are to be announced as inauthentic or imprints of Islamic rule and British colonization. In modern times, the image of Sanskritization as a caste Hindu gentrification of language has gathered strength through the state's promotion of an engineered Hindi in public radio and television, as well as by way of slow, almost unmindful but assured cultural processes that led the marginalization of the once-dominant Urdu from Bombay cinema.

Sanskritization, in this sense, is more than an actual revival of the "language of the gods"; it is the restoration of an aura, a font of oracular authority.[155] The Sanskrit word, which has been left behind by the modern lived life of print or electronic capitalism, or which had once been reduced to decorative signatures of Brahminical authority amid a sea of vernacular pieties, must be politically animated once again in avenues of civic life beyond the sacred. All subcontinental languages must either be returned to her as children or disowned as orphans. The Sanskrit word must become an aspect of the law itself and take on demiurgic power. From that point, there can be a series of hierarchical nominations of 'authentic' Indian languages and exclusions of "foreign" interlopers. In recent times, this spectral Sanskritization has not limited itself to the ceremonies and politics of caste; it has been given, more than ever, a worldly career extending to science, technology, computation, and management.

This complex and modern historical process can be traced back to the Indological centering of Sanskrit with regard to questions of governance, subjectivity, and law of "Gentoo" society during the Warren Hastings colonial administration of the 1770s. This would be followed in 1837 by the state's creation of "official" Urdu—through the vernacular written in Persian script—as the working language for lower courts in North India, and then, from roughly 1860 onward, the production of a counterdiscourse of "Hindi" purged of Persian and Arabic influences. The nationalist Hindi movement would be led early on by the influential figure of Bharatendu Harishchandra (1850–1885) and then institutionalized through Hindi Vardhini Sabha in 1877 and the Nagari Pracharini Sabha in 1893. "Hindi" came into being as a standardized and Sanskritized northern vernacular in Devanagari script, to contend with Urdu, now understood as an 'Islamic' language of what would in time become that other nation.[156] Meanwhile, within the "Hindu" nationalist fold, it was expected that there would be a natural, Sanskritic prioritization of Hindi, the anointed heir, over other paradigmatic vernaculars in the age of print capitalism: Bengali, Marathi, or Tamil.[157] The Hindi–Hindu compact had to gobble up heresies, caste dialects, and sectarian pieties of Hindustan to submit them to an axiomatic Sanskriti as culture and Sanskar as custom. The Brahminical project, in terms of a political theology, would aspire to follow a trajectory of monotheistic Semitization without something similar to the rise of the vernacular Bible and the Protestantism that gave birth to Christian ethnic nation-states in Europe after midmillennial religious wars.[158] It would make Brahminism coterminous with "Hinduism," relationally relegating all other expressions to Prakrit status, belonging to the Dalit, the woman, or the infantile.[159] It would come to give birth, as Agamben would put it, to a new vision of language as a municipal phenomenon with cosmological limits and ends.[160] The act of the sovereign would be to name language itself in Sanskritic terms in order to dispel the fear that at the end we might just be left in solitude with empty words.

The Hindu church under perpetual construction must therefore invent Sanskritization for the stabilization of all semiotic possibilities and conditions of language. The thought of Sanskrit, in that sense, becomes the thought of an originary and pure Indian communicability from which the becoming different of different languages is to be measured and mastered. Indian literature, in that sense, as the official motto of the Sahitya Academy declares, must necessarily be one literature, written in many languages. A Sanskritic Great Tradition must spiritually preside over many little ones, each adjudged to be ripples of the One. The utopian nature of this desire becomes clear when one places it in the intricate historical map of subcontinental language politics.[161] Apart from the panoply of language-based subnationalist assertions that dominate the Indian scenario, this linguistic dispensation also once created the country of Bangladesh and continues to impel the periodic Baloch insurrections in southwestern Pakistan. Meanwhile, with every ascension of a UP- or Gujarat-dominated BJP to national power, chauvinistic regional outfits like the Shiv Sena inevitably seem to turn toward an introspective weighing of their Maratha and Hindu priorities.

The institution of Sanskrit as spiritual parabasis, and Hindi as "panther dialect" in the jungle of languages, is an idealist project to cure the disease of historical time.[162] The extraction of a Shudh Hindi from Arabic and Persian impurities and from the vulgate of Maithili, Hindusthani, Awadhi, or Brajbhasha is a recapitulation of a lost Sanskritic aura. It is a nationalist project to suture back together an original Indian language of being that had been fragmented because of Islamic state power and its imprints on temporal imaginations, life-worlds, and markets. The Sanskritic ontology, in this line of thinking, had provided the bulwark for cultural survival in the dark night of history. But in the present, too, even after the partition of Hindi and Urdu, the state remains alien. It is no longer Persian but is decidedly Anglophone. It is this historical conundrum that expresses itself in terms of Hindi's schizophrenic relationship with English—not just with the language of the old imperial cosmopolitanism and the subsequent "English rule without Englishmen," but also of American-style techno-financial globalization. The installation of Shudh Hindi as the paramount language of national being is always dogged by the emergence of "Hinglish" as the Urdu of a new global dispensation and the lingua franca of money markets.[163] This is, once again, a predicament in time, a conundrum in terms of futural imaginations of being and language. Yet it is this ongoing crisis in language—and concomitant ones of narration and memory—that contemporary urban, technocratic Hindutva tries to ward off and overwrite with a new, spectacular, electronic political theology. As we will see in the final chapter of this book, this new cult of Hindutva 2.0 as advertised modernization promises a fresh clearing. It is, to transpose a thought from Foucault, a momentary postponement of the burning of libraries of Babel, where books gather the murmurings of many books of the past. This is a perpetual dilemma of the Brahminical tyrant, whether it comes to history or plastic surgery: "Either all these books are already contained within the Word and they must be burned, or they are contradictory and, again, they must be burned."[164]

Concluding Remarks

These Herderian pieties have been endemic features of Hindu nationalist thinking in general since the end of the nineteenth century. Postulates of time and origins, landmass, race, language, and cultural memory resonate in these discourses without completing one pan-Indian, providential story of Hindu peopleness. This discourse has to invoke a deep temporal imagination and give it a destinying tilt in order to create a revivalist picture that is more appealing than the story of progress in the homogenous and "empty" time of the modern. It has to stick to Varnasrama as the defining feature of Hindu society and at the same time furnish a nominal sense of equity, redemption, and justice adequate to profane modern desires. In its spurious engagements with modern science and the question of production, traditional Hindutva-speak must also struggle to square its paternalistic promises with the technocratic competence and bureaucratic efficiency people expect from the modern state.

We have looked at the breathtaking scope and the burning edges of this anticipatory discourse, its desire to emerge from deeper origins and then conquer and transcend history altogether. This redemption story is much more complicated than the jealous political monotheisms that Schmitt studied in his immediate context in the West. This is because, when it comes to hardcore Hindu nationalist ideologies, it is not just the instinctive realization of the self and the potential extermination of the enemy that is at stake. The task involves remembering an essential Hindu subject that is apparently different from the profane, modern one, yet one that is lost in an ever-receding past that in itself cannot be viewed other than through the prism of the modern. This recovery also means bringing together the attributes of this phantom Aryan Hindu and presenting him as sovereign amid the clamor of subcontinental identities. In recalling and affirming deep origins, the new Hindu therefore has to commit to a cosmic reckoning of time and agency in relation to which he can only be instrumental. Along with that, the here-and-now historicity of the presently fallen people must be disavowed as one of the prime aspects of a great oblivion.

Then there is the question of space, that of amplifying the heartland microcosm of Brahmavarta—Manu's ideal Vedic village—to cover the national territory. The nation, in that spirit, must be an organic whole, not a federal structure balancing regional powers. This abstract proposition, when placed in a historical field of problems, immediately presents a set of conflicts pertaining to whether revival simply means a north Indian, Brahminical, Hindi-speaking, vegetarian, masculine domination over the Dravidian south, Muslim Kashmir, Dalit India, or Baptist Nagaland. The problem with the organismic national imagination in the subcontinent is not that the model itself does not apply here. It is perhaps that there may be too many such competing imaginaries. India, in other words, is too vast and too diverse to fit into a form that is essentially derived from small and compact European nations marked by one language, one culture, one religion, and one ethnicity. The size of the principality has been a matter of perpetual concern in Western political thinking, from the Greeks to Machiavelli, Rousseau, and beyond, when it came to recommending democratic, aristocratic, or monarchical regimes. In Rousseau, for instance, the possibility of an inorganic fragmentation of the general will increases with the size of territory and population.[165] From such a vantage point, in the historical absence of a focused Hindu general will with monolingual sway, India can never be a Hindu nation, only a Hindu empire.

Meanwhile, it is time to turn away from Golwalkar and his associates in the Hindutva project. Their works have been insightfully analyzed over the decades. I do not wish to add anything more to that corpus. For the rest of this book, I will attempt to illustrate a historical process of Hindu modernization in the longue durée. That is, I will visit two moments, one of the antecedent past and one of the subsequent present, that bookend that early and mid-twentieth-century moment of Savarkar and Golwalkar. I will therefore jump across timelines, going from a nineteenth- and early twentieth-century invention of Hinduism—one derived from literary culture print capitalism and colonial governmentality—to the late twentieth- and early twenty-first-century Hindu media ethnoscape of electronic capitalism. The purpose is to construct a working genealogy of the monothematic Hindu tone of the Indian modernity project itself—of which the Hindutva ideology we have examined is only a part, not the whole. This is an overall process that may be called modernization in the Hindu-Indian context. Modernization, in this restricted sense, is the story of certain historic changes in modes of production, shifts in cognitive universes, and alterations in principles of governance in a set of societies that were largely feudal and agrarian. It is a perpetually mutating arrangement that Rajni Kothari has described in the following manner: "A modernizing society is neither modern nor traditional. It simply moves from one threshold of integration and performance to another, in the process transforming both the indigenous structures and attitudes and the newly introduced institutions and ideas."[166]

I want to take a closer look at a normative Hinduness that has always been contiguous to the mode of secularism that the Nehruvian state adopted after independence. Historically, that secularism has wavered between the principle of *sarvo dharma sama bhava* (the state treating all religions as equal and also actively participating as trustee and administrator for all) and, in moments of expediency, of *dharmnirpekhshta* (the state being indifferent to quiddities of all religions). In sum, this secularism has operated on a plane of benevolent Brahminical tolerance, with a perpetual mission to induct Dalits into caste Hindu society, prevent conversions, and declare most forms of communitarian and regional politics as feudal.[167] In this sense, India, as Upendra Baxi once put it, was always a Hindu secular state.[168] For Nehru himself, that secular architect of modern India, the concept of Hinduization was not to be used in a restricted religious manner, but in "the widest sense of Indian culture."[169] In recent decades this apparently benign Hinduness has increased its powers as a psychological parabasis for a majoritarian nation. It has done so in a pronounced manner, with ritualized pathological expressions, increasingly dispelling the passive notes of sobriety and moderation in the Hindu secular.

3 THE INDIAN MONOTHEISM

The Bhagwad Gita as Holy Book

The invention of Hinduism, from the modern epistemological perspective, began in the last quarter of the eighteenth century. It was guided by the principle that, for Hindus to become a people, they would need a Book, and the Book had to be a good one. The East India Company merchant, typographer, and orientalist Charles Wilkins's (1749–1836) translation of the Bhagwad Gita—a text originally extracted from the Bhishma Parvan of the Mahabharata—was published in 1785 and heartily patronized by Warren Hastings, the first governor-general of British India. The publication was an important moment in the overall textual invention of the "Hindu Tradition" and the emergence of both "India" and "Hindu" as modern political concepts rather than geographical ones.[1]

This form of organizing knowledge, denominating faiths, and identifying populations called for sovereign selections. In 1772, the East India Company administration earmarked the Manusmriti as the standard book of Hindu law, over and above another a dozen and a half Dharmasastras and other Smritis, such as those of Gautama, Baudhayana, or Yajnavalkya. This measure was fortified by the publication of Nathaniel Brassey Halhed's *A Code of Gentoo Laws* (1776), with which the administration invented a paradigmatic Hindu legal template, detaching jurisprudence from the many fluid eccentricities of custom and vernacular interpretation. Such steps toward the determination of a Hindu subject, unity, and justice were taken in an overall climate of early Indological forays into native universes by figures like William Jones, Halhed, and Henry Thomas Colebrook. The discipline itself would assume proper institutional form with the establishment of the Asiatic Society of Bengal in 1784 and with the publications of the first papers on Hinduism by Jones and Colebrook in *Asiatick Researches*. Around the same time and in parallel, with the establishment of the Baptist Mission and Press in Serampore in 1800 by the preacher William Carey and others, the New Testament appeared in Bengali verse styled in the Vaishnava tradition in 1801. The Bengali Bible (Dharma Pustak) was published in 1809.[2]

The beginnings of this great colonial transcoding of Indic faiths into an axiomatic "Hinduism" may be contrasted with a royalist study undertaken two centuries prior by Abul Fazl (1551–1602), the court historian of Jalaluddin Muhammad Akbar (1542–1605), the third and greatest emperor of the Mughal dynasty.[3] The fourth book of Fazl's *Ain-I Akbari* (The Administration of Akbar)—which is itself part of the monumental Akbarnama (Book of Akbar)—is an ethnographic study of the faiths, cosmologies, and literary-intellectual universes of the subcontinent. Fazl begins by dispelling a common opinion that the souls of Hindustan were not nourished by the "full illumination of truth" that came with the worship of a singular God. The monotheistic idea, according to him, is "convincingly attested" in the faith traditions of the land.[4] He then begins a survey of a vast, myriad field, comprising eighteen cosmologies (of which he describes three) and 360 systems of philosophy and conduct, of which he identifies nine as major. Six schools out of the nine—Nyaya, Vaisesika, Vedanta, Mimamsa, Samkhya, and Patanjala—are endorsed by the Brahmins, while the sects of Jaina, Buddha, and the Nastika (Carvaka) are not. Fazl's meticulous reckoning of the six Brahminical orders are often inflected by key Abrahamic concerns like belief in a creator God, apocalypse, or the presence of heaven (*swarga*) and hell (*naraka*). For instance, he discovers doctrinal similarities between Nyaya and Christianity.[5] However, his philosophical study implicitly admits, without much heartburn, that the only common features that tie the six schools together is that they are all Astika (believers in the Vedas). Beyond that, they interpret the scriptures in radically different ways.

Doxa apart, the examination of a broader field of juridical, civic, or practical "agreement" among the learned Brahmins in the *Ain-I-Akbari* extends seamlessly to the eighteen sciences dealing with medicine, law, palmistry (*samudrika*), magic (*indrajaal*), rhetorical composition (*sahitya*), music (*sangita*), or politics (*rajniti*). Fazl finds commonalities of custom in a range of matters pertaining to purity, food, fasting, marriage and funeral rites, or almsgiving. Yet at no point does he gesture toward a singular ontic principle of divinity or even a steady firmament of faith that may be retroactively identified by us moderns as "Hinduism." The six schools themselves, while each "distinct" in doctrine, may be accounted for in sets of two: The Nyaya and Vaisesika agree on many points between themselves, as do Vedanta and Mimamsa, and Samkhya and Patanjala.[6] Meanwhile, the two Sramana schools, the Nastika order of the Carvakas, and indeed the greater penumbra of the rest of the unnamed 360 orders, would all eminently qualify as existing within the belief systems of the "Hindu" people—as would the teachings and creeds of the numerous Sufi mystics who were either born in India or achieved their final resting places there, whom he cites as "Saints of Hindustan" (Awliya-I-Hind).[7]

The colonial logic of administrative taxonomy and identification, launched in the last quarter of the eighteenth century and geared toward the invention of "Hinduism," was therefore remarkably different from Fazl's project. In recent decades, however, there has been a significant body of research challenging this constructivist-orientalist thesis. These works have questioned assumptions that a unified Hindu consciousness, as such, did not already exist before the colonial dispensation and that it was created, ex nihilo, by a modern discourse reaching its apogee with Monier Monier-Williams's *Hinduism* (1877). In an influential 1999 essay, David N. Lorenzen argued in favor of a longer medieval genesis of Hindu consciousness, one deriving from the fifteenth-century Nirguna Sant Kabir, the sixteenth-century Varkari saint Eknath, the fourteenth-century Vaishnava poet Vidyapati, and the works of European missionaries like the Italian Jesuit Roberto de Nobili (1577–1656) or the Franciscan Marco della Tomba (1726–1803).[8] Andrew Nicholson's 2010 work, *Unifying Hinduism*, argued that it was between the twelfth and sixteenth centuries CE that certain thinkers in the Sanskrit tradition initiated doxographical efforts to present the teachings of the Vedas, the Upanishads, the epics, the Puranas, and the six major schools of Hindu philosophy as a constitutive whole. Before this late medieval period, there had been no systematic effort to define a singular tradition for the peoples who followed the Vedas. The genesis of Hinduism was therefore not as far back in time as Hindu nationalists would suggest, nor was it as recent as the nineteenth century, as modernists would aver. Nicholson's enlightening study centers upon the works of the sixteenth-century philosopher Vijnanabhikshu of the Bhedabheda ("difference and nondifference") tradition of the Vedanta. Nicholson argues that it was this medieval doxographical legacy that was inherited by early Indologists like Colebrook and then passed onto modern neo-Hindus like Aurobindo Ghosh, Swami Vivekananda, and Sarvepalli Radhakrishnan. This desire to define the perimeters of orthodoxy was, among other things, prompted by the political as well as theological presence of Islam.[9]

There should be no reason to question the valence of this doxographic terrain. There should be no reason to assume that encyclopedic, universalist lines of thinking about a broader Vedic world did not exist before colonialism. The question once again, however, is whether the phenomenon could be more accurately described as a consolidation of Brahminism rather than a "proto-Hindu" germination.[10] In other words, the efforts of an editorial Brahminism that has always been alert and sensitive to crosscurrents in its own traditions as well as to mutations in competing Sramana orders. It would also beg the larger question as to whether "Hinduism" is itself a garb that modernity throws over Brahminism to anoint it as a new demographic and "religious" identity. This incarnation of Hinduism—as a political phenomenon in reference to the modern state and nationhood, in conversation with colonial ethnology, and pressured by the monotheistic imperative of modern religious anthropology—certainly came into being in the nineteenth century. Seen from this particular, modern vantage point, the medieval "proto-Hindu" consciousness would lack two important things: the "Church" coveted by Savarkar and others, and a precise determination of a wider Hindu laity. Nicholson suggests that during this 'medieval' period the word *nastika* shifted in meaning from its classical designation of those with incorrect ritual practices (heteropraxy) to a designation of those with incorrect opinions (heterodoxy). While it is clear that adherents of Buddhism, Jainism, or Sikhism, along with Islam, would be precluded from this esoteric conception of Astika (affirmer), the status of eccentric formations within what would later become "Hinduism"—for example, Tantra and some Bhakti cults, animists, or untouchables outside the pale of caste society—would at best be ambiguous.

Crucially, from the perspective of modern Hindutva, such a precolonial formation would also represent an incipient consciousness unable to name Islam as the enemy. The Sanskrit texts explored by Nicholson do not mention Islam; the vernacular ones from western India examined by Lorenzen, and the texts from the Gaudiya Vaishnava tradition studied earlier by Joseph T. O'Connell, almost never use terms like *Islam* or *Mussalman*.[11] A panoply of names is used to designate the other in these tracts, from the more ethnogeographic Turk or Afghan to more abstract epithets like Mlechcha—the barbaric, boorish, or impure—and Yavana, a generic term for the foreigner extended to a number of groups throughout history, including the Greeks and Ionians. From the perspective of a Schmittian modern sovereignty, this "proto-Hindu" consciousness would be marked by a critical lack of political jealousy, both toward theological others and the caste unfortunates threatening to leave the modern flock. It is in this sense that the proper project for a Hindu people, and eventually a Hindu nation and state, began in the nineteenth century and not before. This undertaking called upon the Bhagwad Gita to emerge as a singular Holy Book that could set up a gravitational imperative for a vast subcontinental field of awry devotions.

Sibaji Bandyopadhyay's monumental study of the textual career of the Gita—spanning twelve centuries—is one of the most important works of scholarship in recent times on the subcontinental history of ideas.[12] Bandyopadhyay writes that, since the appearance of Wilkins's text, there have been no fewer than three hundred English translations of and commentaries on the Holy Book of the Hindus. If the ones in the vernacular languages are added, it becomes a formidable corpus that includes works by major architects of Indian nationalism such as Bankimchandra Chattopadhyay; Bal Gangadhar Tilak; Swami Vivekananda; Sri Aurobindo; S. Radhakrishnan; Chakravarty Rajagopalchari; and the peerless Mohandas Karamchand Gandhi. Bandyopadhyay's analysis demonstrates how, in this complex terrain, a modern textual apprehension of the Gita becomes central to the task of drawing up an evolving and remembering "Indian" and "Hindu" subject in the world. This, of course, was not a single line of transmission without an internal Hindu battle of the books about whether the Gita should gain preeminence over the Vedas or Vedanta. The divinity of Krishna is denied in Saraswati's *Satyarth Prakash*, for instance: "the One could not have avatars because the One was perpetually inborn; if the Hindus were to be a modern people of the book, that book would have to be the Rg Veda. Saraswati's project is otherwise strongly Semitic. He extracts a set of ten commandments from the Vedic compendium and a form of communion. However, he does not advance a Hindu notion of grace, since the One does not forgive the sins of his devotees. If he did, his system of Karmic justice would be destroyed.[13]

Among many other things, the dominant Gita line reveals how a certain progressivist discourse of modernity tried to induct the text into its own Christological trajectory. For the missionary and orientalist John Nicol Farquhar (1861–1929), the Gita represented a spiritual psychobiography of the Hindu self, a moment in the larger evolutionary schema of *preparatio evangelica* meant for all mankind. Through the Gita, a significant part of humanity reached Christ through the conduit of Krishna, much like the manner in which the pagan works of Plato, or Virgil's *Aeneid*, anticipated Biblical wisdom. The German intellectual Franz Lorinser, in his 1869 translation, followed the same path of natural theology but went a step further to propose that the Gita is not just derived, but partly plagiarized, from the New Testament. It emerges as an authentic theological text precisely because it can penetrate the crust of race, culture, and civilization to reach a human essence already committed to Enlightenment and Christological destinying. For Juan Mascaró (1897–1987), the essence of the Hindu Book can be felt to resonate at almost every axis point of Western literature, as a general historical coming-into-being of humanity itself as singular artwork. It is therefore the spirit of India that one hears echoed in the grand firmament of human consciousness, whether in Wordsworth's "Tintern Abbey" or in the sublime moments in Socrates, Pindar, Dante, Shakespeare, Blake, or Saint Peter of Alcántara. In Bal Gangadhar Tilak's *Gita Rahasya* (1915), the dialectic and the quest in Krishna's sermon becomes akin to the existential meditations of the Prince of Denmark. Contra Farquhar and Lorinser, however, here the tide turns between the East and the West. According to Tilak, the entire German idealist tradition—including Kant, Hegel, and Schopenhauer—is a noteworthy but ultimately failed approximation of Vedantic thought. In the hands of the psychologist Girindrasekhar Basu (1887–1953), Freud's disciple in absentia, the Gita becomes a text of psychoanalysis.[14] Mahatma Gandhi, as we have noted, read the text as an allegorical enunciation of the principle of Ahimsa (nonviolence); the cataclysmic war was not to be taken literally. On the other hand, Bandyopadhyay points out that the Gita was also a central text among armed revolutionaries in Bengal during the first two decades of the twentieth century, operating as the equivalent of Mao's little red book. The British police, at one point, deemed its possession as conclusive sign of sedition.[15] Krishna's call to the warrior Arjuna had thus become, at this particular juncture of organizing national self and imaginary, a readying of the subject for martyrdom.

Traditional "Hindu" doxological or philosophical traditions centered upon the Gita can be traced back to the eighth century at least, to the moment of Adi Sankaracharya. Over the ages this wide interpretive terrain would feature his nondualistic Advaita, the qualified monism or Vishishtadvaita of Ramanuja (11th century), the dualist or Dvaita philosophy of Madhvacharya (13th century), crypto-Buddhist revisions, and warring Shaiva and Vaishnava approaches to the text. However, the cosmopolitan Gita discourse that emerged after 1786 was understandably different in terms of epistemological priorities. What became more important in this framework of religious anthropology was the Gita's conversation with the European Enlightenment and Christian millenarian thinking. This emphasis contained an underlying imperative that the broader tradition of Hindu nationalism would later seize upon: a people cannot be a people without a common journey toward monothematic redemption. In this scenario, there were certain key features identified in the Gita that became crucial in the quest for a modern axiomatic: that it promotes an idea of Swadharma and a social unity of interests (*lokasangraha*) capable of curing mystic worldviews steeped in otherworldliness and universal sorrow; that it furnishes a secure path and destination in terms of Moksha by absorbing and synthesizing the dualism of Samkhya, the monism of Vedanta, and the theistic currents of Bhakti; and that it subsumes the digressions and clamor of the Vedic people into the singular voice and authority of Krishna.

Broadly speaking, the long nineteenth century saw the consolidation of what may be called an affective universe, rather than a civil society, with the spread and settlement of British colonial rule. This would begin in roughly the second decade, with the Third Anglo-Maratha War of 1817–1818 and the parallel institution of European public education in Bengal. It would become a pan-Indian phenomenon with the coming into being of Crown Rule and the British Raj proper after the Sepoy Mutiny of 1857 and the establishment of apex universities in Bombay, Madras, and Calcutta that same year. The questions surrounding an Indian Islam, Islamic Indian modernity, and the future of the traditional Ashrafi elite after the final eclipse of the Mughal empire would become focalized with the coming into being of the Aligarh Muslim University in 1875. The modern split of Hindu and Muslim political identities would be quickened by the colonial population state and its mechanisms of ethnology, linguistics, and electoral representation.

It is against this backdrop that one can locate the tacit or overt impulses of Christophilia, rationalism, and utilitarian positivism in the works of early reformers like Raja Rammohun Roy and Ishwar Chandra Vidyasagar (1820–1891) in Bengal or Dayanand Saraswati in the Punjab. We could place them in this context along with renegade interlocutors of a purported Hindu modernity like the Christian Reverends Krishnamohan Banerjea (1813–1885) and Lal Behari Dey (1824–1892), or the mission-educated, pioneering Dalit thinker and activist Mahatma Jyotirao Phule (1827–1890). This general environment would include innumerable mutations within "Hindu reform" like Keshub Chandra Sen's (1838–1884) breakaway Brahmo Samaj (1866), which many contemporaries found difficult to distinguish from a vernacular Christianity emerging from a natural-theological overwriting of the Vedic compendium. In the course of a critical examination of this complex historical scenario, what I would like to highlight is a set of substantive questions pertaining to being Hindu in a religious—and then, eventually, in a national—monothematic sense. Did becoming Hindu necessarily involve a jealous identity? Could one be a Hindu apostate? Could one convert into or out of Hinduism? What would be the modern principles of inclusion or exclusion in the Hindu demographic fold? Must a Dalit necessarily be in a state of limbo, outside the pale of caste society and yet within the folds of "Hinduism" as a demographic religious identity? By which standard notion of Sanatan Dharma (traditional "Hinduism") could one judge modern innovations like Rammohun's Unitarian Vedic Church of the Brahmo Samaj (1828), Keshub Sen's theology, or Saraswati's austere Vedic Aryanism? In the middle of all this, could someone be a Hindu and a Christian at the same time?

A particularly fascinating instance, in this light, would be the Vedanta-Catholicism of Brahmabandhab Upadhyay (1861–1907).[16] Born into a pious Kulin Brahmin family but educated in Christian schools, Upadhyay converted to the Roman Catholic faith in 1891 after a youthful dalliance with the reformist cult of the Brahmo Samaj and especially Keshub Chandra Sen's Nabobidhan philosophy, which combined the New Testament, Vaishnava piety, and doctrinaire Hinduism.[17] Eventually Upadhyay's experiments with Hindu traditions and Thomist thinking yielded, for him, an *Existentiell* of the Vedanta-Catholic. For Upadhyay the whole thing formed a disjunctive assemblage between Indic ways of life and newly acquired otherworldly expectations. It called for a Brahminical ritualistic purity in everyday affairs, including scrupulous caste discrimination, and a Catholicity of vision in terms of the universal fallenness of man and his providential deliverance: "We are Hindus as far as our physical and mental constitution is concerned, but in regard to our immortal souls we are Catholic. We are Hindu Catholic."[18] Upadhyay's life and his death dramatized two important themes. The first was the amorphous nature of Hindu identity itself, which, for him, was philosophical, customary, racial, or cultural. In essence, it could be categorically separated from a theological commitment to an inclement God elsewhere, from the concept of religion itself in a modern sense. The second pertains to the status of "conversion" in the Hindu worldview he had inherited. This was evident in the mutual exchange of bewilderment between him and the Catholic Church about his syncretic experiments, especially in the monastery he had established in Jabalpur, where Vedanta and Thomas Aquinas were equally valued curricular essentials. Upadhyay obviously did not see any fundamental contradiction between his Hindu self and his Christian faith. As a matter of fact, his intellectual ambitions envisioned a horizon in which Catholicism, in conjunction with Vedantic philosophy, would usher in a second Renaissance that was superior to that of the earlier compact between the Church and Greek thought in Europe. Upadhyay undeniably had a Good Book, but perhaps more than one of them. The Church eventually withdrew its patronage and when Upadhyay, after a phase of strident nationalism, passed away in 1907, it became a matter of conjecture whether he died a reconverted Hindu or a confessing Christian.

Brahmabandhab Upadhyay was not alone in considering his Hindu identity to be a flexible one that could be wrapped around a faith in a different God—or that an alien God Himself could be inducted without guarantees into a mental universe emanating from the Vedas. In contrast to this eclecticism, the Arya Samaj, established in 1875 by Dayanand Saraswati, was a Vedic monotheistic order strictly distinguished from a wider terrain of idol worship and superstition.[19] It would institute the Shuddhi (purification) movement for outcasts and lapsed Hindus as a largely customary measure, one without pronounced confessional imperatives. In primary terms—especially if one keeps the question of caste in mind—Shuddhi could be understood as a rite of entry into the Samaj itself, not necessarily into a sociology of practiced "Hinduism." In the early decades, before the creation of the All-India Muslim League in 1906, Arya Samaj members did not, as a matter of fact, register themselves as "Hindu" in government censuses. On the other hand, more than two hundred thousand "Muslims" would register themselves as "Mohammedan Hindus" during the Gujarat census of 1911.[20] All these measures of stepping into and out of practiced Hinduism, abstracting it as pure faith, culture, or custom, could not admit the category of conversion as central to "religion" as a jealous political mission.

The demographic determination of the Hindu population began with a relatively narrow base in 1872 and expanded subsequently. This expansion was perhaps pressured by congregational and reform institutions as well as by the eventual split along Hindu-Muslim lines in the colonial politics of representation. The 1881 census accorded Satnamis, Kabirpanthis, Nat worshippers, and Kumbhipattias subdenominational status. The 1891 one extended "minor religion" status to deists, atheists, freethinkers, agnostics, positivists, and those without any faith. The term *animist* was applied in a comprehensive manner to groups of forest tribes outside the pale of recognized Hindu Samaj and not yet claimed by Islam or Christianity.[21] In 1906, Sir Sultan Mohammed Shah, the third Aga Khan of the Nizari Ismailis, wrote to the viceroy of India, Lord Minto. The letter made an observation about proportional communal representation accorded by the colonial administration. The Aga Khan argued that, for all practical purposes, the depressed classes (untouchables) were not Hindus and therefore should not be considered as such in future arrangements.[22] If that was done, the ratio of Muslims in relation to the Hindu majority would have increased significantly.

Hindu nationalism, to begin with, was a fierce determination and preservation of a "flock" in reaction to such pendulations of subcontinental identity. This was not an easy task, with a centralizing drive toward a "back to the Vedas" Sanskritization being always complicated by untold vernacularisms of faith, as well as customary cruelty and exclusion when it came to caste unfortunates. Nevertheless, as an Indological environment gradually became influential in the nineteenth century, one could increasingly talk and fantasize about an original "Hindu Indian civilization," retroactively derived and absolved of eight centuries of Islamic culture and almost a millennium of Buddhist dominance prior to that. This modern invention of "Hinduism" involved myriad projects of scriptural interpretation, religious anthropology, history, archaeology, and comparativist studies in philology and philosophy. It was undertaken within the modern disciplinary order that Foucault famously called "power/knowledge" and was increasingly articulated in the disenchanted prose of the modern. In this dispensation, the public discourse of Hinduness—one that spoke to the state, or spoke with the state in mind—could no longer be voiced as priestly dictates (*bidhdhi*) from the absolutist standpoint of old scriptural authorities and feudal institutions. It had to be enunciated with dialogic agon and rigor, in a spirit of creative appropriation as well as moral diffidence toward European enlightenment and its regimes of truth.

Hegel and an Early Moment of Philosophical Interrogation

If it was a modern Orientalist textualism that pronounced the Gita to be the Hindu book of the world, it was also the same order of things that tested the scripture rigorously in relation to humanism and the concomitant theme of the universal. From the outset, Europe had asked whether, and to what primitive extent, the Gita would be amenable to an enlightened subjectivity and an overall charter of freedom. Let us glance at an early but formidable instance in this terrain in order to illuminate some of the challenges that Hindu modernizers and nationalists would keep in mind later while constructing a monotheme of selfhood and belief. G. W. F Hegel, in a short commentary written in 1827, found the Gita to be the poetic work best suited to provide Westerners with a distinct idea of the "most general and most sublime in Indian religion."[23] Hegel's study becomes a civilizational diagnosis here, much in line with early observations made in his *Lectures on the Philosophy of History*, published five years before in 1822. He therefore situates the Gita in the same teleological order that fixes the East as infancy, the Greek as youth, the Roman as individual, and the German as the old age of the Spirit. This story of universal maturation is that of man's rise from the sensuous, animal world to an entity with positive freedom and ego that can forestall immediate gratification in the interest of ends. The historical birth of universal freedom, and the Spirit's consciousness of its own liberty in Hegel's own Germanic philosophical world, is therefore preceded by a Greek order, in which some were free (the rest were slaves), and the order of the oriental despot, in which only one person was.

According to Hegel, an essential pattern of reflective thought that can birth the modern subject is missing in the Bhagwad Gita. He argues that Krishna's call to Arjuna to fulfill the code of the warrior through desireless action is an instrumentalization of the self. It is a duty, a moral obligation, but only in terms of a natural destination, not free will. The most disturbing thing about the Gita's cosmology, for Hegel, is that it leaves no temporal or spatial scope for the exercise of reason: "Acting is being absorbed in knowing or rather in the abstract meditation of consciousness. Religion and philosophy, too, merge here in such a way that they seem to be indistinguishable."[24] Hegel calls Yoga an abstract devotion, a meditation without contents in which the mind "ascends towards the complete emptiness of subject and object and thus towards unconsciousness."[25] The call on the individual is to act without moral intentions or freedom, since the absolute separation between the universal and the concrete renders both devoid of spirit. The universal becomes an empty oneness, while the concrete remains a naturalistic manifold of pluralities. In the absence of a dialectically unfolding self-consciousness—one that marks for itself the goal of finally squaring immanence with transcendence, the fate of the individual with that of world history—meditation becomes an ascetic, total withdrawal from the world while action becomes either decorative or enslaved tasking. Arjuna, at the end of the day, has to war because Krishna commands him to. Krishna does so as the One who has not only already willed the death of enemies, but has arranged for the weaponization of Arjuna himself to that purpose.

Hegel finds the core of Indian philosophy to be pure negativity of thought, and its generated laws (Manusmriti for instance) arbitrary, ritualistic, and superstitious. He recognizes that the Gita is a theistic text, but one that lacks the arsenal of reason to give birth to a public religion that could marry science with faith. It is a theodicy that forecloses individual self-consciousness and, consequently, the categories of rights and justice. This does not mean that Hegel would demur from calling his own philosophy a theodicy, or Leibniz's metaphysics the same. However, unlike the Germanic stage of the Spirit, the theodicy in the Gita is of pure natural origins and is not aligned with a self-conscious Spirit actively present in the world. Unlike the Jesus of the Gospels, Krishna, in his mortal form, cannot bridge the gap between divine wisdom and human praxis.

As a result of these deficiencies, Krishna's declaration of his own status as the One becomes a tirade rather than a constitution.[26] His speech cannot really compel a rational mind to arrive at the idea of one God and accordingly to derive a monism of purpose. As a result, the proposed Oneness is dull and monotonous; it must be repeated ad nauseum, over eighteen books, precisely because it can be neither logically justified nor historically narrated.[27] In the eleventh book, during the Vishwaroopa, or Trikal Darshan, Krishna (presumably tired of repeating himself) reveals his aspect as the three orders of time and creation incarnate. The Oneness here is imposed through a fearful and idolatrous spectacle, a form of "picture thinking" rather than a notion.[28] In the tremendous thickening of cosmic affect in the Trikal Darshan, Indian mythology becomes indistinguishable from philosophy.[29] Arjuna's submission to the will of Krishna is partly out of terror and partly out of his love for the charismatic god. It is not an active self-realization of duty. On the other hand, Krishna, for his part, can only remind Arjuna of his terrible task; he cannot address the Pandava's unhappiness and pain at the prospect of slaughtering his own cousins, uncles, and teachers. The recognition of sorrow as sorrow would have inaugurated the history of the ethical subject, since the pain of unhappy consciousness can only be transcended by a reaching out to objectivity. As we know from elsewhere in Hegel, happy moments, or moments bereft of recognized unhappiness, are the blank pages of history.[30] Both Krishna and the enthralled Arjuna therefore miss the opportunity to register an alienation of consciousness that is a precondition for that consciousness to return to itself. Unlike the case of Sophocles's Antigone, the tragic agon required for the eventual passage from familial law to the law of the state remains missing in the Gita. This is precisely why the predicates of the divine persona—Krishna's enduring love or his fearful power—cannot be translated into a diagram of the rational State. His will cannot be the origin of Right. Instead, it breeds a fanaticism of the void, one of pure contemplation, which can only actualize itself as destruction. The dark god's discourse remains a beautiful instance of the poetic imagination, of which India has some of the most sublime specimens in the world; however, it may not be marshaled to challenge the notorious diagnosis Hegel had made five years earlier: "It is obvious to anyone with even a rudimentary knowledge of the treasures of Indian literature that this country so rich in spiritual achievements of a truly profound quality nevertheless has no history."[31]

Hegel's reading of the Gita in 1827 was thus absolutely consistent with conclusions about the civilization and culture he had arrived at much earlier. The absence of a monotheistic esprit de corps for the nation compromises its security in a world of lordship and bondage. In India, five hundred Englishmen conquered twenty thousand natives at a crucial hour not because the latter were cowards, but because they lacked the basic ability to identify with a universal.[32] Courage, for example, was not the virtue of all mankind; it was only a Kshatriya virtue. In such a situation, it actually becomes necessary for the political constitution to be separated from religion. Yet on the other hand, "If political principles and institutions are divorced from the realm of inwardness, from the innermost shrine of conscience, from the still sanctuary of religion, they lack any real center and remain abstract and indeterminate."[33] The government cannot exhibit itself as anything but a victorious fraction of the general will that automatically becomes guilty in relation to the rest.[34] In the Indian case, this seems to take the form of eternal stasis and inertia. In a highly developed national culture, the caste system creates a theocratic aristocracy, yet the ideality of the imagination remains mired in the sensual world. The spirit does indeed transcend the particular and rise to the universality of God, but, like the fearful spectacle of Krishna's Vishwaroopa that comes and goes, it is only a wild and momentary rise. As a result, India, like the rest of the Orient, can indeed have a state, but that state will be devoid of a providential purpose.

Then there is that old question of Hindu otherworldly asceticism versus the dynamic historical consciousness and action of the West. Hegel insists on a fluidity of thinking and a dynamic liquidation of habit for the global movement of the spirit, as well as for the alignment of peoples and cultures with that force. One can fetch a maritime figuration from the *Philosophy of Right* to illustrate this. Family life, Hegel writes, is dependent on the soil, the terra firma. But the natural element of industry, its medium of outward animation, is the sea. It is in the massive hydraulics of the oceans that one discovers the true flux of history, the joyous discoveries of uncharted possibilities, and the creative destruction of commerce. It is for this reason that rooted cultures like Egypt and India "have become stagnant and sunk in the most frightful and scandalous superstition" while seafaring nations have flourished.[35] In this light, the famous Hindu stricture—that crossing the dark waters results in loss of Varna status—would eminently qualify as superstition and merge with Hegel's overall problem with Hindu law.[36] It is for such reasons that, in the Hegelian universe, there is no possibility for a modern Hindu state. What then should be the unhappy but best possible nature of sovereignty in India?

Hegel's Eurocentric prescription for India and Egypt, expectedly, is in favor of colonization. The spirit of world history has now traveled to the West, and that calls for an infusion of European civil society predicates (law, trade, science, or production) into the stagnant civilizations of the Orient. That, admittedly, would not amount to a warm contact with the universal, but it could ignite historical consciousness in those contexts. The natives, with a new experience of time as historical time, would learn to distinguish themselves from nature and to understand freedom as the universal condition of humanity. Going down the ladder of enlightenment, one would need slavery to awaken humanity among the Negroes.[37] Colonial servitude, by implication, is enough for Hindus who, while not being "animal-men," are obscurantist enough to value animals more than themselves. Both, in different degrees, would learn work as a rationally purposive act rather than as instrumental or naturalized tasks prompted by despotic authority or basic instinct.

Yet for Hegel the implication is that "slavery ought not exist, as it is by definition unjust in and for itself."[38] With the slow maturation of historical consciousness and the universalization of the concept of freedom, both slavery and the colonial state should wither away. Hegel was far from unique on this matter, as far as a general Eurocentric justification for imperialism was concerned. But one can also extract certain radical possibilities in the teleological schema itself, once it is brought out of its provincial repose in Europe. There is that other possibility: that it might be the meek, the slave, or the Indian that may eventually inherit the earth. This sense of secularized providence has, in various ways and in various degrees, touched not only Marx, in his writings on India, but also the pioneering intellectuals of colonial critique: Fanon or Ngũgĩ wa Thiong'o in the wider African context, Nehru in India, as well as his Marxist interlocutors. Keeping this in mind, I will now turn to two nineteenth-century moments in the overall terrain of Hindu nation-thinking that may be considered intellectual ripostes to Hegel on India. What is interesting is that, for one of them, Raja Rammohun Roy, the cornerstone of a pure Hindu religion and culture was not the Gita, but the Vedas and Upanishads. In contrast, for Bankimchandra Chattyopadhyay, the heart of Hinduism lay in the Gita and nowhere else.

Modernity and Hindu Monotheism:
The Literary Moment of Raja Rammohun Roy

A project of Hindu reform had been launched in earnest by the second decade of the nineteenth century, around the birth of Hinduism itself as an epistemological category. This reform-revival enterprise was centered in Calcutta and pursued in a new ecology of European education, spurred by the founding of institutions like the Hindu College and the School Book Society in 1817 or the Medical College of Bengal in 1835. It may be said that this "Renaissance"—spanning decades, headlined by such events as the banning of Sati by the William Bentinck administration in 1829, the irreverent, iconoclastic challenges to caste Hindu practices by the Young Bengal Movement inspired by Henry Louis Vivian Derozio (1809–1831), or movements for widow remarriage and female education in the 1850s led by Vidyasagar—was, in essence, Bengali. This "Bengal Renaissance" had no overt pan-Indian aspirations, even for some time after 1857. Yet within this provincial cast there was a desire to take responsibility for, and speak on behalf of, Indian religion, philosophy, and civilizational complex. There were marked ambitions to do so in a spirit—if one were to draw from the mission of the Asiatic Society—that extended new determinations of Bengaliana to whatever was performed by man or produced by nature.[39] Print capitalism in Bengal was producing rapid translations of Western scientific and medical treatises by the end of the second decade. It would usher in a proper moment of worldliness in the modernizing project with the publication of Reverend Krishnamohan Banerjea's bilingual *Vidyakalpadhrum or Encyclopedia Bengalensis* in thirteen volumes (1846–51).[40] It has been a matter of justifiable debate whether this vibrant intellectual universe can be accounted for in terms of the European idea of the Renaissance. I do not wish to enter the thickets of that controversy, now quite stale.[41] It is sufficient to say that there was indeed an "awakening," a fracture and shift in the elite cognitive apparatus itself. This change in framework was prompted by an early question about the Hindu religion, modernity, and a monotheistic imperative that I intend to explore.

Raja Rammohun Roy (1772–1833) was a polymath extraordinaire, trained in the Sanskrit, Persian-Arabic, English, and Greco-Latin traditions, translator of both the Bible and the Koran, founder of reformist movements like the Atmiya Sabha (1814) and the Brahmo Samaj (1828). Born in a small, high Brahmin Zamindari family, Roy's education was widely eclectic. He was introduced to Aristotle and Euclid via his Arabic education in Patna and to the Hindu philosophical schools through the Sanskrit one in Varanasi. He trained in Buddhist thinking in Tibet and later mastered Greek and Hebrew to explore the Christian traditions. His first major work, *Tufat-ul-Muahiddin* (A Gift to the Believers in One God), was a Persian text with an introduction in Arabic. He subsequently published in English and was one of the pioneers of modern Bengali prose. Roy worked as an official for the East India Company for a period and then, in the last two decades of his life, emerged as a major social reformer in Bengal.

The central impulse in Roy's intellectual project involved recasting the massive Vedic tradition as a modern monotheism. This called, among other things, for the sharpening of an editorial intelligence fit for the times, but in the spirit of the great compiler and redactor Vyasa, to whom tradition attributes the Mahabharata, the origin texts of the Vedanta, and all eighteen major Puranas. The figure of Vyasa appears frequently in Roy's work, as the one who is said to have imparted a manageable shape to the Vedas by dividing the corpus into three and synthesizing all Vedic intelligence by abjuring confusing and contradictory passages.[42] Roy refers to this figure in relation to his own work and his quite overt desire to earmark a canonical Hindu scriptural tradition.

At times one gets the feeling that, for Rammohun, the key figure that is missing in the Hindu fold is not one equivalent to Christ, but to Saint Paul. As a result of this lack, Hinduism never developed into a vertically organized faith on the lines of Pauline Christianity, marked by great redaction, singular dissemination, apostolic succession, and the pastoral guidance of the congregational church. There was no Hindu apparatus to give form to a singular narrative of redemption, to distinguish canonical truth from the gnostic, true believer from heretic, or to determine, at every step, the perpetuation (*agama*) of God's will. In a mélange of subcontinental histories, there was no temporal distinction to be made between the birth of true faith and the pervasive sway of the pagan. The entire body of Hindu wisdom had failed to furnish a sovereign scholasticism of holy catalogues and taxonomy. A modern textual reform of the Hindu tradition thus had to take place along the lines of fixing the New Testament—in twenty-seven books distinct from Gnostic texts and pagan influences—and the Old Testament, by abstraction from the Tanakh, the Septuagint, and other apocrypha, in the progressive construction of the Bible by synods over centuries, guided by the polemics and apologia of figures like Irenaeus, Tertullian, Origen Adamantius, and Eusebius of Caesarea.

Second, for Roy, the modern installation of a Vedic monotheism was not just a process of conventional exegesis or logical abstraction; it had to be literary and anthropological. The project called for a prism of enlightened understanding by which one could comprehend the many eccentricities of Hindu custom, since, apart from the Brahman as One, all other millions of gods and goddesses were earthbound entities imagined by mortals and installed by their mythologies. As manifest will, the One has been symbolically comprehended as forces of nature like the sun or the wind. Yet these myriad forms had to be understood as expressions of an abiding monotheism rather than as an always suspected pantheism. An essential part of Roy's acts of reading and literary elaboration was therefore the translation of the lofty, enchanting style of the scriptures into the critical and disenchanted prose of the modern. The enlightened reckoning of Vedic wisdom could not but be literary because Vyasa takes the supreme being beyond sensory or mental comprehension. The One can only be inferred by gestures of turning and pointing elsewhere, through a reading of his creation in light, in the elements, or in time. The One created the void space from which the universe sprang, and from which also sprang both human error and faith. This is precisely why there is no point quarreling with other religions, since they are all figural approximations of the singular truth that is always beyond rational calculation. Roy therefore takes the theistic question of the One beyond the Kantian distinction between science and dogma. He also, in effect, devolves an axiomatic Hindu anthropology and announces the immense varieties of here-and-now Hinduism itself as the object of that study.

This anthropological stance is evident in two tracts Rammohun Roy wrote in 1817: "A Defense of Hindoo Theism, in Reply to the Attack of an Advocate of Idolatory, at Madras" and "A Second Defence of the Monotheistical System of the Veds; in Reply to an Apology for the Present State of Hindoo Worship." Here he reads the Vedas, the Upanishads, or the Laws of Manu in the spirit of modern logic and realism. He concludes that while the Hindu orthodoxy did, overall, endorse the worship of "330,000,000 deities," this was merely an imaginative "concession made to the limited faculties of the vulgar, with the view of remedying, in some degree, the misfortune of their being incapable of comprehending and adopting the spiritual worship of the true God."[43] It has been in the interest of the Brahmins to encourage superstition and, via the culture of idol worship, rituals, and festivals, to arrogate divinity and pecuniary benefits to themselves. This was a conspiratorial Brahmin exclusivity: limiting thoughts of the Vedic Nirguna—the One without attributes—to their scholastic enclaves, while foisting rituals and idols on the teeming vulgate as mental exercises:

> Permit me in this instance to ask, whether every Mussalman in Turkey and Arabia, from the highest to the lowest, every Protestant Christian at least of Europe, and many followers of Cabeer and Nanuck [in India], do worship God without the assistance of consecrated objects? If so, how can we suppose that the human race is not capable of adoring the Supreme Being without the puerile practice of having recourse to visible objects?[44]

Apart from these observations, there is a moment in Roy's first defense that is remarkable in the light of the literary. He responds to a charge made by a "learned Brahmin" that his translations of sacred texts from Sanskrit to English are filled with inaccuracies and could breed public doubt. Roy declares that authorial intentions, even in original works, are often unclear. Sanskrit was a language that generated sentences amenable "to being explained in different sense."[45] Acts of interpretation and translation therefore could not be monolingual and authoritarian, controlled by the priestly class. The language of the gods could claim a renewed cosmopolitan valence only by reinventing itself as a dialogic democracy. Roy's was a literary exercise that was deliberately internationalist and public, tending, via a "foreign tongue," toward a world republic of letters. The "literary" here is also an admission of fallibility and finitude; it comes with the self-conscious knowledge that error is inevitable when one elaborates the One who is beyond all meaning. For Roy, the question of doubt posed by the learned Brahmin therefore comes from the fear of losing absolute interpretive privileges. On the other hand, a belief in translation can be affirmed by the thought of a cosmopolitan mankind.

Otherwise "we must learn all the languages that are spoken by the different nations in the world, to acquire a knowledge of their histories and religions, or be content to know nothing of any country besides our own."[46] Roy then proceeds to easily debunk a corollary claim made by his interlocutor: that the Puranas prohibit the discussion of Sanskrit scriptures in other languages. An essential part of this new concept of the literary was thus to affirm a new eloquence of the vulgate.

In the course of his defenses, Roy severely criticizes the three dominant strains of Hindu worship in the Bengali Vaishnava, Shakta, and Tantra traditions—especially the "human sacrifices, the use of wine, criminal intercourse, and licentious songs" in idolatrous practices. If these idols and their Puranic exploits stand in for the One, they foreclose the possibility of drawing a public morality from religious faith. Religion then becomes divorced from ethics and practical reason and reduces itself to fatalistic cycles of sacrifice, ritual, and pilgrimage. That apart, piety becomes antithetical to another novel category he introduces in his second defense: that of *common sense*. One story about Brahma, the creator, has him attempting to rape his own daughter. Another one about Vishnu the protector has him fraudulently violating the chastity of Brinda in order to kill her husband. Shiva, the destroyer, is seen to have a "criminal attachment" to Mohini, beyond all limits of decency. In that hall of infamy, a special place is reserved for Krishna, the unethical murderer of Pootna, the debauched womanizer, and the cruel cuckolder of husbands. It was simply a matter of common sense to read these stories either as parables or as mischievous interpolations.

The task of thinking the divine as a literary event involves the scrupulous refusal to see earthbound gods as personifications of the One. It means absolving stories from the trap of the literal and setting them free as allegories or figures, exemplary or otherwise. It is about saving postulates from the prison house of dogma, making them enter into a relational play of contradictions, shock, and affirmations with one another. However, the Hindu religion can be abstracted as a Vedic monotheism only if the task of the literary here is itself made universal by appealing to a natural religion that trumps all exclusive traditions based on revelation. Toward the end of his first defense, Rammohun extends his project to Christ and Mohammad. None of them is a personifications of God. They can be considered—in line with an admirable doctrine he finds in Islam, but not in Christianity—personifications of the mercy of God. Rammohun similarly cannot condone Christian trinitarianism or works involving transubstantiation and the doctrine of real presence.

He makes this amply clear in a later book called *The Precepts of Christ* (1820). This work can be immediately compared with two by Thomas Jefferson, the now lost *The Philosophy of Jesus of Nazareth* (1804) and *The Life and Morals of Jesus of Nazareth* completed in the same year Rammohun published *Precepts*. Rammohan's text, much like Jefferson's deist exercise, is an effort to draw out the universal moral predicates from the Gospels, cutting out enchantment and magic. This text, a Sanskrit and Bengali translation and redaction of the King James' Bible, is founded on the ethical premise that one does not have to believe in the divinity of Christ or the Holy Ghost in order to be a Christian. Christ must therefore come to India with miracles and ritualistic magnificence shorn from his life and works. He must come as a figuration of a pure Unitarian ethics and a harmonious, modernizing sensibility that Roy, in 1829, would call "universal religion."

Is it then desirable that Hindus should convert to Christianity? In a letter written in 1824 to the American theologian Henry Ware on this same matter, Rammohun gives a cryptic reply. He acknowledges that Christianity, or more specifically the Unitarian faith, shorn of the absurd and idolatrous practices of early Greek, Roman, and Barbarian converts, "has a greater tendency to improve the moral, social, and political state of mankind, than any other known religious system." Yet, once one reaches this lofty realm of contemplating the divine—beyond language, reason, or any ostentatious display of identity—the question of conversion itself becomes a nominal one. Roy reminds Reverend Ware of Acts 10:35: "In every nation he that feareth God and worketh righteousness is accepted with him." That is, "in whatever form of worship he may have been taught" to venerate the Almighty.[47]

Rammohun Roy's austere Hindu monism could be conceptualized only in terms of a universal religion, not a jealous one. He tried to institutionalize it with the Atmiya Sabha group in 1814, the Vedic seminary he established, and, most importantly, with the founding of the Church of the Brahmo Samaj, where people of all persuasions were invited and where Rammohun delivered ninety-eight sermons before his departure for England in November, 1830, and his subsequent death in Bristol. The complex history of the Brahmo Samaj, its brief eclipse after Roy's demise, its eventual adoption by Tagore's father Debendranath, and then the internal schisms that led to its split into the Adi and Shadharon factions in the 1860s and 1870s—primarily around questions of worship, marriage laws, and age of consent—is beyond the scope of this project.[48] The mutations and dispersals in this reformist movement were restricted to elite Bengali intellectual circles and limited in their pan-Indian resonances. Despite its significant impact on modern Indian thinking, the Brahmo phenomenon never acquired the institutional power and mass appeal that, to a certain extent, defined the Arya Samaj, and the Punjab- and UP-based North Indian movement inspired by it.

Hindu Modernization: The Literary Moment of Bankimchandra Chattopadhyay

Rammohun's hour inaugurated a general climate of moderate to radical reform, European Enlightenment–style education, and young challenges to the edifices of tradition. These energies set the template for "modern thought" in the subcontinental scenario and, in relation to emergent nationalist discourses later in the century, instituted a vanguard impulse expressed in that pithy slogan attributed to the early nationalist leader Gopal Krishna Gokhale: "What Bengal thinks today, India thinks tomorrow." Over the long nineteenth century, Bengal's myriad intellectual commerce with Europe ranged from Humean skeptical empiricism and Baconian science to Indological and Orientalist disciplines of Anglican and Germanic origin. These worked in concert with Millean utilitarianism, the Social Darwinism of Herbert Spencer, or the positivism of Auguste Comte. A literary project of Hindu revivalism had to locate itself in this basin of contrary affectations and intellectual tendencies. This many-armed enterprise had to inherit, contend with, and absorb the energies of such an intellectual universe while setting up its own providential horizons. It would be, for instance, an essential part of a Comtean schema of social evolution for the Hindu to proceed inevitably, in the theological domain, from a fetishistic or animistic stage to polytheism and then, finally, to monotheism.[49]

In the seminal works of Bankimchandra Chattopadhyay (1838–1894), we witness an effort to abstract a timely Hindu tradition, but also one in consonance with contemporary demands for a nationalist destinying. This extraction is marked by a comparativist reckoning of world religions with an eye on the universal, and it involves the tools of European science, historicism, and logic.[50] Bankim's literary career as a novelist, essayist, and satirist flourished in a political and cultural environment that came into being in the aftermath of the Sepoy Mutiny in 1857 and the transfer of sovereignty to the Crown in 1858. This period was marked by the winds of the second Industrial Revolution in Europe—the settling of technologies like the railways, the telegraph, and eventually electricity—and the rise of a new comprador elite among the

Indian beneficiaries of Western education. The picture of reform and new education, and an Existentiell of speed and machine-driven progress, was now pronouncedly pan-Indian. "India" itself acquired a proper figuration in modern disciplines, with the commencement of the great trigonometrical, botanical, meteorological, and ethnological surveys of the subcontinent.

Meanwhile, with the sublimation of nationalist discourse, Hindu reform, unlike in its early nineteenth-century moment with Rammohun and the ban on Sati by the Bentinck administration in 1829, would cease to call on the colonial state to intervene in matters of customary life. As a matter of fact, nationalism would do exactly the opposite; it would internalize and conserve reform within a purported Hindu national community, and resist any juridical intrusions in that domain. The colonial administration was ready to oblige and stay away from native matters, especially after the debacle of 1857. The question of reform, as Partha Chatterjee has demonstrated, would be restricted to erasing "colonial difference" in relation to native rights, freedoms, and privileges in the public sphere under colonial control, while retaining them in the realm of the private.[51]

It was therefore an hour of fresh intellection that would fix distinct nationalist sensibilities and historical imaginations from the 1870s onward, birth the Indian National Congress in 1885, and offer the first glimpses of organized Dalit assertion, especially on the west coast and in the south. The establishment of institutions variously tending toward Hindu monotheism, congregation, and reform would continue, with the coming into being of the Prarthana Samaj in Maharashtra (1867), the Arya Samaj in Punjab (1875), the Theosophical Society in Madras (1875), and, eventually, the Ramkrishna Mission in Calcutta (1897). The final years of Bankim's life would witness the first tremors of mass nationalist movements with a decidedly Brahminical inflection around matters like the Age of Consent Bill of 1891. Meanwhile, at the other end of the spectrum, the urban Muslims of North India—in the absence of traditional leaders and patrons like Bahadur Shah Zafar, the last of the Mughals, or Wajid Ali Shah, the last Nawab of Oudh—would view social changes with a greater degree of circumspection. British policies after 1857 would distance them from new education and government jobs, holding them primarily responsible for the Mutiny. The Islamic elite would take divergent paths in the aftermath: an Aligarh College–based, loyalist, and Western-educated one promoted by Sir Sayed Ahmad Khan (1817–1898), and another of orthodox revivalism at the influential seminary in Deobandh, inspired by the eighteenth-century Sunni theologian Shah Waliullah Dehlavi (1703–1762).

Bankim was educated in the English, Bengali, and Sanskrit traditions. He was one of the first two graduates from Calcutta University in 1858 and then studied law at Presidency College. He worked as a deputy magistrate and deputy collector for the colonial administration and was part of civil society bodies like the Bengal Social Science Association, established in 1863. Bankim's remarkable literary career flourished amid a veritable galaxy of Bengali litterateurs such as Michael Madhusudan Dutt (1824–1873), Rajnarayan Basu (1824–1899), Bhudeb Mukhopadhyay (1827–1894), Dinabandhu Mitra (1829–1873), Kaliprasanna Sinha (1841–1870), or Girish Chandra Ghosh (1844–1912). It coincided with the first decades of the resplendent literary life of Rabindranath Tagore (1861–1941). Bankim would work in close affinity with intellectuals like the economic historian Romesh Chunder Dutt (1848–1909) and the Indologist Haraprasad Sastri (1853–1931) in *Bangadarshan*, a pioneering journal founded by him in 1872.

From a pan-Indian perspective, Bankim's moment would be marked by greater incursions of print capitalism into the vernacular worlds of Urdu, Hindi, Gujarati, Marathi, and Tamil.[52] This was when many Indian literary commons came into being through standardizations of grammar, lexicon, prose, and punctuation. The period would witness the flourishing of newspapers, journals, dictionaries, encyclopedias, disciplinary textbooks, historical and geographical works, and translations and adaptations of European literature. It would mark the advent of modernizers like Bharatendu Harishchandra (1850–1885), Govardhanran Tripathi (1855–1907), Samuel Vedanayagam Pillai (1825–1889), and Kandukuri Veeresalingam (1848–1919), as well as the first novels in the vernacular languages.[53] The times would demand cultural turns toward historical and linguistic consciousness of various kinds; they would give birth to modern regional and communal identities, as well as the discourses of competing nationalisms.[54] It would be an hour for novel imaginings of the future, of tabulating debts of the past, often in line with British ethnological parameters set out by Alexander Duff (Marathas), James Tod (Rajputanas), or Joseph Cunningham (Sikhs). Meanwhile, the construction of a nation and its history outside these provincial enclaves would continue to be informed by the orientalist metanarrative in texts like James Mill's *History of British India* (1817) or Mountstuart Elphinstone's *The History of India: The Hindu and Mahometan Periods* (1841). Beginning to imagine the nation as an original "Aryan" whole would also come to be indistinguishable from identifying the unhappy lacerations in the "Hindu" social body of the present.

It was at this hour that Bankimchandra Chattopadhyay emerged as a major public intellectual of a modernizing and self-determining India, one with a certain cosmopolitan presence. By the end of his life, Bankim's works had been translated into major Indian vernaculars like Hindusthani, Hindi, Kannada, Gujarati, Marathi, and Telugu, as well as European languages like English, Swedish, and German. It is beyond the ambit of this project to explore, except in passing, the work of Bankim the dialogic novelist who affirmed a Hindu patriarchy while questioning it and exposing its hobbyhorses and ethical impasses—often through a line of charismatic women, including Muslims like Ayesha in *Durgeshnandini*, or Zebunnisa in *Rajsingha*—or of Bankim the biting satirist with acerbic wit and an acute sense of self-irony. I will, for the present purposes, focus on his "Dharmatattva" ("Theory of Dharma," 1888) and "Krishnacharitra" ("Life of Krishna," 1886), two seminal essays written during the last decade of his life, when he took a strong Hindu nationalist turn after spending most of his formative and middle years as a Comtean positivist.

There is a strong sense of disinterest in Bankim toward the austere and esoteric Vedic monotheism found in Rammohun and the Brahmo tradition in general. The One becomes too abstract and distant in such a system; being a pure intellectual postulate, it lacks the warmth to animate a flock and a nation. Bankim, therefore, is not ready to give up the notion of a personal, anthropomorphic God and cast aside the "jungle" of Hindu superstitions, idol worship, myth, or folklore. Rather, he would like to extract from this mélange a vital universal that commands human identification and love rather than mere otherworldly contemplation. The new flock had to be invented from within, through a rational transcription of Puranic cultures and institutions—the adoration for the mother goddess, say, or the evocative powers of Bhakti. A template for Hindu being and action in the world could not come from an asceticism of universal suffering at the expense of sin and redemption. The "jungle" of Hindu faiths required a deeper anthropological evaluation than Rammohun Roy would allow. It had to be subjected to proper modes of identification, separation, and classification. That in itself was also the task of literary imagination and literary redaction. Such a comprehensive project could be illustrated by a reverse scenario, in which similar forests could be located in the heart of Europe itself:

Give to Dante and to Milton in Christianity the place now occupied in the ordinary conception of Hinduism by the Ramayana and the Mahabharata, to Tribonian and Puffendorf, to Montesquieu and Bentham that of Manu and Yagnavalkya, Gautam and Parasara; to the legends of King Arthur and to the romance of the Cid, to Ariosto and to Tasso the place of the Puranas, to Spinoza that of Badarayana; and give to the writings of early Fathers, what they once possessed, the sanctity and authority of the Upanishads; and you will arrive at a notion of Christianity very similar to the notion of Hinduism [to] which the ignorance, the intolerance and contempt of foreigners and the degeneracy of natives have reduced it.[55]

There had to be, thus, equitable clearings in both jungles. If Christian principles were not to be blamed for the Crusades, the massacre of St. Bartholomew, or the Inquisition, then Hinduism, in essence, could not be blamed for the social evil of Sati. If Christian altruism was not to be devalued for the compromised liberty of Catholics and Jews under English statutes, then the spirit of Hinduism could not be blamed for the plight of Sudras under Brahminical dominance.[56]

In "Dharmatattva," a text written in the form of a Socratic dialogue between a Master and a Disciple, Bankim's objective is to draw a composite theory of Anushilan (praxis) from the Gita and present it as a higher form of Arnoldian culture and Western humanism as a whole. In this decidedly modern theory of Dharma, the theme of desireless action (*nishkamabrata*), expressed most famously in Bhagwad Gita 2.47, merges with Enlightenment mantras of concord, balance, harmony, and moderation. In the process, Bankim frees Krishna's idea from the looming specter of otherworldly asceticism that was often seen to afflict the Hindu soul. Bankim traces this ascetic tendency to what he sees as a disastrous merger between speculative philosophy and religious dogma in the Indic tradition, especially in the influential Samkhya school. Samkhya, as he explains elsewhere, is a remarkably skeptical doctrine that develops systems of error and confines them to an orthodoxy based on the infallibility of the Vedas. Thought was thus not allowed to range outside the holy compendium. God himself could be denied, but not the Vedic authority.[57] Action was devalued because it meant the inevitable accrual of Karma.

In contrast, Bankim insists that, according to the Gita—which was a devotional as well as a prescriptive text for him—it is not by renouncing the world but by performing duties with a critical spirit of detachment that one can attain perfection. In this way, potentially, Dharma can now come of age and align itself with the dominant mantras of utilitarianism and positivism. The longstanding duality between right action (Karmayoga) and right knowledge (Jnanayoga) is therefore seen to be resolved. Desireless action in and of itself becomes renunciation (*sanyaas*) in an ontological sense, beyond formalities and ceremonials. Humans become free to practice possessive individualism and other credos of the modernizing, bureaucratizing, and capitalizing world without letting their souls be overtaken by greed. The nation could have its own temporality of industry and progress without surrendering to an essentially Calvinist future.

The theory of Anushilan is achieved by filtering the scriptural by way of modernist skepticism and realism. In order to do this, Bankim must radically relativize and sort received wisdom. He has to disenchant and republish the word of tradition with a daring protestant spirit and keep the operation itself within the limits of rationality. The troubling question of rebirth and the transmigration of souls thus becomes, in his essay, a Pascalian wager for the fictitious Master, a matter of individual belief, inconsequential as far as the core religious purpose is concerned: to create heavenly existence on earth itself by the full expression of the divine in man. The Master's discourse is marked by a new reckoning and a new style, by which the Sanskritic inheritance is vernacularized by the rationality of the Latinate world, and then the resultant Bengali wisdom is again instantaneously re-Sanskritized as "tradition" remembered in sobriety. This task follows a pattern of alternating stentorian statements with earthy analogies and metaphors, worldly postulates with homely figurations. The positivism of August Comte and the utilitarianism of John Stuart Mill become instruments of a worldly revival of Dharma, while the assorted philosophies of Spinoza, Herbert Spencer, Kant, Hegel, and Fichte become illuminating precisely because they approach a Vedanta world view. This new prose and method of enunciation can perhaps be better appreciated through an examination of Bankim's other work, "Krishnacharitra."

The task of constructing a Hindu national icon in "Krishnacharitra" begins with a quandary: "Most Hindus in India, all Hindus in Bengal believe that Sri Krishna is an avatar of Vishnu."[58] Bankim has chosen to refurbish Krishna as a modern Indian figure of adoration that is superior to Christ. Yet perhaps there is a nagging awareness that his project might not be acceptable to all quarters of the Hindu world. Large swathes of people, especially in the north and the west, had a greater attachment to Rama, that other incarnation of Vishnu. Still, that objection aside, what could be common between the religion of the Shiva-worshipping Shaktas and the broader, immensely complex and polymorphic Vaishnavite coalition of Rama and Krishna? After all, Bankim himself declares elsewhere that there is a greater affinity between Mohammadanism and Christianity than there is between Tantra and Vaishnavism.[59]

Nevertheless, it is in his "Letters on Hinduism" that he explains his preference for Krishna over and above the prince of Ayodhya. The Rama in Valmiki's original Ramayana is the protagonist of a tale that, according to Bankim, is either secular history or secular poetry. He is not a divine entity. Second, the nine avatars of Vishnu (with the tenth one, Kalki, yet to arrive) may be imagined as a proto-Darwinian evolutionary series, with the aquatic fish yielding to the amphibian tortoise which in turn is progressively succeeded by the terrestrial boar, the half-man half-beast Nrsingha, the dwarf Vamana, and the raw warrior Parasurama. In this lineage, Rama the virtuous precedes the crowning perfection of man in Krishna, the eighth avatar. The ninth, Buddha, may not be admitted as the Hindu ideal; for Hindus, the Buddha, categorically speaking, is a "deluder and tempter" who is considered "the wisest and greatest of the Hindus" only by Europe. On the other hand, Rama, the model son, husband, brother, friend, warrior, and ruler, lacked the highest attribute of mankind—genius—which Bankim reserves for Krishna alone.[60]

Yet Bankim's presentation of Krishna as Hindu ideal must not betray the provincial bias of Gaudiya Vaishnavism. As a matter of fact, Krishna has to be the construct of an estranging but worldly prose that will reinvent him as a figure of adoration for reasons rightful as well as modern. The Krishna that Bankim is about to create will thus be one that even ardent Bengali devotees might have difficulty in recognizing. This new prose of Hinduness is distinguished especially by an abundance of Arabic and Farsi words, colloquialisms that are at once irreverent and, in terms of affect, endearing and familiarizing. It is thus a dialectical Sanskritization, by which energetic vernacular expressions are not refuted through priestly dictum but embraced in a new commons of language. The trial for Bankim is to forge a congregational plane of address, a stratum of contemporary common sense where the temporalities of reading, writing, translating, drawing aesthetic pleasure, and witnessing the birth of meaning can converge. In "Krishnacharitra," Bankim at one point revisits the quite unreal Khandab Daho episode of the Mahabharata, in which Arjuna, at the behest of Agni, the god of fire, stops the rain with his arrows so that Agni can devour the Khandab forest in peace. But why was

Agni hungry in the first place? Bankim caustically explains that the great god was offered clarified butter (ghee) for twelve long years in the fire rituals conducted by the great sage Durbasa: "Agni was afflicted with dyspepsia, having consumed clarified butter. He went to Brahma and said, '*Thakur*! I am in a lot of trouble. I feel quite woozy, having eaten so much. Now what must I do?' Brahma suggested a treatment like a *Similia Similibus Curanter*."[61]

The prescribed treatment was the great devouring of the forest. Bankim of course disowns the entire episode as imagined hokum but does so with an indulgence that clears the pathway for more profound observations to follow. While Agni is feasting, Arjuna has to fight Indra himself, the god of thunder, who wants to interrupt. When a frustrated Indra throws mountains at Arjuna, the great warrior splits them with his arrows. At this point Bankim comments, as a dramatic aside, that this technique, now lost, could have been used in present times to burrow railway tunnels. Later, while describing an exchange between two figures in the court of King Virata, Bankim writes, "After Baldeb was done with speaking, Satyaki stood up (the reader will notice that there was parliamentary procedure in those days as well) to voice a counterargument" (KC, 471).

The new prose thus becomes immanent to that very space of reason and memory where somber, mythic reminisces work in tandem with wry humor as well as the skeptical spirit of science. It realizes itself between the dictations of gods and the earthbound judgments of man. The prose carries the "reader" with it; he is kept near at hand and occasionally summoned to pay close attention to the historical birth of meaning itself. This relationship between the assumed reader and the author is a playful as well as a pedagogic one. It is seductive and flippant, irreverent as well as conscientious. The call to the second person and the third is an invitation to a novel congregational publicness; it is to partake in an incoming republican revolution of letters in which signs are wonders and there is a general witnessing and authorizing of truth. Sibaji Bandyopadhyay has illuminatingly elaborated this as the "Bankim contract." It is a contract in time, a temporal imagination connecting the traditional past to the modern present. It is being agreed upon even as it is being written out.[62]

Bankim's goal in "Krishnacharitra" is to marshal this style in the restoration of Krishna, the author of the Gita, to the status of a historical "Hindu ideal" by cutting through the mythic crust of the ages obscuring his true self. Krishna therefore has to emerge as an exemplar of monogamous Hindu middle-class values, a householder, and a Karmayogi par excellence. He has to be rescued from the twin images of the deceitful and slippery dialectician in the Mahabharata as well as that of the promiscuous goatherd in some of the Puranas or in the twelfth-century poet Jaidev's *Geet Govinda*. It has to be proven, for example, that Krishna neither fraudulently caused Drona's death in the Kurukshetra War nor kept thousands of wives. The exhuming of the "historical" Krishna from the ground of myth is done with meticulous care and precision by launching an assault of reason on the textual inheritance of the Mahabharata, the *Harivamsha*, and the fifteen Puranas featuring the god. It is accomplished by deploying an entire armada of disciplinary lenses: philology, astronomy, literary criticism, historical skepticism, psychological insight, and a scientific measure of realist plausibility guided by common sense.

Bankimchandra creates the groundwork of Krishna's historical restoration by suggesting that the Mahabharata, the key text to be investigated, has three layers. The bedrock is the authentic account—the history (*itihasa*)—written by the *adikobi*, the singular original poet, while the other two layers are later additions. The second layer is also composed by a magnificent poet, but one susceptible to flights of fancy. It is he who imposes the divine Krishna and his miraculous interventions on the epic. The third layer is the net accrual of many, mostly unworthy and self-serving Brahminical interpolations down the ages. It is to this group that Bankim assigns the most reactionary and savage parts of the Mahabharata, speculating further that this third layer may possibly be dominated by Shaivas hostile to Krishna. It is to these latter that he, for example, ascribes the invective harangue—which we noted via Matilal in the second chapter—that Duryodhana delivers to Krishna at the hour of his death (KC, 513–16).

Bankim points out that the total number of verses in the Mahabharata is more than the number listed in the Parvashangrahadhyay, the second chapter of the first part (the Adi Parvan) of the great epic, which serves as a table of contents. The surplus must therefore be made up of latter-day imaginative embellishments or outright falsehoods that should be discarded. This volume of historically inauthentic material, however, cannot be confined to any fixed part of the massive epic. In Bankim's sovereign analysis, this cluster of falsehoods becomes a mobile entity that can be brought in to question any movement or description in the text. It is marshaled to purify the Mahabharata story of a few decided kinds of adulteration: that which is clearly extrapolated, that which is stylistically anomalous, that which is contradictory to the general grain of story and characterization, and that which is supernatural and therefore not a historical event (KC, 370–73). The restoration becomes a project impelled by the laws of realism, evidence, rational skepticism, and norms of inductive philosophy. There was an original Mahabharata; similarly, insofar as other texts are concerned, Vyasa had written only one Purana—it was his disciples who had multiplied them. The task was thus to untie the text to redact identifiable impurities, to impute original movements to signs and propel them toward a great monothematic center.

It is through such measures that Bankim absolves Krishna of his lusty childhood and youth in the Vishnu and Bhagwata Puranas. In his reading, the amorous adventures of Krishna and the multitude of Gopini women in Vrindavana become the allegorical dance and spiritual play of the Jitendriya—the conqueror of instincts and appetites. Bankim transforms multiple episodes in the life of Krishna into pedagogic parables and metaphysical illustrations, or dismisses them as mischievous poetic departures. He categorically forswears, as historically oblivious and ethically misdirected—an entire tradition of Bengali Vaishnavism with Krishna's mystic consort Radha at the center (KC, 414). The latter phenomenon, broadly speaking, was the outcome of the merging of metaphysical and mystical interpretations of the illicit love between Krishna and Radha (his aunt, by some accounts) with earlier yogic practices of Tantric Buddhism. In this Vaishnava line of praxis, gross erotic love becomes a progressive pathway for the expressive, spiritual realization of *svarupa sakti*, one's ultimate blissful state in a unified cosmos that no longer separates the inner self from the external world.[63]

In "Krishnacharitra," when it came to Krishna's larger-than-life exploits, the kernel of historical truth had to be separated, at every step, from the fluff of devotional imagination. Krishna did kill his uncle—the evil king Kamsa—but without the aid of miracles. The image of the butter-stealing and libidinous god is dispelled by Bankim's presentation of Krishna as the conscientious young man who had mastered the Vedas at Rishi Sandipan's ashram at Kashi and then meditated for a decade in the Himalayas (KC, 422). In the seventh chapter of his treatise, Bankim scathingly comments on the Puranic claim that Krishna had sixteen thousand and seven consorts who bore him a total of one hundred and eighty thousand sons: "It is stated in the Vishnupuran that Krishna dwelled on earth for a hundred and twenty-five years. The math says that Krishna had 1440 sons annually and four each day. Here, we have to imagine that simply Krishna's will was enough to impregnate his wives" (KC, 431). He then pares the number of Krishna consorts down to eight, further dismisses five who are mentioned without any elaboration, announces one—the daughter of Jambuvan, the king of bears—as patently absurd, and, finally, tightens the number to the one called Rukmini (KC, 434–35). Thereafter, he deploys a multipronged textual hermeneutics of suspicion, moral psychology, and a positivist reckoning of Dharma to exonerate Krishna of sundry charges: unjust war, deviousness, allowing Arjuna to abduct his own sister Subhadra, or the apparently treacherous killings of Jarasandha, Drona, Karna, and Duryodhana.

Krishna, as a historical character, thus emerges within the finitudes of the human. Unlike Christ, who combines divinity and mortality in one hypostasis, Krishna is not a performer of miracles, even though it is Bankim's entirely personal belief that he is an avatar of Vishnu. The divinity question is redundant here because if Lord Vishnu had chosen to incarnate himself as human, he would also define human perfection by staying within mortal limits of thought and activity. Bankim's protagonist is thus an exemplar of Anushilan, understood as a greater template of culture, and of Swadharma as duty and ethics. He is a figure of excellence defined by exactitude and not by infinite mysteries. Krishna is the perfect householder, administrator, diplomat, leader, kinsman, social worker, and friend who is always involved with the works of the world. This is where, according to Bankimchandra, the Lord of Dwarka scores higher than both Christ and the Buddha. The latter two renounced the world to propagate faiths, and therefore their Anushilans—the all-round development of human capacities—remained incomplete: "If the Emperor of Rome declared Christ to be the King of Israel, would he be able to rule properly?" (KC, 458). Krishna, on the other hand, propagated Dharma in word and deed; he also cultivated a warrior ethics to actively combat and eliminate Adharma from the world. As Tanika Sarkar points out in her enlightening discussion of Bankim's work, it is Mohammad—the Prophet, warrior, statesman, and householder—who is the passed-over figure in this tripartite illustration.[64]

For Bankim, the superiority of the Hindu ideal is established when one sees the duality of Europe. The icon of the West is an exemplary human being: humble, pious, a messenger of peace, and a renouncer of the world. Modern Europe is its exact opposite; it is interested in material comforts, profit, conquest, and war, precisely because its icon remains otherworldly and mysterious. This duality therefore has to be parlayed into artificial separations like that between church and state. On the other hand, the present malady and inertia of Hindu society is not the result of an endemic dichotomy between worldly works and otherworldly pursuits; it is the outcome of a historical forgetting. This amnesia is largely due to a misdirected literary exercise of the Bhakti tradition, beginning with the Puranas, Jaidev's poem *Geet Govinda* and continuing with other medieval texts like the Padabalis of Vidyapati, Govindadas, and Chandidas. The voluptuousness of Bhakti had obscured the Karmayogi Krishna, the bulwark of the Yadava clan, with the bucolic and fornicating god of Vrindavana.

Krishna, as reincarnated essence of Hindu Dharma, is therefore the exemplum of a more integral humanism. Krishnabhakti, or devotion toward Krishna, is not a pure meditative stance but the thought of a comprehensive monotheme, of adoration indistinguishable from active life. The ideal therefore had to be tactile and tangible, immanent in everyday homesteading values. This is precisely why the ideal must not only point toward right knowledge and right Karma, but also bring glad tidings to the soul that, in "Dharmatattva," Bankimchandra calls *Satchidananda*.[65] This synthesis draws from a lesson that Bankimchandra seems to have learned from two contrasting spheres of Hindu religious activity: Bhakti love traditions and Vedic scholasticism. The first of these proposed an irrational submission to Krishna as beloved, not an ethical universal. The second one, in privileging the Vedas and Manu, ultimately furnished a clerical form of piety devoid of warmth and imagination.

In its radical forms, Bhakti was a subversive energy because—all *bhakts* being equal, feminized devotees in relation to Krishna—it accorded the possibility of negating caste and other hierarchies. Unlike the parochial exclusivity of the Brahminical schools, it had flourished in the literary commons of the vernaculars. Bankim recognized that Bhakti had the warmth to invent a community; it was not the grasping of a remote universal through the rituals and cosmic mysteries of the Vedas, the metaphysics of the Upanishads, or the cryptic clues and hermeneutics of the Brahmasutras, which were, among other things, inaccessible to women and untouchables. In contrast, there were congregational forms in Bhakti modes, especially in the institution of Raasleela, the lyrical plays depicting mythic events from Krishna's life. Bankim saw that this communal religious-aesthetic quest for Krishna as sublime could be ramped up to higher orders of Hindu self-activation. Bhakti, in that sense, could be wedded to reason in order to invent a national community of *deshbhakts*, or lovers of the land itself. *Satchidananda*, in Bankimchandra's elaboration, thus becomes a primal feeling of monothematic commitment and the birth of the political: "I cannot say whether the poets of Mahabharata thought about law at all. But I can say this much, that they well understood that which is above law, from which law originates" (KC, 494). It can, in the fullness of time, yield the once lost and never quite regained righteous Hindu patriarchal order that Bankim imagined and narrated with wistful agon in his late-career historical novels like *Rajsingha, Anandamath* (1882), *Debi Chaudhurani* (1884), and *Sitaram* (1887). That project was to reach its apogee with Bankim's essay on the Gita itself, which he left incomplete at his death.

Bankimchandra Chattyopadhyay was the first major articulator of a militant and modern Hindu patriotism. His project came with the desire for concomitant institutions of discipline and pedagogy along with the emergence of what Gramsci would call a national-popular. The anticolonial ambitions of this undertaking were kept concealed or at best ambiguous by this keen deputy magistrate of British India. The landmark romance, *Anandamath*— first serialized in Bangadarshan and then published as a book in 1882—set up some abiding themes that would unfailingly resonate in subsequent Hindu nationalist discourses. Set in the milieu of the 1773 Sanyasi rebellion of Bengal, the novel imagines the land as the Mother capable of demanding martyrdom and sacrifice from her Hindu sons. The sons themselves form a secret society to inculcate martial and spiritual discipline in a moment of transition from Muslim rule to the English one. This discipline extends to a scrupulous sexual economy, that of the new monogamous couple, that Bankim invents as a utopian "outside" to a historical field marked by the fallenness of caste Hindu polygamy and child marriage. Romantic love arrives in the novel not as a tragic Hegelian impasse between the interests of the family and those of the state, but as a constitutive expression of Anushilan that figures adoration for the nation as a natural ethical extension of the ardor for the beloved. The new Hindu male becomes worthy of being loved consensually—beyond brute feudal entitlements and in line with a modern aesthetic of self-making—only when he stays true to a monogamous commitment and, indistinguishably from that pledge to the beloved, offers himself for martyrdom to the Mother. *Anandamath* went through five editions in Bankim's lifetime. Many early, hostile references to the English were replaced by references to Muslims instead, to merge with a general tenor of contempt and abomination toward Islam that marked Bankim's late career.[66]

There is, however, another aspect of this monothematic project of literary modernization that needs to be emphasized. The Hindu revival pictured in Bankim's writings is not just awesomely messianic but also, from the outset, globally aspirational. That is, a revitalized Hindu nation's tryst with destiny is imagined to be not just an assumption of its rightful place in the durbar of the world, but a status of first among equals. Sibaji Bandyopadhyay has called this an unspoken arrangement with the West.⁶⁷ Per this understanding, the positive role of colonial enterprise was limited to two principle matters: first, bringing India out of the medieval portal of time that had been inaugurated by Islamic rule; and second, providing Hindus with the external knowledge and instrumentation to reset their unique civilizational genius. Once that catalysis is completed, the tide, as it were, would turn in the Hegelian teleology. The Spirit of history would not reach its end in Prussia or anywhere in the West but would return to the reinvigorated Hindu nation, from whence it had emanated. All Western measures of science and techne must therefore be borrowed by India within a deeper invagination of time and not according to the dictates of an empty, metrical logic of progress. Time, in the former sense, can be understood as a curvature bending back to origins, not an irredeemable journey through the void of the modern. It was the new Hindu who could lead the world toward that final humanization of nature while preventing capital and technology from becoming cold monstrosities.

Sarvepalli Radhakrishnan and the Universal Caste of Man

Interlocutors of Hindu reform like the Reverends Krishnamohan Banerjea or William Hastie (1842–1903) argued that Rammohun Roy's Vedism or Keshub Chandra Sen's Nabobidhan philosophy were modern Vedic voyages that could lead either to pantheism or to Unitarian Christianity via natural religion.⁶⁸ For Bankim, it was the other way around. The universal could be found only in Hinduism, and the good substance of other faiths could be understood as imperfect approximations of the Hindu ideal. It was thus a Hindu anthropology—moral, religious, or political—that could train its lenses on the West and ultimately call it to judgment. The European word *religion* was itself impoverished and therefore misleading. Dharma, as a comprehensive method for transcendence and discipline, encompassed faith, life, culture, law, and politics. It was greater than religion and could temper and eventually absorb conflicts of all kinds. Whether it was Kant's categorical imperative, Fichte's harmony of the self and knowledge, Hegel's perfect freedom, Millean agnosticism, or indeed the teachings of Christ, Mohammad, or the Buddha—everything was already subsumed in the essence of the Bhagwad Gita.⁶⁹

Bankim's universalist aspirations came in the wake of Max Müller's rediscovery of Aryan glory and the general cult of the Orient that flourished in the West, spearheaded especially by Henry Steel Olcott and Helena Blavatsky's theosophical movement. This was also the moment of the obscurantist revivalism of Bengali intellectuals like Sasadhar Tarkachudamani or Kaliprasanna Sen, who claimed Vedic origins for all modern sciences; of B. G. Tilak and the Poona revivalists in Maharashtra; and the flourishing of the Arya Samaj in the Punjab.[70] In 1906, for instance, Tilak, a prominent turn-of-the-century Marathi-Hindu nationalist, declared:

> A great change is coming over the West and truths that are discovered by them were known to our Rishis. Modern Science is gradually justifying and vindicating our ancient wisdom. With the establishment of Physical Research Societies and expansion of scientific knowledge they have come to understand that the fundamental principles of our religion are based on truth that can be proved. Take an instance. Chaitanya [consciousness] pervades everything. It is strictly a Hindu theory. Professor Bose has recently shown that this Vedantic doctrine is literally true according to modern science.[71]

For Tilak, the guiding force of a Hindu resurgence had to be an emphatic "energism" drawn from the Karmayogic lessons of the Gita itself, in modern, against-the-grain reckonings of the Holy Book, reckonings that diverged from the traditional lessons of Sankara (renunciation combined with knowledge) or Ramanuja (devotionalism).[72] This line of thought, linking religious revival with the worldly flourishing of a dynamic national society beyond Jati divisions, would be continued by figures like Bipin Chandra Pal (1858–1932), Aurobindo Ghosh (1872–1950), and Swami Vivekananda (1863–1902).[73]

What was common in these thinkers was the instinct to engulf everything—Christian soteriology, the utilitarian notion of progress, and indeed the entire scientific paraphernalia based on Cartesian doubt and Baconian skepticism—into the great cosmic "unseen" (Adrishta) of a neo-Vedantic monism. This Vedanta was "neo" because it had an imperative to be worldly; in other words, it had to range widely outside the Vedas proper before returning to them. It had to dwell and trade in a greater universe of signs, without falling back on absolutist priestly authority bestowed by the language of the gods. In such a neo-Vedanta, the question of the subject, equity, and freedom itself tended to become subservient to the theodicy of the great unseen. This discursive terrain would birth a mode of Indian "spiritualism" that would receive its first memorable articulation as "mother of all religions" by Vivekananda at the World Parliament of Religions in 1893 and would later be globally industrialized as therapeutic cure to the alienation of techno-financial modernity. Vedanta, in this abstracted planetary sense, is something that has the authority to swallow not only egotistic Islam or Christianity, but also historical "Hinduism" itself as an unhappy mélange of ritualism, superstition, and the worship of false idols.[74]

For a figure like C. Rajagopalchari, for instance, it is Vedanta that provides the "spiritual and cultural basis" for Nehruvian socialism as well as for Indian secularism after independence. Writing in 1959, he suggests that the new "regulated cooperative economy" ushers in a moral world compared to which nineteenth-century laissez-faire capitalism appears as a "revised edition of the law of the jungle."[75] The Indian model for tolerance and harmony claims for itself not just the destinying pattern of India after 1947, but the only possible ethical foundation of a postwar world under the specter of nuclear annihilation. The Gita presents God as an immanent principle whose sovereignty is exercised through punctual laws of nature. The universe therefore becomes an elaboration of creative powers inherent in the primordial substance, and Vedanta, in this vein, anticipates all developments in modern biology or physics.[76] In the realm of the social, the Gita lays down a higher form of the socialist doctrine by democratizing a conception of work as true "religious offering."[77] Yet it provides room for individual liberty and expression of skill. Karma, properly understood, is not fatalism, but the "Magna Carta" of free will.[78]

This broad discourse of "soft" Hinduness itself has its benign and sharp versions, with different degrees of philosophical remoteness and worldly embroilment. It wavers between a benevolent, patronizing stance toward Islam and a paranoid and irascible hauteur for what is seen to be a pathologically jealous monotheism engaged in a war without end. Neo-Vedanta combines the thought of an esoteric universalism and a spiritual ignition of humanity with, especially in the cases of Aurobindo and Vivekananda, a disavowal of emasculating Bhakti. In these two influential figures, we also see strong emphases on a new martial discipline and action in the service of the motherland. This terrain, especially in its high-minded moments, mostly does not furnish a clear-cut congregational principle for the Hindu people, perhaps because the true universal for mankind may not, in essence, be expressed in sectarian terms. Yet, at the same time, there is a general self-awareness that Vedic thinking had to be made "practical," in tune with the realities of the modern age. This emphasis on realism and practicality comes with an inevitable political urgency, because the traditional Hindu form of immersion into the question of being—famous for its intuitive turn away from the clamor of the world—had also, according to Vivekananda, created a mindset that would tolerate external slavery as long as there was spiritual independence.[79] Furthermore, such a pragmatic Hindu anthropology adopts some key modes of revision when it comes to addressing caste society, Aryanism as ideology, and the Dravidian question of race and language. I would like to visit a special text in this tradition that addresses the question of caste with a greater amplitude of intellectual concerns, not just in terms of its historical apologia for decadence, but also by way of brave new relations with the modern intellectual world. Its major difference from standard Hindutva texts lies in the fact that it presents the Hindu project as a restoration of an inbuilt principle of dynamic mutation, not as one of reviving origins.

The Hindu View of Life emerged from the Upton Lectures delivered by Sarvepalli Radhakrishnan (1888–1975)—the distinguished Indian philosopher of comparative religions, and eventually the second president of independent India—at Manchester College, Oxford, in the year 1926. In this text, the concept of Hinduism emerges as the great absorbent as well as the great precipitator. "The Hindu view" is that which has imbibed historical novelties down the ages and which has birthed the spiritual foundations for half of humanity, including China and Japan, Tibet and Siam, Burma and Ceylon. This mutating process, involving Vedic Aryans, cultured Dravidians, aboriginal tribes, savages, as well as outsiders, is an exemplary one for a world full of religious and cultural conflict. This is because Hinduism sets up a special accord between a single unifying impulse and the gathering multiplicities of the world. It ultimately provides a primal vantage point—a baseline of experience—that subjugates different dogmatic or doxological expressions of the intellect to a singular resonating impulse. This great encompassing is possible because, according to Radhakrishnan, Hinduism is, in its essence, both supple and experimental. It has neither fixity in terms of belief nor a stable framework of reality; rather, it furnishes a self-certifying (*swatassiddha*), intuitive gateway for perpetually renewing the task of understanding the nature and experience of reality.

From that point onward, the comprehension of reality becomes dependent on the thought of the age, on customs, authorities, social psychologies, and quirks of culture. Such factors sublimate faith, invent gods, and birth institutions of religion as well as of error. The Vedas, in that sense, are mappings of pure intuitive coursings in the elevated souls of the sages. They are neither dogma nor dicta, but tracings of exemplary spiritual experience, or "transcripts of life" endowed with a primal "sense of reality."[80] The expertise of the Rishis and the soundness of the Vedas themselves may be validated by their antiquity and the fact that these truths have withstood tests of time and echoed through the ages. The Vedas are also amenable to many interpretations (*anekarthatam*); they have to be approached with an attitude of trust tempered by criticism (HVL, 15).

There are several significant departures in Radhakrishnan's view of Hinduism, from both its traditional moorings and its settlements in Western religious anthropology. Dharma is not eternal (Sanatan). This is because revelation is an unfinished business; the One never ceases to ripple through creation and expand its phenomenal scope, or, to put it in Abrahamic terms, God never finishes the exposition of His wisdom and love. Revelation is a perennial writing out of the universe that must be understood through constant experimentations with truth, in line with the presiding spirit of the age. This intuitive realization is the beginning of all comprehension; it demands a necessary catholicity of vision and a generosity of the soul since it has to bear responsibility for all fallible theologies and creative graspings of the divine. The Hindu philosophy of religion therefore begins and ends with a trial-and-error imperative that is prompted by the idea of positive ignorance (*bhavarupa avidya*). It is for this reason that this philosophy of religion "becomes as wide as human nature itself" (HVL, 16). This, for Radhakrishnan, is the insight of the nondualistic Advaita in a single stroke, never mind Buddhist claims. Unlike Christianity, which is dependent on the certitude and authority of Jesus, the Advaita cannot dismiss any human spiritual experience or god-realization as false or illusory. All such endeavors become culturally specific, all too human, dualistic quests to identify the godhead in their own image, institute the sacred, and set up protean parables to anchor faith. All anthropomorphic conceptions of the divine are expressions of religious psychology pertaining to local needs, moods, or interests. Advaita holds the preeminent position in this field of relationally valid pieties because it intuits and conceives of the One in its purest essence, without any ornaments. It is a powerful monism that, among other things, renders cultural preferences for polytheism or monotheism redundant.

Radhakrishnan's intuitionism and his notion of experience is in conversation with Henri Bergson, William James, and Rudolf Otto, among others. It is also a clearing to launch explanations for and defenses of practiced Hinduism. The epics and Puranas of miracles and a million gods make a poiesis of religious advancement through shifts in tradition, historical change, continuous psychological mediations of life and custom, or natural benedictions and catastrophes. The idols of polytheism become human approximations of the silence and eternal negation (*neti*) of the Upanishads, and of Nirguna, the One without sensuous properties. With this wide-angle view, one can say that even superstition may have its contingent uses. Hindu mysticism subordinates dogma, and it is because of this mystic tradition that hunting out heresy has not become a fanatical sport in the religion (HVL, 20–29, 42). The Hindus, as in all other milieus, deploy different quirks of culture to galvanize a sociology of the sacred because it is the sacred that motivates common laws, ethics, and moralities. True Vedantic Hindus thus have a double consciousness; they surround themselves with ceremonies and anthropomorphic gods but do not forget the "supra-personal character of the central reality" and the finitudes of human knowledge, including revelation (HVL, 23). Avidya, positive ignorance, represents a wise agnosticism that the world needs, after the cosmopolitanism of the eighteenth century and the nationalism of the nineteenth, because it installs an order "which seeks the unity of religion not in a common creed, but in a common quest" (HVL, 42).

The anthropology of the Advaita, in the same vein, charts a global hierarchy of enlightened religiosity, by which "the worshippers of the Absolute are the highest in rank; second to them are the worshippers of the personal God; then come the worshippers of the incarnations like Rama, Krsna, Buddha; below them are those who worship ancestors, deities, and sages; and lowest of all are the worshippers of the petty forces and spirits" (HVL, 24). This is not just a naturalized order of humans on a scale of mental and spiritual development. It is also one that should be accepted by all of humanity in the interests of tolerance and enlightened peace. However, at another level, Radhakrishnan recognizes a greater paradox: a vast majority of Hindus do not follow the Hindu view of life. It is only a thinking elite that tries to "escape from the confusion of the gods into the silence of the Supreme" (HVL, 25). The crowds, meanwhile, gaze at the heavens or embrace idols of clay. The hierarchical principle furnished by Advaita, therefore, is not only useful in grading the religions of the world in the luminosity of a great Eastern enlightenment. Advaita needs to be applied internally, as a dynamic ordering, to the historical spectrum of pieties within Hinduism itself.

The Vedantic mode begins with and persists in the identification of a deep structure of human psychology. Humans start with an intuitive understanding of the void that lies beyond the limits of their knowledge. At the same time, they are driven by an egotistical desire to solve the mystery of godhead; they therefore invent dualistic fictions that alienate them from the originary intuition itself. Maya (the idea of material universe as illusion), in this sense, is merely a metaphorical admission of the abiding inability of man to round up a story connecting earthly truths to the absolute. It is not a literal assertion that phenomenal life is but a waking dream. The doctrine of Karma, similarly, is not fatalism. It can be squared with freedom, democracy, and a modern system of Hindu ethics. The entire paraphernalia of "wise agnosticism" in Radhakrishnan creates a ground for the emergence of a practical ethics not by privileging the Karmayoga of the Bhagwad Gita, but by a novel transcription of the esoteric heart of Sankara's non-dualistic Vedanta itself. The question of caste, in this light, becomes a global expression of human diversity, psychosis, and intuition. It is to this practical question that I turn, without delving further into the details of his overall metaphysics.

Here is the central question: Why is Karma not fatalism, and how can caste be squared with a modern ethics? According to Radhakrishnan, the fatalism of the lowborn in the cycle of Karma should be mitigated by the fact that God is immanent in all of us and is an active coworker in this life. He is not the transcendent author of an already revealed grand design, or the remote arbiter of salvation or damnation (HVL, 54–55). The study of caste as a practical institution thus begins with a quiet presumption: God is not distant, insofar as his immanent operational presence in the system of Karma is concerned, both in sinners as well as saints. His immense mystery notwithstanding, it may be concluded that God is not indifferent to Karma, and his active participation in the process is sufficient to justify it. Work of all kinds therefore becomes a religious offering. However, the immanent involvement of the otherwise transcendent One brings to the fore that old question about the origination of evil: Is God also a participant in all human actions and practices that are patently unjust or cruel, or at least become so after a threshold of moderation is crossed or an original intention perverted? Insofar as Varna-Jati is concerned, the question pertains to the Christian dualism that Radhakrishnan wants to supersede: How much of the caste system is good, and how much of it is evil? Or, to put it in less moral terms, in the spirit of Nietzsche—that ardent admirer of Manu—how much of the caste system is good, and how much of it is bad?

Radhakrishnan's views on the historicity of caste institutions have similarities and significant differences with Hindu nationalists like Golwalkar. He agrees that in its original form, Varna was a good system based on tolerance and trust, and that in present times it has become a degraded social order based on oppression and exclusivity. What distinguishes Radhakrishnan's elaboration, however, is the global amplitude he gives to the question. Caste in India was an original measure to contain race conflict between Aryans, "sturdy" Dravidians, savage tribals, and then the Persians, Greeks, or Scythians. Such primal scenes of race antagonism were common to all societies in the world. The genius of the Indian caste system was in the fact that it prevented perpetual race war by a process of harmonization rather than extermination or enslavement. Humanity, in essence, bears an indelible caste instinct that plays itself out across color lines. This intuitive feel and experience of caste is universal, even though only select societies choose to organize themselves along such lines. Or, to put it differently, they do exactly the same, but in a state of willful denial. Feudalism in Europe and elsewhere had fostered a military aristocracy; capitalism, despite democratic pieties fashionable in the West, had produced a hierarchy of wealth. In contrast, the caste system in India had produced a democracy of the spirit, not of wealth or political power.[81]

Varna, as race, is also a group psychological formation, with its own cultures, customs, and norms of purity. Racial patriarchies come with their own rules about legitimate commerce (of food, goods, or women) with others. Radhakrishnan weds this question of coexistence with a desired pluralism of life. All races and cultures need to be preserved so that their potentia can be realized in time. The English—by which he presumably means the Celts—were not an impressive race during the times of Julius Caesar. And yet, some two thousand years later, they came to rule a great portion of the earth. Similarly, it could be hoped that the "Red Indians," if conserved in their native cultures—but under the paternalistic care of superior groups—would eventually have their own tryst with destiny (HVL, 68–69). The Indian caste system, in its original intention, ensures such an organic coexistence and evolution. It is the only possible "democratic" solution to a race war perpetually simmering under the social epidermis. It made assimilation a supple process, though rigid enough to ascertain Aryan-Hindu ascendancy. It was, therefore, "democracy" combined with an aristocracy of direction.

Radhakrishnan's notion of democracy accords no natural rights to the subaltern, only a covenant of organic belonging to a familial order under the paternalistic care and external stimulation of superiors. This social belonging mitigates the primal fear of death and enslavement in the weak and transforms wrath and suspicion in the strong to a sense of responsibility. Seen through these lenses, freedom for humanity, in practical terms, can only pertain to the performing of caste duties and giving full expression to Swadharma.

Radhakrishnan explains that this democracy of caste goes against the grain of the social contractualism of Rousseau and Locke, which is based on an abstract and idealistic notion of equality (HVL, 72). Caste does not allow for self-determination based on equitable civil rights or an economism of interest. However, compared with a Western liberal idealism that confuses uniformity and unity, the Indian system is a much more pragmatic approach to balancing natural hierarchies of merit and power. This ingenious harmonizing order dictates that the Brahmins, being spiritual leaders of society, should not covet wealth or power. The Vaishyas, who dominate commerce and wealth, should be subservient to the Brahmins and Kshatriyas. The state, ideally, should be a military organization reducible to a set of Kshatriya duties, leaving all other avenues of life and culture free for a comprehensive spiritual administration of Dharma. The lowly Sudras can receive patronage as well as guidance in an overall dispensation marked by voluntarism of service and trusteeship of power (HVL, 76–77).

Radhakrishnan to a certain extent acknowledges the historical evils of the caste system. He understands that one's being born into a specific caste raises the question of mobility and recognition of individual merit. According to him, the hereditary principle and the social imperative of dynastic training were instituted in caste groups because there was no way of knowing the aptitude of a newborn. Caste, as it was, made no room for the highborn incompetent or the lowborn talent (HVL, 74–79). Yet he offers no theory of mass education or civic liberalization as modern correctives. For Radhakrishnan, the system, as a practical measure, remains a gradualist synergy between the nurture of the social and the primordial of race.

It is because of this understanding—that human nature cannot be "hurried," and that race as ontogenetic destination determines human nature—that Radhakrishnan is not very enthusiastic about miscegenation. The interbreeding between castes, as one sees in Manu or in the epics, is inevitable. Yet this phenomenon must be curtailed as well as controlled at every step. Even in mixed-caste couplings, insemination must travel down from the higher to the lower; an against the grain (*pratiloma*) union, in which a Sudra man impregnates a Brahmin woman, is undesirable because "blood tells" (HVL, 73). The original Varna arrangement, as we have seen, has been repeatedly defended by the Hindu right as an ancient meritocracy. Radhakrishnan, however, emphatically defends a hereditary caste system, summoning ancient Greek wisdom as well as modern science to corroborate his thesis, and making some provisions for exceptional individuals: "We are all familiar with Plato's views of biological selection as the best method of race improvement. Aristotle also believed that the state should encourage the increase of superior types. . . . Darwin's teaching that evolution proceeds by heredity was taken up by Galton and other biologists like Weismann and De Vries, and the science of eugenics rests today on somewhat safe and sound foundations" (HVL, 72–73).

The Western idea of humanity, bookended by Greek wisdom and modern science, completes a full circle, negating an eighteenth-century European constructivist illusion that all men are created equal. What Dumont would famously term *homo hierarchus* half a century later is, in this light, not a postulate of Hindu theodicy; it defines the species life of mankind itself in naturalistic terms, even though a powerful section of mankind disavows that truth in organizing its species being. Logically it follows that just as all human acolytes should eventually submit to the Advaita, all social orderings in a world of race war and abstract justice should emulate, in essence, the wisdom of Varna. The earth can be "one great family" only if the fraternité is recognized as one comprised of unequal races and managed accordingly, in terms of power, knowledge, trusteeship of wealth, and rights to insemination. All natural brotherhoods must, at the end, necessarily recognize elder brothers. Democracy, for Radhakrishnan, is a matter of differential inclusion without fear of death. Caste, to recall Schmitt, is the only solution to an otherwise primordial friend–enemy problem between the races.

Unlike Golwalkar, Radhakrishnan does not attempt to locate a pristine moment of Varna preeminence in the mists of time, nor does he try to defend it in theological or cosmogonic terms. Varna was not immaculately birthed in the ideal Vedic society. Rather, the material form and pragmatic shape of Varna came into being only when the Aryan emerged from his insular repose and faced the practical prospect of race war between the *janapada* (town/village) and the forest. They restricted their wives and daughters from Vedantic study when "women of other racial stocks with different customs were accepted in marriage" (HVL, 59). The Varna system had settled itself during that hour, after a bellyful of fighting between the races. It was never a perfect static arrangement but rather a dynamic evolution in time. It did not decay from an impeccable state but was displaced from a perfect arc of becoming. Evils like untouchability were thus social consequences of Islamic colonization (HVL, 75). Modernity, in that sense—indeed in both India and the world—should be about reviving the rational predicates, restoring a dynamism of the Varna imagination, rather than letting matters languish in a fixed form of caste society.

What remains a compelling but perhaps unresolved question in Radhakrishnan's text is the one about the means and ends of human history. He suggests that humanity's journey to complete self-consciousness should entail a final and entirely rational submission to Vedanta, overcoming all jealous monotheisms. Now, in such an evolutionary schema, should the caste system—as disciplined sexual endosmosis combined with the management of inevitable miscegenation—disappear? Or become redundant after a critical stage of hybridization? Even though he does not state it clearly, one could say that the end of caste is not a hoped-for event within the logical parameters of Radhakrishnan's text. This is because, in his Hindu view, the relational transfer of merit or depravity is a strictly patrilineal process. The spiritual democracy of caste has already foreclosed the biogenetic equity between the sexes. The woman in the illicit union is merely the passive bearer of an ancestral essence inherited from her father that is largely negated by insemination. Brahminical insemination traveling downward is thus always of more value than that of the Sudra man traveling upward. All proliferating hybrids are not equal; they do not nullify but only increase the catalogue of qualitative race differences. When human nature is "hurried" and hybridization is uncontrolled, what is achieved is progressive anarchy, not the end of history. That possibility aside, it is not desirable to do away with race individualities and race differences because, for Radhakrishnan, humanity is defined by its racial pluralism, and its richness can only be conserved by manifold expressions of difference admitted in a gradualist scale of recognition. This hierarchy itself and its perpetuation must be accorded positive value. Miscegenation, in that sense, can only diminish or scatter pure, elemental essences—the spiritual energy of the Brahmin, the valor of the Kshatriya, or the labor power of the Sudra. Uniformity and abstract liberal schemas of justice and equality can only weaken and dissipate the spectrum of human expressions at their finest. Caste is therefore not an unhappy consciousness that needs to be transcended.

Radhakrishnan's project is a figuration of Hindu life as true and universal human condition. What is extractable from the picture is also an idea of tolerance that, one could argue, in many ways informs a Hindu-normative modernity and an Indian secularism of the twentieth century. It proposes an order in which a naturally hierarchical caste democracy of the "spirit" should customarily guide the nominal equalities of law and rights in the modern republic. However, in the course of his elaboration, Radhakrishnan introduces another critical question in relation to a changing India and a changing world. He is alert to the fact that the "unhurried" order of caste, as he imagines it, presumes an artisanal universe. In 1926, he could see the latter besieged by two templates of modernization—an irreverent and alienating schema of capitalistic industrial development in the West and the Soviet-plus-electricity model in postrevolutionary USSR:

> A building craftsman of the old days had fewer political rights, less pay, and less comfort too, but he was more happy as he enjoyed his work. Our workers who enjoy votes will call him a slave simply because he did not go to the ballot-box. But his work was the expression of his life. . . . He was dominated by the impulse to create beauty. Specialization has robbed the worker of pride in his craft. (HVL, 80)

Contemporary materialism has produced a modern economy of desire based on wealth. This brings the danger of a great modernist overwriting of caste consciousness—as an aesthetic, spiritual, and existential project—by the political theme of class interest. The organic composition of caste society based on paternalism, sacrifice, and service is therefore imperiled by an outpouring of "suspicion and hatred, envy, and jealousy" beyond the affectional regime of "tolerance." People are no longer content to bring up children in a dynastic order of life, but demand that all doors be opened, that hereditary and customary hierarchies of talent be radically levelled (HVL, 81). This trouble with the modern world, as we know, would be a persistent theme in anxious as well as celebratory imaginings of India's transformational movement, from agrarian paternalism and ground rent to bourgeois avenues of capitalist modernization and surplus. For Radhakrishnan, the contemporary philosophical challenge lay in the mutation of the caste system to adjust to these new realities and maps of desire.

From the perspective of Hindutva, the problems with Radhakrishnan's 'Hindu view of life' begins with the fact that few Hindus actually follow it. In terms of caste, it precludes the idea of an ethnonational uniformity and the idea of a Hindu political congregation. Radhakrishnan proposes a frosty and distant universal that lacks a principle of exclusion and war. It is too protean in character and accords no principle to designate the foe. In Savarkar for example, it is Buddhism and not Hinduism that is accorded the status of universal religion. It is done precisely in order to jettison the former from the field of the political. It was thus Buddhism that could embrace all of mankind; the Hindu, meanwhile, could have his clear and present enemy. The point, however, is whether it is at all possible to speak of a perennial

Hindu people, civilizational ethos, way of life, or a Hindu craft without the nineteenth-century prism of the Anglophone colonial. Is it possible to do so without mourning? We had broached this question via Aamir Mufti and G. N. Devy in the previous chapter. We could accentuate it when it comes to a relationship between soft and hard Hindu assertions. Is it possible to speak of a benign Hindu harmony and a modern Hindu mitigation without nation-thinking, without the state in mind?

With its discursive influence as well as its industrial dissemination since Vivekananda, this form of Advaita spiritualism sets up a horizon of the universal and the normative within the discursive apparatus of the modern. It inaugurates a zone of comfort and transfer between contrary principles and affectations. It mitigates a potentially schizophrenic split between what A. K. Ramanujan memorably described as the two lobes of a brain engaged in an "Indian way of thinking."[82] As such, it sets up an epicenter of normalcy with differential degrees of accessibility, belonging, and marked deviation for all humankind, even the Muslim, the Dalit, or the woman. It is in this light that one can revise the early postulate derived from Schmitt, that the political is a monotheistic religiosity for a provincial God; it cannot, in essence, claim all of mankind since mankind has no enemies. In contrast, one can say that hard Hindutva acutely needs the universality of soft Hinduness. Chauvinistic nationalism must always gesture toward the universal, since the "political" is established exactly along the lines of a psychopathological retraction from it, in the muddied and blocked pathways to it. One is compelled to retract from the universal, to step away from the norms of humanity, precisely in order to destroy enemies, save the universal, and affirm the notion of humanity itself as Hindu. The political determines the enemy as the one who stands in the way of squaring the home with the world, and achieving the country as well as a singular mankind blessed with perpetual peace. It is thus an enemy that has already lost its humanity.

Ambedkar and the Annihilation of Hinduism

Radhakrishnan's Hindu view of life accords a prism of "realist" philosophical perception. It does not justify caste as theodicy, but essentially as a custom. The "Hindu view" becomes a tripartite arrangement, between an elite enlightenment of Vedanta; millions of gods and forms of worship as dualist illusions that have their own situational virtues; and caste as way of life. An abstracted Hindu "religion," in the Western sense, is a part of this culture—

faith complex, not the whole of it. It is because of this tripartite arrangement that Radhakrishnan can, at times, step outside a metaphysics of the One to defend caste as a matter of the practical management of race psychologies. Conversely, he can also step back into Vedanta to anoint the caste system itself as spiritual democracy. Hindu tolerance, in that sense, presumes a pluralism of life that is hierarchical and not immanent. There can be no tolerance without caste, for caste is the foundational principle of tolerance. That is because the life of a man in the natural state is not just nasty, brutish, and short: he is also driven by a primal, indelible race instinct.

Radhakrishnan's reckoning does not necessarily imply the usual distinction between Varna and Jati that was common to Gandhi and the moderate reformers or to the Arya Samaj. The history of caste, in that sense, is a secret history of miscegenation by which positive race identities like the Aryan or the Dravidian are submerged, and what gradually replaces it is a priestly system of regularizing originary race probabilities in a hierarchically divided people. A social order has to define itself in terms of hereditary professions and exclusive institutions of training to rationalize merit expectations in a historical field of illicit unions. Caste, in that contemporary sense, is not so much an assertion of race purity; rather, it is a holding on to differential memories and mythologies of race corruption, admittedly with weak messianic power. There is only a relentless scientific management of unfolding caste realities—ending untouchability, finding ways to lift the talented Sudra or relegate the unworthy Brahmin—and not a return to an original system. That return is as much a biological impossibility as it is an epistemological one amid the random pulsations and speeds of the modern, the unstructured spaces and transports of the industrial city, and the clamor of assertive class interest.

It is at these crossroads that one can turn to the formidable work of Bhimrao Ramji Ambedkar (1891–1956), polymath intellectual, jurist, principal architect of the Indian Constitution, first law minister of the republic, and iconic leader of the modern Indian Dalit movement.[83] I intend to visit his seminal tract *Annihilation of Caste* (1936) and a few other texts in order to interrogate Radhakrishnan's tripartite arrangement of the Hindu view. Questions arising from this critical interface include the following: Does a modern critical reconnaissance of "Hinduism" call for the separation of Hindu philosophy from Hindu theology and ritualism? Is there a consistent Hindu theology or, ultimately, just Hindu caste ethics? Can caste, as Hindu harmony, really furnish a principle of Hindu democracy?

Is a Hindu religion—even a composite of Vedantic monism and a million idolatries—possible without caste? That is, can the postulate of Dharma be isolated from the comprehensive vision of Varnasrama Dharma?[84] Conversely, does the annihilation of caste actually mean the annihilation of Hinduism itself?

Annihilation of Caste was drafted as a presidential address for the 1936 Lahore conference of the Jat Pat Todak Mandal (Organization to Eradicate the Caste System), a body of social reformers troubled by untouchability. The address and the conference itself were canceled due to Hindu uproar over an advance copy of the speech. It was clear to bewildered respondents that, in order to eradicate caste, Ambedkar was calling for the "the complete dismantling of the Hindu religion" itself.[85] The aborted speech was later published by Ambedkar as *Annihilation*. Having looked at Radhakrishnan on this topic, we could begin our explorations of this remarkable text at the point where Ambedkar addresses and dismisses the question of race in relation to Jati discrimination. He declares that, from the ethnological point of view, there could hardly be any group in India untouched by interracial commerce. There was nothing racially common between the Brahmin of the Punjab and the Brahmin of Madras; conversely, there was no difference in stock between the highborn and the pariah from the same regions (AC, 39–40). The caste imagination could not be based on a phenomenology of biological race precisely because it otherwise insisted on strict customary notions of purity and marriage. The fair-skinned Sudra was as much ostracized in this order of things as the dark Brahmin was privileged. It is here that Ambedkar invokes a key feature of his overall critique: there is no biogenetic justification to prevent free interbreeding between humans. If the basic principle of eugenics argued for improving the human stock through judicious breeding, then one would fail to comprehend how caste could systematize such a practice when it "is not a positive method of selecting which two among a given caste should marry" (AC, 40–41). Furthermore, if the creation of subcastes is not eugenic because it despoils "blood," then there could be no natural reason to prevent further intermarriages between these already lapsed human groups. On the other hand, the science of heredity actually unveils a radical democracy of genetic possibilities, since there is no single mode of transmission. The development of mental and physical powers depends more on a cluster of factors than on the progression of any single hereditary element. Nature, along with nurture, is thus more multidirectional and anarchic than Radhakrishnan had imagined.

The essence of caste must be identified in order for the annihilation of caste to take place. Ambedkar does not necessarily deny the imprints of race consciousness or race nostalgia in customary manifestations of caste bias. However, the question itself cannot be settled in that dimension, since the man of race is born while the man of caste is twice-born. Similarly, from the vantage of political economy, caste could not be understood as a division of labor. It was instead a calibrated division of laborers following a logic that is not fully anticipated or conquered by economism. The study of the essence of caste must therefore begin with illustrations of Jati prejudice, not only to identify a plane of commonality but also, at another level, to highlight arbitrariness as the consistent principle of caste dominance. This is because caste consciousness is always a sublimation in time, in a historical field of problems pertaining to shifts in custom, culture, production, theology, or the aesthetics of self-making. Ambedkar illustrates this point with a catalogue of disparate local phenomena.

In 1928, the high-caste Hindus (Kalotas, Rajputs, and Brahmins) of Indore district informed the lowly Balais of more than a dozen villages that they could not wear gold jewelry or apparel with colored or fancy borders and that they would be forced to render bonded labor. On refusal, the Hindus took away their rights to water and grazing fields. In 1935, the untouchables of Kavitha, Gujarat, were told not to send their children to government-run schools. In the village of Zanu, Dalit women were attacked for having the temerity to use metal pots. A prosperous untouchable in Jaipur State was assaulted for serving ghee to his untouchable brethren (AC, 24–25). Elsewhere, Ambedkar mentions a class of unseeables called the Purada Vannas of Tamil Nadu. These people were not allowed to come out during the day because their appearance itself was considered polluting. The unfortunates had thus become nocturnal, scurrying home at dawn like the badger or the hyena.[86] Such brutish discriminations followed no standard scriptural logic or customary injunction. Rather, they established the phenomenology of caste as a perpetual reinvention of masters and slaves in shifting semiotic universes and scenarios of production.

Caste demands a special docility from the lowly. However, it is not the kind of docility that the underling can prove at every step by emulating the exemplary ways of the master. Rather, in its essence, the imagination of caste stipulates difference itself as means and ends. Caste is therefore Swadharma as a consistent principle of relational difference in shifting historical configurations; it is not a universal way of life to be followed. Ambedkar describes how relatively affluent untouchables like the Sonars and Pathare Prabhus of Maharashtra were denied the civil rights to emulate Brahmins and accrue new markers of respectability, style, and honor. The Sonars were prevented from wearing dhotis of a certain kind and from using the word *namaskar* for salutation. The Pathare Prabhus were stopped from following the Brahminical example and proscribing widow remarriages in their communities in order to raise their caste prestige (AC, 48–49). For Ambedkar, it is this absolute monopolization of virtue and of the avenues of virtue by the highborn, along with the absolute relegation of the lowly to vice, that separates the Hindu system from Muslim proselytization by the sword or the terror of the Spanish Inquisition. In the latter two cases, the oppressed had a way out by abandoning lesser gods and embracing the universal that the oppressor offered.

Caste is thus a perpetual arbitration of privilege based on changing affectations of honor and propriety. Its operation is a dynamic one, involving a shifting bricolage of bodies and objects (jewelry, metal pots, government schools, or widows), customs and ethics, monopolies of education, or means of war. Ambedkar indicates that caste—as theodicy, as psychologism, or as pathology of power—may be comprehended only to a limited extent by speculating about its historical origins. Rather, the entire phenomenology of caste—from instinct to concept, consciousness to institutions—may actually be understood by the intellectual rehearsals of its death, by radical imaginings of what exactly might succeed in "killing the spirit of caste." Jati animosity cannot be mitigated through measures of reform such as the abolishment of subcastes or the settlement of customary incongruities. Nor can caste be rationalized or humanized by instituting interdining between groups, or by transcending taboos related to touch, food, or water. Caste can only be destroyed by way of intercaste marriages (AC, 72–73). Such unions would not birth a new "race" or despoil the purity of originary ones, but create a brave new democracy of mongrels beyond sacralization. This is the case precisely because caste perpetuation is strictly a matter of patrilineal overdetermination, which is not true for race reproduction as pure biogenesis that must accord positive recognition to the mother. The sexual economy of caste, in that sense, may be affiliated with what Gayatri Chakravorty Spivak has called reproductive heteronormativity, "the world thing with which we have always secured the space between making and need. The child as excess has assured the father an immortality of which the mother is the custodian."[87] What intercaste marriages would therefore devastate is a process of making holy the "twice-born" and the enthralled mentality that facilitates it. The birth of the caste body and its rights of insemination are consecrated measures. What miscegenation—as rule and not exception—would do is rupture a moral economy of grading all births according to differential degrees of nobility and profanity, and of marking others outside its pale as "untouchables." The proposal—which would have come across as positively indecent to Ambedkar's intended audience at the Jat Pat Todak Mandal—deliberately invokes a vision of sexual congress as the limit scenario of "touch" between sacred and desecrated skins. It violates a metaphysical circuit that already privileges and relegates bodies and souls trapped inside such skins. It is this metaphysical skin that may or may not enter into tactile relation with fabric, clarified butter, or metal pots; it is this skin that accrues pollutants by crossing the dark waters or is condemned by birth to be in touch with corpses, gutters, bones, or night soil, regardless of actual race pigmentation.

In an early paper delivered at Columbia University in New York in 1916, Ambedkar had declared that any given caste may not be understood in isolation, but only in relation to an entire system of caste divisions.[88] This idea, in other words, goes against the grain of the general argument—based on uniqueness—that Radhakrishnan would make ten years later, according to which "any group of people appearing exclusive in any sense is a caste" (HVL, 74). That apart, in *Annihilation*, Ambedkar argues that purity, while being an important secondary expression, is not the defining feature of caste since it might be a priestly imposition on any religious group. In the Indian context, it is endogamy that marks the essence of caste, since caste groups of a region may otherwise share common predicates of custom, religion, or language. Ambedkar finds this to be unlike endogamous American white, black, or native groups of his time who may be historically distributed in the same land but with strictly segregated cultures. Hindus, Ambedkar clarifies, are otherwise strictly exogamous, with marriage prohibited not just among immediate blood relations, as it is in most posttribal societies, but also among members of the same clan or Gotra, mythically understood, descending from five or seven sage patriarchs of deep antiquity. Caste is therefore the superimposition of an endogamous diagram on what is otherwise a general field of strict exogamy (AC, 137). This proposition by itself, according to Ambedkar, invites rational scrutiny as to why, historically, otherwise exogamous humans would agree to such a system, especially given the problems pertaining to surplus men and women that it would automatically generate. He notes that traditional Hindu societies have tried to solve this problem of surplus bodies by burning widows or bestowing eternal widowhood on them, compelling a widower to a state of ascetic existence, or getting him remarried to a girl not yet of marriageable age (AC, 140–43). In order to explain this phenomenon, Ambedkar proposes a theory of beginnings: the system could be organized as such precisely because caste is enclosed class (AC, 147). This enclosure becomes an originary event in the mystical preservation of Brahminical class interests, with other castes defining themselves negatively; through imprecise and incomplete imitations of hegemonic priestly norms. The caste of the powerful invents itself as an endogamous unit by closing its doors; the subaltern classes follow suit partly from the desire to imitate and partly because the doors are closed.

Jat-pat (caste discrimination) can therefore be understood as an engine of discipline that inextricably combines a libidinal economy of desire with a political one of interest. Ambedkar's formulation of caste as the theological patina wrapped around raw class interest points to a great concealment: "[No] civilized society of today presents more survival of primitive time than does the Indian society" (AC, 136). Yet what he would powerfully resist in his subsequent work are instrumental as well as idealistic solutions to the problem. On the one hand, his radical fiction of beginnings demolishes the Radhakrishnan line of argument: caste was not race at all, but class interest fortified by priestly ministrations. Conversely, in *Annihilation of Caste* and elsewhere Ambedkar criticizes orthodox Marxist analyses of caste as a superstructural expression, a false consciousness that will wither away as soon as the submerged class war is activated and made to resurface. Ambedkar's complex formulation therefore presents the skin of caste not as a virtual epidermis that conceals the real within, but one that is material precisely because it points to the materiality of desire and abomination in the world.

Ambedkar, of course, is well aware of the utopian, rhetorical, and deliberately provocative nature of his demands. He pronounces the impossible, the absolutely forbidden, in order to test limits and to glimpse the anarchy that lies beyond the edges. The irreverent rationalism and scathing irony are also directed at a form of temperate Hindu reform that found its most famous expression in Gandhi. According to the latter, the ideal Varna system was, among other things, a necessary imposition of sexual discipline for the careful nurture of an organic society. Ambedkar points out that his proposal for free sexual commerce between the castes was no more "absurd" than Gandhi's ascription of sexual discipline to a religion that allowed Kulin Brahmin men to marry a hundred times. However, taken to the limits of its own exertion, what could be the endgame of Ambedkar's own project? What tectonic transformation would be required to break endogamous taboos of caste existence?

Skin cannot be restored to a natural state of sexual desire precisely because of the Hindu consecration of the skin. Hindus, according to Ambedkar, observe caste "not because they are unhuman or wrongheaded. They observe caste because they are deeply religious" (AC, 74). Caste can end only if the consecrating framework of the religion itself is destroyed by a radical refuting of the Shastras. Contra both Radhakrishnan and Gandhi, Ambedkar declares that the problem cannot be solved purely within the realm of custom or culture, by a spiritualization of politics, or a modern institution of a revised fourfold system as spiritual democracy. Instead, what must be abnegated is a scriptural tradition that makes no distinction between theology, epics, customary rituals, and treatises on law like Manusmriti.[89] Manu especially forecloses the exercise of reason even when there is a conflict between the Vedas and other scriptures. For him, stipulated Sadachar (ancient custom), good or bad, must be obeyed, without human skepticism or doubt. According to Ambedkar, it is this absence of reflexive thought that helps the Hindu to partake in the whirlpool of the modern: to lose caste while traveling in a public bus and to get it back immediately after disembarking. In such a scenario, "what is called Religion by the Hindus [becomes] nothing but a multitude of commands and prohibitions," and the Shastras, at best, present a legalized class ethics (AC, 82). What Ambedkar invites is a messianic departure on the lines of the Buddha and Nanak, of fulfilling the caste law by closing the door on it.

In the course of his argument, Ambedkar also preempts and dismisses that other apology in the Gandhi–Radhakrishnan reformism which argues that caste is not a unique product of the Hindu religion, and that it is also not even peculiar to Hindus in the subcontinental civilizational complex. This line, as we have seen in the previous section, tends towards a naturalistic, race-based exoneration of Jat-Pat. It would suggest that since there was a general human instinct to make caste distinctions, there was nothing ontologically unique about the Hindu arrangement, apart from the fact that it was, in original essence, a wiser, practical, and more harmonious system than the others. Ambedkar refutes this by making an important distinction between the Hindu system and the presence of caste and tribal arrangements in South Asian Muslim, Sikh, or Christian communities. Caste, in the non-Hindu groups, is closer to a raw formation of custom, uncooked in religious culture. There is no mechanism in these theological universes to sacralize the segregation itself (AC, 66–71). Caste, in non-Hindu quarters, is thus mere practice or xenophobic prejudice. It is not a dictate of the gods or a cosmic arrangement of pure elements and dross pollutants. Different non-Hindu caste groups, therefore, may share organic filaments to recompose them into a higher state of unity, spiritual or otherwise. On the other hand, there "is no integrating force among the Hindus to counteract the disintegration caused by caste" (AC, 68).

It is precisely for this reason that Ambedkar, in 1935, after witnessing the transformed scenario of the nationalist movement under the Indian National Congress and Gandhi, would take a less optimistic view about the Indian cultural unity that he had argued for in 1916. Hindu society, according to *Annihilation of Caste*, is a myth. "It is only a collection of castes" that come together during riots (AC, 42). A society exists by communication, including channels of exchange pertaining to primal instincts and procreation. Parallel activities dictated by caste segregation, even if similar, do not constitute an organic or contractual whole. Caste is therefore a calibrated distribution of ressentiment without any mitigating principle that allows for horizontal alliances. Insulated caste histories prevent a unified project of memory and a sense of common ancestral belonging. Decedents of Englishmen who fought on opposite sides of the War of the Roses have long forgotten their feud; this is not true of Kayasthas who have still not forgiven Brahmins for Shivaji's infamy. In such a scenario, nationalist projects of assimilation and shepherding, like the Shuddhi movement of the Arya Samaj, are thus instances of "folly and futility" (AC, 50). In such undertakings, lapsed Hindus are not saved from the lures of Sikhism or Islam and reconvened into Hinduism; instead, Shuddhi merely inducts them back into an Existentiell of caste, since "[in] every Hindu the consciousness that exists is the consciousness of his caste." This is also why there can be no caste Hindu democracy, since democracy, for Ambedkar, is an idea drawn from his teacher and colleague John Dewey. Its meaning is not restricted to liberal institutions of representation and pedagogy, or merely to a form of government; democracy is instead "primarily a mode of associated living, of conjoint communicated experience" (AC, 55).

It is in this light that Ambedkar, in *Annihilation of Caste* and elsewhere, conducts a profoundly anticipatory critique of the Indian modern nationalist project as he saw it developing, especially after the Depressed Classes resolution was taken in the Calcutta session of the Indian National Congress in 1917. Indian nationalism was an ideology that had decided to postpone the question of social revolution in favor of a political one. History, for Ambedkar, provided the exact opposite illustrations. Great political transformations had always been preceded by social ones: Luther in Germany, Puritanism in England or America, and Mohammad in Arabia. It was the rise of Buddha that had led to Chandragupta the Sudra Emperor, and the Saints of Maharashtra had paved the way for Shivaji (AC, 30). In contrast, modern Hindu reform had been largely restricted to the improvement of the caste Hindu family. At the level of the social, the new Hindu covenant offered by the Congress via Gandhism was an idealistic Brahminical paternalism that magically aspired to induct the four thousand Jatis of India into the fourfold Varna. It intended to do so without dispelling the aura of skins and without unleashing novel energies of love between them. For Ambedkar, the whole thing begged the question as to whether the Hindu nationalist deserved political power, since the Swaraj this Hindu envisioned was founded on a fundamental denial of civil rights to a large section of the people (AC, 25–26). It was also not clear what his arrangement had in store for women, even in the age of female barristers and teachers. The revival of Varna was a project to retain caste and Brahminical dominance in the modern era while breaking strict rules about profession, exposure to pollutants, mobility, or the rights of women, their education, and their presence in civic spaces. It was designed to absorb the novelties of history and perpetuate the same "notions, sentiments, and mental attitudes" (AC, 57).

The Gandhian ideology, despite its censure of untouchability, must necessarily promote Varna to foreclose class war as an inevitable feature of a modern consciousness. In Gandhi's early thought at least, the revision of Varna as a realm of trusteeship, voluntarism, and service transcends the historical field of exploitation and Jati discrimination. The Mahatma understood that, in its modern incarnation, the system had to address an expanded order of worldliness and desire. One could thus hunt in the morning, fish in the afternoon, or criticize in the evening, but strictly as hobbies, with caste duties otherwise defining the entire realm of political economy. Ambedkar illustrates this norm by citing a 1925 passage from Gandhi:

> The varna system is connected with the way of earning a living. There is no harm if a person belonging to one varna acquires the knowledge or science and art specialized by persons belonging to other varnas. But as far as the way of earning his living is concerned he must follow the occupation of the varna to which he belongs which means he must follow the hereditary profession of his forefathers.[90]

After making the caustic observation that the barrister Mahatma certainly did not do what he preached by observing his Baniya duties, Ambedkar places the commitment to caste as central, and not peripheral, to Gandhi's antimodernism. Gandhi's aversion for industrial development and the modern state, according to Ambedkar, emerges from his Varna idealism. That is because it is the apparatus of the modern that democratizes leisure and, in effect, creates the epistemological possibilities to distinguish hobbies from labor power.[91] Modernity also offers mass education and extends the rights to property and some juridical and civic means of self-defense to the masses. In contrast, Varna, as in Radhakrishnan or Gandhi, systematizes an agrarian and artisanal Indian society based on presumed natural inequalities of man. Its untimely enshrinement in the modern world brings about a pedagogic fatalism that Ambedkar, summoning Dewey, cites in *Annihilation* as that which "tends to make the past a rival of the present and the present a more or less futile imitation of the past" (AC, 95).

What Congress and Gandhi Have Done to the Untouchables was written shortly before India's independence and the drafting of the Indian Constitution of which Ambedkar would be the prime architect. On the eve of momentous changes, what he saw, with much consternation, was the saintly specter of Gandhi affirming a Varna abstraction as the natural destination for the nation and civilizational complex. The specter was doing so by absorbing all disaffections and evils of everyday Jati exploitation into its incarnate saintliness. This phenomenon had become clear to Ambedkar long ago, when Gandhi foreclosed the possibility of the depressed classes' gaining a separate electorate by way of the British Prime Minister Gordon Ramsay's Communal Award of 1932. The Mahatma had gone on a fast to compel both parties—Madan Mohan Malaviya leading the Savarnas and Ambedkar himself the Dalits—to sign the Poona Pact of 1932 and preserve the integrity of the purported Hindu society and its political representation. Gandhi, in effect, would enforce this unity as indistinguishable from the integrity of the Congress and the nationalist movement itself. The larger-than-life 'Bapu' "fathering" the nation was thus mitigating vices and affirming virtues at once through the exercise of a Weberian charisma. Gandhism was a powerful ontological shepherding of signs that would later threaten to displace Ambedkar's constitutional revolution to a state of abject formalism. This apparently benign but assiduous Hindu paternalism would perpetually occupy the space between *nomos* and the law, establishing an underlying vernacular Swaraj that would spell Sudra slavery or obsolescence at the level of customary and pastoral life. Gandhism promised to cure untouchability with a simultaneous spiritual ennobling of Sudra poverty. This psychologism of Varna, its professed debts to ancestors and its hierarchical naturalism, would imperil the nominal equality of citizenship and spiritually obscure the project of class struggle and social justice. The lure of Gandhian ideology was, to Ambedkar's eyes, the lure of a temperate Brahminism, which he describes elsewhere as a regime based on certain absolutist principles: graded inequality between classes, complete disarmament of Sudras and untouchables, a ban on their acquiring property or positions of authority, and indeed, a complete subjugation of women.[92]

Gandhism's overwriting of and strategic mergers with the works of the modern could, in time, create the parabasis of a new Hindu normal. The affective powers of this benevolent Hinduness, Ambedkar clearly understood, would render the Indian constitutional revolution passive by foreclosing a constitutional morality. The prime architect of the Indian Constitution would spend the last years of his life deeply skeptical about the permanence and strength of the democratic republic he himself had helped to birth. He would expend the rest of his formidable intellectual powers in forging a revolutionary assemblage of Marxist and Buddhist thought to ward off the impending perversion of democracy into caste Hindu majoritarianism. In October 1956, weeks before his death, Ambedkar would convert to Buddhism along with roughly half a million of his followers to fulfill a promise he had made decades earlier—that he had been born a Hindu but would certainly not die one.

Concluding Remarks

Ambedkar's Jacobin critique strikes at the heart of a Hindu-normative project toward national peopleness—even the paternalistic version of tolerance and "Savarna secularism," much less the militant right-wing Hindutva of a Savarkar or Golwalkar. What he also exposes is the parabasis that the benign and the strident share as a secret choral unity. This parabasis is one that allows for the mutual transmission of principles and prejudices in a sublimated plane of caste Hindu common sense. It variously births both the energies of militant bigotry as well as the culture of patronage and clientelism that seeks to neuter republican virtues. The first, as we have seen, is directed at punishing the minority or the caste betrayer; the second makes toleration indistinguishable from principled subjugation. Both forbid the imagination of a revolutionary India that is not Savarna in essence; both foreclose a Hindu equity of virtue, class, and *potentia*.

The separation of Varna destinies means a separation of passional commitments, imaginative horizons, and responsibilities. The idealistic project of a Hindu-Indian political monotheism, for Ambedkar, is thus bereft of genuine spiritual qualities that can replenish the void of the modern. In his eyes, Hindu reform in general craves an axiomatic that does not allow for the separation of religious principles from custom or culture, ancestral obligations from contemporary common sense, superstition from science, or jurisprudence from priestly dicta. It cannot, therefore, detach an authentic historical consciousness from the mythological firmaments of the human imagination. "Hinduism," for Ambedkar, is a schizophrenic order that fatally infects all particulars of narrating a nation into being: realism, logic, history, the subject, and the law.[93] A majoritarian Hindu normativity, with its antiquarianism and its refusal to submit caste Dharma to the rule of democratic law, would always bear this schizoid character.

Ambedkar would present the split between Brahman the cosmic universal and the violent earthly inequalities of Varnasrama Dharma as one of the abiding riddles of Hinduism. Discussing the need for a social foundation of democracy rather than just a formal superstructure of electoral politics, he would make a distinction between three impulses in the Hindu Tradition. He calls the first one Brahmaism, or the doctrine that suggests that Brahma is the only abiding reality behind the multiplicity of creation. The second, Advaita, does the same, but announces the phenomenal world itself, including its cruelties and injustices, to be Maya or unreal. The third, "Brahmanism," focuses on Chaturvarna (fourfold Varna system), the infallibility of the Vedas, sacrifices, and salvation. For Ambedkar, it was crucial that, unlike Advaita, Brahmaism does not deny the real world but sets up a network of radical correspondences between three postulates: *Sarvam Khalvidam Brahma* (All this is Brahma), *Aham Brahmasmi* (I am Brahma), and *Tattvamasi* (Therefore thou art also Brahma). Since the unknowable Brahman is shared by all, "no doctrine could furnish a stronger foundation for democracy than the doctrine of Brahma."[94] It leaves room for no other form of associated living. The tragic failure of historical Hinduism was that its society was not organized according to this powerful cosmic principle of equity. Instead, the religion became a latitudinarian arrangement by which the One of Advaita did not have to be presented in courts of social justice while the inequities of Chaturvarna could be insulated from tribunals of philosophy.

What we have examined in this chapter is a constellation of moments—from the Vedantic reform of Rammohun to the pacific paternalism of

Gandhi—in a general path of monothematic Hindu becoming in anticipation of the nation-state, and in dialogue with that thing called modernity. We glimpsed a discursive terrain that had the narrative form and an idea of historical epigenesis at the heart of its operations. Modern Hindu reform involved scriptural reinterpretation, historical-sociological transcriptions of mythic material and dogma, and anthropological understandings of traditional institutions. The project had to furnish imagined communities and personages with a subjectivity and a historical agency pertinent to an overall invention of a Hindu past. The texts we have looked at had to, therefore, inevitably engage with worldly regimes of truth; they had to argue reasonably with Reason, and anxiously gather the ambiguous and the scattered in order to translate traditional memory into antiquarian or monumental histories. In Ambedkar we have seen the limits of this Hindu Reason and its crippling impasses. If indeed one were to claim Spinoza or Kant as honorary Hindus, as Bankim did, which castes would their beef-eating selves belong to?

I end this chapter by invoking the figure of Rabindranath Tagore (1861–1941), who strode across this discursive terrain like a colossus, but will largely remain outside the ambit of this study. That is because a wider discussion of the evolution and complexity of Tagore's thinking would require a separate book, or two. Nonetheless, it is crucially important to nod in his direction because, along with figures like Ambedkar and Periyar E. V. Ramaswamy, the literary explorations of progressive and secular Urdu modernism headed by Saadat Hasan Manto or Faiz Ahmad Faiz, or the voices of many women across ages and provinces, it is Tagore's thinking that should be reignited in our perilous times. This gesture is therefore to mark, among other things, the finitude of the current book itself and the possibilities that lie beyond it. The trajectory of Tagore's journey would be illustrative of the entire modern Indian quest we have traced so far, from a Brahmo childhood, a Vedic orthodox Hindu phase in his early forties, and finally to a position of an increasingly radical humanism between the great wars that was marked, among other things, by a trenchant critique of nationalism and untouchability. Tagore's thinking was deeply inflected by the Upanishads, Gaudiya Vaishnavism, Buddhism (especially the concept of Maitri, or amity, in the Theravada school), folk traditions of Bengal, and Sikhism and the Nirguna traditions of Nanak and Kabir. It was internationalist, enriched by travels and a keen interest in other civilizational formations in the Americas, the USSR, China, and Japan. It was nomadic and pantopic; unlike that of Gandhi, it bore no aversion to science and technology. Tagore's work was marked by creative and vital movements of dance, play, struggle, and poiesis between the polarities of the age. Over the decades, his dynamic engagements with the concept of the nation, caste realities, or the human essence would take place in diverse expressive forms such as the novel, in *Gora* (1910), *Ghare Baire* (1916), or *Chaturanga* (1916); the essay and the polemical tract in *Nationalism* (1918) or *Kalantar* (1937); the dance drama in *Chitrangada* (1936) or *Chandalika* (1938); and a trove of songs and poems of breathtaking range. It is perhaps in this corpus that the Indian search for a vernacular modernity with cosmopolitan ambitions reached one of its pinnacles, in terms of intellectual and creative powers, abiding enigmas, noble flaws, and magnificent irresolutions.

What we can mark apropos of Ambedkar's point about Brahmaism and its aborted democratic possibilities, is that for Tagore the finest commitment to the universal is one that is unencumbered by parochial guarantees of caste sociology or nation-thinking. In other words, he would not allow fatal ties to a static Hindu Samaj, or an India abstracted from Asiatic and worldly horizons, to stand in the way of expressing a human fullness. It could certainly be claimed that one or some of the many incarnations of Tagore that emerge from his vast, many-armed oeuvre were normative "Hindu" thinkers coming from a general Vedic horizon. In the arc we have traversed, Tagore could be repeatedly summoned to bear witness against Tagore. He could justifiably be accused of harboring fears and suspicions about an "aggressive" Islam and of having a general aversion to Abrahamic monotheisms (such charges could be brought against Ambedkar as well). The problem for the nationalist, however, would be to chain Tagore to a consecrated land, a people, and a singular memory. The nation, for Tagore, was simply a European template for organizing peoples for a "mechanistic purpose." That is because a national imagination can be marked only as part of a network of "mutual jealousy" with other nations in the age of competition and industrial slaughter.[95] Analogously, he would severely critique a Gandhian antimodernism centered upon the idolatry of the *charkha* (spinning wheel) and its atavistic ennobling of poverty. One had to be touched by the "spirit" of the West, and all other forms of worldliness, without being entrapped either by agrarian conservative nativism or by the state of man as a political and commercial animal with limited ends. In affirming a human universal without insular interests, Tagore thus avoided the Western conundrum that afflicted a long line of thinkers from Hegel to Heidegger: How does one magnify an essentially national vision into a picture of the world?

Despite early enthrallments to Vedic revivalism and qualified attachments to Varna as an original Indic harmony, Tagore would eventually announce

India as the land of the Sudras, marking the misfortunes and inertia of the nation as a whole indistinguishable from the entrapment and depression of its lowly. In stark contrast to Radhakrishnan, he viewed the ironclad notion of Swadharma not as matter of artisanal joy or pride, but as a dynastic crushing of the Sudra imagination, soul, and creativity. The hereditary and endogamous caste system was simply an ossified system of marking sectarian differences; it was blind and deaf to the vital mutations of life.[96] Despite their epistemological, experiential, and generational differences, there was thus a line of inquiry and interrogation that Tagore shared with Ambedkar. Both thought that the tragic flaw of Savarna Indian nationalism was its decision to postpone the social revolution for the political one. Nationalists, all in all, viewed the communitarian and spiritual work of the nation, apart from a few touches of reform and revival, as already accomplished thousands of years ago. They were thus engaged in the task of building a "political miracle of freedom upon the quicksand of social slavery."[97]

4 HINDUTVA 2.0
AS ADVERTISED MONOTHEISM

From Print Capitalism to New Media

This is what we have done so far. We have traced a persistent monotheistic imperative in the anthropological invention of "Hinduism," which was a requirement built into the modern political marking of the faith and the denomination. This conceptual line was crucial in the emergence of a form of nation-thinking that aimed to affirm a Hindu essence, conquer spatial and temporal imaginations, institute memory and providence, and furnish what might be called a compelling political theology. Our explorations have taken place in relation to a provisional dictum extracted from Carl Schmitt: in order for there to be a Hindu nation as an artwork of public religiosity, there had to be a Hindu monotheism or a secular equivalent of the same. This dictum is an insular one, as we have noted; it does not provide a universal explanatory model regarding the historical formation of nation-states and peoples, nor does it in any way exhaust the possibilities of imagining India. Yet we have mobilized it as a ruse of reason for examining the modern invention of a Hindu axiomatic and a national peopleness. We have, accordingly, sketched a constellation of themes and ideas in this historical field of problems. This tracing is not meant to provide a total reckoning of the many streams of soft and hard Hindu nationalism, their spectrum of culturalist transpositions, intricate caste politics, or regional and linguistic variants. Nevertheless, it could be said that the quest for a Hinduism with an Abrahamic inspiration—or a comparable ethnonationalist form of culture—has been consistent in Hindu nationalist efforts to determine an abiding self and nation. A naturalized image of an essentially Hindu India—an organic whole rather than an associational pact—has always been summoned to judge regionalisms or to condemn the secular, democratic, and federal features of the modern republic. This form of monotheistic passion—with or without the religion itself—was deemed necessary for this nationalism to acquire a jealous character, and sort friends and enemies in differential measures of infidelity or apostasy. In this vein, the discourse of Hindu nationalism, and its reflections regarding self and other have always been tinged by an envy toward Islam's monotheism, as that which is able to birth fanatic faithfuls committed to a single God and a single destination.

This Hindu search for an axiomatic involves finding a singular principle for the ontological gravitation of signs, one that can cut through provincial clamor and caste divisions and institute a unitary narrative of being with a naturalized Aryan-Brahmin heartland bias. Ideally this principle should be able to wear the apparent pluralism of Indian traditions as a badge of tolerance, but also be able to reduce the pluralities themselves to decorative status and arrange them in descending hierarchies. But Hindutva's engagements with the immense varieties of faith and memory also reveal its many points of agon. We have glimpsed certain key moments of this project as a literary undertaking in the nineteenth and twentieth centuries. At this point, it is time to skip a few decades, from the mid-1960s ruminations of Golwalkar to a period commencing in the late 1980s when Hindutva emerged as a mass ideology with the broadcast of the television adaptations of Ramayana and Mahabharata, the Sangh Parivaar's accrual of new ritual values and modes of mass mobilization during the Ram Janmabhoomi movement, its global spread in the Hindu diaspora, the eventual liberalization of the Indian economy, and the ushering-in of a planetary media ecology in the 1990s. We are shifting, if you will, from an order of print capitalism to an electronic one.

Apart from what we have seen in the work of ideologues like Golwalkar or Savarkar, or in soft-Hindu men of letters like Radhakrishnan or Rajagopalchari, a greater print-based, twentieth-century publicity devoted to a Hindu-Hindustan imaginary will escape a detailed study here. This enterprise involved an increasing mercantile capitalist interest in defining a national culture in terms of Sanskritic reform and parabasis. Animated by high priests like K. M. Munshi or B. V. Keskar, it had a formidable armature in the age of mechanical reproducibility, covering traditional arts, theater, and literature, as well as new mass media like film and radio. The project was impelled by a special sense of Savarna urgency and panic around matters like pan-Islamicism, the floating of the two-nation theory, and what was seen to be a Gandhian capitulation to increasing Dalit impertinence in the Poona Pact of 1932. It was marked by a greater middle-class interest in the shaping and monitoring of a high Hindu cultural ethnoscape. Such efforts to secure a normative, pan-Indian "mainstream" would include Rukmini Devi Arundale's extraction of a classical template of Indian dance absolved of Islamicate or courtesanal traditions, V. N. Bhatkhande or V. D. Paluskar's missions to invent a classical Indian music purged of Tawaif forms like Thumri or Kajri, or Ananda Coomaraswamy–inspired perennialist inventions of an artisanal Indian Swadesh and Volk. These efforts involved, among other things, absolving literary and cinematic narratives of what Kaushik Bhaumik has called the "bazaar energies" of imperial cosmopolitanism—the Victorian Gothic, the Masnavi poetic, the Punjabi Qissa or the Farsi Dastaan traditions, and the impulses of Urdu modernism and Afsana literature in general.[1] This Sanskritic mode, of course, was more easily manifested in parlors than accomplished in the streets. Nevertheless, with the flourishing of hegemonic institutions, state patronage, and the promotion of a highly engineered "Hindi" in official media organs, it would lay a powerful claim in the determination of a modern Indian culture. In subsequent decades, the cleaned-up ethnoscape would be extended to disparate avenues such as television, the audio cassette revolution, advertising, textbooks, and comics for children.

A good part of this epoch, especially the years between Gandhi's assassination in 1948 and the Indian Internal Emergency of 1975, was one of quiet, pastoral work for the RSS; Hindu political units like the Jan Sangh or Ram Rajya Parishad were marginal to Indian politics. It would be pertinent to catch a glimpse of the Savarna soft-shepherding of culture in the age of print capitalism, but, from a wider civil society perspective that is not restricted to core Hindutva entities like *Organiser*, the RSS mouthpiece. Akshaya Mukul's insightful and comprehensive study of the Gita Press phenomenon provides a vivid illustration of the many-armed Hindu publicity of the twentieth century.[2] A brief exploration of Mukul's book is important to this project for two reasons. First of all, it reveals a terrain of normative Hindu meditations on modernity, ethics, culture, and nationhood that is indeed affiliated with the Sangh Parivaar institutions but also extends to institutions, markets, and civic avenues beyond it. Mukul's study, in that vein, points to key complicities between Hindutva and Congress-style mainstream nationalism's soft determinations of the secular. Second, it provides us with a glimpse of orthodox Hindu (rather than Hindu reformist or ethnocultural Hindutva) desires to administer the modern language games of science, morality, technology, and economy. These desires have been subsequently rendered voluble and kinetic in the media age.

The Gita Press was established in 1923 by Jaydayal Goyandka and Hanuman Prasad Poddar, two Marwari businessmen turned spiritual entrepreneurs. Located in the city of Gorakhpur in Uttar Pradesh and operating like the Bible Society, the institution emerged as the largest publisher and mass circulator of Hindu religious texts in multiple languages, including millions of copies of the Bhagwad Gita and Ramcharitmanas. It distilled a new iconography from the Nathdwara and Bengal schools of painting, built hagiographies, and published primers for women and children. These books were cheap, often printed in portable editions, and frequently distributed free in orphanages or religious missions. Backed by powerful entities in the mercantile world who viewed the venture as religious philanthropy and nation-building, the firm started the influential monthly journal *Kalyan* in 1927 (and the English-language *Kalyana-Kalpataru* in 1934) to espouse caste Hindu values in relation to civic and political life. The objective was to secure a Brahminical hegemony in an age of great upheavals, but one that would now be shared by an emergent Baniya "neo-Kshatriya" mercantile capitalist class. It was accordingly patronized by the conservative Hindu wing of the Congress and other mainstream political actors and public intellectuals.

Gita Press, according to Mukul, promoted a Baniya model of profiting from Bhakti, in which its mass products like the pocket-sized Ramcharitmanas or Hanuman Chalisa could become part of a mass Hindu diurnal, involving worship, ablutions, and chanting with rosaries (GP, 229). These, along with good works (including donations to the Gita Press itself), were seen to add tangible benefits in earthly existence itself, both for the individual and to the spiritual coffers of a burgeoning nation. These core products aside, over the decades the institution would market a range of items from herbal balms, confections, medicines, tea, or aphrodisiacs to finance its own existence as well as to infuse a micropunctual, ritualistic Hinduness into the thickness and speed of modern life. The Gita Press would open a chain of Ayurvedic dispensaries and an all-male Vedic school in Churu, Rajasthan, open to only the three higher castes. Over the decades, it would publish material in concert with Hindu issues and institutions concerning proselytization, cow protection, popularization of the great epics, or promotion of Hindi as national language. It would print Ram Lila plays, as well as notations of devotional songs emerging from the Hindustani classical tradition. The publication house would start its own unit called Geeta Seva Dal for social work, charity, and disaster relief, and set up Kalyan Ashram to stop tribal populations from embracing Christianity. Gita Press, in other words, was an early pioneer in what would eventually become a global Hinduism industry.

The monthly journal *Kalyan*, currently in the ninth decade of its career, has been the flagship entity in the operations of the Gita Press. Mukul points out that, along with usual Hindutva suspects like Golwalkar or Karpatri Maharaj, Congress stalwarts and public intellectuals like Dr. Rajendra Prasad, C. Rajagopalchari, Purushottam Das Tandon, and S. Radhakrishnan wrote for *Kalyan*, as did reputed scholars like the Sanskritist Kshitimohan Sen or the linguist Suniti Kumar Chatterjee. Major litterateurs like Mahadevi Varma, Maithilisharan Gupt, and Harivansh Rai Bachchan graced the pages, as did the celebrated Urdu-Hindi novelist Munshi Premchand, who was also the first president of the decidedly left-wing Progressive Writers Association. The journal regularly featured Muslim intellectuals like Muhammad Hafiz Syed, professor of philosophy at Allahabad University, or the journalist Syed Qasim Ali. This eclectic field was supplemented by some international writers like the Gandhian American missionary Ralph T. Templin or the German Indologist Otto Strauss. The theme-based issues were decorated with carefully selected excerpts from "great men" as disparate as Abul Fazl, Edmund Burke, George Bernard Shaw, Oscar Wilde, and indeed, Adolf Hitler (on dutiful women).[3] Mukul attributes the wider cosmopolitan pretense of the journal—featuring essays and excerpts from people resistant or indifferent to the Hindu nationalist cause—to a simple operating principle. Keeping the Brahminical sanctum sanctorum intact, outside authors would be chosen for a very specific purpose to lend prestige and heft to the general platform. All writers could address, from their own vantage points, transformations and crises of the age in relation to Hinduism. That is, they had to acknowledge, directly or indirectly, for good or bad, that a Hindu way of life was in crisis or was being transformed. Such writings would then be immersed into the overall choral unity of the Hindu project (GP, 223–24). The journal, in its entirety, was thus an attempt to provide a state-of-the-faith report to the nation and to the world, calling both to judgment. It involved a continual reactivation of the scriptural in an age diseased by civilizational decadence, immorality, Islam, and materialism.

Kalyan largely operated without the immediate political stigma attached to the RSS or the *Organiser* after Gandhi's assassination. Yet it was greatly informed by the personal ideology and obscurantist worldview of its founding editor Hanuman Prasad Poddar, who was associated with the Hindu

Mahasabha and was eventually a founding trustee of the VHP. The journal was, for all practical purposes, to the right of prominent Hindu nationalist forces, especially when it came to matters of caste and untouchability. The Gita Press worked more in line with an orthodox and austere vision of Sanatan Dharma (eternal religion) than the reformist legacy of the Arya Samaj or the ethnocultural one of the reputed atheist Savarkar. It would remain steadfast in its support for Varna discrimination and untouchability, bitterly opposing Ambedkarism and other democratic enthusiasms like intercaste marriages. It would vociferously oppose the Child Marriage Restraint Act of 1929, widow remarriage, and the Hindu code bills of 1955–56 that extended rights of inheritance, property, and divorce to women. *Kalyan* would be staunch in opposing birth control and family planning, and allowing females to work or receive an education beyond what it considered natural, Dharmic limits. The journal would staunchly decry Western education, remain suspicious of modern medicine and lament modern desegregation of spaces, such as efforts to abolish separate Hindu and Muslim arrangements for tea, food, and water on the Indian railways. *Kalyan* would repeatedly assert that there could be no Swaraj without Hindu ascendency; it would categorically describe the entire Pakistan project in terms of primal usurpation, murder, conversion, and rape. Immediately after partition and independence in 1947, Poddar published a twelve-point program sketching out a desired majoritarian nation that would be called Hindustan or Aryavarta. It would be organized along the lines of a Hindu culture, under a saffron flag and with Hindi as national language. Military service would be made mandatory, and only Hindus would be allowed in the armed forces. Muslims had to be debarred from high posts and could get government jobs only proportionate to the population (GP, 254–55). When this dream was formally shattered by the republican revolution of 1950, *Kalyan* would subsequently focus all its energies on distinguishing and protecting an eternal Hindu Samaj from the encroachments of an activist state.

The dominant mode of enunciation in *Kalyan* was that of a paranoid style inflected by a perpetual sense of victimhood and angst. The stance was to disavow and indict the entire apparatus of the modern—including the twin specters of barbaric Islam and godless communism—aimed at the destruction of the rural and artisanal base of Varnasrama. The urban industrial order quickened by Nehruvian development was a monstrosity of irreverent energies, illicit transports, and circulations of impure objects and bodies, ranging from biscuits containing eggs to toothbrushes made of pig hair.[4] Birth control and female higher education were looked upon as plots to destroy the fabric of the Indian joint family, imperil the future of the Aryan race, and lose the demographic war against Islam. Such positions were defended by way of pseudoscientific hokum or mythical data merged into the obsessive style: mathematics caused depression in women; 40 percent of British women suffered from premarital pregnancy; or 60 percent of American women were single and past the age of marriage (GP, 356; 367–68). One of the most ingenious arguments against contraception declared it to be unsuitable for tropical climates (GP, 385). On the other hand, a set of pieties and measures of self-control could enable a woman to deliver a Dharma-inclined male child: not getting noses pierced, avoiding conversations with cunning people, and, indeed, refusing food from Sudras (GP, 378). In an age of decadence, Poddar, as late as 1953, wanted female actors to be banned from the cinema (GP, 399). At the same time, he extolled things like the "magic" of Sati, which, in its ideal form, involved the widow's principled grief crossing a physiological threshold to activate the thyroid gland, such that the body, without any external coercion, underwent spontaneous combustion (GP, 374).

The Gita Press, unlike other Hindutva forces, did not editorialize Shastra discourse to mitigate the social inequities of caste. It employed only caste Hindus, practiced scrupulous Savarna discrimination at home, and preached it to the world. Such absolutist scriptural fatalism aside, it also tried, unsurprisingly, to justify caste in pseudoscientific or economistic terms. It parried questions about temple entry by invoking the infallibility of the scriptures or by the paternalistic suggestion that Dalits and tribals should take care of that other important department of Hinduism that deals with nature worship and animism (GP, 268–72). Similarly, *Kalyan* would deal with the scourge of communism with the usual tactic of principled disavowal followed by neurotic appropriation: the most cherished ideals of the commune had already been perfectly achieved in the caste Hindu joint family (GP, 331).

The only principle of equity that this version of Hinduism could accord was the esoteric one of the soul, shared not just by men and women, but also cats and dogs. Contrary to the long reform tradition that we examined in the previous chapters, this Sanatan nationalism therefore foreclosed an organic uniformity of the flock or a congregational sociology. Yet the Gita Press would extend a spiritual claim over not just Dalitbahujans but also over followers of Jainism, Buddhism, and Sikhism as all being branches of the same spiritual tree. It required dogmatic adherence to a Manuvaadi segregation of bodies and spaces, while simultaneously insisting on a principled continuum of Hindi, Hinduness, and Hindusthan. The project, which continues to this digital day, would remain "incomplete" in terms of its own idealistic horizons, as would contiguous Hindu missions of reform or ethnocultural nationalism. The task, at this point, is to see whether and how their distinct operations and mutual concert shift in nature and amplitude in the age of new media and Hindu political ascendency.

The Age of Information and the Question of Hindu Fascism

It was from the early 1990s that the project for a Hindu political theology began to acquire informational powers that resonated with increasing frequency across the Indian landmass and abroad. As Arvind Rajagopal's illuminating study has shown, the Ram Temple movement that culminated with the destruction of the Babri Masjid on December 6, 1992, congealed a particular climate of religiosity. It drew energies from a new Hindu commons inaugurated by the Ramayana and Mahabharata tele-epics, grand symbolic undertakings like Advani's Rathyatra, and urban-industrial expressions of Savarna masculinity by way of bumper stickers, bandanas, T-shirts, or buttons. The movement featured novel use of technologies like VHS tapes and audiocassettes to circulate speeches by firebrands like Sadhvi Ritambhara, and an advertising drive by significant sections of the vernacular press in Hindi, which circulated rumors, reported miracles, and galvanized myths for the cause.[5]

This was not a mere augmentation of older forms of propaganda or ceremony. Informational Hindutva would begin to define the ground rules of discursive and affective engagement with an increasingly greater range of issues and would go from strength to strength over the decades that followed. For the first time, it would decisively influence the policies of the Anglophone state, in terms of security, economy, culture, and jurisprudence. Manisha Basu understands this order as one in which Hindutva's metropolitan project was marked "by its adoption of English as a type of globally cybernetic form to an increasingly Sanskritized national culture." This was a new syntactic assemblage, a new performance of information that "dissolve[d] the differences between contingent pasts, presents, and futures" and collapsed the narrative of decolonization.[6] Basu notes the emergence of a new mode of language and style in an increasingly smooth electronic ethnoscape, dominated by a new breed of technocratic intellectuals like Chetan Bhagat or Jay Dubashi. Here, tradition and modernity, old patrimony and Chicago-style economism, were orchestrated together by an "elaborate poetics of management speak."[7]

We can understand this phenomenon, in a cumulative sense, as advertised modernization. That is, "modernization" as a concept we had drawn earlier from Rajni Kothari: a scenario in which "Tradition" and modernity do not necessarily trump each other but shift to a new symbiotic arrangement and register of performance. The advertised form is an ethereal and spectacular public Hinduness that transcends an older, conflict-prone, and segmented landscape filled with the babel of languages. It seeks to invent a new flock in a virtual realm of urbanity that besieges, electrifies, and inducts the countryside. This assemblage of Hindutva 2.0 is, in essence, not reliant on the institutional paraphernalia of modernity: the book form, the museum, the academy of fine arts, or the university. It is also not beholden to traditional orders like the seminary, the *shakha*, councils of holy men, or the temple of cautious priestly mediations—even though it undeniably draws significant resources from them. Hindutva 2.0 works primarily by way of loose, fungible distributions of affect, spectacle, and what we will call the substance of the advertised. It does not aim to resolve the ancient debates about theology, philosophy, science, history, or tradition that we have explored in previous chapters. Instead, it seeks to particularize and synchronize key words within the debates themselves—*Vedic* and *science*, for instance—into instantly consumable mythograms. It deals with the troubles of the historical by hollowing out historical consciousness and memory. It inaugurates a new synergy between the state of being Hindu and neoliberalism, one taking place on a plane of marketable desires and terrors. In its most sophisticated forms, Hindutva 2.0 transcends representation, identity, story, or ideal. The political rise of core Hindu nationalism is indeed a very important expression of this dispensation, but not all of it. The ecosystem of Hindutva 2.0 is that which tends to settle a national normal by spreading soft and hard proclivities of an urban Hindu normative across the entire political spectrum. It is one that shifts what political scientists call the Overton Window—the permissible range of ideas and voiced feelings in a given climate of public opinion—itself to the right.

Let me, however, preface such a discussion with something else, since we are shifting to a contemporary moment in which the RSS is by far the largest voluntary mission in the world, the VHP is global, and the spectacular political rise of the BJP over the last three decades has peaked in a Narendra Modi premiership with an absolute majority in parliament. Since we began this study by invoking a Schmittian idea of political theology and tracing affinities between Indian authoritarianisms and European fascism, perhaps at this point one needs a discursive clearing for that old question: Is it fair to compare the varieties of Hindu nationalist assertion to hard-right historical formations in Italy or Germany prior to World War II? It is a good time to ask that because, for many, another hour of arrival has indeed come for that strange beast that had begun to slouch toward Ayodhya in the winter of 1992.

As we have seen, the category of fascism has been broached with both positivist fervor and trepidation, and it has also been dismissed as irrelevant to the Indian context. Dismissals of the thoughtful kind have been based on three major premises. First, the progression of Hindutva has been a slower shepherding of an ethnonationalist ideology over almost a century; its temporal arc does not match that of a fascist movement that necessarily flares up only to be extinguished. Second, India's greater pluralisms aside, the pluralism *within* Hindu nationalism itself renders a fascistic mobilization on a pan-Indian scale difficult to achieve. Third, India—as a complex formation, with its unique past—is simply different in both cultural and historical terms. Ergo, while such fascistic tendencies might exist, India is hardly the platform to manifest or maximize them in terms of expressive state power.

Institutional Hindutva is undoubtedly part of a wider assemblage of Hindu chauvinism. In terms of European parallels, the broader formation has contained energies mobilized along the lines of both Italian fascism and German Nazism, but it has also featured conservative powers akin to that of the Spanish Carlists during the Civil War or the Catholic corporatism of Salazar in Portugal's Estado Novo after 1933. In the current dispensation, the assemblage includes media-driven missionary or godman-centered cultish formations that have been politicized in a manner similar to American megachurch evangelism and New Religious movements since the 1960s. With the coming into the forefront of organizations like Sanatan Sanstha and Abhinav Bharat, cellular organizations of Hindu terror have entered the picture. Next on the list would be a spectrum of parochial chauvinisms following a militant "Sena" model that includes the Marathi Shiv, the Rajput Karni, or the upper-caste North Indian Ranvir and Hindu Senas. It would therefore be useful at this point to critically separate strands in a general specter of European fascism itself, both in the interest of historical precision and to preempt standard complaints from the twenty-first-century right about the casual and banal use of the "f-word" by hypersensitive liberals and leftists. Conversely, it is also to look at that other possibility: that, while in the past Hindutva was just a fascist ideology, the moment has come at last when it threatens to become a bona fide fascist movement.

In her classic study on the origins of totalitarianism, Hannah Arendt makes a distinction between fascism in predominantly agrarian Italy and Nazism in industrial Germany.[8] The former, at least until 1938, existed on the lines of a nationalist party dictatorship—a template followed in the 1930s by an impressive array of Western countries, including the Baltic States, Franco's Spain, Portugal, Poland, Romania, and Hungary after the dissolution of the dual monarchy. Mussolini's fascists merely used the movement to bring the party to power in an otherwise multiparty democracy. It was what Arendt calls the "party above all parties" model, which aspired to conquer the government and foster a cult of state worship. Nazism, in contrast, was a totalitarian movement proper, in her estimation, owing more to pan-German, anti-Austrian, anti-Jewish sentiments mobilized against the multinational legacy of the Catholic Hapsburgs. For the Nazis, therefore, the existing state form of the Weimar Republic was to be despised absolutely until their tribal but transnational Germanism conquered it and in doing so protected the people from the pan-European Jewry. The Nazi movement as such did not have any determinate goals that could be defined within the time–space limitations, existing socioeconomic realities, and constitutional parameters of the given nation-state.[9] The movement simply had to move, without a clear and present charter of class interests. It had to recruit, not just people who were ignorant of politics, but people who had grown to abhor all politics. It had to do so in a plane of language marked by nihilism and vulgarity and it had to be animated by fantasies of resurrection from defeat and oblivion. The mass, in a totalitarian sense, therefore comes into being when the movement is actually able to make the "people" fugitive from its own composite self; the mass becomes an agglomerate of lonely and anxious individuals that can come together without common interests or pursuits. Unlike that of the party above all parties, Nazism's final objective was to make a utopian tribalism triumphant in a worldly sense, or to render the state order itself suicidal in the process. Arendt insists repeatedly that Nazism was essentially about world empire; the *Volksgemeinschaft* was merely propaganda. Along with a disavowal of the Weimar constitution it did not bother to abolish, the movement, in its purest form, also did not identify with a racially corrupt, defeated, and emasculated German people after the Treaty of Versailles. Nazism was therefore 'totalitarian' precisely because it could sacrifice all for ideology.[10] Himmler wanted to open a fourth military front within Germany itself, against a German population suffused with pacifist temptations and internal enemies.[11]

As a concomitant measure, Hitler vowed to gas Germans to a painless death in the event of defeat.[12]

Arendt also distinguishes between Nazi or Stalinist totalitarianism and a Mussolini-style national corporatist dictatorship in terms of land and population size. Totalitarianism, as a rule, is deemed possible only in a scenario in which a total Schmittian settlement of the political—the domestic sorting of friend and enemy through an exterminating war—may be carried out without seriously depleting the population. It is in this precise context that Arendt earmarks China and India as potential candidates for a totalitarian turn should such politics arrive and flourish in some future moment.[13] This hypothesis assumes a particularly chilling form when we return to that old question: What would a Hindu Rashtra do with its population of roughly 200 million Muslims? Genocidal fantasies targeting 14 percent of the population are floated imperiously in contemporary India, much more often than in the past, alongside that other solution—sending them to Pakistan. Currently there is also that other prospect of "detention camps" for those who fail the citizenship test and are excluded from the reactivated National Register of Citizens (NRC).

If we bring Arendt's models, of Italian fascism as an authoritarian cult and Nazism as a totalitarian one, into a state of critical proximity with Hindu nationalism, we see that the Indian situation, in various degrees and forms, has contained both impulses, often acting at odds with each other. That aside, there have also been insular caste Hindu tribalisms that do not conform to any of these models. In the atomic age, the idea of world empire may perhaps be set aside as a quaint nineteenth-century throwback, and the total decimation of Indian Muslims deemed too impractical and too disruptive for markets. However, there is that abiding Sangh Parivaar territorial desire for a maximum India (Akhand Bharat), achieved through goodwill or firepower, and a providential yearning for the nation to become the Vishwa Guru, the world teacher with global spiritual dominance. This uncompromising idealism of RSS-style nationalism, now extended to the pan-Hindu diaspora, has always been in a state of tension with the parliamentary pragmatics of the BJP. The chief issues of contention have been the construction of the Ram Temple at Ayodhya, the abrogation of Article 370 of the Indian Constitution granting special status to Kashmir, the replacement of personal laws with a uniform civil code, the ending of reservations, and sundry other matters pertaining to Pakistan and minority rights. These things aside, there is yet that purist Brahminical desire to revisit the fundamentals of the constitution in quest of Hindu Rashtra. So far, however, a high Hindu disdain for Westminster parliamentarism has always been complicated by the inevitable realities of Hindu Westminster parliamentarism.[14]

Until 2014, the clear and present emergence of a Hindu party above all other parties was prevented by the sparseness of what I am calling a compelling political monotheism. Nevertheless, in relation to Arendt's elaboration, we should freshly identify certain bullet points of Hindu authoritarian desire that have become pronounced in recent times. These have a critical pertinence in relation to the mass psychology that Arendt investigates in Hitler's propaganda machine, a psychology that Deleuze would later call a hypnotic spiritual automaton of fascism.[15] These bullet points would include the yearning for an actionist majority beyond existing consensual institutions, marked by a contempt for life, peace, and common sense. They would feature a zeal to render all politics that do not respond to ontological questions of millennia and self-certifying ideas of time and memory as fraudulent. Then there would be the will to dismiss all historiography as forgery and, at the same time, the resolve to gain sovereign access to history even at the price of destruction. In its purest forms, this mindset would be marked by an actual derision for a historical Hindu people afflicted by pacifism, emasculation, defeat, egalitarian dissipation, and Sudra impudence. The discourse of Hindu nationalism, as we have already seen, promises to usher in a Hindu Rashtra where right will be determined by what twice-born men want, law will be indistinguishable from caste ethics, and Islam will be marked as a clear and present corruption in the body politic.

Lately, the specter of Hindu fascism—if we can now return to using this word in a qualified sense—has grown to haunt modern India, perhaps like no other time in the past. One can say that with a sense of historical introspection and with the awareness that postponing the study of fascism till it assumes or abuses state power is already studying it too late. This illuminating idea comes from Benjamin Zachariah, for whom the topicality of the term becomes irresistible precisely at the point when it becomes far more awkward to avoid it than to use it.[16] I am not interested in a presentist diagnosis of Modi's still unfolding tenure, but, in light of Arendt's elaboration, I will mark a few key symptoms that are telling. They do not necessarily function as signs of an inevitable propulsion toward a "classic" totalitarian movement, but they are certainly expressive of an emboldened Hindu will to sovereignty and the possible reduction of Indian constitutional democracy and its public institutions to mere formalisms.[17]

The India of the present features elements of what Arendt calls an essential culture of paramilitarism and gangsterism, involving activist groups engaged in "beef lynchings" and preventing—often by terminal measures—intercaste marriages and what is called love jihad.[18] The new normal has fostered a culture of pronounced assaults on free speech, summary killings of left and liberal intellectuals, murders of journalists, condemnations of mainstream media, and systemic attacks on Dalits, Muslims, Christians, LGBTQ+ people, and students. A pathologized urban patriarchy, bolstered by social factors like the catastrophic gender ratio in northern states like Haryana, Rajasthan, or UP, has birthed a trend of rape and macabre violence against women. Such lumpen energies are being ennobled and recruited, in alarming measures, by a moral engine of Hindu cultural vigilantism. The Modi government, in concert with the extraparliamentary organizations of the Sangh Parivaar, has organized and abetted the undermining of educational institutions at the level of culture, curriculum, and freedom of speech. It has made significant advances toward the "Saffronization" of the bureaucracy, media, police, and the judiciary, plus key autonomous institutions like India's Election Commission, the Reserve Bank of India, and the Central Bureau of Investigation (CBI).

These invoices for a Hindu-normative, strong statism did not arrive with Modi. Indeed, many of them were already at work in various degrees throughout the 1990s and were very much present or incipient during the decade-long rule of the Indian National Congress–led United Progressive Alliance (UPA) between 2004 and 2014. The presiding image of Modi, as decisive leader, is in many ways a figural congealment of a long-incubating decisionist desire of the Indian ruling elite in the wake of liberalization, the Hindu Bomb, and impending superpower status. As a human manifestation of this desire, Modi may be seen to have radically aggravated or accelerated such tendencies. He has merely globalized feelings and statements that were already present as a voluble discursive murmur. In this order of masculinist temper and paranoia, the minority may never be perceived as a small number enclosed within the given borders of the nation-state; the minority is that which renders the Hindu triumphant as well as endangered.[19] "*Hindu khatre mein hain*"—the Hindu, despite constituting almost 80 percent of the Indian population, is perpetually in peril because the minority is always suspiciously worldly, working as fifth columnists or merchants of terror for the global Caliphate or a transnational Vatican plot. The minority, in other words, is much like the Jew of early twentieth-century Europe, seen to be working in secret toward a Hebrew domination of the world. The Dalitbahujan, meanwhile, is a pathological betrayer or an easily tempted juvenile who is always an outward-looking potential convert. On the other hand, this persistent angst of the twice-born is accompanied by a bipolar celebration in our times that may be affiliated with Arendt's "party above all parties" model. It pertains to a brave new BJP declaration of a *Congress mukt Bharat*, an India eventually free of the INC and the secular socialist-liberal ethos of the passive revolution it represents.[20]

It is, however, necessary to distinguish the person Modi from this new will to leadership and homogeneity, much in the same manner in which Marx separated the ordinary individual from his iron death mask of power in the *Eighteenth Brumaire*. This mantle of leadership is created through a historical alignment of forces, mutations in structures of power and class interests, in a particular Indian conjunction of urbanization and neoliberal development. Modi repeatedly insists on his humble roots and his *fakir* (ascetic) disposition in public speeches; he speaks of the "leader" only when he speaks of himself in the third person. The leader is constituted not just by his talk, but also by his emphatic silence—in this case, when it comes to public lynchings, threats, murders, and other atrocities committed in the name of protecting cows, preserving caste honor, and keeping minorities and women in place. The leader is not at all diminished by his failure to keep his men in check, since, as Arendt explains, a movement with a totalitarian impulse is not supposed to be managed well. The movement can move only with surplus energy in its burning edges, operating beyond the limits of constitutional ethics, morality, or law. It must be guided by immanent will, and not by the finitude of words or the clarity of orders. The power of the leader begins exactly where his secrecy and reticence begin; and he is to exercise that secrecy in broad daylight. Professional experts, academics, the media, or the secret service cannot say anything new about the Pakistani intelligence services (ISI), resident antinationals, or Muslims that the leader does not already know better. The leader's silence is therefore meant to evacuate the language of institutions. The emptiness is then occupied by the clamor of his radical supporters, calling for a total destruction of habitual norms and categories. Vulgarity, nihilistic iconoclasm, and ressentiment must become the rule if the movement is to preserve its shock appeal.[21] In this register of massification, the desire to curate new realities must become one with the desire to escape from reality. As a result, nothing can be judged as lies within the cult of the leader, because all sayings are prophetic, beyond contemporary experience and existing frameworks of validation and reasoning. These include claims about the economy, governance, security concerns, as well as a special set of memorable pronouncements made to the Indian public in recent times: that some kind of internet and social media existed in the age of the Mahabharata, that cows have radioactive horns, and that the elephant-headed Hindu god Ganesha was the product of ancient organ transplant technology.[22] These remain lies only until the inevitable Vedic moment when Western history as well as science are revealed to be forgeries and the entire modern framework of truth, justice, and equity explodes. That aside, what can be identified as mendacity or doublespeak on the part of the leader becomes strategically essential to the devoted, meant to delude treacherous renegades and deadly enemies.

I want to theorize these different forces in the Hindu fold—the pastoral RSS, the parliamentary BJP, the still-extant Gita Press, or the provincial Karni Sena—in terms of a new diagram of sovereign power. That is, in terms of a networked relationship in which they are no longer defined by their distributions in a historical landscape but by their informational synergy. This dispensation is Hindutva 2.0 as a form of advertised modernization. It is an ecology that does not dialectically resolve traditional disputes between Hindu parties themselves or between them and their opponents. Rather, it manages arguments, tensions, and embattled desires to precipitate a new metropolitan Hindu normal. This is a resonance machine (rather than an enclosure or echo chamber) whose affective powers and flows increasingly redefine the state of Indian secularism and compel even enemies to participate in a center that it creates like the eye of a storm. To the Dalit, especially the elite sections of Dalit communities, it offers the tempting prospect of finally being part of a majoritarian Hindu identity in times of tumult, terror, and precarity. This atmospheric Hinduness—a new dynamic regulation of signs and references—pertains to that paradigm shift that the BJP leader L. K. Advani perhaps had in mind when he declared after the destruction of the Babri Masjid in 1992, "Now all parties have to respond to us."[23]

Hindutva 2.0 is therefore a figuration of informational power that brings together a Hindu sense of being and a neoliberal credo of development. It gives that assemblage itself an aura of religiosity and destination. Hindutva 2.0 does this by bringing matters that were once incommensurable into a new state of concert. It weds paternalism with technocracy, syncs fakiri with finance, and merges doxa with science by orchestrating opposing propositions on a pure plane of the advertised. Such a dispensation essentially does not have a unified "subject" at the heart of its operations. It does not necessarily cure all forms of unhappy consciousness in opposing parties: conservative angst about Westernization, for instance, or, on the other side, the urbane, technocratic Hindu's unease with hard-core Manuvaad. Nor does it foster an actual organic Hindu unity by resolving the issue of caste. Instead, the logic of the majoritarian normal seeks to furnish the mass perceptual prisms and terms of engagement when it comes to older ideological wars about class, gender, caste, ethnic identities, nation, memory, myth, progress, science, aesthetics, justice, or terror. Hindutva 2.0 is thus a plane of consistency and transmission, an informational enrollment of Indian thought and feeling amid the welter of the neoliberal profane, centering itself upon what Andrew Murphie has called the "ontogenetic politics of cognition."[24] It presumes a neuropolis of populations—rather than a historical city of peoples—when it comes to representation, self-determination, or *thymos*. Unlike past forms of the habitually Hindu normative secular, this normal sustains itself on industrialized instincts of jealousy and anxiety.

The Rise to Power of Narendra Modi as a Media Phenomenon

Let us be a little more illustrative at this point and turn to two public instantiations of Hindutva 2.0 as advertised modernization. The first is the media construction of Modi himself as a messianic figure invested with millennial expectations. The second one has to do with the informational wind behind Modi that raised him to power in 2014 following what, in the Indian context, was the first campaign conducted along the lines of American presidential elections. Both of my invocations will be figural and therefore brief, without detailed analyses of them as parallel historical processes. The image of Modi here is especially important, as a "brand" in itself, since its affective powers clearly extend beyond the traditional Sangh Parivaar ideological axiomatic. It is now an accepted truism that the BJP with Modi and without him are two significantly different political propositions.

Modi's political rise began when he, until then a relatively obscure general secretary in the Gujarat unit of the BJP, rose to the chief ministerial position in 2001 almost by default. This was followed, shortly after, by the notorious massacre in Gujarat, a systematic bloodbath inflicted on Gujarat's Muslim population across a hundred and fifty urban centers and close to a thousand villages from the end of February to the first few weeks of April, 2002.[25] If one went by broad estimates offered by more than forty human rights groups, more than 2,000 people lost their lives. Countless others were raped and maimed, and about 150,000 were rendered homeless with their properties and means to a livelihood destroyed. The phenomenon was a torrid activation of what has been called the "institutionalized riot system," which had come into being after the Babri Masjid demolition, and it was the first anti-Muslim pogrom in which the propertied middle classes took an active role. It was also the first Indian genocide to take place as a media event, coming after the arrival of 24-hour news and the mass usage of cell phones.[26] Conversely, the traditional defense from the Hindu right was that the slaughter was the result of a spontaneous overflow of powerful Hindu emotions after the Godhra incident, in which a train compartment of the Sabarmati Express was allegedly set on fire by Muslim arsonists on February 27, 2002, killing 59 Hindu pilgrims (*karsevaks*).[27] It was further said that Modi, who would later emerge as a decisive leader who exercises absolute control over his administration, was helpless to prevent the carnage that went on for weeks, with active aid of the state machinery. Modi, for his part, would later say in a media statement prior to the 2014 elections that he did not feel guilty about the massacres in Gujarat. He felt sad, as one would feel if a car ran over a puppy.[28]

Back in 2002, the Indian metropolitan elite had reacted with pious outrage immediately after the mayhem.[29] It was bad for the nation's image and, as venerable industrialists like Ratan Tata reminded people, bad for business. However, in the years that followed, Modi emerged as a messiah of development, armed with sophisticated perception management machinery. He became a genial man of humor and vision to the urban chattering classes. The media also transformed him into a fashion and yoga icon. Modi courted celebrities and the filthy rich; he hosted "Vibrant Gujarat Summits" to invite capital, and floored erstwhile critics like Tata with astounding business proposals, offering soft loans from the state exchequer at 0.1 percent interest and land at below-market prices, often displacing fishermen and farmers, at steep ecological cost and in frequent contravention of the state's own laws for the acquisition of *gaucher* (grazing) land. This was touted as the now-fabled Gujarat Model of development. The media was largely silent while Gujarat's state debt was trebling as this was going on. It did not matter that development in Gujarat was essentially top-down; that, for a traditionally rich state, it had relatively shocking poverty levels; that it scored poorly in terms of Human Development Indices, hunger rates, child malnutrition, and minority protection and prosperity. That thousands of farmers, pastoralists, fishermen, Dalits, and tribals had their home and work habitats destroyed, or that around sixteen thousand of such utterly precarious and disposable people had committed suicide in the course of Modi's tenure.[30] What would also progressively diminish in terms of recall value were the documents of 2002, the mountain of evidence pertaining to systemic witness and victim intimidation, and summary "encounter" killings by the Gujarat Police for years following the genocide.[31]

During the campaign season for the 2014 elections, the electronic and print media was quite brazen in its bias. Apart from the wholesale support from Network 18, which belonged to ardent Modi supporter and billionaire industrialist Mukesh Ambani, Modi was in general accorded a wildly disproportionate 32 percent of the coverage. Arvind Kejriwal of the Aam Aadmi Party (AAP; Common Man's Party) came in a distant second with 10.3 percent of reporting and Rahul Gandhi third with 4.3 percent.[32] Modi was barely fact-checked, and his repeated factual howlers were not just given easy passes but often invested with what the American comedian Stephen Colbert has called "truthiness." This happened when Modi mixed up dates and figures, or when he said that women in Gujarat were malnourished because they chose to be slim. This temperamental man, known to have walked out of nationally broadcast television interviews in the past upon being questioned about the atrocities in Gujarat, was pampered, choreographed, and fawningly advertised in media engagements. The Indian media in general and the American image-management firm APCO imbued Modi with a crucial Teflon quality. He was cleansed not just of the blood of Gujarat, but also of other issues, like allegations that he used the state machinery to spy on a young woman or, for that matter, stories about the wife he had abandoned in his younger days.

The "Modi wave" was consolidated, accentuated, and amplified from the major cities to the small, midcaste, middle-class townships that were entering the aspirational universe of globalization through shopping malls, broadband, and multiplex theaters. This was done by projecting him personally as a transformational figure, rather than the BJP in general as a claimant to the anti-incumbency sentiment. The epic election campaign involved 437 mass rallies, for which Modi was flown across a distance totaling seven times the circumference of the planet on private jets provided by industrialists like Gautam Adani. These were supplemented by 200 "Namo Raths" (vehicles equipped with 54" LCD screens), which visited 19,000 villages in Uttar Pradesh to show recorded speeches, as well as by video conferencing outreach drives in which the humble, former tea-seller Modi interacted with common people in 4,000 tea stalls across 24 states.[33] Two studios were set up in Delhi and Gandhinagar for a massive "shock and awe" campaign, as journalist Rajdeep Sardesai described it, for which 3D hologram technology was procured from the British company Musion. If the sheer number of rallies at which Modi spoke was impressive, what was more impressive was the fact that millions of people in more than a thousand other locations were "touched" by the magical projection of his three-dimensional electronic image, like the coming down to earth of a distant god.[34]

The key to Modi's victory was a campaign which involved a grassroots-level informatization and a fine techno-calibration of messages, target populations, and spaces by the "IT cell" of the BJP. The aforementioned massive populist mobilizations and grand symbolic gestures were complemented by policing, trolling, propagandizing, and myth-marketing on social media and in the Twitterverse. In select places, Modi played up his lowly Teli caste background; in upper-caste areas he did not mention it. The poor were reminded that Modi was once a humble tea vendor, while to the wealthy he was sold as an apostle of development; to the frugal middle classes as a beacon of "minimum government, maximum governance," and a bulwark warrior with a fifty-six-inch chest who would keep Pakistan in its place. To the public in general, which was tired of financial scandals, Modi promised to confiscate and repatriate black money from offshore accounts.

Hard-core Hindutva was used selectively, especially in western Uttar Pradesh, around the carnage grounds of Muzaffarnagar, to alienate the powerful Jats from their traditional Muslim and Dalit allies.[35] Indeed, the campaign itself followed a classic pattern of doublespeak. While powerful sections of the media were working assiduously to clean up the image of the man once known as the butcher of Gujarat, foot soldiers were out and about, periodically reminding people of core friend–enemy relations. Subramanian Swamy, a right-wing economist trained at Harvard, announced that it would be correct to take away voting rights from those Muslims who did not acknowledge their Hindu ancestry. The BJP leader Giriraj Kishore declared that Indian citizens opposed to Modi should be sent to Pakistan.[36] At the end it was this precision campaigning that maximized the seats from a relatively modest vote share. It was a campaign that borrowed its central promise—"*Achche Din*" (Good Days)—from a landmark cola advertisement: "Happy days are here again."

This was an electronic mobilization that, in terms of critical breadth and penetration, would not have been possible in the general elections of 2009.[37] In the Indian media landscape of 2009, there had been 584.32 million cellular phones, with 192.88 million of these in rural areas; and there were 16.8 million internet subscribers, including 8.77 million broadband users. By 2014–15, there were almost a billion mobile phone users, with 377.73 million of them in villages; and the number of internet subscribers had grown exponentially to 251.9 million, with revised broadband (512 kbps) users numbering 60.87 million.[38] A significant chunk of the population—among urban elites as well as from the midtown, midcaste quarters—had taken to social media with passionate intensity. With novel forms of sociability, the electronic commons birthed new interactive networks which cut across lines of religion, caste, trade, region, kinship, and ethnicity. These were electronic abstractions that rose above traditional barriers and set up new avenues of ideological and affective commerce between the Anglophone world and the vernaculars, and between the country and the city. It was a new congregational plane, animated by instantaneous and wide dissemination, beyond stigmas of touch, food, liquor, or custom. It was audible and imagistic beyond the protocols and institutions of the lettered city. Marked by speedy information flows and feedback loops independent of traditional institutions of news and veracity, here one could freely disperse affects and expressions without disciplinary enunciation or narrative form. This was, in a sense, a great liquidation of the hardened pathways for stories and statements, in a new metropolitan order in which the historical city had been redrawn by virtual lanes of data and information flow, and in which the virtual urban diagram itself had been stretched to the countryside. In this realm of capital as information and emotion industry, all things solid tended to melt into ether.

For many pundits, the election of 2014 was game-changing because the singular charisma of Narendra Modi had effectively nullified a theory that had become a truism: that the immensely pluralistic India was, essentially, a coalition.[39] With this absolute majority, the polity would no longer be mired in that long tradition of king making, ideological compromises, backroom deals, horse trading, and common minimum programs. The ironclad figure of Modi was thus a congealing of the long-gestating decisionist desires of a metropolitan Indian elite that had, in the past, hedged their bets in terms of inevitably hung parliaments. Now, circa 2014, a significant portion of them invested tremendous emotional and financial resources behind a single man. It is of course immensely difficult to envision and describe a pan-Indian formation that operates as a homogenous ruling class, but what I intend to do here is abstract two broad figurations of power across the feudal-bourgeois spectrum that might offer a glimpse of a Modi constituency beyond the traditional BJP-RSS flock. In other words, a passionate group that draws both from politics and from an aversion to politics.

For crucial reasons, the ascension of Modi appeared to be a dream scenario for the industrial elite, the financial aristocracy, and the professional, urban middle classes beholden to them. Let us bring these otherwise disparate groups under the umbrella term *Gentoo*. Historically, as we know, this word derives etymologically from the Portuguese *gentio* that designated the pagan; it was used by most early European colonial administrations specifically to refer to the "Hindu" population, as distinguished from Islamic groups. Here I use it to mark an educated, Anglophone, techno-financially oriented Indian population that is strongly Hindu-normative in its bearings without necessarily being cadres of the BJP or the wider Sangh Parivaar. In other words, the contemporary Gentoo is the classy Indian (male) who would like to finally bury his Gandhian, Nehruvian, and other differentially pagan ancestors and realize a destinying tryst with gentility and gentlemanliness, now understood in neoliberal terms. The lot of the Gentoo is a many-armed coalition of comprador and traditionalist urban forces, dominated by Savarna powers but often including other community elites. The Gentoo—despite existentialist predilections of many kinds—would like to consolidate a national life and language of metropolitan Hinduness. That is, he would like to reinvent an urban "Hindu" way of life that can, in the fullness of time, seamlessly merge with the civic religiosity of contemporary market structures. He stands committed—often with distinct spiritual fervor—to a specter of globalized "development." He yearns for a long-awaited historic emergence from the "waiting room of history" (after overcoming the final historical roadblock of Nehruvian socialism) and find a place in the sun. This desire comes with a feisty, irascible impatience, without any guaranteed tempering by way of classic liberal bourgeois ethics.

I therefore use the term *Gentoo* in a sense slightly different from that of Dipankar Gupta, who has marshalled the word to identify a "westoxicated" elite (rather than a westernized one) in the general arc of India's Anglophone modernity.[40] In terms of specific timelines, the Gentoo I have in mind gestates from the time of the Emergency and comes to his own after liberalization. He is thus the historical progeny of the new middle class that—as Arvind Rajagopal has pointed out—was birthed by the state in the 1980s in order to create and consolidate a new desire for statism. This was a class that would identify communication as a central feature of the coercion or consent question, affirm a perpetually Caesarist character of the Indian state, and replace the old Nehruvian theme of "national integration" with the maturing vision of a Hindu India. For Rajagopal, the specter of "soft emergency" in state activism, impelled by memories of 1975–77—including grand technocratic welfare schemes, strikes falling to record lows, record profits in private businesses, urban beautification, and forced sterilization—would now be the desired norm. Henceforth, state reasoning would enter the realm of publicity; visual and aural dramatization of the economy at work would become part of a new governmentality. That is, it would enter an increasingly informational arena where, unlike in the past, the state—with its Films Division and organs of radio and television—would no longer be the arch-archivist or documentarian. This new sphere of gradual electrification, computerization, and broadcasting would not be monopolized by the government, but would be a wider world increasingly dominated by the Hindu middle class.[41]

The other key figure that we may draw from the host of the eclectic Indian elite is that of the vernacular Dehat (rustic), who emerges from among the rich farmers and other privileged caste groups.[42] These latter classes usually do not see themselves as benefiting as much from free market reform and are against such measures unless they can extract heavy tributes out of them. This agrarian assemblage of forces—complicated as it is in terms of caste, class, and religious, regional, and linguistic affiliations—has, aside from preventing land reform since independence and ensuring perpetual surplus for the farmer capitalists, exerted myriad pressures of a "demand politics" on standard coalitionary formations at the federal level. The Dehats are habitually seen by Gentoos as entities who create a multitude of provincial and provisional sovereignties instead of an axiomatic one for India. From the original Jat Supremo Chaudhary Charan Singh to the big Yadavs Mulayam and Lalu of today, this particular prototype has been viewed by English-speaking urban India with bemused anthropological curiosity during the best of times and absolute fear and loathing during the worst. As a matter of fact, there is a metropolitan habit of addressing and judging the workings of the Dehat as Rajniti (statecraft), which, perhaps because of an incurable vernacularism and rustic crudeness of method, is not quite politics. 'Rajniti,' in common metropolitan understanding, is a word that is to be necessarily used as a pejorative with recidivist associations: feudalism, casteist chicanery, insular regionalism, and corruption. It is often adjudged to be that which forecloses or corrupts a metropolitan politics proper, in terms of discipline, circulation, and management. The fiscal sultanisms of the Dehat—patronage, tribute, extortion—hinder the smoothening of space and the rationalization of time in accordance with market efficiency and the historical consolidation of value exclusively as capital. Before Modi, the Gentoo had been resigned to the fact that his own class could never operate as a nationalist bourgeoisie but could only enter into provisional Gentoo-Dehat alliances in the great coalition of things. Too much navel-gazing was a luxury the Gentoo could ill afford, for it always came with the sneaky suspicion that there was, somewhere, a Dehat inside him as well.

Until 2014, the problem for the Gentoo was that, traditionally, he could exercise his influence on Indian politics largely through the upper house and the bureaucracy of the central government, as well as by controlling the rarefied echelons of the electronic and print media. As a result, when it came to actual heavy lifting of the political kind, the techno-financial Gentoos or their comprador underlings could not do without their intimate enemies. The Dehati masters of Rajniti had been, for the last three decades at least, the mass leaders of India, mobilizing the teeming millions of illiterates, the unwashed, and the poor. They were the ones who could get things done on the ground, while the Gentoo elite—as Frank Wisner, the former U.S. ambassador to India once pithily expressed—could only watch the real workings of Indian politics as a spectator sport. Yet Wisner's observation is only a half-truth, for what the Gentoo had hitherto done was precisely to ensure that politics remained a spectator sport, sufficiently isolated from core spheres of governance and bureaucratization in the Anglophone state.

Before 2014, the Gentoo never felt as if he had his own man at the center of things, one with absolute neoliberal commitment. But around that time, he saw in Modi something he had not seen in any other Indian politician in recent memory. Modi was a Dehat who could talk the talk of the Chicago boys and walk it as well. Even more promising was his endearing knack of vernacularizing the discourse of international finance in the Indian context. By conquering Delhi's Raisina Hill, and that too with absolute majority, he achieved what other "CEO" chief ministers of the past, such as Chandra Babu Naidu, had failed to do: translate regional appeal into pan-Indian mass popularity. And then, finally, judging from the manner in which he stymied the Parveen Togadia–led VHP forces in his home state of Gujarat, and then swatted the formidable L. K. Advani-Sushma Swaraj challenge to his leadership in the BJP itself, Modi looked like a man more than capable of keeping his own house in order. As a matter of fact, prior to his 2014 ascension, the BJP itself, as a political formation, was being described as a de facto conglomerate of six or seven state parties.[43]

We can postulate three kinds of Gentoo investment in the Modi wave of 2014. The first is the least interesting of the lot because it came from the Gentoo already committed to hard Hindutva. His was an unequivocal and unapologetic support backed by neoliberal economism, Savarna pride, and a primordial hatred for Islam. The second mode of Gentoo support was more nuanced, since this Gentoo imagined being Hindu as indistinguishable from a metropolitan way of life. Precisely for this reason, he perhaps remained uncomfortable with the doctrinaire religiosity of the Sangh Parivaar, especially when it came to rigid caste matters, the proscription of meat or alcohol, strictures against conspicuous consumption, and some measure of female emancipation. For such a Gentoo, the expectation in 2014 was that of a great, "postpolitical" abstraction, one by which a constellation of factors would allow Modi to operate only as a manager and not as a fascist. Categories like "fascist" or "communist," therefore, were essentially twentieth-century terms; in the present circumstances they operated, for all practical purposes, as empty signifiers in the shadow play that we call representational politics. Within the auspices of development (*vikas*), whether it was India's Modi or France's left-wing Hollande, all had to submit to a greater planetary administration of things.

The third archetypal Gentoo was the voter who insisted on defining himself as secular-neoliberal. That is, he was a fiscal conservative who did not consider himself to be a part of the Hindutva brigade, either in a religious sense or as a participant in an agenda of cultural nationalism. Without a doubt this third man was the Modi voter with the unhappiest consciousness and who never tired of announcing his support as provisional, even to the extent of it being a Faustian wager.[44] Unlike the second group, he did not believe in the pure abstraction of a managerial Modi and therefore admitted—to himself, at least—that a political price had to be paid. What he was unsure about was the magnitude of the price in the long run and the nation's ability to absorb it. Even as he committed himself to the celebration of a proper Thatcherite or Reaganite revolution in the Indian context, Gentoo III must have been worried by the fact that, for Modi, the model was neither Thatcher's Britain nor Reagan's America, but Deng Xiaoping's China or Lee Kuan Yew's Singapore.

The Modi campaign, as an instance of advertised modernization, functioned as a resonant monotheme of development that brought the three Gentoos in alliance with hitherto non-BJP Dehats who, no longer satisfied with the agrarian affluence and caste power of the older days, were looking to get a piece of the metropolitan pie. The Jats of Haryana and western UP and the Patidars of Gujarat, both agitating at the time for OBC status and affirmative action benefits, would be the prominent members of this latter group.[45] They thus joined traditional Hindutva voters in the Modi camp, along with vast swathes of India's millennial youth driven by the hope of techno-financial growth and jobs in the New Economy. As far as economic vision was concerned, in 2014, there was nothing much to choose between this monotheme of national advancement and the manifesto declarations of most opposing parties, including the Congress.

For the Indian elite, Modi was supposed to cut through the clamor and implement, with an iron hand, a Gentoo template of development that was already ready and waiting. He had to restore the investment cycle by replenishing institutions and creating infrastructure necessary for business. He had to make the Foreign Investment Promotion Board more dynamic and bring new stringency to intellectual property laws and patent rights. The strong leader had to cure India's ancient Nehruvian predilection for welfare and planning. He had to continue the informalization of work and the relaxing of labor protection laws, like the Industrial Disputes Act (1947), Contract Labor Act (1970), and Factories Act (1947). The use of raw state power to quell labor agitation—witnessed during the UPA years in the Sriram piston factory in Rajasthan or the Maruti car plant near Delhi—had to become the norm rather than the exception.[46] The neoliberal elite expected Modi to set aside ecological considerations and ease land acquisition even further for corporations and mining interests, especially by weakening Schedule 5 of the Constitution, which recognized and protected the way of life of tribal populations. Tax holidays aside, the Gentoo would be pleased if the next phase of gentrification in the big cities followed the Sabarmati Riverfront Project model in Ahmedabad, Gujarat, in which, over a decade, thousands of lower-caste and Muslim evacuees were removed from a newly rationalized urban space and safely ghettoized in policed suburbs.[47] In the same vein, Gentoos would welcome a more emphatic militarization of civic spaces in areas like Kashmir, the northeast, and heartland areas with rich mineral deposits.

The emergence of the image of Modi as a leader invested with millennial passions—cleansed of all moral or criminal responsibilities for the 2002 genocide—thus happened at a particular historical conjunction. It was one that included reconfigured class interests, an altered mediascape, a critical spread of virtual and real urbanization, and an overall middle-class and elite desire for turbocharged neoliberal growth. What was relatively new was that a former RSS *pracharak* (Proselytizer), with his clear ideological priorities and suspected pathologies, could now be readily admitted into the heart of this convergence. This was decidedly an augmentation of Hindu power in the raw, crossing an earlier threshold of "moderation" best represented by the BJP's pragmatic choice of the "softer" Atal Bihari Vajpayee over the radical L. K. Advani as the face of the party in the late 1990s. Modi's rise signaled a generational shift away from that dispensation. The desire for modernization had focalized a new will to sovereign exception and a majoritarian desire along economic, political, and cultural lines. This was a will beyond the tepid consensus of what Achin Vanaik had called the Hindu secular state. A critical portion of the Indian electorate was now ready to accept a social price for greater development by appending it, more emphatically than ever, to the ongoing agenda of the Sangh Parivaar. That is, India was now ready to tolerate a new normal of muscular Hinduness that would cast a perpetual shadow of expendability over Muslims, Dalits, women, and other minorities.

The Idea of Advertised Modernization

The rise of Modi as a media phenomenon merged energies of Hindu pride with the paraphernalia of techno-financial growth. It promised a Digital India with a hundred smart cities, millions of jobs in the New Economy, bullet trains, advanced militarization, and space research. It promised all of that in conjunction with a vision of greater authoritarianism that would, in time, radically transform democratic institutions, revise constitutional fundamentals, and unfold a new realm of common sense that would eclipse the dual legacies of Gandhian tolerance and Nehruvian secularism. This was the specter of a political monotheism that would merge a rapidly urbanizing Hinduness with a metropolitan economism. The state of the minority would, at every step, be determined in accordance with the terms of that merger. It was a picture that was not just acceptable to one third of a massive voting population, but affirmed with passionate religiosity.

I would like to begin this section by emphasizing something which should already be clear. First of all, Hindutva 2.0 is not reducible to Hindutva propaganda or "messaging," even though the latter are undeniably major components of the former.[48] The spectacular rise of Narendra Modi was an insurrection in a general field of electronic culture and politics resting on a bedrock of the Hindu normative. It was not just the outcome of traditional

Hindutva hegemony, but something motivated by new forms of desire, affectations, and terror. This is also why I have no interest in speculating here either on the durability of the BJP's electoral mandate or on Modi's own political future after 2019. The greater question, for me, pertains to the state of an overall Hindu modernization with a monotheistic bent that has eroded what Ambedkar once called "constitutional ethics," endangered the republic, and compromised as well as exposed the Indian secular.

Let me, at this point, properly locate the concept of advertised modernization and its changing dynamics in an informational world. There has always been information, but it was only in the last quarter of the twentieth century that it was electrified as a livewire principle of governance and sovereign power in and of itself. That is, in terms of human-computational synergies, we speak of a shift from a mainframe era of defense computing and bulky data processing to PC-dominated microprocessing and finally to our era of ubiquitous computing via the internet and other virtual technologies. This unfolds an epoch in which human anticipation is automated, greatly so, with the imminent arrival of further miniaturization through 5G wearable technology that promises to cover sensory operations as well as biopathological processes. As we know, in advanced metropolitan scenarios the micropunctuality of information technologies has birthed serious concerns as well as conspiracy theories about surveillance, privacy, truth, and democratic procedures.

In the realm of culture, the new order has prompted a convergence of content along with a divergence of hardware in the capitalistic production of social life itself. The digital has engulfed all vertical twentieth-century institutions like print, film, radio, or television. In a planetary "internet of things," Nike shoes now converse with iPhones. To many, this mid-twentieth-century dream of a total cybernetic reordering of society threatens to emerge as a full-blown Orwellian nightmare, featuring the Chinese government's use of facial recognition technologies to monitor citizens, Google's behavior prediction models, and governments' use of biometric data to target minorities and immigrants. A planetary security system driven by satellite imagery and drone technology tends to obliterate the temporal and spatial distinction between movements of war and those of policing. Media and culture become synonymous when the accelerated timeframe of the media tends to obliterate all other temporal imaginations. The future itself becomes one with the futurity of the media.[49] Meanwhile, the speed of information tends to compress memory and consolidate an absolute vision of the past.[50]

As such, this dispensation has been subject to fresh philosophical investigations by eminent minds, from Gilles Deleuze to Katherine Hayles.[51] The challenge here has been to understand a new temporal tension between humanity and technicity; it has been to account for a sense of disorientation that occupies a widening gap between technical systems and older principles of social organization. The intellectual trial has thus been to ask and endure again the Heideggerian question concerning technology without his conservative confusion of technicity as inevitable inauthenticity. This impulse, of secular philosophy meditating its own obsolescence in the age of information, may be traced back to the moment of Benjamin and Adorno, with their insightful witnessing of a return of aura and myth in the age of technological reproducibility and mass culture. They deduced a paradoxical socialization of technology by which the masses, as a condition of massification itself, could increasingly experience philosophy only as forms of faith.

Contemporary media ecology electrifies and opens out the previously enclosed institutional spaces that Foucault studied—the school, the prison, the clinic, and the army barracks. It ushers in an order of randomness and distraction to replace contemplation or disciplinary focus. In the modes of hyperlinked society, statist pedagogy can merge instantaneously with surveillance, therapy, religious evocation, consumer culture, or entertainment, and the spatial and temporal boundaries of the factory or the workday become redundant. The electronic city, like the bank, never sleeps. In its overall production of social life, capital, as screen-city or as nocturnal television, exploits not only the conscious and voluntary activity of the subject, but also the somnambulist energies of the mass. It solicits desire and affect at the level of preindividual erotics, as Amit Rai has theorized in relation to the Bollywood media assemblage. The new Indian urban sensorium, in Rai's work, comes into being at the point at which body and population meet.[52] Perception, as a Bergsonian principle, becomes a necessary and interested subtraction from a sea of mutations, durational intensities, and stochastic experiences of variously nested temporalities. As Derrida observed, "news," as a determinate local abstraction of "actuality effects" from dynamic and uncontrollable planetary flows, becomes "spontaneously ethnocentric."[53]

Bernard Stiegler understands this planetary regime as one of an industrial temporalization of consciousness and memory.[54] Mass information is osmotic, neurological, and operates, to a large extent, below the radar of human consciousness or Gestalt psychology. The idea of massification here is thus not the humanist predicament that Arendt postulated—that of an agglomeration of alienated individuals. Rather, it is one that works at a sensory level, in the first instance, in the erogenous zones between atomized bodies and majoritarian "lumped" populations—in other words, as an industrial erotics of elation, unease, anxiety, race instinct, or xenophobia. The accelerated speed, incessance, and volume of information flows are too much for the conscious citizen to process, and, in that light, democratic societies are seen to be increasingly dominated by tribes locked in cognitive bubbles rather than by publics. The radical aesthetic departures, incessance, and political relativisms of the age therefore come with a necessary "post-truth" specter to the tired and overwhelmed eyes of the modern. That is because planetary flows become unbound from the spatial and temporal limits of traditional institutions of authentication—the news agency, the government, civil society, or experts. The phenomenology of news becomes part of an overall movement of the "fake." The end of linear writing in the age of the hyperlink spells a profound crisis of the book form and a system of enlightenment founded on axiomatic governing entities committed to *veritas*: the Humboldtian academy, the great lexicographers, Diderot's *Encyclopedia*, the national academies of art, literature, and science, the national museum, the model Bibliotheca Augusta under Leibniz, and, in the twentieth century, public radio and television.

Information, in this contemporary scenario of dazzling speed and planetary compass, is therefore an aggravation of that old Benjaminian problem: it is already "shot through" with explanation and feeling.[55] If language, at every step, has to meditate on its own finitudes, information, as the instrumentalization of language, imperils the very notion of finitude. As a figuration of power, information is not to be confused with the technology-facilitated exchanges of gnosis, perception, or data among human communities, such as, for example, the worldwide electronic lines of solidarity that had been established with the protestors in Tahrir Square in the spring of 2010. There is no dearth of examples in the Indian scenario of communities using media technologies to empower themselves, especially in relation to cultures of feudal absolutism.[56] The essence of "information power," on the other hand—as capital pertaining to affect, emotion, or news industries—is nothing informative. The essence is an emotive "shooting through" of explanation rather than the explanation itself (which might be good or bad). There is thus, strictly speaking, no subject of information. The subjective is necessarily a slow, vernacular moral retraction or an agoraphobic recoil from a global whirlpool of counteracting industrial perceptions and memories. Massification of political will, in this scenario, becomes a matter of immanent flows of affects and disaffections between body and population.

It is perhaps because of this primary realization that a critical consideration of affect has deterritorialized regimes of the subject in psychoanalysis, ideology critique, phenomenology, and other domains of Cartesian humanism. That is, in spheres of humanist thinking about the subject that were marked by an assured hierarchy of the mind over body.[57] Instead, in affect theory, the political human may be reimagined in terms of a parallelism between the mind and the body, as Deleuze suggested via Spinoza. Affect as embodied psychosomasis therefore flouts a general Cartesian rule: that affection (*affectio*) is directly of the body, while affect (*affectus*) solely refers to the mind. For Deleuze, therefore, the idea of affect is to affirm the powers of the body beyond the knowledge we have of it, and the powers of the "mind" beyond the consciousness we have of it.[58] The critical considerations of embodiment and affect point to a neuropolitics of the twenty-first century in which multidirectional stimulations, attention spans, diversions, ennui, or boredom become potent political factors. To put it in colloquial terms, the micropolitics of media have, among other things, industrialized "gut feeling."

It is in this scenario that I propose advertised modernization as a particular stance of contemporary political gesturing. "Advertised" is obviously a conceptual metaphor here. We have long since adjusted ourselves to a certain civic indulgence of the phenomenon of the advertisement, as long as it deals with identifiable commonplace feelings and objects. That is, we accept its hyperbolic declarations about beer, clothes, or cars, without actually believing that such procurements will absolutely live up to their primary product promises, or contribute ancillary effects like improving one's love life or professional success rate. The advertisement is supposed to render an innocuous "take away," a "feel good" sensation, or, in some cases, a consumable fear. It is designed to fix an often intangible sense of prestige, pride, or belonging in relation to a particular brand. It is supposed to do so without narrative obligation to truth or closure and without reference to a realistic world-picture to formally authenticate its claims. The advertised is also, by its nature and terms of engagement, instinctively majoritarian.

This general phenomenon may be partially illuminated by the political lies of our times. In recent years, it has been a matter of scholarly and journalistic concern that politicians, especially right-wing demagogues from different countries, are growing used to lying with impunity. That is, with the full knowledge that they will be fact-checked—often in real time—and with the full realization that in a democratic and free public sphere, even their loyal followers will be exposed to discourses challenging or exposing those very lies. Let us call this the Trumpian lie, in honor of the man who, perhaps more than anyone else, has made this a matter of global concern. Trump-speak might often sound like the proclamations made by dictators, but in contemporary democratic ecologies of information, they do not actually operate as such. Unlike in cases of absolutely controlled totalitarian environments, they can be scrutinized and publicly called out. For the devoutly faithful Trump or Modi constituency, such oratorical transmissions have been operating as pure gestures advertising a new covenant between tradition and modernity, rather than as dialectical matters of an Aristotelian politics aimed at virtue, noble action, or means and best of ends. Advertised statements come already embalmed with an affective insulation of tribal authenticity and already having transcended ordinary questions of veracity and falsehood. They therefore come "from the heart," regardless of the words chosen, the policy details mangled, the mythologies floated, the dystopian nightmares invoked, or the hyperbolic claims made. The Trumpian lie arrives as a libidinal gesture of pleasure and perpetuation in perilous times. It functions in a scenario of assurance in which there may be an insiderist convergence between the political podium and reality television in a cult of race and class nativism.

The Trumpian lie does not exhaust the broader political phenomenon of advertised modernization. As "frontal" gestures of solicitation, they are a very small segment of such ecologies. In order to understand this, we need to update the concept of advertising itself, from its twentieth-century incarnation in the age of industry and vertical institutions of mass culture to an order of convergence marked by nondirectional flows between platforms, instant audience migrations, and corporate cooperation. That is, from a moment in the 1960s when advertisers could reach 80 percent of U.S. women with a prime time slot on three networks to the mediaverse of scattered, horizontal dispersals in which the same content would have to run on a hundred channels to gather nearly as many eyeballs.[59] In the age of the hyperlink and the industrial temporalization of consciousness, advertising does not work according to David Ogilvy's "push model" anymore.[60] Campaigning becomes interactive, driven by continuous feedback loops and data processing, operating between partial attention and complete immersion. It becomes a matter of acquiring "lovemarks" across a range of media "touch points," blurring the lines between entertainment and product placement, and passing the brand through a circuit of emotive experiences.[61] This, in a sense, is the cultivation of "Google juice" or positive patterns of linkage in "pull media" like the internet, where it is the public that seeks out information and decides which news should rise to the surface. Contemporary campaigning involves navigating a sea of variables, no longer under expert editorial control, in order to achieve a workable signal-to-noise ratio. It is about infusing the brand into the overall picture of a secure metropolitan life worth living.

Advertising in the digital age is therefore an enterprise that ideally looks to reduce the purely informative, the purely pedagogic, or the purely doctrinaire to degree zero of top-down execution. As Rai points out, the generic fifteen- or thirty-second ad has reached the end of its shelf life. The future belongs to uninterrupted branding of digital content "that integrates the marketing interval into the attention of consumers contagiously."[62] The aim, accordingly, is to insert and circulate informative or doctrinal particulars immanently, in a wider realm of infotainment which, in itself, is a chaosmos of industrial attention and diversion. Branding becomes a matter of controlled chaos, leveraged in order to achieve critical densities of affect, recall value, or regularities of reference. The keywords in advertising jargon therefore become the microsegment, the mosaic, the hide and seek, or the creation of "affinity spaces" for visitors who are "loyals," "zappers," "minglers," or "casuals."[63] This playfulness is achieved not just by negating rival clusters of energy, but also by "piggybacking" on others, and entering into synergies with others still. The advertised, in an ideal form, should therefore merge with the pulsations of the city itself, its forms of customary life, and its horizons of expectation. This, in other words, is the paralogous line of thought I am tracing: a monotheme of Hindutva 2.0 that no longer operates simply by way of a real congregation of believers and the categorical exclusion of infidels and apostates, but rather in virtual affinity spaces that cut across older dividing lines between the caste Gentoo and the caste Dehat.

The thought of the "Modi brand" and Hindutva 2.0 as a contemporary political monotheism for a virtual Hindu congregation involves just such an advertised realignment between tradition and the modern. It may be understood, after Rancière, as the informational distribution of the Brahminical sensible.[64] The energies in this distribution may "touch" upon the diverse works of the world contagiously, without enclosing them into the truth of a singular and realist Hindu metafiction. This is exactly what gives Hindutva 2.0 an affectional latitude, a nonobligatory flippancy and verve that the older discourse of Hindu nationalism lacked. That older revivalist discourse, as we have seen in the case of the Gita Press for example, struggled to subsume the modern disciplines and the physical sciences into an apex Hindu vision. It had to world the caste question afresh in an altered universe of rights, freedoms, and irreverent democratic tempers. It attempted, at every turn, to reconcile mythology with history, science, and realism, or theodicy with justice. Such discursive efforts—rarely sublime, often ludicrous—have had a long history and continue to this day. However, in this new ecology, they acquire fresh powers of particularization and shooting through.

The Tripura Chief Minister Biplab Deb's recent assertion that some sort of internet existed during the age of the Mahabharata, is, in that sense, no different from the postulates that have regularly come up in Hindu discourse, right from the moment of the Calcutta or Poona revivalists.[65] The difference, however, is that Deb's comment arrives in an informational environment saturated with random Hindu emotives. This ecology of audacity and indulgence offers instant transmissions between town and country, Sanskrit and the vernacular, between the Bhagwad Gita and labor management, or between Vedic cosmogony and astrophysics. The energies of Hindutva 2.0 can, accordingly, advertise a new Hinduness by curving around, piggybacking on, or assembling with a much wider spectrum of objects and postulates than in the past. It can thus bravely "touch upon," without obligation, many matters that traditional Hindu nationalist discourse has either avoided or approached gingerly. It can make Deb's statement itself Trumpian by placing it in a wider, but increasingly homogenous spectrum of neurosis and laughter. The specter of the majoritarian normal becomes apparent exactly when we realize that there are indeed available "Hindu" ways—both city-slicker and rustic—of taking Deb seriously, indulging him, making fun of him, or even dismissing him altogether. It is this stance of the advertised that I will illustrate in a wider realm of culture, this time in terms of "Bollywood" as affect industry.

The Bollywoodization of Hindutva

I began the previous section by outlining an ethereal diagram of power, the scenario of a total cybernetic rewriting of species life dreamt up by idealists like Claude Shannon, Norbert Weiner, or Nicholas Negroponte. It is undeniably a sensationalist and scandalous picture of a global electronic Big Brother. It would be quite fair to ask to what extent this metropolitan diagram is pertinent to contexts like India, where vast swathes of a population of 1.3 billion belong to what Manuel Castells has called the fourth world on the other side of the digital divide.[66] I have two defenses to justify my invocation. The first is that information as power is neither a selective outcome nor a reflection of capital. It is money circulating as capital. The informational is money in its pure form as a mental relation rather than the coin, as Marx presciently observed in the *Grundrisse*.[67] As a mode of planetary governmentality, it operates through distant metropolitan terminals and immanent, networked pressure points of investment, copyright, lawfare, speculation, surveillance, militarization, or debt control. It would be an error to limit its pertinence to a positivistic terrestrial sociology of its operations. Information virtualizes; it abstracts and transforms life processes into capitalizing data at a planetary level. It does not enclose or occupy space, but it solicits, presses, and controls. It can render entire populations and forms of life disposable by way of long-distance speculations, remotely controlled "structural adjustments," or, in a more elementary manner, by predator drones. The pertinence of this metropolitan diagram of power in the era of globalization therefore lies in the fact that all traditional societies have to respond to it in various ways. Without information, or access to it, there is increasingly no money, recognition, or security. Perhaps the rice farmers in Luzon and the hungry populations of Ethiopia or Sudan know this instinctively, without tracking the intricacies of tariff walls, deregulated speculation on commodity futures, oil prices, national debts, or the leasing of arable land to foreign powers. People largely prevented from entering the digital age in Turkmenistan, Eritrea, or North Korea are, likewise, invested with new forms of loneliness.[68] The Islamic State, cornered and almost extinguished in western Asia, has now virtually tweeted its bases to Burkina Faso and the southern Philippines.

My second defense has to do with a specific elite Indian imagination, one that pictures information technology as transformational power of the messianic kind. As Ravi Sunderam or William Mazzarella have pointed out, e-governance has had a magical ring in the Indian political imagination, in terms of traversing the "last mile" and solving the impasse between middle-class globalization and grassroots resistances to it.[69] E-governance, in that sense, has been viewed as that power that will lead to the proper invention of the techno-financial Indian state and effect what Marx would call the real subsumption of capital. Ergo, there has been a persistent tendency to look at the historical differences between town and country, between north and south, or the heartland and the periphery as essentially problems of communication. Within the auspices of what Mazzarella calls the "charisma of the new media," the picture of a digital transcription of the statistical state and the colonial bureaucracy—from land records to weather reports—arrived with the religious fervor of purifying the corrupt and balancing the uneven. It came with a Gentoo desire to reboot history and subsume Dehati nonsynchronous temporalities into the neutrality of net time. This overall yearning for absolute transparency, security, and frictionless delivery systems inflects heated present-day debates about the biometric database–linked Aadhar Card issued by the Unique Identification Authority of India (UIDAI) and the Digitization of the National Register of Citizens (NRC) in the state of Assam to distinguish the citizen from the immigrant or infiltrator. The desire for a total cybernetic rewriting of uneven Indian realities was on vivid display in the aftermath of the Indian demonetization of 2016.[70] What was illuminating was one of the many defenses mounted by the Modi government and technocracy at the time. It was declared that demonetization was strong medicine to bring about a digital or cashless India.[71] Hundreds of millions of people, suddenly rendered precarious and unable to access their own money held in banks, were, in effect, being told not just to get cell phones, but also to smarten them up. It was an elite demand for a bold leap in time, since the nation, at that point, had less than 30 percent smart phone penetration. Such pronouncements were in stark contrast to that other temporal imaginary simultaneously at play in other parts of India, one in which people remembered their ancestors and abandoned the money form altogether. They had temporarily returned to the economy of barter.

The aura of informational financialization was one that the Gentoo had instantly warmed to. An emboldened nationalist imaginary, in the wake of globalization, deemed it vital for a spiritual unification of the country itself, and then for the extension of that virtual nation to the diaspora. In political debates and culture wars, this phenomenon has often been understood as an interface between an Anglophone India and a vernacular Bharat. Advertised modernization is a form of publicity that tends to informationalize the ontological distance between the two. "India" is therefore to diagnose, manage, archive, electrify, and digitally rewrite Bharat. Hindutva 2.0 is a shorthand for how this will to majoritarian identity sets up a plane of urban caste Hindu normalcy as the default position from which anarchic transmissions in the world are to be uniformly absorbed and reckoned with. In doing so, Hindutva 2.0 also naturalizes an updated Hinduness as the only natural and viable stance of competitive patriotism that globalization inevitably calls for. It advertises a spectral metropolitan India where the ambitious Gentoo and the aspiring Dehat can meet, overcome their sectarian jealousies, and a purported national being can merge with a singular monotheme of techno-financial progress. This is also why Hindutva 2.0, as a resonance machine, must operate with greater amplitudes than the traditional discourse of Hindutva. It must "touch upon" a greater paraphernalia of the profane—boundless capitalism, conspicuous consumption, technology and science, certain measures of cosmopolitanism, and so on—that earlier, more austere Hindu fathers were circumspect about.

Beginning in 1991, Indian cultures began to absorb the transformational impacts of globalization, the pulsations of a transnational media universe, and the million allures of a world of consumer goods. By May 2007, India was posting its highest growth figures (9.4 percent) in more than two decades. This was a new form of urban development—involving financialization, technocratic governance, information networks, post-Fordist manufacturing, dynamic supply chains, and the industrialization of agriculture—that was besieging the countryside as well as transvaluating spaces of the historical city. Such transformations created Fortune 500 hubs like Gurgaon out of sleepy feudal hamlets like Gurgram.[72] It led traditional Kannadigas of Bangalore or Marathas of Mumbai to feel differentially excluded by a new cosmopolitan gentrification that tended to erase the historical striations of the city—the caste enclaves, the refugee colonies, the slums built on land claimed from the sea, or the informal nooks of immigrant survival—into smooth and secure spaces of prime real estate.[73] Multiplex and shopping mall cultures penetrated small towns and midsized cities along with the cell phone and the internet. The era birthed many Existentiells of accelerated time and space; it congealed local cosmologies of desire as well as sharp abomination and unease. On the one hand, globalization threatened to erode traditional forms of privilege, or at least to render them precarious. On the other, there was the increasingly popular and fervent technocratic desire for nuclear superpowerdom and big-time growth.

There have been many significant studies detailing the rapid media transformations in India during this era.[74] I will thus not provide an exhaustive account of that story and will limit myself to a few pertinent headlines for the uninitiated, if only to underscore the breathtaking dimensions and accelerations of the spread. The story of the electronic expansion of the public sphere should begin in the early 1980s, around the time of the Delhi Asian Games of 1982 and the launching of the INSAT-1A and -1B satellites. Doordarshan, the state-owned terrestrial network, would grow exponentially in the next two decades, from 19 transmitters in 1982 to 1,041 in 1999.[75] This was the dispensation that created a significant hour of prime time religiosity during the telecast of the great epics *Ramayan* (Ramanand Sagar, 1987–88) and *Mahabharat* (B. R. Chopra, 1988–89). Cable television would enter the Indian skies in the early 1990s, around the time of the first Gulf War and the liberalization of the Indian economy. This would lead to a rapid extension and privatization of the televisual landscape within a very short interval. Indian television would go from a handful of state-owned channels on the eve of 1995 to around three hundred by 2008, with more than fifty 24-hour news portals operating in eleven languages.[76] This growth would continue unabated in the direct-to-home (DTH) and streaming eras.[77]

The epoch was marked by the corporatization of the culture industry, with big intercontinental mergers, such as that between Reliance Entertainment and DreamWorks SKG, and the coming into being of conglomerates like Network 18 or Essel. Meanwhile, Sony, Warner, Fox, Disney, and eventually Netflix would successively enter Indian markets through production and distribution arrangements.[78] The Indian media and entertainment industry would grow from $9 billion in 2005 to $22.3 billion in 2018. Indian advertising would emerge as the fastest growing in the Asian market after China, standing at $9.4 billion in 2018 and projected to double in the ensuing five years. There would be similar growth patterns in animation and VFX, gaming, FM radio, the music industry, multiplex screens, and advanced digital distribution systems like DTH and DAC (digital address cable) television. By 2018, Google's YouTube was projecting an Indian user base of 400 million people.[79] This transformational landscape of change was marked by an acute compression of time and space that in itself became a political phenomenon. In little more than a decade of the new millennium, India's tele-density had increased from 14 percent to 83 percent. From around 1992, information and communications technology (ICT), grew at 60 percent per year; in a single eleven-week span, from November 1999 to January 2000, it grew by 117 percent.[80]

Hinduism, as an industrial and marketable religion, acquired new powers of augmented presence in this dispensation. Today, it offers online Darshana of idols, virtual pilgrimages—such as a VR experience of the Kumbh Mela—remotely purchased rituals in Varanasi for the souls of ancestors or the atonement of sins, desktop deities, and a plethora of other activities hitherto hierarchically mediated by the priest and caste society.[81] The "postmodern" Hindu assemblage globally markets a variety of goods and services pertaining to "new religious" or motivational therapy, feel-good nostrums, pop philosophy, yoga, Ayurvedic, lifestyle products, Vaastu, gemstones, and astrology.[82] It features a bevy of jet-setting celebrity god-men with multimillion-dollar incomes and global spiritual empires. The Vedic market includes designer real estate, interior decoration, education, hospitality, and tourism industries, as well as theme park projects. It has percolated through all avenues of culture, from techno music to animation, advertising, commodity culture, or graphic novels. It has readily adopted many modes of American televangelism and product marketing through 24/7 channels like Aastha TV or Sanskar TV.

All this aside, overseas Hinduism has been able to accomplish mergers that the forbidding walls of insular cultures did not allow in the past. Arvind Rajagopal has illustrated this ecumenical aspect of a globalizing Hinduism by citing the Shiva-Vishnu temple in Pittsburgh as a symptomatic assemblage.[83] This novel formation is one that closes the door on centuries of Shaivaite and Vaishnavite conflict and becomes emblematic of a desire to unite contrary strands of the faith into a cosmopolitan axiomatic. The temple rests on a mental geography created by hitherto unimaginable exports of matter and memory. The global Hindu of today locates the Shiva-Vishnu site in an extended realm of the Hindu spiritual by superimposing the holy cartography of the Triveni of Aryavarta, the confluence of the rivers Ganges, the Yamuna, and the mythical Saraswati, on Pittsburgh's Three Rivers Crossing of the Allegheny, the Monongahela, and the Ohio. This, of course would be in stark contrast to Savarkar's absolutism—that the Hindu could live elsewhere but not seek the sacred elsewhere. Increasingly, therefore, there seems to be a Hindu way of doing, feeling, and transporting everything metropolitan.

The ideology of Hindutva, too, has followed the same pattern and has come a long way from promoting a kind of Gandhian agrarian socialism in BJP's election manifestos of the 1980s. Today the Sangh Parivaar is global in its reach, with institutional circuits of money, ideas, commodities, and information extending well into the Indian diaspora on all continents.[84] It has made adjustments with finance capital and neoliberalism and, as the Modi campaign proved beyond any doubt, has become immensely media savvy. In the course of the last three decades, it has unleashed a pronounced Anglophone culture of its own, infusing an updated Hindu message and a majoritarian Gentoo normalcy across a spectrum of fields, including economic management, national defense, and science and technology.[85] Among other things, this transformation has been made possible by Hindutva's strategy of adopting the "think tank" model of the American right and garnering greater control over mainstream electronic and print media to compensate for its relatively sparse presence in the academy. In terms of international politics, the Hindu technocratic diaspora has sought to normalize a natural affinity between Hindu India, Trumpian white nationalism, and the right-wing Zionism of Israel's Likud Party against global Islamicism. This transnationalism and neoliberal economism have been balanced by a relentless parochial vigilantism of culture, involving agitations against artists like M. F. Hussain, condom ads, rock concerts, and a long line of films from *Fire* (1996) to *Padmavat* (2018).[86]

It is in this context that I want to illustrate a part of Hindutva 2.0 in terms of a "Bollywoodization" of the modern religion, the nationalist ideology, and its predicates in culture. That is, I want to demonstrate how these forces now operate within an overall immersive experience of the contemporary metropolitan digital order, birthing neo-Hindu versions of what Shanti Kumar has called the "unimaginable communities" of electronic capitalism.[87] This new virtual dispensation has fostered planetary Hindu publics and congregational forms that were historically 'unimaginable' in previous decades that were dominated by Gita Press–style print capitalism and the older culture industry, and marked by the caste-segmentation of spaces.[88] "Bollywood," as it has been understood in recent times, is a media assemblage which cuts across a variety of avenues: television, cinema, radio, travel, fashion, jewelry, music, consumer goods, event management, internet, cellphone ringtones, and advertising. As an urban resonance machine and sensorium, it strongly inflects shopping mall environments, marketing, and contemporary presentations of a brand India in general.[89] It infuses advertising energies into state overtures to the NRI (Non-Resident Indian) communities, international diplomatic missions, and state projects of cultural ambassadorship like the "India Everywhere" campaign in Davos, 2006.[90]

Bollywood's consumable India became central to the imagining of a rising nation-in-the-world, both in international spheres as well as in Gentoo self-perception. The primary objective of this machine was to market a key virtuality: the picture of an English-speaking, tech-savvy, 300-million-strong Indian middle class—democratic and non-Islamic—waiting to exhale in the neoliberal order. That is, when barely 5 percent of the Indian population would qualify as such—in terms of purchasing power, relative to developed markets—and when well over three quarters of the Indian economy belonged to the informal sector. This auratic construct of a technocratic class with a millennial vision was put in place not only to solicit foreign investment, but also to allow that class to speak fervently for the nation at large and to define its policy priorities. The media drive was, of course, overwhelmingly and disproportionately driven by a Gentoo elite. A study conducted in 2006 of journalists and decision makers in twenty-seven national Hindi and English media outlets revealed that 86 percent of them were from upper castes representing only 16 percent of the population—and none was a Dalit.[91] This class-caste consensus was also bolstered by a relatively new stratum of homogeneity and national narcissism, long after the language wars of the 1950s and 1960s. Robin Jeffrey, for instance, has observed that it was the age of cable television that made Hindi more acceptable to other parts of India.[92] This media dispensation also presumed colossal shifts in the linguistic map and in demographic distributions between town and country. The era of liberalization had witnessed unprecedented urbanization in India and an ebbing of the country's much vaunted historical pluralism. A recent survey by the Bhasha Research and Publication Centre, conducted under the leadership of G. N. Devy, has concluded that about 220 Indian languages have disappeared in the last fifty years; another 150 could become extinct in the next fifty.[93]

Elsewhere I have theorized the Bollywood cinema of the 1990s and after in terms of a geotelevisual and informational aesthetic with a pronounced high-Hindu ontology.[94] That is, as a cultural dispensation that absorbs the geotelevisual pressures of metropolitan globalization by setting up "advertised" relationships between them and the ethical postulates of "tradition." A template of Bollywood cinema was one among many modes by which Hindutva 2.0 absorbed and adjudged new sensations, hermeneutics of desire, and visions of vice that either had arrived or were out in the open: unapologetic consumerism, the profit motive, living overseas, premarital sex, adultery, or homosexuality. Bollywood thus represented a shift in gears from a more "protected" postindependence cinematic template which M. Madhava Prasad called the feudal family romance, a master genre that attempted to induct the wonders of the world—from James Bond to *Arabian Nights*—into the moral universe of the caste Hindu, North Indian, extended feudal clan.[95]

The visual and aural kinesis of the informational 1990s challenged and pressured the older moral economy from multiple directions. The challenges were on the grounds of aesthetics, propriety, austerity, permissiveness, and aspirations, in a globalized environment where desire was democratized, even if the means to it were not. The aphoristic energies of information strained older modes of ethical governance and narrative resolution. Hindi cinema thus adopted what is now known as the signature Bollywood style, involving sudden transportations to fantastic scenarios beyond the determined milieus of the story, or nonobligatory breakaways into MTV-friendly song and dance capsules. Then there was the introduction of opulent and utopian assemblages of "home"—"panoramic interiors" as Ranjani Mazumdar calls them—that merged visions of richness, consumerism, or techno-fetishism with a spectacular staging of ritualistic Hindu life.[96] Bollywood cinema, in that sense, reserved a space for the purely advertised, a space beyond the control of contextual storytelling. This was a zone of affects and immersions celebrating a spectral form of life that connected metropolitan India across cultures and languages to the diaspora and the world.

The infusion of the nondirectional powers of advertised modernization began at the level of colors, saturations, textures, magical transportations, luminosities, and sonorous resonances. In most cases, they operated at the semiotic plane, not in the spheres of ethical propositions, problems, and solutions. The cinematic image of Mumbai itself—as a stage for gathered metropolitan desires and plenitudes—often became a compact of the real and the geotelevisual. In Sanjay Gupta's *Aatish* (1994), the cinematic city becomes a hybrid of the historical Mumbai and Mauritius of the golden coasts and the deep blue sea. In David Dhawan's *Yaarana* (*Friendship*; 1995), the protagonist starts driving a car in the dusty streets of Mumbai and continues until the vehicle comes to a stop in a lush, touristy landscape in Switzerland. In Shankar's *Nayak the Real Hero* (2001) the skyline of Kuala Lumpur is superimposed onto Mumbai to visualize a desired skyline of development. Similarly, in Rajiv Kapoor's *Prem Granth* (*Book of Love*; 1996), the agrarian heartland of village India is upgraded as manicured vistas of South African locations.

"Bollywood" came with alluring new textures of Tradition and a lush heritagism perhaps best seen in the famous joint-family-marriage melodramas of the late 1990s and early 2000s. In these influential films, the ritualistic paraphernalia of the Savarna home could be assembled alongside conspicuous consumables and exotic locales around Europe and the world at large. The superrich Raichand Mansion in Karan Johar's *Kabhi Khushi Kabhi Gham* (*Happiness and Tears*; 2001) is a filmic combination of lavish neotraditional interiors melded with the European aristocratic exteriors and grounds of the Waddeson Manor in Buckinghamshire, UK, expansive enough for a private helicopter to land in the driveway. The neo-Hindu Gurukul in Aditya Chopra's *Mohabbatein* (2000) is a rather draconian Hindu spiritual makeover of British public school education. The campus is an assemblage comprising Longleat, a country house in Wiltshire, England, and spots in the Oxford and Cambridge universities, while the Indian world at large outside the school premises is shot in quotidian locations in Maharashtra and Hyderabad.

Increasingly, during this period, it seemed that a cinematic high-Hindu "Tradition" could no longer be staged without a concomitant richness of worldly paraphernalia. The Oberoi farmhouse in David Dhawan's *Chal Mere Bhai* (*Let's Go Brother*; 2000) flouts visual distinctions between the private home and the shopping mall, or between the suburbs of Mumbai and alpine Europe. What is striking in this film and many others of its ilk is that the setting collapses the walls between the private and professional spheres. Almost all the employees of the Oberoi firm are inducted into an extended kinship network headed by the family patriarch. The house-office becomes a utopian world in which principled Hindu paternalism cures the malaise of alienated caste labor. Here there could be no temporal distinction between business and leisure, romance and secretarial work, or bossing and bride hunting. This form of utopian melodrama mitigated key transformational anxieties of an irreverent globalization and reassured the maintenance of a caste-class patriarchal status quo. It presented mega-"business" in the era of finance capital as essentially interiorized "family business," always under the spiritual control of the caste father, where authority is never dispersed among a body of anonymous shareholders.

The Bollywood geotelevisual aesthetic was thus an advertising mode by which a new, urban Hindu elite presented its life and aspirations as artwork. In a global distribution of the Brahminical sensible, spaces, movements, bodies, objects, customs, and rituals of the world were imbued with new spiritual animations and resonances. It was precisely because of this opening-out that such cinema required a dimension of the advertised, beyond narrative, as master organizer of effects. Storytelling had to concede a volume of signs in the mise-en-scène that were voluptuous and libidinal beyond measure. These too-hot-to-handle objects, spaces, lifestyle signatures, and forms of urbanity could only be segmented off by way of music, dance, and various touch points of spectacle. The Brahminical moral and ethical universe could not always manage, justify, or resolve them in a total manner, at least with a happy consciousness. The faithful wife in Yash Chopra's *Darr* (1993) could thus partake in a lusty dance sequence with her stalker in the dreamscapes of his psychopathic mind, in assemblage with forbidden objects like the swimsuit or the Champagne bottle. The Hindu woman in Karan Razdan's *Girlfriend* (2004) could display a lesbian side, but only when drunk out of her wits.

This does not mean that there was no relationship between a caste Hindu moral cultural governance of narration and the spectacular mounting of desires that flirted with the forbidden. The relationship may be called disjunctive in a Deleuzian spirit, marked by osmosis and diverted channels of energy. It was usually a wrapping-around, in which sensations and principles were brought into a state of dangerous proximity rather than frontal collision or dialectical exchange. This was a delirium of affects in the preindividual space between the subject and the population, between two mutually exclusive domains of postulation and possibility. Hindutva 2.0 as Bollywood could thus be a thrilling orchestration of signs between the father's absolute "no" and the million worldly allures that the prodigal had to navigate and "lovemark" before returning home. The "take away" consequently became a photosynthesis of moralisms and pleasures, both transformed by mutual exposure and semiosis. This Bollywood style pointed to a spectral nation and an extended mosaic of "window-shopped" Hindu culture that no longer had to be narrated into being.

In the digital age, Bollywood neo-Hinduism has inserted Vedic and Puranic cosmologies into the generic Hollywood-style superhero film, as in Rakesh Roshan's *Krrish* (2006) and *Krrish 3* (2013), science-fantasies such as Anubhav Sinha's *Ra.One* (2011), or the animated feature.[97] It has infused energies of a messianic patriotism across hitherto cinematically unexplored domains of a national civic religiosity, including into the sports film, the biopic, films on entrepreneurial heroism, and on techno-military achievements such as space exploration or the 1998 nuclear tests in Pokhran. What has been especially illuminating in the digital dispensation is the emphatic return of the historical, the period piece, or the folklore film after a protracted twilight. Films like *Bajirao Mastani* (Sanjay Leela Bhansali, 2015), *Mohenjo Daro* (Ashutosh Gowrikar, 2016), and the recent, controversial *Padmavat* (Bhansali, 2018) each variously presents a new Hindu will to the past. This involves not just the insertion of marketable myths into the field of the historical or the fauxhistorical; that is, for example, the introduction of the horse and unicorn in the Indus Valley setting of *Mohenjo Daro*. Other than monumental canvases and antiquarian mise-en-scènes, what distinguishes this will is a phatic retexturing of the pictures of the bygone. The idea of the phatic-textural here is in line with the Lyotardian figure that Christopher Pinney invokes qua the politics of popular images in the Indian context: the phatic is the zone in which propositional meanings are no longer conveyed, but in which intensities are felt within a semiotic structure of auratic nationalism, its allegories, and the charismatic staging of the technology itself.[98] The acute resolutions, colorations, and imaging possibilities of the digital are deployed in the service of a new sovereign desire to monarchically direct the energies of memory toward an absolute vision of the past. It imparts new epic animations, breathtaking vertical looms, a burrowing acuity of Dolby sound, plus a critical buoyancy, musculature, and luster to pictures of an imagined bygone. As such it can conjure up a panoptic perspective that is no longer earthbound or human, but adequate to a cosmic moral governance. The image of the past becomes haptic and tactile like never before; it is now meant to be felt in the inner recesses of being rather than merely witnessed.[99] As an assemblage of affects, it presents the thrill of two temporal visions—that of a techno-determined future of the nation and of the ornaments of a great Hindu recapitulation. A technologically emboldened Hindu nation is finally able to birth pictures and an invasive experience of sound that are adequate to the profound nature of Hindu remembrance. Once it was only Hollywood that could plausibly part the Red Sea.

The arrival of Bollywood proper in the 1990s involved a particularly ecstatic cultural tryst with a new horizon of metropolitan desires. This was a special accentuation of what I have earlier called an ongoing Epic of Tradition. Rural India virtually disappeared from top-line films, apart from featuring as disaster zones. The figures of the Dalit, the Muslim, and the poor were gradually excluded in terms of custom, attire, speech, food, hygiene, habitat, and other details of lived life. In recent years, however, with multiplex and consumer culture entering suburban centers, the small town and the village had returned with a vengeance in big-budget films like *Dangal* (Nitesh Tiwari, 2016) as well as in smaller-scale, more cerebral fare like *Newton* (Amit Masurkar, 2017). This terrain is marked less by geotelevisual song and dance routines and more by a relatively grounded sociology of many vernacular approximations of globalization. It is a far more complex scenario, one in which the Dehati and semiurban middle classes enter into a cinematic conversation with the metropole, featuring crosscurrents of desire and ethics, changing class and caste configurations, and generational shifts of aspiration.

This is an immense field, ranging from the food film to the sports or horror genres, covering issues and themes as disparate as conjugality, communication, the agrarian crisis, village entrepreneurship, elections, or shifts in market realities and customary values. Such films have dramatized historically recent transformations, featuring objects and facilities ranging from electrification, computers, and information to sanitary napkins, and hygienic toilets. There is no universal political or aesthetic field theory to thread them together—that is, apart from nonmetropolitan settings and a relative avoidance of purely advertised geotelevisual excursions. I am therefore casting a wide net here, including both arthouse films like Anusha Rizvi's *Peepli Live* (2000), which visits the themes of farmer suicides and media cannibalization in a darkly satirical mode, and commercial potboilers like *Chennai Express* (Rohit Shetty, 2013), which attempts to dissolve the pathology of honor killings into new forms of schizoid laughter. Nevertheless, I would like to argue that, despite their wide variety in terms of ideological proclivities, form, and substance, this mass of cinema, in different ways, registers not so much the positive imprints of a globalized Hindutva 2.0 but the inevitable pressure points and solicitations of this ecology—even in the very gestures of retraction from or gravitation toward it. Here is a nonexhaustive list: the city's electronic besiegement of the countryside; finance capital and customary life; new libidinal technologies; new temporal and spatial imaginaries; new forms of loneliness and insecurity; new Existentiells of speed and inertia; and, above all, an electronic monotheme of patriotic development. These films, in ways both original and trite, respond to that nova that normalizes and advertises a caste Hindu metropolitan existence as the only form of life worth living. The films do so in terms of an ontogenetic mode of cognition when it comes to locating selves in town or country in the world. It is within this framework that we can locate disparate tropes like the lottery ticket in *Malamaal Weekly* (Priyadarshan, 2006), the American president in *Phas Gaye Re Obama* (Subhash Kapoor, 2010), or the Hindi novel that sold two copies in *Bareilly ki Barfi* (Ashwin Tiwari, 2017).

"Encounters" on the Other Side of the Spectral City

Let us return to the city once again and focus on the other side of the great metropolitan caste Hindu normalcy. This pertains to that obverse aspect of the Janus-faced Gentoo, which reveals the fact that he is always—in all playgrounds of desire, amid all his affirmations of a neotradition and participations in a fresh congregational peopleness—speaking about the state, or keeping the state in mind. This dark side comes with the desire for a stronger, decisionist entity beyond the liberal socialist parameters of the constitutional republic, with key provisions of majoritarian exception well beyond the old "Hindu secular." The will to sovereignty lodges itself exactly in that existential gap between the virtual metropolitan dreams of Bollywood and the realist nightmares of the city. That is, between the spectral South Mumbai of the movies which can extend itself instantly to alpine Europe and the historical Bombay which houses the great Asiatic slums like Dharavi.

The elemental Mumbai—of gritty life, squalor, poverty, and crime—may be seen in a spectrum of middle-of-the road genres that ushered in the multiplex era. The changing metropolis in such films is one in which a diagram of development, security, and surveillance is superimposed on an older urban map marked by lines of tension between a Gujarati-Parsee industrial and mercantile elite, a Marathi peasantry and lumpen proletariat, the cosmopolitan professional classes, and various Islamic energies hailing from the coasts of Konkan and the Arabian Sea at large.[100] From the vantage point of South Mumbai, this historical city is filled with premodern tribalisms and extralegal urban technologies of survival that obstinately resist a modern schema of management and governmentality. When seen through such lenses, the city appears less as a civic arena and more as a differential flow of illegalities, with the legal order being only one of the participants. These spaces and their denizens are cinematically expressed with what Moinak Biswas has called a new will to realism tied to the sovereignty question.[101]

I want to elaborate one regular feature of this cinematic underbelly as a theme of sovereign exception.[102] "Encounter," in the legal sense, designates an event in which there is an exchange of gunfire between the police and certified criminals or suspects. In such situations, cops can shoot with extreme prejudice for purposes of self-defense, the protection of citizens, or to prevent detainees from escaping. However, in popular parlance, *encounter* is also an expression for extralegal killings by policemen. It is, in that sense, understood as categorically "fake." Such actions are usually conducted in desolate areas outside the city; suspects are picked up, taken to the remote outskirts, and shot. The encounter is depicted or invoked as a commonplace facet of urban existence in a wide range of genres in Hindi cinema, from the gangster film—from *Satya* (Ramgopal Verma, 1998) to *Raees* (Rahul Dholakia, 2017)—to social dramas like *Chandni Bar* (Madhur Bhandarkar, 2001) and even comedies like *Dhamaal* (Indra Kumar, 2007). Then there is another batch of films, such as *Ab Tak Chhappan* (Shimit Amin, 2004) or *Shootout at Wadala* (Sanjay Gupta, 2013), that exclusively deal with the trope, basing themselves on real-life events and characters.

Historically, the practice of the encounter is said to have become prevalent in Mumbai from the early 1980s onward, after the closing of the city's famed textile mills created a fertile ground for mafia recruitment.[103] However, it was roughly from 1993, in the wake of the bomb blasts and a full-scale war between gangster Dawood Ibrahim and his former subordinate Chota Shakeel, that "encounters" were irresistibly systematized by the Mumbai police.

This was accompanied by a shift in the legal and civic cognitive framework that communalized the underworld question as a whole. A coterie within the police force's special branch came to be known unofficially as the Encounter Squad. Consisting largely of personnel from the detection unit, the Squad launched a widespread purge operation in the underworld, eliminating alleged mobsters without giving them the chance to defend themselves in court. The major operatives of this special branch unit gradually became folk heroes, often touting their kill numbers to the media with impunity.[104] Some of them became virtual celebrities and media stars, giving interviews, making public appearances, and often serving as consultants to the film industry. *Time* magazine pegged the number of Mumbai encounters at 1200 over a period between 1982 and 2003.[105]

The "encounter," in vernacular parlance, is thus a popular reckoning of the executive state practicing secrecy in broad daylight. It pertains to a candid, civic acceptance of extrajudicial terminations of life, with a willed suspension of the rule of law and rights. This is a measure of urban common sense that operates with the full knowledge that the people in the crosshairs are predominantly Muslims, Dalits, and the poor. In cinema, the encounter becomes an indelible aspect of the city in and of itself, for it is advertised as a primal instrument of the fear that founds the city and the horizon of security that preserves it. As it is depicted in *Kaagar* (N. Chandra, 2004), the body of the condemned—as legal grapheme—is the work of a meticulous technique of writing. The face is covered with jute or hemp to muffle the shot and restrict the spread of carbon. The distance is carefully measured; subjects are sometimes fired upon from behind to simulate attempts to escape. Cops carry a host of illegal weapons along with their service revolvers to plant at such sites. The "encounter" therefore takes place in transit, in a unique interval between the norm and the fact. The body of the condemned falls in a bare space between nature and the polis, capitulating as a third figure who is neither the citizen nor the subject, instantaneously invented and killed between the grounds of natural justice and civic law. The slaughter becomes an event of exception that does not have to formalize itself into institutions like the prison at Guantanamo Bay. Along with the Indian state's greater use and abuse of laws like the Terrorist and Disruptive Activities (Prevention) Act (TADA; 1985–95) and its more draconian sequels in the Prevention of Terrorism Ordinance (POTO) of 2001 and Prevention of Terrorist Activities Act (POTA; 2001–4), the encounter is woven into the fabric of a new urban existence built on security management. This form of statist monopolization of violence and quick will to suspend writs of habeas corpus, nondiscriminatory citizenship, and the evidence act, efface the distinction between policing and war.

The Dirty Harry–type cop dramas glorifying vigilante justice are certainly not rare in world cinema or, for that matter, new to Indian film. However, what makes the cinematic encounter unique is the fact that extrajuridical killings of helpless unarmed suspects or detainees are often imbued with a baroque moral heroism. I use the word *baroque* here in a Benjaminian sense, as that which is an expression of unremitted sovereign desire. It is perhaps quite rare in a democracy for the exercise of state power in the raw, disproportionally targeting minorities, to be not just accepted as part of diurnal existence but culturally valorized. Among other things, it presents a jealous normative of urban, Savarna common sense that challenges modern liberal perspectives about citizenship rights, and about policing itself as an instrument of social justice. The mass habituation to vigilantism has grown stronger over the decades, with periodic terrorist attacks on the city: the Gateway of India and Zaveri Bazaar blasts in 2003, the seven explosions in the local commuter trains of Mumbai that killed more than two hundred people in 2006, and, indeed, the notorious "26/11" Mumbai Attacks of 2008. Even aside from the film portrayals, such representations have been a major part of what Daya Kishan Thussu has called the Bollywoodized news cycle, as well as of television programs devoted to crime, urban security, and policing such as *Red Alert* on Star News and *Dial 100* on NDTV.[106]

This baroque will to sovereign execution, as well as that which Rajagopal has called "Hindu National Realism," both emerge from the great metropolitan normal of Hindutva 2.0.[107] This normal threatens to abjectly instrumentalize principles of constitutional democracy, courts of justice, and other public institutions for its fantasies of purification. It invents and lays a total claim to key postulates of an ethnonational monotheme in the age of shock and welter: security, territory, development, home, and essence. When the normal expresses itself in an ultimate form of sovereign execution, the encounter's extreme prejudice eviscerates the notion of the suspect. This is another lesson that we can recall from Arendt: there are no suspects in the totalitarian imagination.[108] The minority is already guilty of all imputed crimes unless the merciful leader delays the inevitable punishment or says otherwise. Similarly, within the auspices of the Savarna informational ecology, the encounter simply becomes a first information response to a chronicle of betrayal already foretold.

The history of exception in the career of the Indian state is a long one. It perhaps began in earnest with the coming into being of the Armed Forces Special Powers Act (AFSPA) in 1958 to quell unrest in the Naga Hills; continued with successive Congress governments periodically imposing President's Rule in states governed by opposition parties; with the mobilization of the state machinery in combating Maoism and agrarian unrest; the notorious Emergency between 1975 and 1977; the Indian state's responses to a spectrum of secessionist movements in the northeast, Punjab, Kashmir, and other areas reaching a fever pitch during the 1980s; the communalization of politics during the 1990s; and finally with the neoliberal security management of urban spaces and mineral deposits in the era of globalization. In the contemporary scenario, the encounter works in tandem with cynical deployments of the Information Technology Act of 2000 (amended in 2008), the Prevention of Insults to National Honor Act of 1971, and the colonial-era Anti-Sedition Act.

This climate of exception—determined in metropolitan caste Hindu terms—was not inaugurated with the Modi era. It has marked the governance of all Congress-led coalitions in the recent past. In the course of Modi's tenure, as is well known, there has been a further informalization of what the task of the encounter really is: eliminating the "suspect" as a civic or juridical category by a "shooting through of explanation." Vigilantism under Modi has spread to Hindu militia and WhatsApp network groups protecting cows, protecting women from "love jihad," and protecting impressionable Dalits from the lures of conversion.[109] Snuff pornography created from some of these ghastly murders are now part of the information ecology. Meanwhile, the Uttar Pradesh government under the stewardship of hard-right Hindu zealot Yogi Adityanath has advertised, with characteristic impunity, an annual track record of more than 3,000 police encounters under its watch. The police, for its part, has invited journalists to "watch and film" on one occasion in the Aligarh district, gunning down two men in front of their cameras.[110]

The advertised modernization of heritage cinema and the "Hindu National Realism" of Mumbai Noir pictures are the Jekyll and Hyde aspects of Hindutva 2.0. The first of these may be understood as a benign plane of planetary desires. It presents a metropolitan caste Hindu existence as the only form of life worth living. It is, among other things, an aesthetic plane for the differential inclusion for all phenomena, even Islam. That is, an "Islam proper" determined by the Hindu secular and a global credo of multiculturalism and diversity that expects all nonmajoritarian entities to merge into an overall civic religiosity of the market. Islam becomes a matter of phobia for this normative state only when it becomes a matter of public rights and recognition. Hindutva 2.0 and the Bollywood assemblage may thus readily include the dapper, clean-shaven Khan trio as India's biggest movie stars; embrace Azim Premji as one of India's greatest entrepreneurs, or champion A. P. J. Abdul Kalam as India's "missile man" and one of the finest presidents of the nation. On the other hand, the demographic figure of the "Muslim" becomes apparent exactly from the point at which the identified attributes of Islam enter the realm of public visibility. That is, when he presents a form of "Turko-Arabic" existence and piety that is automatically antithetical to majoritarian determinations of life and market procedures, combining a range of imputed sociological and aesthetic "vices" like the Urdu language, ghettoized underdevelopment, high rates of breeding, multiple wives, beef consumption, alien attire, or the Islamic beard. The "Muslim" as such can thus be affectively disarticulated from the moral economy of the city, while the follower of Islam, as a juridical figure, can be readily included. This mode of "inclusion" is also precisely why, in this dispensation, there is no escape for the "other"; for one can deliver oneself from an identity through conversion or death, but from vice there is no exile or martyrdom.[111] A "good" follower of Islam is also, in differential terms, a figure of vice; if one acquires a degree of urban chic beyond that—that is, finds ways and means to render one's Islam decorative or invisible—one stops being a "Muslim" altogether, no matter what one's identity is.

The second aspect of Hindutva 2.0, illustrated via the trope of the encounter, pertains to the fierce side of the majoritarian Hindu normal. It presents an urban caste Hindu existence as the only *secure* form of life worth living. It is in this arena that the state encounters the Muslim as the targeted profile for security management and for calibrated, informational distrust. As the visible, poor face of Islam in broad daylight, he becomes "shot through with explanation" relating to criminality, terror, a transnational *umma*, and the pathology of an untimely, absolutist ethics.[112] The perception of Islam as an absolutist ethics is important for the cult of the encounter because it authorizes the state to respond with fearful symmetry and an instant theodicy of its own. This statist monotheism is one that confuses law or duty with a divine ontology of justice in the very act of killing. Law, as Agamben reminds, is for judgment, not justice.[113] Law is a discursive phenomenon among humans, amenable to error and adjustment; justice is a divine ideal which procedures of judgment aspire toward but never quite grasp. Law is replaced by theodicy when the temporal gap between judgment and justice is closed. The presumptive image of the Muslim as driven by an absolutist ethics (which conflates juridical and political categories) allows the state to exercise extreme prejudice toward a pathological enemy with whom there can be no political or juridical engagement.

The Indian Muslim—despite being part of one of the largest Islamic populations in the world in a single country—assumes, by default, the face of the immigrant, the suicide bomber, the criminal, or the infiltrator. He becomes the object of a ready-at-hand majoritarian fear of small numbers. The encounter of the Muslim, likewise, becomes an anecdotal expression of "intense localism" in the greater metropolitan order of things. I use *intense* keeping in mind its etymological variant *intendere*, to intend. Encounters are always accidents (of self-defense, public safety, or escape attempts); yet they are always intended. When the state and the informational order disguise the retailed intentional as systematized anecdotal, the numbers do not add up as genocide. The Muslim as the target of encounter is to be understood within the auspices of Hindutva 2.0 as a phenomenon of singularity and individuation—on a case by case basis—without which the state would be guilty of protracted war against Islam and other enemies.

Conclusion: Toward a Proper Sociology of Hindutva 2.0

I have used some sketches from Bollywood cinema—pertaining to a new Hindu heritagism and a new Hindu security—to illustrate certain signatures and processes of Hindutva 2.0. But that should bring us to a troubling question: Does that mean that we are declaring all films that have come out of the Hindi, Tamil, or Telugu industries in the last three decades to be essentially Hindu nationalist in gross ideological terms? That certainly is not the idea, since Hindutva 2.0 is an ecological principle of solicitation, orchestration, or contagion. It is also, thereby, a mode of capital that tends to assign value to all expressions of publicity or art already within the networked flows of the affect industry. It is not an ideological or doctrinal enclosure like the older discourse of Golwalkar. As a form of capitalization, Hindutva 2.0 "touches upon" all gestures of aesthetics or instrumentation. That is, it exerts pressures, presents allures, and offers supplications even when it comes to film, television, or radio works that might be scrupulously "secular" or decidedly against Hindu bigotry. Hindutva 2.0, in this sense, becomes apparent as a normative informational ecology when a filmic gesture enters it and finds the range of possibilities pertaining to narration, aesthetics, or ideology already narrowed and already committed to a majoritarian ontology of being. This is a constriction not in the range of formal choices in and of themselves, but a constriction of the affectional possibilities of these choices. It is experienced in the moment when one discovers that—in the plane of the industrial temporalization of consciousness—there are increasingly limited ways of being nationalist, being a "responsible citizen," or simply being human. Conversely, it is important to understand that Hindutva 2.0, as a diffusion of profane energies, may actually foster unhappiness and repulsion among the puritan and agrarian-conservative old guard of Hindu nationalists fiercely against cola culture, beauty pageants, or different modes of sexualized, consumer-driven urban life.

What the ecology of Hindutva 2.0 does is precipitate a new Hindu "social" with greater latitudes of worldliness and sharper monothematic jealousy. This is also why the phenomenon may not be reduced to that old foot soldier of Golwalkar, now armed with a smart phone and Twitter handle. The technology, the network, or the instrumentation are not simple mediators or force multipliers in an otherwise unchanged Hindu society. Rather, they, along with humans, become participants in a wider conception of the social that may be drawn from Latour.[114] "Society," or Hindu society in this case, is only a peculiar moment of reassociation and reassembling that mutates with every technology invented, every satellite launched, every vaccine administered, or every forbidden love consummated. A proper sociology of Hindutva 2.0 may proceed along this particular line of thinking, which Latour traces from Gabriel Tarde rather than Émile Durkheim. The problem with traditional sociological studies of Hindutva 2.0 is that they often rely on an ethnography of the subject, imagined in the tradition of the confessional and the extracted "truth" that sets one free. That sociology, as Latour explains, is a Christian tautology of the social by which pure social ties are made of pure social ties.

Let me illustrate this with an example. Steve Derne's work on globalization and Indian television, based on ethnographic studies in Varanasi and Dehradun, presents a picture of a "localized" Indian small-city middle class earning less than 10,000 rupees a month. According to Derne, this class, at least in the 1990s and the first decade of the new millennium, was looking at liberalization as an opening up of economic opportunities rather than as a cultural transformation. Derne illustrates his thesis with an ethnography of audiences staunchly sticking with caste-based "arranged marriages," even though they were watching glamorous love marriages on cinema and television all the time. His work is insightful in terms of providing a picture of how subjects, in a certain order of change, might cope and existentially affirm traditions. There is no reason to think that his interviewees could have been lying or stating half-truths. The problem, however, is that the method of the subjective confessional hardens categories and insulates them from each other. That is, "culture," "global," "local," or "television" as positive, unchanging determinants. As a result, Derne fails to ask whether the cluster of social resonances and affects around "love" or "marriage" remain the same as they were the past. In other words, whether the concepts and institutions remain untouched by the desires and plenitudes of geotelevisual information. Derne's study therefore does not account for the perpetual difficulty of that question: Where exactly does the local end and the global begin? The Hindu social ties of marriage or love beget the Hindu social ties of marriage and love, with television as a mere instrument of entertainment that may be walled off from the scene of the social. Instead, there could be an alternate scenario in which the principled subject may insist on disavowal at every step, but the thing that he disavows (love marriage) itself, along with what he affirms (caste-based arranged marriage), shifts in terms of a sociology of affectations. Both, in other words, are incessantly *modernized*.

Apropos of Latour, we can postulate that dominances, asymmetries, inertia, or temptations are not made of already existing social stuff. They are outcomes of nonsocial intrusions and innovations impinging onto an imagined society. The social is simply a mode of transmission; it is a movement, a transformation, a web of solicitations and enrollments.[115] The industrial speed of information culture, its charismatic machines, and its virtualities are thus materially consequential actors exactly in the same manner in which we earlier, via Ambedkar, saw objects and networks like jewelry, dhotis, metal pots, public buses, or railroads transforming a sociology of caste. That is, a metal pot does not become just a supplementary marker of caste prestige; as a new, active ingredient in the caste assemblage, it transforms customary imaginations and practices of the system itself. If we account for the word *socius* in its oldest etymological sense of "someone following someone else," that "someone" at either end could be a nonhuman actor.[116] A new sociology of Hindutva 2.0 demands a critical admission and reckoning of these active components and their intensities, while avoiding both a technological determinism as well as a sociological one.

The thought of Hindutva 2.0 is not guided by a technological determinism, in the sense that it is not a technologism of closed systems that operates here with predictable outcomes. It presents the picture of an electronic political monotheism and a virtual ethnoreligious congregation, albeit one that is historical and "social" as much as technological. The spectral and advertised Hindu nation, as a dynamic cluster of particularized feelings and memories, promises to ward off the nightmare of perpetual postmodern instrumentalization, the hypertrophy of will, and an empty time without the heroic. It promises, in a spectacular manner, a new Hinduism, beyond the ascetic tradition, that can square the *Gemeinschaft* of old pastoral enclaves with the *Gessellschaft* of the new metropole. In the process, it can also claim to absolve the rawness of capital itself as a cultic religion without a dogma or theology that, as Benjamin once put it, produces guilt without atonement.[117]

Am I crediting Hindutva 2.0 with too much of a totalitarian presence in the Indian ecosystem? That is not my intention, for it is not the only game in town. It "touches upon" without extinguishing older counterpublic spheres, including myriad folk forms of theater, music, painting, or narration. Hindutva 2.0 is a cloud formation in the world of finance capital; it sublimates a normative image of the nation amid the tumult of globalization and terror. It is an electrolysis of older and newer forms, in an Indian epoch of unprecedented urbanization, the industrialization of agriculture, and the fast-track expansion of information culture. Hindutva 2.0 deserves critical evaluation on its own terms because it has transformed an older normative of the Hindu secular and has also denuded the evocative powers of traditional liberal and left discourses. That is, it has birthed a conjunction in which even ideological opponents of Hindutva are increasingly compelled to respond to issues in the terms set by an informational environment of Hinduness, whether they are talking about militarization and human rights abuses in Kashmir, the economy, affirmative action, the rights of women and minorities, or the game of cricket. Opposing left and liberal discourses face a crisis not necessarily due to any lack of rigor, innovation, or logical consistency in arguments, but because they discover their categories themselves to be presently drained of affectional power. In other words, classic ideas, references, and universals of political liberalism—indeed, ones on which the Indian constitutional revolution itself was founded—such as secularism, social justice, equity, rights, or citizenship seem to lose emotive value unless they submit to a basic "Hindu minimum" of memory and belief. In defining the very terms of engagement and dissemination, Hindutva 2.0 as parabasis—a electronic choral murmur of thought and feeling—has, for the most part, left all purported friends and enemies circling their wagons around the same categories of neoliberal economism, governmentality, and "development." Among other things, it has birthed a new affectional assemblage to make it possible for Modi to run on development in 2014, with the Hindu pride being acceptable to urbane Gentoo classes as an incidental accruement or expense. This ecology came into being much before Modi and looks to remain in place regardless of whether he wins or loses the elections that are still impending as I write.

Yet it is important to remember that while affect is industrial in our times, it is also the absence of thinking. Affects work in terms of intensifications and rarefactions; they release energies that a "movement" can capture, but only to use them up in their usefulness. Hindutva 2.0 is not an enclosed propaganda machine (even though it includes propagandist operations); it inevitably births viral antagonisms to its majoritarian trends. The ecology dominated by the electronic monotheism of a new age Gentoo Hindutva has lately been infused with fresh pluralist energies, counteracting ideologies, and images of alterity. There are emergent feminist voices, Dalit assertions, and new Marxisms challenging both this metropolitan normal and the old pieties of left and liberal establishments. There is thus hope that a generational shift will pose serious challenges to the current monolingual advertising of a new age jealous nationalism. The new Ambedkarite-Marxist-feminist language of resistance, however, cannot afford to be insular and nativist in turn. It must be, and perhaps is already becoming, subcontinental, Asiatic, and planetary.

The question is whether the fierce expressions of Hindutva 2.0 are to be seen as insurrections germane to an insulated story of Indian modernity. Or, whether they need to be connected to two temporal axes: that of the long incubation of Hindu India and that of a general rise of revanchist nativisms across the world in the era of competitive globalization and a planetary war against terror. In other words, connected to an increase in shrill, irascibly impatient, and acute assertions of self and peoplehood coming from an agoraphobic reaction to the greater financialization of the planet. What I find especially remarkable about this late Hindu nationalist effort—via the National Register for Citizens and other measures at the level of language, culture, or memory, ranging from education to banalities like renaming streets or railway stations—is the utopian desire to remit a core Hindu India from the greater history of the subcontinent. It aims to purify borders and 'belonging' in Assam or Bengal at the level of electrification, data, and the archive.

Is the current Hindu quest for a home in the world itself ironically driven by an intuitive feeling that a home of absolute familiarity is no longer possible, that the agrarian-artisanal repose of the Brahminical Manuvaadi is itself increasingly besieged and redrawn by a world of circumspection? This seems to be a general malaise of pathos and anxiety across the world. The nation, by organic adoption or unhappy imposition, is the theater provided by modernity for the playing out and congealment of emotions, memories, and affections pertaining to the self and peopleness. It is the singular horizon of that abstract thing called belonging, under the auspices of which wounded masculinities are supposed to heal, principles of identity and tradition restored, thymotic energies expended, and habitats and ways of life reconstituted. Yet fretful and insecure assertions of nationhood in the present day are perhaps always informed by an intuitive understanding that the nation-state is no longer the ontological terminal of sovereignty. In a world dominated by a cartel of international banks, a transnational plutocracy, and North Atlantic military powers and their constable states, the nation is no longer the seat of those two immense themes of the liberal tradition: self-determination and the rights of the people. Yet paradoxically, and perhaps precisely because of this, the nation has to be defined as a progressively more insular cosmology of justice. It has to be relentlessly purified and made to close in upon itself; the country has to be at once achieved and repeatedly taken back.

These nativisms are informational formations themselves. They capitalize on an all-too-human desire for "voiding," at some limit of tolerance and cognitive mapping, the endless stream of information and the relentless fever of the archive. Twenty-first-century fascism is about focalizing these intense localisms and threading them into a nationalist politics of rage and revenge banks. The strongman is the one who, in existential terms, closes the door on the relentless kinesis. It is he who formalizes the shooting-through of explanation by declaring that—in terms of diagnosing the malaise of the social and identifying the enemy that causes it—no further explanation is necessary. The strongman is he who replenishes the masculinity of the nation by monopolizing any civic skepticism about information culture. He simplifies matters and makes choices stark and elemental. In doing so, the father with pithy explanations does not abnegate information culture, but advertises absolute command over the positivism of information culture.

Perhaps what I am suggesting, apropos of this ecology of the metropolitan Hindu normal, is akin to what Charles Taylor has called a "nova effect" in his exploration of the malaises of modernity. The collision between globalization and a purported Hindu tradition provides a strange illumination that is not beholden to the aura of the original entities, "spawning an ever-widening variety of moral/spiritual options, across the span of the thinkable and perhaps even beyond."[118] It aspires to occupy an evacuated space and revenge a great neoliberal replacement of the transcendental time of the ancestors with a horizontal, empty temporality of capitalist-bureaucratic development. It is in this sense that we can submit the Indian theme of advertised modernization to the wider global scenario of rising authoritarianisms driven by tribal anomie and ressentiment. Such nova effects congeal, with their situational particulars, in a world where millions have been lifted from the abject poverty of old agrarian-feudal orders and thrust into a new relative poverty and precarity that is, in turn, marked by rising inequalities, the specter of climate change, and the brazen plutocratic hijacking of democratic systems. Nietzsche had said at the end of *The Genealogy of Morals* that man becomes an ailing animal when he suffers but is, at the same time, unable to answer the question, "What is the meaning of my trouble?"[119] The nova of advertised modernization does not promise to end suffering, at least not completely. In the first place, it seeks to set up an epicenter for the chaos—or rather a nostalgia for one—and thereby donate meaning to suffering.

NOTES

INTRODUCTION

1 Ilaiah, *Why I Am Not a Hindu*, xi.
2 Ilaiah, *Why I Am Not a Hindu*, 1.
3 A complete breakdown by caste of the Hindu population of India—in terms of marking the OBCs who are 40–44 percent of the population—has been avoided in modern Indian censuses. However, the 2015–16 survey commissioned by the Ministry of Health and Family Welfare, reached the following conclusions: "Forty-three percent of women and 44 percent of men belong to other backward classes (OBC), while 20 percent each of women and men belong to scheduled castes, 9 percent each of women and men belong to scheduled tribes, and 26 percent of women and 27 percent of men do not belong to scheduled castes, scheduled tribes, or other backward classes." The Savarna Hindus, however, control 41 percent of the total wealth in the country. See International Institute for Population Sciences, *National Family Health Survey*, 53.
4 Schmitt, *Political Theology*, 36.
5 See Connolly, *Capitalism and Christianity*, 10.
6 Gyan Prakash has, with reason, pointed out that the Hindu right, in essence, seeks an ethnic majoritarianism, not religious dominance. According to him, the Bharatiya Janata Party (BJP) does not want to dismantle the secular structure of the state but to declare Hindutva as the secular reason of the state. It is only the fringe elements that actually want Hindu Rashtra. See Prakash, "Secular Nationalism, Hindutva, and the Minority." His formulation presumes a calculating Hindu subject of the political mainstream presiding over and balancing a complicated field of zealots and moderates. I would rather look at the "movement" as a mutating historical assemblage of events, powers, and affectations that can take opportune hegemonic directions as well as become a suicidal statism. The Hindu might be making his own history, but not the way he would like it.
7 The RSS was established in 1925 as a voluntary paramilitary organization intended to foster a spirit of European-style ethnic nationalism rather than

reform the earlier Arya Samaj (1875) or the community interest–based politics of the Hindu Mahasabha (1906). It came into being in a particular climate of anti-Islamic sentiment after the Minto-Morley Reforms of 1909 (granting a separate electorate to Muslims), and it came into its own with rising fears of pan-Arabism, the Khilafat Movement, and the Moplah revolt of the early 1920s. The RSS was also formed as a primarily Marathi Brahmin organization in response to rising Dalit assertion, the latter already having taken an Ambedkarite turn in terms of demands for rights, social justice, and representation. For a brief overview, see Sumit Sarkar, "Indian Nationalism and the Politics of Hindutva."

8 The word *Savarna* refers to the twice-born castes: the Brahmin, the Kshatriya, and the Vaishya. *Sangh Parivaar* is an umbrella term used to designate the RSS and its many affiliate organizations, like the VHP, the student-wing ABVP (Akhil Bharatiya Vidyarthy Parishad), and the labor union Bharatiya Mazdoor Sangh.

9 See especially chapter 1 of *A Critique of Postcolonial Reason* for Spivak's de Manian take on allegory and parabasis.

10 See Deleuze, *Foucault*, 7, 56.

CHAPTER ONE. QUESTIONS CONCERNING THE HINDU POLITICAL

1 See Fukuyama, *The End of History*, and Rawls, *A Theory of Justice* and *Political Liberalism*. Since Fukuyama's reading of the notion of *thymos* in book 4 of Plato's *Republic* as desire for recognition, Charles Taylor has read the political condition of belief in the age of the secular in terms of a spiritual quest for fullness that marks the human condition and a paradoxical modern demand that we pick only *one* option for fullness. Also, unlike the ancients, for whom fullness was eschatological, moderns have "internalized" the question. The mercurial Peter Sloterdijk, on the other hand, has proposed a historical humanism in terms of rage, and not the Hobbesian fear or the neo-Hegelian desire for recognition. See Taylor, *A Secular Age*; and Sloterdijk, *Rage and Time*.

2 See for instance Abu-Lughod, "Going beyond Global Babble," for an interesting early reckoning of this globalization unrest and of its similarities to late nineteenth- and early twentieth-century imperial cosmopolitanisms in the era of what Karl Polyani called "The Great Transformation." On neoliberal transformations in haunted maps of old empires, see also Ann Laura Stoler's *Duress: Imperial Durabilities in Our Times* and *Imperial Debris: On Ruins and Ruination*. For classic reckonings of the globalization phenomenon, see Saskia Sassen's *Globalization and the World System* and Joseph Stiglitz's recently updated *Globalization and Its Discontents Revisited*.

3 See Carl Schmitt's *The Concept of the Political* (1976) and *Political Theology* (1985).

4 See Hegel, *Philosophy of Right*, 168–69.
5 A passage from book 4, chapter 8, of Rousseau's *The Social Contract* becomes particularly interesting in light of what I am calling a monotheistic imperative in Western political theology: "From the mere fact that God was set over every political society, it followed that there were as many gods as peoples. Two peoples that were strangers the one to the other, and almost always enemies, could not recognize the same master; two armies giving battle could not obey the same leader. National divisions thus led to polytheism, and this gave rise to civil intolerance, which . . . are by nature same." Rousseau, *Social Contract and Discourses*, 298–99. It was ancient Rome that began that process of political transcription, by inducting the gods of the vanquished into the pantheon, making paganism an axiomatic religion for the first time. This axiomatic is essential for people to cast aside a state of primitiveness in which they are more scared to break oaths to their sectarian gods than they are of breaking laws. It can be detected variously in other thinkers important to Schmitt: in Hobbes's tirades against the religions of the Gentiles in the *Leviathan* (part 1, chapter 12, "Of Religion"; part 4, "Of the Kingdom of Darkness"), or in the Machiavelli of the *Discorsi*, for whom the essence of any religion must be based on one main principle and the channel of trust must consequently be made singular in that spirit. Rome entered a crisis when people began to suspect Delphi; on the religion of the Romans, see Machiavelli, *The Prince and The Discourses*, 145–50. Machiavelli, of course, famously preferred pagan religions, for their liberty and virtue, over the Christian meekness and otherworldliness.
6 Spear, *A History of India*, 15.
7 Wittfogel, *Oriental Despotism*.
8 Khilnani, *The Idea of India*, 9. The idea of "India" here is that of the "political" union beyond regional, self-disciplining communities, with the federal platform being the arena of negotiations between various contending groups. Both Khilnani and Ashish Nandy, among others, have insisted that "politics," in that sense, has been an "external" apparatus, entering the picture only when vernacular fractions need settlement of mutual conflict.
9 See, for instance, John Locke's "An Essay Concerning Toleration" and "A Letter Concerning Toleration" in *Political Writings*, 186–209, 390–435. Locke was writing at an hour when England was trying to break not just with Catholicism, but also with mainline Protestant churches like Calvinism or (Scottish) Presbyterianism.
10 The Kumar Suresh Singh–led project for the Anthropological Survey, entitled *People of India* and published in 43 volumes (1985–94), was a massive project involving 47 scholars studying 4,694 communities. It concluded that one-sixth of the communities in India could not be identified as belonging to any particular religion, conventionally defined. See Nandy et al., *Creating a Nationality*, vii.

11 See Jalal, *Partisans of Allah*. Jalal points out that modern reckonings of Islam are overdetermined by Arabic culture, despite the fact that some of the key innovations of early modern and modern Islamic thought have taken place in the subcontinent, which is home to more than a third of the total world Muslim population. Among other important distinctions, South Asian Islam never severed its connections with the mystical tradition, especially the Sufi one based on the ethical writings of Ibn Miskawayh (11th century), Abu Hamid al-Ghazali (1058–1111), and the poetry of Jallaluddin Rumi (1207–1273). The *Wujudi* line of thinking entered into intellectual and devotional commerce with the Bhakti traditions, as well as with formations like Kashmiri Tantrism. The mystical bent was present even in the more orthodox traditions of Jihadist thinking that Jalal traces back to figures like Shah Waliullah (1703–1762). See Ronit Ricci's *Islam Translated* for an account of the cultural and linguistic mutations involved in Islam's move from an Arabic world to the east and the south. For a comparative analysis of Hindu and Muslim nationalisms in the subcontinent, see van der Veer, *Religious Nationalism*.

12 See Tejani, *Indian Secularism*. An illustrative text in terms of a late nineteenth-century invention of communities would be David Pococks's *Kanbi and Patidar*. There were four Muslim households in the village where Pocock conducted his anthropological research (two Voras and two Sipais). They did not distinguish between Shia and Sunni worldviews. The Prophet was represented as a holy man, one of many, who was born in India. The Voras and Sipais gave Muslim names to their children and circumcised them, but they also followed "Hindu" rules of property, succession, and custom and were treated as just another caste by the villagers. See also Gyanendra Pandey's discussion of Pocock's work in "The Secular State and the Limits of Dialogue."

13 See for instance Brunner and Lelyveld's "Islamic Mysticism in India," in Embree, *Sources of Indian Tradition*, 447–90.

14 Azfar Moin, *The Millennial Sovereign*.

15 Ahmad, "The Islamic Tradition in India."

16 For the present I am thus sticking to a German notion of organicity and natural destination marking nationhood. In an extended sense, this can also be found in Rousseau or Giuseppe Mazzini. This terrain of thinking about the nation is of course different from a liberal or constructivist tradition exemplified by Hans Kohn or Ernest Gellner, or a Marxist-Gramscian one represented by Eric Hobsbawm, Benedict Anderson, and, especially in relation to debates about India, by figures like Ranajit Guha and Partha Chatterjee. As for the Hindu right, there is no clear consensus: the desired state is largely an organic expression in Golwalkar, while it may be contractual in Deen Dayal Upadhyay. The idea of peopleness, however, is organic in both.

17 The primacy of fear in Hobbes is often overplayed. He writes in *Leviathan* (book 1, chapter 13, article 14) that the passions that incline men to peace are "fear of death, desire of such things as are necessary to commodious living, and a hope by their industry to obtain them." See Hobbes, *Leviathan*, 86.
18 Schmitt, *Concept of the Political*, 26–29.
19 Rousseau cites Grotius on this, with qualification. Each man "can renounce his membership of his own State, and recover his natural liberty and his goods on leaving the country" (*Social Contract*, 273); i.e., provided he is not escaping his obligations or his duty to serve in hour of need. After the Social Contract is drawn, residence constitutes consent. What Rousseau also concedes thereby is that the General Will lies in the majority opinion (278).
20 See chapter 9 of Arendt, *Origins of Totalitarianism*, 267–92.
21 Schmitt, *Concept of the Political*, 37, 48.
22 Schmitt, *Concept of the Political*, 33.
23 Schmitt draws this postulate from a long European tradition of defending the personal sovereignty of the monarch in theistic terms. See Schmitt, *Political Theology*, 36–41. A modern, Kantian notion of democracy (which Schmitt reads in a figure like Hans Kelsen) is an "expression of political relativism and a scientific orientation that is liberated from miracles and dogmas and based on human understanding and critical doubt." Schmitt, *Political Theology*, 42.
24 Giorgio Agamben's work, especially, has been exemplary on this matter.
25 The National Citizenship Register was developed in 1951 to address population movements across borders during partition. It gained new political valence in the Indian state of Assam, which shares a border with Bangladesh, after the liberation war of 1971. After lying dormant for decades, it became politically relevant once more after Modi came to power in 2014. See Lauren Frayer and Furkan Latif Khan, "Millions in India Face Uncertain Future after Being Left Off Citizenship List," NPR, May 10, 2019, https://www.npr.org/2019/05/10/721188838/millions-in-india-face-uncertain-future-after-being-left-off-citizenship-list.
26 Schmitt, *Political Theology*, 5. This would be not just the Jehovah of the Old Testament but also the God of the Gospel of John that speaks of a violent Christ as the harbinger of Millennial Rule.
27 The most famous contrast, of course, would be with Rousseau's social contract and a body politic based on General Will. Here the people are constituted more by *amour propre* and compassion than by Hobbesian fear (Rousseau's primitive man is wild rather than wicked). The people have two bodies. They are citizens because they share sovereign authority and they are subjects because they are under the same laws of the state. Yet for the *foreigner*, the sovereign body politic has to be expressed as one indissoluble individual, an incarnate General Will. The people, as active sovereign, cannot be bound to itself; it cannot impose on itself a law it cannot break. See Rousseau, *Social*

Contract, esp. 193–95. The sovereign, in this sense, ceases to exist as soon as the ascension of the Master, just as people cease to exist when the populace decides simply to obey. Hence, there can be no *exception* to the "voice" of the General Will expressed by the people, and the greatest expression of the sovereign is the assembled people of Rome, who can potentially break all laws, including the Social Contract itself. In Rousseau, when it would seem that people are deluded about the General Will, it may be assumed that it is actually not the people but powerful interest groups in an unequal society who are masquerading as the people. As a matter of fact, the sovereign cannot actually be represented precisely because all people cannot gather in one place.

28 An interesting parallel example from the European "liberal" tradition would be that of John Locke. In him, we see four different kinds of laws: divine, human, fraternal, and individual (or private) law. Divine law is given to men by God: it becomes known by implanted natural reason or is revealed by supernatural revelation. The jurisdiction of human laws, ones decreed by the magistrate, extends only to those things to which the divine or moral law is indifferent. As a matter of fact, man's free will, or choice, is restricted to such domains only. Yet perhaps what makes Locke liberal is that the sphere of "freedom" itself is quite capacious, since, as he explains, Christ talked of no kingdom other than the spiritual one and was silent about the authority of magistrates. Paul confirms, in Corinthians 1:7, that Christianity in no way alters the secular conditions of men. Slaves remain slaves. It is this constriction of the moral sphere—its separation from the contractual spheres and the rules of property—that allows a potential separation between the church and the state. See Locke, "Second Tract on Government," in *Political Writings*, 161–71. Mill too follows in the same trajectory. Christianity, for him, while undoubtedly *summum bonum*—the foundation of morality—is in its original form largely silent on public affairs. Capitalism and the profit motive, for Mill, is therefore a form of *mitigated* Calvinism that would otherwise say, "Whatever is not duty is a sin." See Mill, *Utilitarianism, On Liberty, and Considerations on Representative Government*, 117–29.

29 See Schmitt, *Crisis of Parliamentary Democracy*, 32.

30 Schmitt, *Concept of the Political*, 19.

31 Schmitt, *Political Theology*, 36.

32 Schmitt, *Political Theology*, 47–49. It is also there in Rousseau's "Discourse on Political Economy": "The most general will is always the most just also, and . . . the voice of the people is in fact the voice of God" (*Social Contract*, 133).

33 For further elaboration, see Schmitt, *Crisis of Parliamentary Democracy*, 42–43.

34 Schmitt, *Political Theology*, 42.

35 Schmitt, *Concept of the Political*, 64.
36 Schmitt, *Concept of the Political*, 54.
37 For the Machiavelli of the *Discorsi*, a dictatorship instituted by public law during exceptional times was always beneficial for Rome. Such a dictator figure, ratified by the free suffrage of an uncorrupted republic and nominated by consuls, was called into being only for a limited term and had to act and decide in a manner that bypassed the slow and talkative procedures of the republic. He had no right to alter the abiding shape of government, diminish the people or the senate, destroy institutions, or create new ones. Ideally, he was to emerge from the honorable poverty of the Roman citizen, like the exemplary Quintius Cincinnatus, who came from his four-acre farm to assume the dictatorship and deliver Rome from the menace of the Equeans. He had discarded the trappings of exceptional power once the task was accomplished and receded to his humble background. See Machiavelli, *The Prince and The Discourses*, 121–22, 201–4, 258–60.
38 Schmitt, *Concept of the Political*, 46.
39 Mohamed, "I Alone Can Solve."
40 See for instance Jaffrelot, *The Hindu Phenomenon*; and Vanaik, *Situating the Threat of Hindu Nationalism*. For a counterpoint to this position, see for instance Radhika Desai, "A Latter-Day Fascism?"; and Banaji, ed., *Fascism*. I will take up this question again in the final chapter.
41 Zachariah, "Fascism in India."
42 Gandhi, much against the advice of Romain Rolland, met with Mussolini in late 1931. Later, this is what he had to say about the Italian dictator: "Mussolini is a riddle to me. Many of his reforms attract me. He seems to have done much for the peasant class. I admit an iron hand is there. But as violence is the basis of Western society, Mussolini's reforms deserve an impartial study. His care of the poor, his opposition to super-urbanization, his efforts to bring about co-ordination between capital and labour, seem to me to demand special attention. . . . What strikes me is that behind Mussolini's implacability is a desire to serve his people. Even behind his emphatic speeches there is a nucleus of sincerity and of passionate love for his people. It seems to me that the majority of the Italian people love the iron government of Mussolini." Quoted in Gordon, *Brothers against the Raj*, 277. Gandhi was, of course, not alone in this. His qualified admiration for El Duce was shared early on by figures as diverse as Winston Churchill and George Bernard Shaw. However, here, and in his infamously naïve response to Hitler in 1940, it was clear that while Gandhi opposed war and violence of all kinds, he was not necessarily against forms of strong authoritarian paternalism on the national stage. Disagreeing with Nehru's disavowal of fascism, Bose wrote in 1934: "Considering everything, one is inclined to think that the next phase in world history will produce a synthesis between Communism and Fascism. And will

it be a surprise if the synthesis is produced in India? In spite of the antithesis between Communism and Fascism, there are certain traits in common. Both Communism and Fascism believe in the supremacy of the State over the individual. Both denounce parliamentary democracy. Both believe in party rule. Both believe in the dictatorship of the party and in the ruthless suppression of all dissenting minorities. Both believe in a planned industrial reorganization of the country. These common traits will form the basis of the new synthesis. That synthesis is called . . . 'Samyavada'—an Indian word, which means literally 'the doctrine of synthesis or equality.' It will be India's task to work out this synthesis" (Bose, *The Indian Struggle*, 313–14). Bose would later famously solicit the help of the Third Reich and Japan to consolidate the Indian National Army and lead an armed struggle against the British in 1944–45.

43 In early 2015 a survey of high school and college students from eleven Indian cities revealed that about half of them would prefer military rule over democracy. Around 65 percent of them believed that boys and girls from different religions should not mix. See Nikita Niraj Arora, "Young India Says 'Yes' to Military Rule," NDTV, January 23, 2015, https://www.ndtv.com/india-news/young-india-says-yes-to-military-rule-no-to-inter-religious-mingling-survey-731336.

44 See Suman Gupta, "On the Indian Readers of Hitler's *Mein Kampf*." Leaders of the Hindu right from M. S. Golwalkar to Bal Thackeray have regularly expressed admiration for him, and surveys have shown that Hitler is a figure who is startlingly popular and admired among the educated youth. In recent years quite a few business establishments from cafes to boutiques have been named after the Führer of the Third Reich, and there have been a number of films made about him in multiple languages. State board history textbooks for schools in Gujarat have chapters hailing the greatness of Adolf the patriotic savior of the German selfhood and economy after the Treaty of Versailles.

45 Khilnani, *The Idea of India*, 51.

46 M. S. Golwalkar, for example, compares it to driftwood, devoid of any *swadeshi* concept, and argues that its federal structure also betrays a distrust of a homogeneous nationhood. He demands that it be redrafted. See Golwalkar, *Bunch of Thoughts*, 227, 438.

47 See Jaffrelot, "Hindu Nationalism and Democracy." Jaffrelot discusses, among other things, the similarities and differences between conceptions of a Hindu majoritarian democracy and a tradition of agrarian paternalism that can be traced from Aurobindo Ghosh to Gandhi, Vinoba Bhave, or J. P. Narayan.

48 I use the word *Brahminical* here and elsewhere as a signifier denoting graduated caste Hindu dominance over the Dalit, the woman, or the tribal. The Brahminical, in other words, can operate in situations where the Brahmin itself is not the "dominant caste."

49 Katju, *Vishwa Hindu Parishad and Indian Politics*, 68–74. She points out that the number of ascetics in the Mandal was 41; by 1992 it had increased to 160, and the recent formation in 2017 had 250 such figures. See "VHP Kendriya Margdarshak Mandal Meet Gets Underway at Haridwar," *News Bharati*, June 1, 2017, http://www.newsbharati.com/Encyc/2017/6/1/VHP-meet-begins-at-Haridwar. In Christophe Jaffrelot's reading, the VHP was set up in 1964 to group the heads of various Hindu sects in a central hierarchized structure along the lines of a Christian consistory. The VHP instituted the Dharma Samsad in 1984, in line with what Jaffrelot calls "strategic syncretism" toward building a Hindu Church and a Hindu ecclesiastical tradition. See Jaffrelot, *Religion, Caste and Politics in India*, 66–68, 226–46. See also van der Veer, "Hindu Nationalism and the Discourse of Modernity."

CHAPTER TWO. THE HINDU NATION AS ORGANISM

1 See Chatterjee, *Nationalist Thought and the Colonial World*, 29–30, 43–48.
2 Casolari, "Hindutva's Foreign Tie-Ups in the 1930s." For more detailed histories of Hindu Nationalist movements and institutions, see Tapan Basu et al., *Khaki Shorts and Saffron Flags*; Jaffrelot, *The Hindu Nationalist Movement in India*; Andersen and Damle, *The Brotherhood of Saffron*; Hansen, *The Saffron Wave*; and Udayakumar, *Presenting the Past*.
3 Savarkar, *Hindutva*.
4 Savarkar, *Hindutva*, 24.
5 Golwalkar, *We*, 86–87.
6 Golwalkar, *We*, 57.
7 See Pollock, "Deep Orientalism?" Pollock argues that unlike the French or English versions, the "vector" of German orientalism was directed inward. That is, the primary purpose was not to "other" the colonized subject, but to construct "the conception of a historic German essence" as an attribute of a Master Race (in relation to the Semite) and define "Germany's place in Europe's destiny" (83). This Indology was thus part of the "German romantic quest for identity" and "what was eventually to become one of its vehicles, the emerging vision of *Wissenschaft*" (82). This project called for a double move: one was to celebrate "Aryan supremacy" and thus acknowledge kinship between the European and Indian. The second was simultaneously to avow "the degeneracy of the South Asian Aryans," to the point of "proposals for a eugenics program in India" (83). See also Aldhuri, "Pride and Prejudice."
8 Cheah, *Spectral Nationality*, especially 15–60.
9 See Hobbes, *Leviathan*, especially part 2, "Of Commonwealth" (111–245). In the same vein of Anglican social contractualism, Locke, too, takes pains to distinguish political from paternal power, the august office of the

magistrate from common husbandry. See especially chapter 6, "Of Paternal Power," in "The Second Treatise on Government," in *Political Writings*, 286–99.

10 Cheah, *Spectral Nationality*, 59.

11 See Kautilya, *Arthasastra*. The totalitarian state outlined in the text proposes a strong welfare and safety network for the people, including surprisingly liberal attitudes toward women in relation to divorce, widow remarriage, and good maintenance and property rights.

12 See Kautilya, *Arthasastra*, book 1, especially chapter 10, "Ascertaining by Temptations Purity or Impurity in the Characters of Ministers"; and chapters 11 and 12 on "The Institution of Spies." The range of spies is breathtaking, from the sauce maker, the shampooer, the doorman, or the domestic servant within the palace walls to widows, mendicants, hunchbacks, and actors in public places and abroad. In book 2, chapter 25, on the duties of the superintendent of liquor, Kautilya specifies that the state shall allow only men of well-known character to take home wine in small doses. The rest have to drink in public houses, closely monitored by spies while they inebriate themselves. Book 2, chapter 27, also makes it clear that the king owns and leases out all sex workers. They and entertainers always have to be on duty for state-assigned tasks of espionage, assassination, or deluding foreign spies. Kautilya intermittently provides immensely detailed lists of suspicious markers, psychological or psychosomatic, for government agents to track, including ulcers and fatigue from a long journey, people in a hurry to get boils or wounds cured, or even people roaming with broken garlands or footwear. See also book 4, chapter 4, and the entirety of book 5. The prescriptions for the control of the economy are equally meticulous and totalitarian.

13 See Kautilya, *Arthasastra*, book 1, chapter 18, "The Conduct of a Prince Kept under Restraint and the Treatment of a Restrained Prince." This overall note of caution was perhaps prompted by events like the Magadha prince Ajatsatru's murder of his father Bimbisara around 493 BCE. Kautilya himself provides a list of kings murdered by sons, queens, and brothers.

14 See Kautilya, *Arthasastra*, book 2, chapter 1.

15 See, e.g., Upadhyay, *Integral Humanism*. Upadhyay's concept of the nation is organismic and based on a Jungian concept of group feeling. It, unlike the state, is not subject to the social contract.

16 See Fichte, *Addresses to the German Nation*, especially 136–38, 143–45.

17 In this context, see, e.g., Dalmia, *The Nationalization of Indian Traditions*.

18 Suleri, *The Rhetoric of English India*, 24–48.

19 Mufti, *Enlightenment in the Colony*, 15. See also Devy, *After Amnesia*, 10.

20 These are some of the recent "greatest hits" of contemporary Hindu nationalist publicity. I discuss them in greater detail in the last chapter.

21 Surendranath Dasgupta, *A History of Indian Philosophy*, vol. I, 16. Here and elsewhere I will be referring to the 1981 Penguin edition of the Rg Veda, translated by Wendy Doniger.

22 Dasgupta, *A History of Indian Philosophy*, vol. 1, 18.

23 Surendranath Dasgupta, *A History of Indian Philosophy*, vol. I, 20. The compendium would mean the four Vedas, collated for perhaps a millennia, ending at around 500 BCE; several expository texts based on them, called the Brahmanas; the symbolic and mystical explanations of rituals, called Aranyakas; and the later speculative, metaphysical elaborations called the Upanishads. The Upanishads, which represent the end of the Vedas, were called Vedanta. The six classical schools of Hindu philosophy that followed were based on the Vedanta.

24 M. Hiriyanna understands the Vedic schema to develop along three lines— monotheism, monism, and ritualism. This Vedic monotheism, however, lacks a creator god with demiurgic power: "This tendency . . . does not result in a fully crystallized conception of a supreme God, as required by Monotheism in the ordinary conception of the term. It aims rather at the discovery, not of one god who is above other gods, but of the common power that . . . is immanent in all of them" (12). The unitary god (Prajapati) is more an abstraction than an anthropomorphic entity. The One in the Upanishads is likewise not pantheistic, since it involves both transcendence and immanence and is never exhausted by its creation. This monotheistic drift was more philosophical than religious. See Hiriyanna, *Essentials of Indian Philosophy*, 11–18. See also hymn 10.121 of the Rg Veda, which begins with a philosophical question—"To which god should we offer homage with our oblation?"—and ends with a later addition that answers the question by positing the unitary figure of Prajapati. See also Rg Veda 1.129 on the "golden egg" (*hiranyagarbha*) as the One.

25 Surendranath Dasgupta, *A History of Indian Philosophy*, vol. 1, 50–52. This strain of thought, especially in its Advaita Vedantic incarnations, has obviously invited comparisons with the monism of the One in Plotinus and the neo-Platonic philosophers. See, e.g., Radhakrishnan, *History of Philosophy*, 2:114.

26 See Surendranath Dasgupta, *A History of Indian Philosophy*, especially 1:258–59, 1:325–26, 1:363–66, 1:399–403, 1:475–76. In contrast to the Judeo-Christian God, Matilal abstracts two models from the Indian tradition: that of the potter and the spider. The potter model is present in Nyaya-Vaisesika, where God is only the efficient cause, fabricating the universe out of preexisting clay. The spider analogy comes from the Upanishads. God creates as an emanation of his own essence. See "On Omnipotence" in Matilal, *Ethics and Epics*, 361–62 (this work is cited in the text hereafter as EE). Elsewhere Matilal talks of a medieval god who is like a prince whose desires have been

already satisfied by the father. He thus creates the universe as a plaything without any desire to be satisfied or fulfilled; see "Karma and Renunciation," EE, 133.

27 Two exemplary figures in this context would be the philosophers Ramanuja (11th century) and Madhava (13th century). Ramanuja, the founder of the Shri Vaishnava movement, disagreed with Sankara that Jnana marga (the path of true knowledge) was the besteay to achieve Moksha. It was rather devotion, expressed as Bhakti, which was the true path, within a Calvinistic kind of framework in which deliverance is determined by preordination. Romila Thapar reads Ramanuja as a historical bridge between devotional movements and Brahminical theology. She suggests a more pronounced similarity between Madhava's Bhakti and the concept of grace, probably inspired by the Christian church in Malabar. See Thapar, *Interpreting Early India*, 400–402.

28 EE, 99. See Vyasa, Mahabharata, book 14, Ashwamedhika Parvan, sections 53–59, for the Krishna–Uttanka episode. I will restrict my broad references to the epic to the English translation of the Nilkantha edition by Kisari Mohan Ganguly, first published between 1886 and 1893. An online edition of this translation can also be browsed at https://www.sacred-texts.com/hin/maha/index.htm.

29 Bhagwad Gita, 11.22.

30 See the Mausala Parvan (book 16) of the Mahabharata.

31 It is decided here that, ethically, abandonment is the same as killing. See Matilal, "Rama's Moral Decisions," in EE, 86–87.

32 Matilal theorizes a "Krsnology" rather than a theology from his studies of the Mahabharata, one devoid of omnipotence or a creator God and understood along the lines of Samkhya-Yoga and Nyaya-Vaisesika schools of philosophy (EE, 102–3).

33 Indology has always highlighted the fact that the problem of evil never appears as a serious flaw in the Hindu conception of God. That is because here God is neither all good nor omnipotent (EE, 99–100). The question of evil, as it appears in the Book of Job, has of course resonated across the Christian theophilosophical tradition, from Augustinian theodicy to Lutheran predestination, Leibniz's "best of all possible worlds," and beyond.

34 On this, see Connolly, *Capitalism and Christianity*, 17; and Blumenberg, *The Legitimacy of the Modern Age*.

35 Matilal provides a basic etymology and gloss of this complex term: "It is from the root *dhr*, meaning "up hold, support, sustain [*dhr dhāranya-posanayoh*]" (EE, 37). Dharma thus can mean religious duty, code of conduct for a group, natural proclivity, or morality, usually related to activity (*pravrtti*) or retirement from life (*nivrtti*). Rta in the Vedas is a cosmic order, one that is similar to the physical universe. Dharma and an incipient question of Moksha replaces Rta in later texts, beginning, for instance, in the dialogue between

Sage Nachiketa and Yama, the god of death in the Katha Upanishad. It also thereby starts to dominate the question of nivrtti, or retirement. Matilal points out that neither in the Vedic Brahmana tradition nor among the recalcitrant Sramana sects, such as the Buddhist, Jaina, or Ajivika groups, does one find God referred to as the ultimate authority on Dharma. In the Isa Upanishad, it is said that the face of truth remains hidden by a circle of gold. The Kena Upanishad posits Brahman as that which is beyond the known and the unknown. In the Chandogya three sets of Dharma are mentioned: rituals (*yajna*), the study of the scriptures (*adyayana*), and austerities (*tapas*). In his laws, Manu himself outlines an eclectic, potentially conflict-ridden process of deriving the Dharmic from five sources: the Vedas, Dharmasastras, virtues cultivated by the Vedic scholars, the good conduct of the honest, and mental satisfaction—with mental satisfaction, in Matilal's reading, gaining pragmatic precedence over others in cases of conflict (EE, 37–51).

36 In later texts, Moksha (salvation) was added to the list. Raghavan and Dandekar suggest that it was Arthasastra ideology that "completely dominated the polity of ancient India." Only periodic attempts were made to assert the superiority of the Dharmasastras, during intervals of Brahminical ascendancy, as with the works of Manu, written during the rule of the Sunga dynasty (2nd to 1st century BCE), or those of Yajnavalkya during the Gupta period (4th to 5th centuries CE). See chapter 9, "Artha: The Second End of Man," in Embree, *Sources of Indian Tradition*, 234–37.

37 Vatsayana, *Kamasutra*, 3.
38 Vatsayana, *Kamasutra*, 8–10.
39 Vatsayana, *Kamasutra*, 24–25.
40 Matilal, EE, 23. See also, e.g., Weber's assertion in *Economy and Society*: "The catalog of sins and penances in the Hindu sacred scriptures makes no distinction between ritual and ethical sins, and enjoins ritual obedience (or other forms of compliance which are in line with the status interests of the Brahmins) as virtually the sole method of atonement. As a consequence, the pattern of everyday life could be influenced by these religions only in the direction of traditionalism. Indeed, the sacramental grace of the Hindu gurus even further weakened any possibility of ethical influence" (561). In Weber's evolutionary schema, Bhakti infuses energies of "savior religion" into Hinduism much later. But here too salvation largely depended on the techniques of devotion rather than moral conduct (572). The Hindu scriptures, for instance, forbid adultery not for moral reasons but because proscription of all forms of sexuality was part of severing the soul from worldly attachments in general (604). This was thus different from Pauline celibacy undertaken for the purpose of maintaining the personal charisma of religious virtuosi or the Lutheran reckoning of sex within marriage as a lesser evil to avoid whoredom (604–6).

41 Matilal points out that the author of the Mahabharata uses the dying Duryodhana to list Krishna's many misdeeds. As a matter of fact, it could be argued that Krishna breaks almost all the stipulations of the Kshatriya code of conduct listed in book 6, the Bhishma Parvan (EE, 92–94). See also Mahabharata, book 9, Shalya Parvan, section 61.

42 See Matilal, "Elusiveness and Ambiguity in *Dharma* Ethics," in EE, 45–46. Matilal also notes that in the Mahabharata it is none other than Arjuna, the middle Pandava, who emerges as a critic of Rama. In the Drona Parvan of the epic, he bitterly compares the "white lie" of elder brother Yudhisthira, which lures their guru Drona to his death, to Rama's immoral slaying of Valin. See Mahabharata, book 7, Drona Parvan, section 197.

43 See Ramanujan, "Where Mirrors Are Windows," in *Collected Essays*, 6–33.

44 The landmark essay to visit in this context is of course A. K. Ramanujan's "Three Hundred Ramayanas," a text that was purged from University of Delhi's BA history course, following protests and vandalism by activists from the student wing of the RSS, Akhil Bharatiya Vidyarthi Parishad (ABVP). See *Collected Essays*, 131–60.

45 As Romila Thapar, among others, has pointed out, this does not take into account colonialism as a factor in the development of capitalism, on the one hand, and Buddhist and Jaina mercantilism, on the other. See Thapar, *Interpreting Early India*, 8. See also Peter van der Veer's *Imperial Encounters* for an insightful account of how the experience of empire shaped religiosity in both the colonies as well as the metropole. Weberian nineteenth-century Protestantism did not exist before the empire.

46 See Matilal, "Karma and the Moral Order," in EE, 408–9.

47 See Bhagwad Gita, especially chapters 1–6.

48 In the broader Hindu nationalist tradition, this persistent theme of replacing a perverted, endogamous Jati system with a revived pure Varna meritocracy perhaps begins with Dayanand Saraswati (1824–1883). See Saraswati, *Satyartha Prakasha*, 97–104. It continues with later reformers like Pandit Madan Mohan Malaviya (1861–1946), Lala Lajpat Rai (1865–1928), or Swami Shraddhanand (1857–1926). A key text calling for a unified Hindu laity in this light is Shraddhanand's *Hindu Sangathan*, which prescribes the fourfold absorption of all castes, the gradual introduction of *pratiloma* (against the grain) marriages, interdining between castes, and common schools and congregational institutions called Hindu Rashtra Mandirs in every township.

49 The other conundrum here is—as Thapar, among others, has pointed out—whether the Varna diagram can be proposed at all as a principle of individual destination, subtracting clan and kinship realities. Thapar thus inverts the Jati caste and Varna timelines. It was caste as Jati that was reformulated as Varna in kinship-based societies. Vertical mobility was possible for groups rather than individuals. See Thapar, *Interpreting Early India*, 122–25.

50 See Matilal, "Dharma and Rationality," in EE, 53–54. When Nahusa inquires about the proper Dharmic designation of Brahminhood, Yudhisthira declares that a Brahmin should be marked by virtues such as truthfulness, wisdom, or generosity. Each birth, on the other hand, is the outcome of lusty copulation over which the individual born had no control. In the Upanishad story, Satyakam, the son of the lowly maid Jabala, goes to the sage Gautama to be accepted as a student. He learns that he has no paternal identity (Gotra) and fearlessly says so in front of his teacher and the students. Gautama, at that point, makes a moral decision and embraces Satyakama, calling him a true Brahman who deserved to be initiated. Adopting his mother's name as his Gotra identity, Satyakama grows up to be a great Upanishadic sage himself.

51 See chapter 15, "Sects and Sex in the Tantric Puranas and the Tantras," in Doniger, *The Hindus*, 406–44; and Shashibhushan Dasgupta, *Obscure Religious Cults*.

52 Universes featuring a godhead without attributes (*nirguna*), as opposed to those featuring anthropomorphic icons of devotion (*saguna*) like Krishna or Shiva. This group of poet-saints belongs largely to the Sant tradition that swept northern India from the fourteenth century onward, with Kabir of the Kabirpanthis, Ravidas, and Nanak, the founder of Sikhism, being the most famous names. The Sants had affinities and links with Sufi mysticism, as well as with Tantric traditions, centering upon shared ideas of love, suffering, pantheism, and union. See, e.g., Embree, *Sources of Indian Tradition*, 371–73.

53 See Pollock, *Language of the Gods*, 39–42. "Theodicy of privilege" is an idea Pollock draws from Weber via Bourdieu.

54 See Matilal, "A Note on Sankara's Theodicy," in EE, 429–30. In the Mahabharata, the word *Daivya* is frequently used to mean fate or destiny.

55 Matilal has responded to a frequent assertion that the term *theodicy* (as Weber famously used it in relation to Karma theory), does not apply to ancient India because evil, along with creation itself, was accounted for by many schools as a grand illusion. He suggests that an Advaita thinker like Sankara is not ready to jettison the realist perception of creation and the creator God. It is on this "firm footing" of *vyavarhika* (the here and now) that Sankara argues that the ultimate truth transcends diversity and tends toward the monism of Brahman. The problem of evil, as Matilal illustrates through the *Brahmasutra*, the Jaina *Mahapurana*, or the Buddhist Nagarjuna's *Twelve-Door Thesis*, was always apparent and discussed. See Matilal, "A Note on Sankara's Theodicy," in EE, 421–23.

56 See Weber, *Religion of India*, 144.

57 See Louis Dumont, *Homo Hierarchus*.

58 For a critique of Weber and Dumont, see Matilal, "Elusiveness and Ambiguity in Dharma-Ethics," in EE, 36–48.

59 EE, 23. In the OED, the given etymological strands are "Anglo-Norman *religiun* [and] French *religion*, system of beliefs and practices based on belief . . ."; "classical Latin *religiōn-, religiō*, supernatural feeling of constraint . . ."; and "*re-, prefix* + a second element of uncertain origin; by Cicero connected with *relegere* to read over again . . . but by later authors (especially by early Christian writers) with *religāre* (religate, *v.*), 'religion' being taken as 'that which ties believers to God.'" See "religion, n.," OED Online, accessed January 3, 2020, https://www.oed.com/view/Entry/161944.

60 See Asad, *Genealogies of Religion*, especially chapter 1, "The Construction of Religion as an Anthropological Category," 27–54.

61 It is now a common assumption that Golwalkar's work is not entirely his own. A good part of it is written by others, including RSS secretaries who drafted his public speeches and statements.

62 Saraswati, *Satyartha Prakasha*, 217–18.

63 See, e.g., Thapar, "Secularism, History, and Contemporary Politics in India." There has been a new age Hindu effort to Aryanize the Indus Valley Civilization, to push the composition of the Vedas back to 3000 BCE with "evidence" such as a bovine, computer-distorted image of a Harappan seal as a horse. This project is also based on a dogmatic insistence that the lost Saraswati River mentioned in ancient literature must be located in modern-day India and could not be located, for instance, in what is now the Haraxvati area of present-day Afghanistan. In recent times, especially during the Vajpayee administration (1998–2003), the Archaeological Survey of India has been politically mobilized to establish the Ghaggar River as the ancient Saraswati, and generally to superimpose the map of mythology on the topography of history by finding evidence of the Ram Temple in Ayodhya, the lost city of Dwarka, and the remnants of the Ram Setu (bridge of Ram) mentioned in the Ramayana.

64 Golwalkar, *We*, 40.

65 Golwalkar, *We*, 44–45. See Tilak, *The Arctic Home in the Vedas*.

66 See Blavatsky, *Isis Unveiled*, vol. 1, especially chapter 14.

67 Peter van der Veer makes a very pertinent observation that the anticlerical and anticolonial impulse of theosophy was central to Indian politics, influencing figures like Gopalkrishna Gokhale, B. G. Tilak, and Motilal and Jawaharlal Nehru. This impulse ebbed after Gandhi entered the scene and took nationalist ideology to the countryside. See van der Veer, *Imperial Encounters*, 73–78.

68 See Foucault, *Society Must Be Defended*, 124.

69 Lal, *Hindu America*.

70 Jones, "On the Hindus," 256.

71 Lal, *Hindu America*, xvii.

72 Historians and Sanskrit scholars like Romila Thapar and Sheldon Pollock have been targets of constant attacks by ideologues of the Hindu right. A

recent major addition to this list has been the banning of Wendy Doniger's *Hindus: An Alternative History* in India at the instigation of the right-wing Shiksha Bachao Andolan Samiti (roughly translated as Committee for the Movement to Save Education).

73 See Thapar, *Time as a Metaphor of History: Early India*. On deep time, see also Goswami, *Producing India*, 154–64; and Chatterjee, *The Nation and Its Fragments*, especially chapter 4, "The Nation and Its Pasts," 76–94.

74 Thapar, *Time as a Metaphor of History*, 10–16.

75 The idea of deep cycles of time is of course not unique to India or to Hindu India, abounding in staunchly anti-Brahminical Buddhist, Jaina, and Ajivika texts. Some Greeks, especially the Stoics, had similar imaginations. Such ideas abound in creation myths in ancient Mayan, Egyptian, Taoist, and Norse cultures. In Aristotle, profane time is sublunar time, while the stars belong to eternity. It could be broadly postulated that Hindu cosmogonies kept the concept of the eternal (*anadi*, in the Vedic tradition) separate from earthly time and matters of human fate in terms of birth, death, salvation, or even relationships with divinity. Charles Taylor has pointed out that it is in the Christian epoch that salvation becomes a matter of transcending time in the Western world. In Augustine's *Confessions* eternity becomes time gathered into an instant—*nunc stans* as an attribute of His divinity. Rising to eternity was rising to participate in God's instant. See Taylor, *A Secular Age*, 55–57.

76 Debord, *Society of the Spectacle*, 76.

77 Doniger and Smith, eds., *The Laws of Manu*, 1.23. Hereafter cited parenthetically in the text as *Manu*.

78 Ramanujan, "Is There an Indian Way of Thinking?," in *Collected Essays*, 45.

79 On this see, e.g., Udayakumar, *Presenting the Past*.

80 I refer to recent Hindu right-wing revisionisms of history at the school textbook level. One of the major controversies was about the outcome of the Battle of Haldighati, in which Mughal forces clashed against Rana Pratap's army. Both forces consisted of a mix of Hindu and Muslim soldiers. The Mughals were led by the Rajput Man Singh, and Pratap's host included Afghans led by Hakim Shah Suri. Pratap lost the battle and was forced into hiding in a wounded state. In recent Sangh Parivaar revisionism, backed by Vasundhara Raje's government in Rajasthan, the battle was fought *between* Hindus and Muslims, and Pratap is held to have been the winner. See Mahim Pratap Singh, "Breaking History: Maharana Pratap Won Battle of Haldighati," *The Indian Express*, February 9, 2017, http://indianexpress.com/article/india/breaking-history-maharana-pratap-won-battle-of-haldighati-rewrite-rajasthan-government-raje-4514897/.

81 See Thapar, *Interpreting Early India*, 137–50. The Gana Sanghas largely did not follow Vedic rituals or Varna. Buddhism and Jainism flourished in them. Mahavira belonged to the Jnatrika clan which was part of the Vrijji confederacy

located in Vaishali; Buddha grew up in Kapilavastu town of the Sakya clan. The heterodox sects they birthed therefore held sway outside the eastern perimeter of Aryan Vedic dominance, or what Manu would call Aryavarta, in modern-day Bihar and eastern Uttar Pradesh.

82 See Thapar, *Interpreting Early India*, 232–47.

83 This historical issue has been one of the most important lightning rods for recent Hindu political mobilization, especially around the destruction of the Babri Masjid. It was positioned in Hindutva discourse as a symbolic settling of more ancient debts with Islamic iconoclasm. This simplistic and linear view of Islamic marauders, looters, and temple-destroyers (with no distinction to be made, for instance, between Arabs or Tajiks and Turks or Turushkas) has been massified in the last few decades. As in other instances of the Sangh Parivaar historical imagination, this issue does not admit nuances. Mahmud of Ghazni (971–1030 CE), for example, was indeed an ardent Sunni iconoclast who looted and destroyed temples in Mathura, Thanesar, Kanauj, and Somnatha for two decades. However, his destructive ire was directed as much against the Shias and Ismailites. There were other religiously motivated destroyers, like Sikander Lodhi or Aurangzeb, but temples were also destroyed throughout the ages for political reasons and looted simply because they were rich institutions that were administrative centers (iconoclastic ire was hardly ever directed at rock-cut temples and murals at Buddhist, Jaina, Vaishnava, or Shaiva temples at Ajanta, Ellora, Elephanta, or Aurangabad). Romila Thapar, for instance, has pointed out that there was no recorded "Hindu" trauma about Mahmud's invasions or his Islamic iconoclasm, when, around the early tenth century, it was standard practice for many victorious forces to do exactly the same. The "Hindu" and Jain Rashtrakutas destroyed the "Hindu" Pratihara temples; the predominantly Shaiva Paramaras razed Jain temples built by the Chalukyas as well as the mosque built for Arab traders. The Shaiva Cholas destroyed Vaishnava, Buddhist, and Jaina institutions in enemy territory. Kalhana's *Rajtarangini* details the Buddhist destruction of temples in Kashmir under the Devotpatan Nayak, an officer appointed especially for this purpose. See Thapar, *Interpreting Early India*, 428–30. Accounts of Mahmud's fanatic iconoclasm come almost entirely from Persian sources like Al-Biruni (11th century) or Firishta (17th century). Contemporary literature on this subject, from both the political right and the left, is voluminous. It must be said that many intellectuals of the left have not served their cause well by trying to sweep Islamic iconoclasm totally under the carpet. For a snapshot of the recent turmoil surrounding statements by historians like Richard Eaton, Audrey Truschke, or Ram Punyani, see, e.g., "The Myth of Destroyed Hindu Temples," The Muslim Debate Initiative, January 11, 2016, https://thedebateinitiative .com/2016/01/11/the-myth-of-destroyed-hindu-temples-and-forced-conversion -of-hindus-by-historical-muslim-rulers-of-india/.

84 Golwalkar, *Thoughts on Some Current Problems*, 14.
85 The discourse of the manly Englishman as opposed to the weak and girlish Hindu informed controversies like that surrounding the Age of Consent Bill of 1891. The bill itself was presented as a cure for Hindu effeminacy, diabetes, and racial weakness; conversely, many nationalists like Tilak saw it as an attempt toward Hindu emasculation. See van der Veer, *Imperial Encounters*, 86–103. For insightful overall critiques of Hindu masculinity in the Sangh Parivaar imagination as well as mainstream Indian nationalism, see Chakraborty, *Masculinity, Asceticism, Hinduism*, especially 168–213; and Tanika Sarkar, *Hindu Wife, Hindu Nation*.
86 P. N. Oak, president of the "Institute for Rewriting World History," is the author of many booklets that have had a strong influence on the populist Hindu imagination, foregrounding ideas of unjust history that are now getting institutionalized and entering the mainstream of mass culture. See, e.g., *The Taj Mahal Is a Temple Place* and *World Vedic Heritage: A History of Histories*.
87 Foucault, *Society Must Be Defended*, 115–16.
88 Nehru, *Discovery of India*, 477.
89 Nehru, *Discovery of India*, 509–10.
90 Nehru, *Discovery of India*, 520.
91 When it comes to ancient Sanskrit literature, the instances of dark tribes (short, wild, with bloodshot eyes and speaking barbaric languages) being deemed demonic and essentially outside the pale of caste Hindu society are too many to list. Mlechcha, strictly speaking, is a linguistic marker of identity, while the Nishadha and Dasyu are ethnic ones. An especially noteworthy example would be the burning of the Khandava forest by the Pandavas (in book 1 of the Mahabharata, Adi Parvan, sections 224–36) to displace the Nagas under King Takshaka and to build their new capital, Indraprastha. In the Ramayana too we see a categorical distinction between the kingdom of Kosala in the Ganges valley and the forest domains of the Rakshasa tribes. Conversely, as Thapar points out, the youngest and least prestigious Atharva Veda was perhaps a compendium of rituals to induct local tribes into the Vedic community. The Nishadhas were associated with some rituals. See Thapar, *Interpreting Early India*, 122.
92 Manu Goswami traces an early, protonationalist Hindu understanding of "Aryanness" to Raja Shiva Prasad Sharma's three-volume *Itihas Timirnashak* (A History of India), published in 1864. Sharma describes the present people of the subcontinent with the term *Hindu*, which, in his case, is of strict geographical derivation. He ascribes all the ills of Hindu society (Sati, female infanticide, purdah, caste/Jati discrimination, etc.) to historical degeneration under Muslim rule. Goswami, *Producing India*, 174–82.
93 See, e.g., Trautmann, *Aryans and British India*; Robb, *The Concept of Race in South Asia*; Leopold, "The Aryan Theory of Race in India, 1870–1920";

chapter 6 in van der Veer, *Imperial Encounters*; Ramaswamy, "Remains of the Race"; and Jaffrelot, *Religion, Caste and Politics in India*, 123–43.

94 See van der Veer, *Imperial Encounters*, 145–50. Among other things, the science of race was an instrument of colonial demographics and the basis of a colonial statistical assertion that Indians were too racially diverse to form a nation. In this light, van der Veer discusses the work of Sir Herbert Risley (1851–1911), the administrator in charge of the 1901 census, in which a nasal index was used to classify castes in terms of an evolutionary schema that, in line with a radical transformation of the Aristotelian *scala naturae*, places progressively darker skin closer to monkeys, with the "fully evolved" white Victorian man at the other end of the spectrum.

95 Saraswati, *Satyartha Prakasha*, 266.

96 See, e.g., Romila Thapar on the complicated birth of Rajput identities during the ninth and tenth centuries in *Interpreting Early India*, 418–21.

97 Thapar suggests that *Manu* and other early Dharmasutras were written when heterodox sects were challenging and overwhelming the Vedic order and when India was opening up to trade and new ideas. This explains the sense of existential threat and paranoia, along with a deep suspicion of urbanization, in these texts. Vedic Brahmanism received royal patronage under a smaller (compared with Buddhism) set of ruling dynasties, like the Sungas, the Satavahanas, and the Iskhvakus. It was in competition with not only the Sramana orders but also emergent Bhagwata and Shaiva sects which would, in time, toward the end of the first millennium, give birth to a terrain of Puranic Hinduism based on the Agamas (devotional scriptures of Shaivism, Vaishnavism, Shakti and Tantra schools), the Mahatmyas (chronicles of sacred sites, idols, and heroes), and the Puranas (mythologies)—together eclipsing Vedic gods as household deities. See Thapar, *Interpreting Early India*, 260–75. In the complicated history of "Hinduism," Brahmins would eventually begin to appropriate and dominate traditions and rituals of Puranic idol worship. Follow-up texts to *Manu*, like the ones by Medatithi (10th century) and Kulluka (13th century), continued the same process of rearranging Varna according to emergent political realities.

98 This broad cosmological imagination is complex and variously articulated in Indic traditions, beginning with the cosmogony of the Rg Veda emerging out of consumables that are at once primal forces and appetites. Consider the example of 6.70: "With ghee are covered heaven and earth, glorious in ghee, mingled with ghee, growing in ghee" (trans. Joel Brereton, cited in Embree, *Sources of Indian Tradition*, 10). These traditions often propose a vertical vitalist chain linking human fate with the elemental alchemy of nature, plants, beasts, and insects, as well as with the metabolism of the gods. See, e.g., Yajnavalkya's Brihadaranyaka Upanishad: "While those who conquer the worlds through sacrifices, charity, and austerity, reach the deity of smoke, from him

the deity of night, from him the deity of the fortnight in which the moon wanes. . . . Reaching the moon, they become food. There the gods enjoy them as the priests drink the shining soma juice. . . . and when their past work is exhausted, they reach [become like] ether, from the ether air, from air rain, and from rain the earth. Reaching the earth, they become food. Then they are offered again in the fire of man, thence in the fire of woman, whence they are born (and perform rites) with a view to going to other worlds" (6.2.16). The Brahminical administration of sacrifice therefore involves the accurate sacerdotal use of sonic wind pressure (the cosmic *Vayu*) in the uttered mantra, coupled with the correct use of fire, water, and ghee (clarified butter).

99 See "Introduction," in Doniger and Smith, *The Laws of Manu*, lv.
100 The distribution of Varna groups inside the city is clearer in the Arthasastra (book 1, chapter 4). The royal palace occupies one-ninth of the land inside the fort and is at the center, along with the abode of the gods and the honorable house for liquor. The Brahmins and Kshatriyas stay north and east of the palace. The Vaishya groups, the commercial district, liquor shops, and brothels occupy the edge of the city, south of the palace and the temples. The Shudras and artisans are confined to the west. The burial grounds are located east or north of the city. Heretics and Chandalas live beyond the burial grounds.
101 See sections 5 ("King Dasaratha's Kingdom and Capital") and 6 ("The City of Ayodhya") in Valmiki, *The Ramayana of Valmiki*, Book I, Balakandam, 17–20.
102 See Foucault, *Society Must Be Defended*, 172.
103 On this, e.g., see Mohanty, *Classical Indian Philosophy*, 98–99. In *Manu* there are four sources of law: the Vedas, memory and tradition, good custom, and approval of conscience. Dharma is between ethics and law. The law, in the Hindu theories, was made neither by God nor the state. It was not the command of the sovereign (except in special cases) nor based on natural law. It does not derive from legislative acts or juridical decisions. Dharma theory thus cannot be founded on metaphysics. It is only the form of legitimation that can be metaphysical. Custom is the highest determinant of Dharma in *Manu* and other Dharmasastras, with immemorial usage trumping jurisprudence. This is akin to Hegel's ethical reality of *Sittlichkeit*, which undercuts the authority of the state as well as that of the scriptures. And then, further, we have the doctrine of Kali-Varjya: customs may change with time.
104 It is indeed possible to complicate the textual integration and the reading of the Manusastra, as Arvind Sharma, for instance, has demonstrated. See Arvind Sharma, "How to Read the Manusmriti?" It is possible to make the inherited text converse with the Mahabharata and many others in the broader tradition like Varahamihira's *Brhatsamhita* (6th century) or Asvaghosa's *Vajrasuci*; texts belonging to other schools of jurisprudence like the *Parasrasmriti* or *Naradasmriti*; or the conjectural, expansive versions of the Dharmasastra

itself in *Vrdhdha Manu* (Older Manu) and *Brhan-Manu* (Greater Manu). In Manu's exegesis itself, it is often not quite clear in the hermeneutic cycles when exactly he is summarizing his rivals to refute them (*purvapekhsha*) and when he is offering his own postulates.

105 Ramanujan, "Is There an Indian Way of Thinking?," in *Collected Essays*, 49.
106 Ambedkar, *Thoughts on Linguistic States*, 22.
107 For references to the Dharmasutra, see Olivelle, *Dharmasutras*, 133–34.
108 See Mahabharata, book 6, Bhisma Parvan, sections 7–12; and Bandyopadhyay, "Utopia and Dystopia," in *Three Essays on the Mahabharata*, 222–26.
109 See Kautilya, Arthasastra, book 9, "The Work of an Invader," chapter 1.
110 See Eck, *India: A Sacred Geography*.
111 Goswami, *Producing India*, 194.
112 On this, see Bandyopadhyay, "The Mahabharata"; van der Veer, *Imperial Encounters*, 116–22; Belvalkar, "Introduction"; Sukhthankar, "Prolegomena"; and Bhattacharya, "Methodology of the Critical Edition of the *Mahabharata*." The Bhandarkar Research Institute (established 1918) was strongly patronized by Hindu nationalists like B. G. Tilak.
113 See van der Veer, *Imperial Encounters*, 117–18. The principle, Latin for "the more difficult reading is the stronger," suggests that, when texts are in conflict over a particular word, the more unusual one is likely the most authentic one.
114 See van der Veer, *Imperial Encounters*, 125; and Pollock, "The Ramayana Text and the Critical Edition."
115 Golwalkar, *Bunch of Thoughts*, 98, 112. This source is hereafter cited parenthetically as BOT. The long and complex history of Dravidian anti-Brahminical nationalism, perhaps seen in significant institutionalized forms since the Justice Party of the 1920s and 1930s, is beyond the scope of this project. Sumit Sarkar points out that there was ample British support for it quite early on, in the spirit of an overall "Divide and Rule" policy; see *Modern India*, 57–58. On the linguistic and ethnological work of the Scottish Presbyterian Missionary Robert Caldwell (1814–1891), who based his theory of Dravidian languages and peoples on a fundamental Aryan-Dravidian distinction, see van der Veer, *Imperial Encounters*, 49–50, 141. According to van der Veer, it was Caldwell's *Comparative Grammar of the Dravidian or South-Indian Family of Languages* (1886) that laid the ground for Dravidian nationalism in the next century.
116 Sheldon Pollock has pointed out that the Buddhists also used the term *Arya* (noble) but democratized it beyond the monopoly of the twice-born; see *Language of the Gods*, 52.
117 Golwalkar, "Students Are Not the Pillars of the Nation." Golwalkar's statement raises the historical specter of a northern Brahmin colonization of the south and the creation of a landed aristocracy through land grants in the

era of the Pallavas, Cholas, or Hoysalas during the second half of the first millennium. See Thapar, *Interpreting Early India*, 340–41, 361–86. It was an epoch in which, until the seventh century at least, the Mlechcha rulers of the north (the Sakas, the Indo-Greeks, the Kushanas, and the Hunas), who had replaced the mighty Guptas, extended greater royal patronage to Jainism and Buddhism.

118 For the first case, regarding Algeria, see Foucault's magnificent elaboration of this connection between history and public rights in *Society Must Be Defended*, especially 123–25. For the case of South Aftica, see Derrida, "Racism's Last Word," 294. Among other things, Derrida's is an insightful reading of the Calvinism inherent in South Africa's apartheid state. The National Party excluded Jews until 1951. The Boers, coming out of nomadic origins and long travels, excluded any other chosen people.

119 Ramaswamy, *Lost Land of Lemuria*.

120 Ramaswamy, *Lost Land of Lemuria*, 55–60.

121 Ramaswamy, *Lost Land of Lemuria*, 103–4.

122 For a comprehensive and insightful account of a production of the "Bharat" imaginary as a "smooth" national space between 1858 and 1920, see Goswami, *Producing India*. The idea of Akhand Bharat functions as a "deep structure" of mythic belonging, nostalgia, and resentment to interrogate the pragmatics of modern geopolitics. In a sense that Goswami draws from Pierre Bourdieu, its construction involves a "historical labor of dehistoricization" (16–20).

123 The Invasion theory originates with Friedrich Max Müller (1823–1900), stemming from his reading of episodes in the Rg Veda like that of Indra attacking Dasa settlements. See Thapar, *Interpreting Early India*, 87. In the Avesta, the hierarchy is reversed. Indra is demonic and Ahura/Asura is the highest deity. Thapar also points out that the earliest evidence of the Indo-Aryan language (not identical to Vedic Sanskrit) comes from modern-day Syria, in the form of a peace treaty between Hittites and the Mitannis (107–8).

124 See "Law for Two Children Should Be Framed: Praveen Togadia," DNA India Report, January 13, 2015, http://www.dnaindia.com/india/report-law-for-having-only-two-children-should-be-framed-praveen-togadia-2052242/.

125 See Shyamlal Yadav, "RSS and the Idea of Akhand Bharat," *Indian Express*, January 4, 2017, http://indianexpress.com/article/explained/rss-akhand-bharat/.

126 Savarkar, *Hindutva*, 29.

127 Savarkar, *Hindutva*, 107–8.

128 See, e.g., Golwarkar, *We*, 123. Golwalkar traces this to the inception of the Indian National Congress under A. O. Hume in 1885. *Serai* means a roadside inn/resting place in North Indian languages.

129　Golwalkar considers the attitude of Zoroastrians exemplary in this regard. According to him, the Zoroastrians arrived in India to escape Islamic Persia and abjured beef, respected mother cow as a national symbol, lived in peace, and assimilated themselves into the mainstream of national life (BOT, 133).

130　The VHP revived the older Arya Samaji practice of *shudhdhi* (purification) as *paravartan* (return); the recent concept of *ghar wapsi* (return home) is related. See Nandy et al., *Creating a Nationality*, 92.

131　See Nehru, *Discovery of India*, 146–56, 192–246.

132　Nehru, *Discovery of India*, 149.

133　See Ramanujan, "Repetition in the Mahabharata," in *Collected Works*, 162.

134　See chapters 82–84 of *Markandeya Puranam*. On this see also chapter 6, "The Goddess Mahisasuramardini," in *Myth, Representation and Historical Role in the Hinduization of India*, in von Stietencron, *Hindu Myth, Hindu History*, 115–72.

135　See, e.g., "This Is Why Smriti Irani Mentioned Goddess Durga," *ZeeNews*, February 25, 2016, http://zeenews.india.com/news/india/this-is-why-smriti-irani-mentioned-goddess-durga-and-mahishasur-in-parliament_1859153.html.

136　There are, of course, numerous scholarly accounts of Puranic memories being marshaled by subaltern castes against the grain of Brahminical hegemony. See, e.g., O'Hanlon, *Caste, Conflict and Ideology*, 164–65.

137　Sumit Sarkar, *Modern India*, 39.

138　Sumit Sarkar, *Modern India*, 154.

139　See Sumit Sarkar, *Modern India*, 44–50. For a wider and more detailed view of peasant uprisings, see Ranajit Guha's seminal *Elementary Aspects of Peasant Insurgency in Colonial India*; and, e.g., Tanika Sarkar, "Jitu Santal's Movement"; and Hardiman, "Power in the Forests."

140　A classic literary instance would be the great Dalit intellectual Jyotirao Phule's (1827–1890) *Ghulamgiri* (in Marathi with an English introduction) published in 1885. Here Phule radically reinterprets the Puranic tradition, reading the Avatars of Vishnu as purveyors of a violent Aryan colonization. Vishnu's archenemies, the demons and ogres, become folk heroes of the dispossessed. Valin, who was treacherously killed by Vishnu as Rama, becomes Bali Raja, the original and righteous king of Maharashtra. The object of Dalit remembrance and desire for restitution therefore becomes the kingdom of Valin, not the kingdom of Rama. See Omvedt, *Dalit Visions*, 19–20. This would be followed by innumerable assertions of Dalit countermemory in the twentieth century, including Ambedkar's burning of Manusmriti and Periyar's setting fire to the image of Rama in 1956 and his accompanying valorization of Ravana.

141　See Ramanujan, "Who Needs Folklore?," in *Collected Essays*, 544.

142　See Thapar, *Interpreting Early India*, 294.

143 Ashis Nandy has founded his critique of Western secularism on a Gandhian reckoning of the fluid, faith-based identities of South Asia. Modern secularism, in his estimation, imposes a Semitic model on this spread by splitting religions into faith and ideology, both distinguished from cultures and composite ways of life (bypassing, for instance, the distinctions between Persian and Indonesian Islam). This forking inaugurates a sociology of religion that views all pieties through the lens of Anglican Christianity. Secularism, as an expression of this arrangement, views religion only as a competing ideology to the ideology of modern statecraft. Nandy correctly identifies the problem of what I am calling the Indian Monotheism but at the cost of championing an agrarian-romantic view of the everyday, village-based community without considering the micropolitics of power in those very communities. See, e.g., Nandy, "A Critique of Modern Secularism."

144 See, e.g., Amin, "Gandhi as Mahatma"; Parekh, *Gandhi's Political Philosophy*; and chapter 4, "Gandhi and the Critique of Civil Society," in Chatterjee, *Nationalist Thought and the Colonial World*.

145 Gandhi's ardent admirer, follower, and unlikely political heir Jawaharlal Nehru would never take his asceticism and artisanal worldview seriously. Nor would he subscribe to the Mahatma's spiritualization of politics, by which great transformations could be achieved through the portals of personal salvation and eradication of sin. Nehru famously speculated that perhaps Gandhi did not really believe that modernity could be undone. He was, to Nehru, the consummate "philosophical anarchist." See Nehru, *An Autobiography*, 510–14; also 76–77, 370–71. Partha Chatterjee, in his reading of Nehru in terms of the moment of "arrival" of the dominant cast of Indian nationalism, points out that the first Indian prime minister realized that the Indian peasantry could not be organized purely by principles of rational political mobilization. This is where the communists, following "European labor standards," failed. The task would require the political genius of Gandhi, that spellbinding magician of Indian mass psychology. Nehru found the phenomenon at once exemplary, quaint, and anachronistic, as well as "reactionary" from the vantage point of the modern. Yet he was "powerless" to intervene. Reason and modernity, in the circumstances, could only offer a "blank check" to Gandhi. See Chatterjee, *Nationalist Thought and the Colonial World*, 150–51.

146 In recent times there have been some excellent intellectual evaluations of this powerful Gandhian category from the standpoints of class, gender, and caste critique by scholars across generations. For a brilliant critical view on the modern concept of nonviolence, see Bandyopadhyay, "A Critique of Non-violence," in *Three Essays on the Mahabharata*, 267–307. Bandyopadhyay draws from the concept of *anrisamsa* (noncruelty) in the Aranyak Parvan (book 4) of the Mahabharata. For a remarkably insightful critical exposition of B. R. Ambedkar's nonabsolutist critique of *ahimsa*, one based on the ideas

of John Dewey and Buddhism, see Kalyan Kumar Das, "Encountering John Dewey's 'Pragmatism' in an Indian Context." See also Anirban Das, "Of Sleep and Violence," for yet another insightful take on the question of violence in the Mahabharata.

147 On the Jaina Ramayans, see Ramanujan, "Three Hundred Ramayanas," in *Collected Essays*, 131–60; and Shah, "Ramayana in Jaina Tradition."

148 See Udayakumar, *Presenting the Past*, 75–108, on the tussle between Gandhi, Gandhians, agrarian conservatives, and Hindutva ideologues over the concept of Ram Rajya.

149 Letter to Narandas Gandhi, July 22, 1930, in Gandhi, *Essential Writings* 232.

150 "Crusade against Non-co-operation," *Young India*, August 4, 1920, in Gandhi, *Essential Writings*, 336.

151 "Talk with Manu Gandhi," in Gandhi, *Essential Writings*, 407–8.

152 "My Mission," *Young India*, April 3, 1924, in Gandhi, *Essential Writings*, 33.

153 The modern Hindu patriarchy and its quest for the state, was, in Nandy's understanding, a modernist insurrection against the ultimate authority in "the Indian mind," which has, in his estimation, always been the feminine *Adyashakti*, the fecund principle of nature. Nandy, *At the Edge of Psychology*, 36. Nathuram Godse, the RSS man who assassinated Gandhi, was brought up as a girl. In Nandy's psychoanalysis, he emerges as a figure who militates against a weak father who failed to prevent the partition of the nation as mother (78–91).

154 It was the sociologist M. N. Srinivas who coined the term *Sanskritization* to designate a pattern of change in social behavior (involving meat and alcohol, conjuring up fictitious caste histories, etc.) that lower castes often follow to rise in status. See Srinivas, *Social Change in Modern India*, and also "A Note on Sanskritization and Westernization." I am using it in a slightly different sense, as largely a semiological principle of creating the Hindu axiomatic, which would include the creation of a majoritarian culture and a pan-Indian Hindu aura overriding regional differences. This would, of course, include a standing invitation to enter the Sanskritization process as Srinivas describes it.

155 See Pollock, *Language of the Gods*, for an account of a Sanskrit cosmopolitanism that flourished from Afghanistan to Java in the beginning of the first millennium, only to be challenged and replaced by the vernaculars from the second millennium. The interesting thing that Pollock points out about this "cosmopolitanism" was that while the language had to acquire a supraregional dimension (*cosmos*) and a political dimension (*polis*), it did not try to theorize its own universality. It had to come out of its sacerdotal cocoon but did not foster grand cultural themes like Hellenism, Arabiya, and Farsiyat—or a political form like the *imperium romanum*. The elites expressed their power in Sanskrit, in the form of inscriptions (*prasastis* on rock faces,

copper plates, or temple walls) that Pollock calls the aesthetics of the state (with grammarians, metricians, and lexicographers becoming instruments of power). Yet there is little evidence to suggest that Sanskrit, as the language of the gods, was used for any practical matters of governance. Unlike other sacred languages like Latin, Greek, Arabic, or Chinese, it was not used for trade or any significant form of quotidian activity (12–15). It is in this sense of singular and austere usage that the language, imagined thus, becomes the immediate expression of theodicy. Pollock derives the title of his monumental work from Dandin's *Kavyadarsha* (7th century): "The language called Sanskrit is the language of the gods, taught [to men] by the great sages of old" (44).

156 See Mufti, *Enlightenment in the Colony*, especially the section "Urdu, Hindi, Hindustani: The Dialectic of Dialect in Colonial India" (140–53) for a brilliant exposition of the Hindi-Urdu question in relation to what he calls "nation-thinking" and the overall experience of rupture that colonial modernity automatically entails. See also, e.g., Alok Rai, *Hindi Nationalism*; Orsini, *The Hindi Public Sphere*; Faruqi, *Early Urdu Literary Culture and History*; Hakala, *Negotiating Languages*; and the essays in part 5, "The Twinned Histories of Urdu and Hindi," in Pollock, *Literary Cultures in History*. Mufti, among others, notes that the period that witnessed the gathering of the most divisive energies across the Hindi-Urdu aisle was also marked by the greatest flourishing of secular Urdu literature (180).

157 See, e.g., Savarkar, *Hindutva*, 41: "Hindi or Hindustani is the eldest daughter of Sanskrit."

158 I speak, strictly, of an impulse of the Brahminical here, as opposed to a general vein of anticlerical Hindu reformism that merged Protestant asceticism with a neo-Hindu spiritualism in the scenarios of nineteenth-century reform and twentieth-century nationalism. See, e.g., Barton Scott, *Spiritual Despots*. The allure, as well as the disavowal, of the Protestant specter has been a dualism at the heart of the Hindu project since the days of the Arya Samajis and the Sanatan Panthis.

159 Here and elsewhere in the book, I generally use the term *Dalit* as a perpetual figuration of the oppressed that includes, from the modern constitutional perspective of the Republic of India, the Scheduled Castes, the Scheduled Tribes, women, and others disadvantaged by class and religious exploitation. That is, I use it in the sense that Kancha Ilaiah uses *Dalitbahujan*. He settles for this term to account for key historical shifts in caste configuration from the late nineteenth-century moment of Mahatma Jyotirao Phule to the mid-twentieth-century moment of Ambedkar, up to more recent times that witnessed the Mandal agitations of the early 1990s. Phule used the terms *Sudra* and *Ati-Sudra*, which were apt for his times but not for a later age that saw the emergence of Sanskritized Sudra "upper castes" like the Reddies, Velamas, or Kammas. Ilaiah calls these latter groups Neo-Kshatriyas, since they

become saviors of Brahminism in the era of industrialization and urbanization. Ambedkar abandoned the "Depressed Classes" identified by the colonial bureaucracy for *Dalit* to denote the Scheduled Classes in the 1950s. Ilaiah extends it to *Dalitbahujan* to include OBCs and STs, after the emergence of the Bahujan Party under Kanshi Ram in the 1980s. The term *Dalitbahujan*, in that sense, becomes the figuration of an oppressed majority. The Dalitization of the nation automatically points toward a true democratization. See *Why I Am Not a Hindu*, vii–ix, 36–39.

160 Agamben, "Language and History," in *Potentialities*, 47.
161 For a general overview of events and debates, see, e.g., Brass, *Language, Religion, and Politics in Northern India*; and the essays in Sarangi, *Language and Politics in India*.
162 I allude, of course, to Dante Alighieri's *De vulgari eloquentia*.
163 Two recent works on this wider domain of an emergent Anglophone, cosmopolitan Hinduness are Manisha Basu's *Rhetoric of Hindu India*; and Srinivas Aravamudan's *Guru English*.
164 Foucault, "Language to Infinity," in *Language, Counter-memory, Practice*, 67.
165 See, e.g., Rousseau, *Social Contract*, book 3, chapter 1.
166 Kothari, "Caste and Modern Politics," 58.
167 See, e.g., Nigam, "Secularism, Modernity, Nation"; and Ilaiah, "Towards the Dalitization of the Nation."
168 Baxi, "The Constitutional Discourse on Secularism."
169 See Nehru, *Discovery of India*, 74.

CHAPTER THREE. THE INDIAN MONOTHEISM

1 See Marshall, *The British Discovery of Hinduism*.
2 Sukumar Sen, *History of Bengali Literature*, 179–80.
3 Fazl, along with his elder brother, the court poet Faizi, was instrumental in diminishing the influence of the Sunni orthodoxy in Akbar's court. His thinking on kingship was influenced by Shiite teachings and mediated Greek thinking such as the Platonic idea of the philosopher-king, as filtered through al-Farabi (10th century) or Ibn-Rushd (12th century). The Shiite idea of a chosen one, illuminated by God's light and bestowed with esoteric knowledge and immunity from sin, was parlayed by Fazl into the figure of Akbar the temporal ruler as Padshah. See Embree, *Sources of Indian Tradition*, 425.
4 Fazl, *Ain-I-Akbari*, vol. 3, "Prefatory Remarks," 1.
5 See Fazl, *Ain-I-Akbari*, vol 3, x: 127.
6 See Fazl, *Ain-I-Akbari*, vol. 3, x: 127.
7 See Fazl, *Ain-I-Akbari*, vol. 3:349–79.
8 Lorenzen, "Who Invented Hinduism?"
9 Nicholson, *Unifying Hinduism*.

10 I am grateful to Sibaji Bandyopadhyay for pointing this out to me.
11 See O'Connell, "Vaisnava Perceptions of Muslims."
12 Bandyopadhyay, "Atho ma faleshu kadachon." For an English-language version of this work and Bandyopadhyay's other essays on the epic, see Bandyopadhyay, *Three Essays on the Mahabharata*.
13 See Saraswati, *Satyartha Prakasha*, 214–20.
14 For a detailed discussion, see Bandyopadhyay, "Atho ma faleshu kadachon," 66–117.
15 Bandyopadhyay, "Atho ma faleshu kadachon," 182–83.
16 For an exhaustive account of Upadhyay's life, see Lipner, *Brahmabandhab Upadhyay*.
17 Partha Chatterjee illustrates an interesting aspect of Keshub Chandra Sen's project, namely, that his Christ had to be reinvented in an Asiatic avatar, since Christianity itself was born in the East: "Why should you Hindus go to England to learn Jesus Christ? Is not his native land nearer to India than to England? Is he not, and are not his apostles and immediate followers, more akin to Indian nationality than Englishmen? Why should not one, then, recover Christ for India?" To the Englishmen, Sen declared, "If you wish to regenerate us Hindus, present Christ to us in his Hindu character." See Chatterjee, *The Nation and Its Fragments*, 41. For more on Keshub Chandra, see, e.g., Scott, *Keshub Chunder Sen*.
18 Cited in Lipner, *Brahmabandhab Upadhyay*, 209.
19 Coming primarily from the non-Brahmin mercantile castes of Punjab, the Arya Samajis had a contentious relationship with the orthodox Brahmin-dominated Sanatan Dharmis of the Uttar Pradesh region. In 1893 it would split into a moderate "College" faction and a hard-line "Gurukul" one, around "Hindu" questions of vegetarianism and Anglophone education.
20 See Sumit Sarkar, *Modern India*, 74–75.
21 See, e.g., Office of the Registrar General & Census Commissioner, Ministry of Home Affairs, India publications, http://www.censusindia.gov.in/data/Census_2001/Publication/India/41020_2001_REL.pdf, accessed October 31, 2017.
22 See Tejani, "Reflections on the Category of Secularism in India," 52.
23 Hegel, *On the Episode*, 9. Hegel of course commented on the Indian "spirit" and its expressions in philosophy, poetry, and art in his *Encyclopedia of the Physical Sciences* (first published in 1817) and in what would later come to be collated as his *Lectures on the Philosophy of History* (1837). His idea of "India" was largely derived from Wilkins's translation of the Gita and developed separately from the general environment of German Indology. Hegel was taken to task for his ignorance of India by many, including Schopenhauer, Schlegel, Humboldt, and Schelling. Wilhelm von Humboldt presented two lectures on Schlegel's Latin Gita on June 30, 1825, and June 15, 1826, at the Royal Prussian Academy of Sciences, Berlin. The lectures were published in 1827. Hegel

interrupted his work on the *Encyclopedia* to write a review of Humboldt's work. The review was published in *Wissenschaftliche Kritik* in January and October of 1827.

24 Hegel, *On the Episode*, 25.
25 Hegel, *On the Episode*, 45.
26 Hegel, *On the Episode*, 127.
27 Hegel, *On the Episode*, 129.
28 Hegel had covered this ground earlier in the *Phenomenology* while discussing natural religion and religion in the form of art. In accounting for matters like the contradictory actions of the gods in the pantheon, the unhappy self-consciousness of the stoics, or the oracle's eventually becoming dumb, he had written that the journey of consciousness from "picture-thinking" to the "notion" was essential for the birth of a modern subjective horizon. See Hegel, *Phenomenology of Spirit*, 424–53.
29 Secular consciousness in Hegel is consciousness free not of the love of Christ but of dogma. The discourse of Krishna is, in that line of thinking, accepted by Arjuna as dogma. In this phenomenology, cognition is always caught between fear of error and doubt; it cannot be the instrument to discern the absolute. See also the discussion on natural religion in *Phenomenology of Spirit*, 416–24. In idolatrous faiths, the spirit as artificer struggles to fill inner forms with outer realities as projections of *kenosis*: the sphinx of the Egyptians, the obelisks of the pagans, or the Black Stone of Kaaba at Mecca.
30 Hegel, *Philosophy of World History*, 78–79.
31 Hegel, *Philosophy of World History*, 135.
32 See Hegel, *Philosophy of Right*, 296. Hegel alludes to Robert Clive's 1751 battle in Arcot, in which he reputedly led five hundred men against Indian and some French troops.
33 Hegel, *Philosophy of World History*, 104.
34 Hegel, *Phenomenology of Spirit*, 359–60.
35 Hegel, *Philosophy of Right*, 151.
36 In Baudhayana's Dharmasutra, for instance, the sin of crossing the sea is grouped together with stealing a Brahmin's property or deposit, bearing false witness with regard to land, trading in all sorts of merchandise, serving Sudras, fathering a child by a Sudra woman, or becoming a child of a Sudra (book 2, verse 2, 1–10). See Olivelle, *Dharmasutras*, 168. One also, of course, has to point out that this was far from universal in the Hindu fold, especially in the south. Interestingly, Nehru, in his *Discovery*, chides Akbar, the Mughal Emperor he greatly admired, for not realizing the importance of sea power even after the arrival of the Portuguese. See Nehru, *Discovery of India*, 260–61.
37 See Hegel, *Philosophy of World History*, 177. The Indian is more advanced than the African Negro because the Indian can speak with the European and

thus submit himself to tutelage. The inhabitant of the Dark Continent is an "animal man in all his savagery and lawlessness," and the Negro can communicate better with the Mohammadan than the European.

38 Hegel, *Philosophy of World History*, 184.
39 For an introductory look into Bengali reform, education, and print culture in the course of the long nineteenth century, see Sivanath Sastri's classic *Ramtanu Lahiri o totkalin bongosamaj*. See also Chakravarty, *Mudroner shongskriti o bangla boi*; Chaudhuri, *Calcutta*, vol. 1; and Bandyopadhyay, *The Gopal-Rakhal Dialectic*.
40 Sukumar Sen, *History of Bengali Literature*, 184.
41 For a critical overview, see Sumit Sarkar, "Calcutta and the Bengal Renaissance." See also the classic studies in Susobhan Sarkar, *Bengal Renaissance and Other Essays*; and Asok Sen, *Iswar Chandra Vidyasagar*.
42 The Vishnu Purana states that all human ages (*manavtaras*) have their own Vyasa. There have been twenty-eight such incarnations in the massive churnings of the temporal order; he will continue to be born as long as creation exists.
43 Roy, "A Second Defence," 127.
44 Roy, "A Defense of Hindu Theism," 114.
45 Roy, "A Defense of Hindu Theism," 109.
46 Roy, "A Defense of Hindu Theism," 109.
47 Roy, "Letter," 251.
48 The classic text is Sastri, *History of the Brahmo Samaj*.
49 See, e.g., Comte, *The Positive Philosophy*, book 6, chapters 7–9, 531–636.
50 To see more on Bankimchandra and the literary-intellectual moment I am describing, one can turn to Bandyopadhyay, *The Gopal-Rakhal Dialectic*, 18–36; Kaviraj, *The Unhappy Consciousness*; Tanika Sarkar, *Hindu Wife, Hindu Nation*, 135–62; Guha, *An Indian Historiography of India*; Chatterjee, *Nationalist Thought and the Colonial World*; and Raychaudhuri, *Europe Reconsidered*—in addition, of course, to the rich body of work in Bengali.
51 Chatterjee, *The Nation and Its Fragments*, 6–10.
52 Using an estimation arrived at by Mahadev Govind Ranade, Sumit Sarkar points out that there were only 3 publications in Marathi between the years 1818 and 1827. The number was 102 in the decade from 1847 to 1857; 1,530 publications between 1865 and 1874; and 3,824 from 1885 to 1896. See Sumit Sarkar, *Modern India*, 83.
53 For a more detailed canvas of the late nineteenth-century literary scene in India, contemporaneous with Bankim, see Sisir Kumar Das, *History of Indian Literature*, 8:203–11. Works such as Reverend Lal Behari De's *English Bengal Peasant Life* (1874) and Hari Narayan Apte's *Marathi madhali sthiti* (1885) attempted to present lowly peasant or middle-class life with a touch of ethnographic or psychological realism. Similarly, the English-educated Christian

Samuel Vedanayagam Pillai's 1879 novel *Prathapamudaliar charitram*, the first in Tamil, explored matters of caste and female emancipation. Kerala's first modern novel, Chander Menon's romance *Indulekha* (1889), sought to combat the social domination of Namboodri Brahmins. See also Sumit Sarkar, *Modern India*, 161.

54 Raja Shiva Prasad's three-volume *Itihas timirnasak* (A history of India, 1864), for instance, was perhaps the first modern study of India as Bharat, one extending the concept to Vedic times, but also impelled by a rationalist critique of the Puranas and Sastras as well as a disavowal of the Islamic Mughal inheritance. See Goswami, *Producing India*, 172–82. This overall protonationalist vision of a glorious Aryan past would be augmented by other works like Bhudeb Mukhopadhyay's utopian *Swapnalabdha bharatbarsher itihash* (Indian history acquired in a dream, 1862) or Rajani Kanta Gupta's *Arya Kirti* (Aryan achievement, 1883). Meanwhile, in 1870, Sir Sayyid Ahmad Khan would publish the English version of his *Essays on the Life of Mohammed* as a riposte to William Muir's orientalist *Life of Mohamet* (4 vols., 1856–61), borrowing the polemical methods of the Christian apologia. The text arrived at a moment of the reassertion of an axiomatic Muslim identity after 1857, against the grain of traditional Sufi syncretism. See Jalal, *Partisans of Allah*, especially 149–52.

55 Chattyopadhyay, "Letters on Hinduism," 234–35.
56 Chattyopadhyay, "Letters on Hinduism," 239.
57 See Chattyopadhyay, "Buddhism and Sankhya Philosophy."
58 Chattopadhyay, "Krishnacharitra," 353. Hereafter this work is cited parenthetically in the text as KC.
59 Chattyopadhyay, "Letters on Hinduism," 230.
60 Chattyopadhyay, "Letters on Hinduism," 248–50.
61 KC, 446, translation mine. The italicized words are European terms that Bankim himself uses.
62 Bandyopadhyay, *Bangla uponyashe 'ora,'* 26–27.
63 See Sashibhusan Dasgupta, *Obscure Religious Cults*, 113–46; and also Partha Chatterjee's elaboration of the complex tradition of Gaudiya Vaishnavism, its Brahminical annexation in the sixteenth century as well as popular, subaltern deviancies, in *The Nation and Its Fragments*, 181–87.
64 Tanika Sarkar, *Hindu Wife, Hindu Nation*, 182–83.
65 Chattopadhyay, "Dharmatattva," 604–6.
66 See Sisir Kumar Das, *History of Indian Literature*, 8:213–14.
67 Bandyopadhyay, "Punar bishoye punarbibechona," 219.
68 See, e.g., Banerjea, *Dialogues on the Hindu Philosophy*.
69 Chattopadhyay, "Dharmatattva," 610–12.
70 See Sumit Sarkar, *Modern India*, 73–75.
71 Bal Gangadhar Tilak, speech delivered at the Bharata Dharma Mahamandala, Benaras, January 3, 1906. In Tilak, *Writings and Speeches*, 40.

72 See Andersen and Damle, *Brotherhood in Saffron*, 14.
73 For a detailed discussion of the commerce between Advaita and Indian nationalism, see Bandyopadhyay, "Non-dualism and Nationalism."
74 See Sharma, *Hindutva*. Sharma suggests that the discursive lineage that ties Aurobindo and Vivekananda with later figures like Radhakrishnan and Rajagopalchari conjures up a "soft Hindutva" that provides a worldly, cosmopolitan platform for more chauvinistic expressions. For a critical account of Vivekananda, especially regarding the soft and hard Hindu line he pursues in his English and Bengali works, respectively, see Bandyopadhyay, "Punar bishoye punarbibechona."
75 Rajagopalchari, *Hinduism*, 6.
76 Rajagopalchari, *Hinduism*, 46–47.
77 Rajagopalchari, *Hinduism*, 22.
78 Rajagopalchari, *Hinduism*, 69.
79 Vivekananda, *Complete Works*, 5:361–62.
80 Radhakrishnan, *Hindu View of Life*, 14. Hereafter this work is cited parenthetically in the text as HVL.
81 See HVL, 83: "Democracy is not the standardizing of everyone, so as to obliterate all particularities.... While the system of caste is not a democracy in the pursuit of wealth or happiness, it is a democracy so as far as the spiritual values are concerned." A social hierarchy based on the superiority of the Brahmin is thus more rational than a feudal one based on military valor, or a capitalistic one based on wealth.
82 Ramanujan, "Is There an Indian Way of Thinking?," in *Collected Essays*, 34–51.
83 On biographical and critical evaluations of Ambedkar, see, e.g., Keer, *Dr. Ambedkar*; Omvedt, *Ambedkar*; and Jaffrelot, *Dr. Ambedkar and Untouchability*.
84 V. Raghavan and R. N. Dandekar pose this question in the course of their otherwise conservative elaboration of "The Hindu Way of Life": "[In] popular parlance, dharma almost came to mean just *varna-āsrama-dharma*, that is, the dharmas (ordained duties) of the four classes and the four stages of life." Cited in Embree, *Sources of Indian Tradition*, 215.
85 In a letter from a certain Har Bhagwan to Ambedkar, dated April 22, 1936. Cited in Ambedkar, *Annihilation of Caste*, 6–9. Hereafter this work is cited parenthetically in the text as AC.
86 Ambedkar, *Writings and Speeches*, 5:139.
87 Spivak, *An Aesthetic Education*, 464–65.
88 Ambedkar, "Castes in India," in *Essential Writings*, 242–62.
89 This "absurdist" proposition is interesting precisely because it illuminates the only path to ending Brahminical hegemony, and to general emancipation, that Ambedkar could envision in the circumstances. The solution pictures a powerful Weberian rationalization backed up by the power of a

modern state committed to equity as a foundational principle. All Shastras, except for one, had to be banned or deprived of their sacred status. Priesthood had to be abolished or at least made nonhereditary. Priests had to be salaried servants of the state and subject to ordinary laws; they had to be chosen through an entrance examination, much along the lines of the Indian Civil Services (AC, 89–90).

90 Ambedkar, *What Congress and Gandhi Have Done*, 289.
91 Ambedkar, *What Congress and Gandhi Have Done*, 294–95.
92 See Ambedkar, "Caste, Class and Democracy," in *Essential Writings*, 146.
93 See Ambedkar, "Krishna and His Gita," in *Essential Writings*, 193–203. The Gita, for Ambedkar, is not a Gospel. It is neither a book of religion nor a treatise of philosophy. It defends the dogmas of counterrevolution in Jaimani's Purva Mimansa and Badarayana's Brahmasutras and is not concerned with actions or knowledge in general. Ambedkar blames Tilak for the modern elevation of the Gita to the status of a self-contained book that has severed all connections to preceding literature. The antiquity and pure origination of the Gita is maintained by a stubborn refusal on part of figures like Telang, Radhakrishnan, or Gandhi to admit that the text is younger than Buddhism, and that the Gita's Brahmana-Nirvana theory is derived from Buddhist sources like the Mahaparinibbana Sutra of the Thedavada tradition.
94 Ambedkar, "Riddle No. 22," in *Riddles in Hinduism*, 176–77.
95 Tagore, *Nationalism*, 8–12.
96 See Tagore, *Nationalism*, 116–24; see also "Shudradharma" in Tagore, "Kalantar," 362–67.
97 Tagore, *Nationalism*, 122.

CHAPTER FOUR. HINDUTVA 2.0 AS ADVERTISED MONOTHEISM

1 Bhaumik, "The Emergence of the Bombay Film Industry."
2 Mukul, *Gita Press*. Hereafter this work is cited parenthetically in the text as GP.
3 For a survey of contributors, see GP, chapter 3, 167–224; for the Hitler reference, see 367.
4 See Mukul's discussion of an extract from a speech made by Shankaracharya Niranjan Dev Tirth in Delhi in 1967. GP, 272.
5 See Rajagopal, *Politics after Television*, especially 72–116.
6 Manisha Basu, *The Rhetoric of Hindu India*, ix.
7 Manisha Basu, *Rhetoric of Hindu India*, 17.
8 Arendt, *Origins of Totalitarianism*.
9 Arendt, *Origins of Totalitarianism*, 227–60.
10 Here, to illustrate the movement superseding the state and the people, Arendt cites Schmitt: "The Movement . . . is State as well as People, and neither

the present state . . . nor the present German people can even be conceived without the Movement." Arendt, *Origins of Totalitarianism*, 266.

11 Arendt, *Origins of Totalitarianism*, 266, 421.
12 Arendt, *Origins of Totalitarianism*, 348.
13 Arendt, *Origins of Totalitarianism*, 308–11.
14 On this, see especially Amrita Basu, *Violent Conjectures in Democratic India*, especially 52–82.
15 See Deleuze, *Cinema 2*, 262–70.
16 Zachariah, "Fascism in India," 181.
17 See Gudavarthy, *India after Modi*.
18 See e.g., Iwanek, "Love Jihad."
19 See Appadurai, *Fear of Small Numbers*.
20 See, e.g., "Congress-mukt Bharat," *The Economic Times*, February 7, 2019, https://economictimes.indiatimes.com/news/politics-and-nation/55-years-vs-55-months-narendra-modi-lays-down-his-governments-achievements/articleshow/67885812.cms.
21 Arendt, *Origins of Totalitarianism*, 363–70.
22 The list of BJP and Sangh Parivaar claims of ancient Hindu scientific advancement has become inexhaustible in contemporary public culture. See, e.g., Ayeshea Perera, "Cows to Planes," *BBC News*, September 22, 2017, https://www.bbc.com/news/world-asia-india-41344136.
23 See Rajagopal, *Politics after Television*, 117.
24 See Murphie, "The Fallen Present."
25 There have been many scholarly studies of the 2002 pogrom in Gujarat and its juridical and political aftermath. See, e.g., Berenschot, "Rioting as Maintaining Relations"; Spodek, "In the Hindutva Laboratory"; Baxi, "The Gujarat Catastrophe"; Jaffrelot, "The 2002 Pogrom in Gujarat" and "Gujarat 2002"; Ghassem-Fachandi, *Pogrom in Gujarat*; Shani, *Communalism, Caste, and Hindu Nationalism*; and Lobo and Das, *Communal Violence and Minorities*. For recent book-length accounts of investigative journalism, see Ayyub, *The Gujarat Files*; and Mitta, *Modi and Godhra*. For a historical perspective on communal riots in general, see Brass, *The Production of Hindu-Muslim Violence*.
26 The term *institutionalized riot system* comes from Brass, *The Production of Hindu-Muslim Violence*. In 2002, the Muslim wounded were often turned away from public hospitals, and the police, on a regular basis, either refused to lodge First Information Reports (FIRs) or did so erroneously, leaving out names of perpetrators mentioned by witnesses. There were no DNA samples recorded, no postmortems commissioned; cell phone CDR records were suppressed initially; and recordings of police radio communications were effaced. There were reports of police personnel actively participating in the slaughter or, as a Hindu leader once boastfully declared to a reporter on hidden camera, equipping the Saffronazi with cartridges. Nearly two hundred thousand

people took shelter in relief camps, and a Concerned Citizens Tribunal Report reported that the state government refused to give them even basics like water, sanitation, and food. See Jaffrelot, "Gujarat 2002," 78–80, for an overview. See also Rajagopal, "The Gujarat Experiment"; Anuja Jain, "Beaming It Live," and Nalin Mehta, "Modi and the Camera."

27 According to the 2005 report of the Banerjee commission appointed by the Central Railway Ministry, the forensic evidence pointed toward a fire that started inside the compartment. The Concerned Citizens Tribunal Report, conducted under retired Justice V. R. Krishna Iyer, reached the same conclusion. See, e.g., K. S. Subramanium, "Truth behind the Fire in Sabarmati Express," *Mainstream Weekly*, April 14, 2011, https://www.mainstreamweekly.net/article2684.html. On the other hand, the precise cartographic knowledge of Muslim houses, flats, and business establishments, or the logistical efficiency in terms of the supply of arson materials and weapons that marked the "spontaneous" Hindu response were eerily suggestive of a Hindu version of the Kristallnacht.

28 See, e.g., Sruthi Gottipati and Annie Banerji, "Modi's 'Puppy' Remark Triggers New Controversy," Reuters, July 12, 2013, https://in.reuters.com/article/narendra-modi-puppy-reuters-interview/modis-puppy-remark-triggers-new-controversy-over-2002-riots-idINDEE96B08S20130712.

29 I refer to the times when *India Today*, then the nation's most popular newsweekly, put Modi on the cover of its issue of April 29, 2002, with the caption, "Hero of Hatred."

30 On Modi's "Gujarat Model," see, e.g., Hirway, Shah, and Shah, *Growth or Development*; Kohli, *Poverty amid Plenty*, especially 179–91; Sood, *Poverty amidst Prosperity*; and Sud, *Liberalization, Hindu Nationalism and the State*.

31 These would be data and testimonies collected by the NGOs (the Concerned Citizens Tribunal, for example, which collected 2,094 written and oral testimonies), recordings of Modi's inflammatory public speeches, recorded by filmmakers like Rakesh Sharma, the dozen or so secret camera interviews of boastful rioters by the undercover Tehelka journalist Ashish Khetan in 2007, official statements by the renegade BJP Minister Haren Pandya, or the deposition in January 2010 by the IPS officer Sanjiv Bhatt to the Special Investigative Team (SIT) appointed by the Supreme Court. Both Pandya and Bhatt stated that in a high-level meeting on February 27, 2002, at the chief minister's residence, Modi had commanded that the administration stand down and let the Hindus vent their righteous fury. Pandya was mysteriously murdered in 2003 and Bhatt has since been suspended from service, harassed, and arrested. See Jaffrelot, "Gujarat 2002," 78.

32 "The Fourth Estate That Vanished."

33 See Jaffrelot, "The Modi-centric BJP." Jaffrelot talks about "vote mobilizers," a section of people indifferent to politics who attached themselves to the

campaign, to the extent that only about 19 percent of people canvassing for Modi were regular BJP party cadres. Special among them was a group of U.S.-trained IT experts and professionals who had a game-changing effect on digital media mobilization.

34 See Sardesai, 2014; for another journalistic account, see Price, *The Modi Effect*.
35 On the Muzaffarnagar riots that began around the last week of August 2013, and in which more than 50 people were killed and about 50,000 displaced, see, e.g., Hilal Ahmed, "Muzaffarnagar 2013." For a visual documentation, see Nakul Singh Sawney's brilliant film *Muzaffarnagar baki hain* (2015).
36 See Faizan Ahmad, "Those Opposed to Narendra Modi," *Times of India*, April 20, 2019, https://timesofindia.indiatimes.com/news/Those-opposed-to-Narendra-Modi-should-go-to-Pakistan-BJP-leader-Giriraj-Singh-says/articleshow/33971544.cms.
37 See Jeffrey and Doron, "Mobile-izing," for a fascinating account of the 2007 UP elections as the first mass mobile phone elections in India, when the Dalit Bahujan Samaj Party (BSP) under Mayawati used them to circumvent the mainstream media.
38 See Telecom Regulatory Authority of India, 2009–2010 Annual Report, https://trai.gov.in/sites/default/files/ar_09_10.pdf; and 2014–2015 Annual Report, https://trai.gov.in/sites/default/files/TRAI-Annual-Report-%28English%29%3D01042015.pdf, accessed December 23, 2018.
39 For the first two decades after independence, India was ruled by massive absolute majority Congress governments. However, this Congress, under that Fabian socialist Jawaharlal Nehru, was not just a political party; it was a singular mode for organizing and giving a functional form to a clamorous polity quite breathtaking in the range of its subsurface realities. One could call it a brave new consociationalist arrangement between competing powers at best and a catastrophic balancing act at worst. The "Congress System," as Rajni Kothari famously described it, was about absorbing, often with considerable political endurance, multitudinous energies of the local kind and producing a working consensus at the top. In the decades that followed, the inevitable happened. Instead of splitting left and right into bipolar "big tent" entities, the Congress became the mother of a thousand parties in the course of its long dispersal. From the late 1960s onward, with the surfacing of regional nationalisms, the Dalit organizations, the Lohia socialists, and a series of internal ruptures in the Congress itself, the ground for the "essentially coalitional" reality of Indian politics was laid. See Kothari, *Politics in India*.
40 Gupta borrows the term from the Persian intellectual Jalal-e-Ahmad, who had declared that if the Iranian middle classes were truly westernized, they would not have allowed a Khomeini. Westoxification, in that sense, is "traditional snobbery with contemporary artefacts." See Dipankar Gupta, *Mistaken Modernity*, 21–24.

41 Rajagopal, "The Emergency as Prehistory." See also van der Veer, "Virtual India." The essay connects what I am calling the figure of the Gentoo to the informational India with a diasporic extension, with Narayana Murthy of Infosys as middle-class icon. For insightful sociological studies of the postliberalization middle class, see Fernandes, *India's New Middle Class*; Deshpande, *Contemporary India*; and Derne, *Globalization on the Ground*.

42 The concept of Dehat here undeniably refers more to North Indian "cow belt" ruling groups—traditional upper castes like the Thakurs and OBC caste elites like the Jats—than to South Indian agrarian sections. See Jaffrelot, *India's Silent Revolution*. The traditional polarization of identities between Congress and the BJP had been that of the KHAM alliance (Kshatriya, Harijans, Adivasis, and Muslims) versus the upper castes like the Brahmins, the Baniyas, and the Patels.

43 For a glimpse of the internal schisms within the RSS and the BJP in the run-up to the 2014 elections, see Guichard, "How Autonomous Are the Branches?"

44 A classic example would be that of the public intellectual Gurcharan Das; see "The Modi Mirage," *Foreign Affairs*, April 11, 2019, https://www.foreignaffairs.com/articles/india/2019-04-11/modi-mirage.

45 As of now, only Jats of Rajasthan are entitled to OBC reservations for Central Government jobs.

46 See, e.g., Chandru, "Ad-hocism."

47 See, e.g., Renu Desai, "Governing the Urban Poor."

48 In the recent run up to the 2019 elections, Hindutva publicity has focalized itself more acutely around the figure of Modi. His administration has spent an astronomical amount of resources advertising the man and his schemes. There is now an entire television channel, NAMO TV, and a Namo app dedicated to his life and words. That is, apart from Fox News–style strong propaganda machines like Zee News and Republic TV. Bollywood has just finished a biopic of the prime minister set to be released on the eve of the elections. Over the years, there has been a pronounced revisionist desire to build a celluloid mythology of Indian militaristic achievements under the first and second NDA governments: for example, *Paramanu: The Story of Pokhran* (dir. Abhishek Sharma, 2018), on the Indian nuclear test explosions conducted by the Vajpayee administration in 1998, or *Uri: The Surgical Strike* (dir. Aditya Dhar, 2019), a fictional account of the Indian army's reprisal against the Uri attacks of 2016.

49 On this, see Zielinski, *Deep Time of the Media*.

50 See Stiegler, *Technics and Time 2*.

51 See, e.g., Deleuze, *Cinema 2*, 262–80; Agamben, *Means without Ends*; Rancière, *The Future of the Image*; Hayles, *How We Became Posthuman*; and Janich, *What Is Information?* For a useful view of this terrain, see Hassan, *The Information Society*; or Poster, *Information Please*.

52 Amit Rai, *Untimely Bollywood*, 3–4.
53 Derrida and Stiegler, *Echographies of Television*, 4.
54 See Stiegler, *Technics and Time 2*, 97–187.
55 Benjamin, "The Storyteller," 89.
56 For microlevel, situated, and vivid studies, see, e.g., Singh, "Citizen Journalism"; or Saeed, "Negotiating Power."
57 See, e.g., the essays in Clough and Halley, *The Affective Turn*.
58 Deleuze, *Spinoza*, 18–22.
59 Jenkins, *Convergence Culture*, 66.
60 See, e.g., the essays in Turrow and Tsui, *The Hyperlinked Society*.
61 Jenkins, *Convergence Culture*, 20. The term *lovemark* was coined by Kevin Roberts, CEO worldwide of Saatchi & Saatchi.
62 Amit Rai, *Untimely Bollywood*, 87.
63 Jenkins, *Convergence Culture*, 66, 280.
64 I allude to Rancière, *The Politics of Aesthetics*: "The system of self-evident facts of sense perception that simultaneously discloses the existence of something in common and the delimitations that define the respective parts and positions within it" (12).
65 See, e.g., Bikash Singh, "Internet Existed in the Days of the Mahabharata," *The Economic Times*, April 18, 2018, https://economictimes.indiatimes.com/news/politics-and-nation/internet-existed-in-the-days-of-mahabharata-tripura-cm-biplab-deb/articleshow/63803490.cms.
66 Castells, *The Information Age*, esp. 69–170.
67 See Marx, *Grundrisse*, 191–228.
68 This is, of course, not to say that internet cultures are the same in all societies or to forget the fact that the net is still overwhelmingly Anglophone. See, e.g., Poster, *Information Please*, 81–83.
69 Mazzarella, "Beautiful Balloon"; and Ravi Sundaram, "Beyond the Nationalist Panopticon."
70 The measure in itself—taking around 86 percent of currency notes out of circulation in an economy where more than 90 percent of all transactions are in cash—has been panned in general by economists around the world. Over 170 people died standing in bank queues; millions of jobs were lost and thousands of small-scale industries and businesses closed down. See, e.g., Michael Safi, "Demonetization Drive," *The Guardian*, August 30, 2018, https://www.theguardian.com/world/2018/aug/30/india-demonetisation-drive-fails-uncover-black-money.
71 See, e.g., Sumit Agarwal, "India's Demonetization Drive," *Forbes*, September 1, 2018, https://www.forbes.com/sites/nusbusinessschool/2018/09/01/indias-demonetization-drive-a-necessary-jolt-towards-a-more-digital-economy/#5650d7453dc3.
72 An excellent work on this new form of urbanization is Ravi Sundaram's *Pirate Modernity: Delhi's Media Urbanism*.

73 See Nair, *The Promise of Metropolis*; and Prakash, *Mumbai Fables*.
74 For book-length studies, see, e.g., Anustip Basu, *Bollywood in the Age of New Media*; Butcher, *Transnational Television, Cultural Identity, and Change*; Kumar, *Gandhi Meets Primetime*; Kohli-Kandhekar, *Indian Media Business*; Manteca, *Screening Culture, Viewing Politics*; Mazzarella, *Shoveling Smoke*; Nalin Mehta, *Television in India*; Punathambekar, *From Bombay to Bollywood*; Amit Rai, *Untimely Bollywood*; and Rajagopal, *Politics after Television*.
75 Kumar, *Gandhi Meets Primetime*, 46.
76 See Kohli-Kandhekar, *Indian Media Business*, 64.
77 According to the Broadcast Audience Research Council's (BARC) Universe Update of 2018, television penetration had more than doubled since 2001, having climbed from 32 percent to 66 percent. In 2018 there were 197 million television homes in India, an increase of 7.5 percent from the 2016 numbers. The total number of viewers had increased by 7.2 percent to a gargantuan population of 836 million. See BARC India Universe Update, July 2018, https://www.barcindia.co.in/resources/pdf/BARC%20India%20Universe%20Update%20-%202018.pdf.
78 See especially Punathambekar, *From Bombay to Bollywood*.
79 India Brand Equity Foundation, "Media and Entertainment," February 2019, https://www.ibef.org/download/media-and-entertainment-feb-2019.pdf.
80 The auratic grip of IT on the Indian millennial imagination, nevertheless, was an outsized one. Currently estimated at $167 billion, the Information Technology-BPM industry is less than 10 percent of the Indian GDP and a fraction of the global IT industry, whose value is estimated at around $5 trillion. See the analysis in the India Brand Equity Foundation report at https://www.ibef.org/industry/indian-iT-and-iTeS-industry-analysis-presentation. A good chunk of the industry comprises emotional labor in call centers, backroom work, and other outsourced functions by what have been called the "coolies of the digital world." See, e.g., Mazzarella, "Beautiful Ballooon"; and Bryson, "The 'Second' Global Shift."
81 See Mallapragada, "Desktop Dieties."
82 See, e.g., Urban, *Zorba the Buddha*.
83 Rajagopal, *Politics after Television*, 239–46. The VHP organized the Global Vision Conference, Washington, DC, in 1993. The VHP's pastoral activities in the United States involved templates familiar to the culture like youth camps, seminars, lecture tours, family counseling, and social service. It would also be pertinent to remember that the VHP in India protested GATT, while the one overseas endorsed it.
84 On this, see Sudeep Dasgupta, *Hindu Nationalism*; and Mallapragada, *Virtual Homelands*.
85 See Manisha Basu, *The Rhetoric of Hindu India*.
86 See, e.g., Mary E. John, "Globalization, Sexuality, and the Visual Field."

87　Kumar, *Gandhi Meets Primetime*.
88　This does not mean that print media is in eclipse. Unlike most Western democracies, newspaper circulation has been growing in India. See, e.g., Ram, "The Changing Role"; and Neyazi, "Politics after Vernacularisation."
89　See the essays in Punathambekar and Kavoori, *Global Bollywood*; especially those by M. Madhava Prasad, Ashish Rajadhyaksha, Tejaswini Ganti, Shanti Kumar, and Daya Kishan Thussu.
90　See Hall, "India's New Public Diplomacy"; Thussu, *Communicating India's Soft Power*; and Punathambekar, *From Bombay to Bollywood* on the Bollywood, and IT modes of branding India and its soft power, and on mitigating bad international perceptions about freedom of press, corruption, health, transparency, and so on.
91　Yogendra Yadav, "Social Profile of India Media," *The South Asian*, June 12, 2006, cited and discussed in Maxine Loynd, "Politics without Television," 71.
92　Jeffrey, "The Mahatma Didn't Like the Movies."
93　See Devy, *People's Linguistic Survey of India*, vol. 1.
94　Anustup Basu, *Bollywood in the Age of New Media*.
95　Prasad, *Ideology of the Hindi Film*.
96　Mazumdar, *Bombay Cinema*, chapter 2.
97　See for instance Anustup Basu, "The Eternal Return."
98　Pinney, "The Politics of Popular Images." Also, on the circulation of images as embodied value, see Kajri Jain, "More Than Meets the Eye."
99　See Anustup Basu, "The Passion of the Digital."
100　See Prakash, *Mumbai Fables*; and Suketu Mehta, *Maximum City*.
101　Biswas, "Mourning and Blood Ties."
102　See Anustup Basu, "Encounters in the City."
103　The practice, as a culturally identified phenomenon, has a longer pan-Indian history, stretching back at least to the state's suppression of Maoist insurgency in Bengal and in other parts of eastern India from the mid-1960s.
104　Pradeep Sharma is said to have led the pack, allegedly with more than a hundred killings, followed by other stars like Praful Bhonsle, Ravindra Angre, and Vijay Salaskar. Daya Nayak, allegedly with eighty-odd notches on his belt, has perhaps been the most famous of the encounter specialists. See Sagnik Chowdhury and Neeraj Chauhan, "The Dirty Harrys of Indian Police," *The Indian Express*, March 27, 2008, http://www.indianexpress.com/news/the-dirty-harrys-of-indian-police/288872/2.
105　See Alex Perry, "Urban Cowboys," *Time*, January 6, 2003, http://http://content.time.com/time/magazine/article/0,9171,404315,00.html.
106　See especially chapter 4 in Daya Kishan Thussu's *News as Entertainment*, 91–112.
107　See Rajagopal, "The Gujarat Experiment."
108　Arendt, *Origins of Totalitarianism*, 423.

109 See Khalidi, "Hinduising India," for an insightful indictment of Indian secularism on the conversion question. The Congress government of Madya Pradesh had pioneered anticonversion legislation in 1954. This practice took an especially urgent form when several hundred Dalits converted to Islam in Meenakshipuram, TN, in 1981–82. Between then and 2007, eight states—Andhra Pradesh, Chhattisgarh, Gujarat, Himachal Pradesh, Madhya Pradesh, Orissa, Rajasthan, and Tripura—have passed anticonversion legislation. The Gujarat model is particularly blatant, making it impossible to convert to Islam, while Buddhists and Jains may become Hindus. For an overview of the historical role of the Indian judiciary on such matters, see Ronojoy Sen, "The Indian Supreme Court."

110 See Piyush Rai, "Yogi Govt Lists Encounters as Part of Achievements," *The Economic Times*, January 26, 2019, https://economictimes.indiatimes.com/news/politics-and-nation/yogi-govt-lists-encounters-as-part-of-achievements-to-be-highlighted-on-r-day/articleshow/67699717.cms.

111 See Arendt's discussion of French anti-Semitism and the Dreyfus Affair in *Origins of Totalitarianism*, especially 86–87.

112 See Judy, "Democracy or Ideology," for a brilliant exposition of this central tendency in contemporary international Islamophobia. According to a 2006 report furnished by a governmental committee appointed by the Indian Prime Minister Manmohan Singh and chaired by Justice Rajinder Sachar, the condition of Muslims in India was worse than that of the Dalits. Fifty-two percent of Muslim men were unemployed, compared with 47 percent of Dalit men. Among women, the ratio was 91 percent to 77 percent. Almost half of Muslims over the age of 46 couldn't read or write. While making up 11 percent of the population at that point, Muslims accounted for 40 percent of India's prison population. Meanwhile, they held less than 5 percent of government jobs. See Ministry of Minority Affairs, *The Sachar Committee Report*, accessed March 21, 2016, http://minorityaffairs.gov.in/reports/sachar-committee-report.

113 See Agamben, *Remnants of Auschwitz*, 18.

114 Latour, *Reassembling the Social*.

115 Latour, *Reassembling the Social*, 64–65.

116 Latour, *Reassembling the Social*, 108.

117 Benjamin, "Capitalism as Religion."

118 Taylor, *A Secular Age*, 299.

119 Nietzsche, *The Birth of Tragedy; and The Genealogy of Morals*, 298.

BIBLIOGRAPHY

Abu-Lughod, Janet. "Going beyond Global Babble." In *Culture, Globalization and the World System: Contemporary Conditions for the Representation of Identity*, edited by Anthony King, 131–38. Minneapolis: University of Minnesota Press, 1997.

Agamben, Giorgio. *Means without Ends*. Translated by Vincenzo Binetti and Cesare Caesarino. Minneapolis: University of Minnesota Press, 2000.

Agamben, Giorgio. *Potentialities: Collected Essays in Philosophy*. Edited by Daniel Heller-Roazen. Stanford, CA: Stanford University Press, 2000.

Agamben, Giorgio. *Remnants of Auschwitz: The Witness and the Archive*. Translated by Daniel Heller-Roazen. Stanford, CA: Stanford University Press, 1998.

Ahmad, Imtiaz. "The Islamic Tradition in India." *Islam and the Modern Age* 12, no. 1 (1981): 44–62.

Ahmed, Hilal. "Muzaffarnagar 2013: Meanings of Violence." *Economic and Political Weekly* 48, no. 40 (October 5, 2013): 10–13.

Aldhuri, Vishwa P. "Pride and Prejudice: Orientalism and German Indology." *International Journal of Hindu Studies* 15, no. 3 (December 2011): 253–92.

Ambedkar, B. R. *Annihilation of Caste: With a Reply to Mahatma Gandhi; and Castes in India: Their Mechanism, Genesis, and Development*. Jullundur: Bheem Patrika, 1968.

Ambedkar, B. R. *Essential Writings of B. R. Ambedkar*. Edited by Valerian Rodrigues. New Delhi: Oxford University Press, 2004.

Ambedkar, B. R. *Riddles in Hinduism*. Edited by S. Anand and Shobhna Iyer. New Delhi: Navayana, 2016.

Ambedkar, B. R. *Thoughts on Linguistic States*. Aligarh: Anand Sahitya Sadan, 1989.

Ambedkar, B. R. *What Congress and Gandhi Have Done to the Untouchables*. Bombay: Thacker, 1946.

Ambedkar, B. R. *Writings and Speeches*. Volume 5. New Delhi: Ambedkar Foundation, 2014.

Amin, Shahid. "Gandhi as Mahatma: Gorakhpur District, Eastern University Press, 1921–22." In *Subaltern Studies III: Writings on South Asian History and Society*, edited by Ranajit Guha, 1–61. Delhi: Oxford University Press, 1984.

Andersen, Walter K., and Shridhar D. Damle. *The Brotherhood of Saffron: The Rashtriya Swayamsevak Sangh and Hindu Revivalism*. London: Westview, 1987.

Appadurai, Arjun. *Fear of Small Numbers*. Durham, NC: Duke University Press, 2006.

Aravamudan, Srinivas. *Guru English: South Asian Religion in a Cosmopolitan Language*. Princeton, NJ: Princeton University Press, 2005.

Arendt, Hannah. *The Origins of Totalitarianism*. New York: Harcourt, 1973.

Asad, Talal. *Genealogies of Religion: Discipline and Reasons of Power in Christianity and Islam*. Baltimore: Johns Hopkins University Press, 1993.

Ayyub, Rana. "The Gujarat Files: Anatomy of a Cover Up." Foreword by Justice B. N. Krishna. Self-published, 2016.

Azfar Moin, A. *The Millennial Sovereign: Sacred Kingship and Sainthood in Islam*. New York: Columbia University Press, 2014.

Banaji, Jairus, ed. *Fascism: Essays on Europe and India*. New Delhi: Three Essays Collective, 2013.

Bandyopadhyay, Sibaji. "Atho ma faleshu kadachon." *Anustup Sharodiya* (2003): 2–232.

Bandyopadhyay, Sibaji. *Bangla uponyashe 'ora.'* Calcutta: Papyrus, 1996.

Bandyopadhyay, Sibaji. *The Gopal-Rakhal Dialectic: Colonialism and Children's Literature in Bengal*. Translated by Rani Ray and Nivedita Sen. New Delhi: Tulika, 2015.

Bandyopadhyay, Sibaji. "The Mahabharata." In *Indian Keywords*, edited by Peter de Souza and Rukmini Nair. London: Bloomsbury, 2019.

Bandyopadhyay, Sibaji. "Non-dualism and Nationalism." In *Sibaji Bandyopadhyay Reader: An Anthology of Essays*, 38–144. Delhi: Worldview, 2012.

Bandyopadhyay, Sibaji. "Punar bishoye punarbibechona." In *Alibabar Guptabhandar*, 217–74. Kolkata: Gangchil, 2009.

Bandyopadhyay, Sibaji. *Three Essays on the Mahabharata: Exercises in Literary Hermeneutics*. Hyderabad: Orient Blackswan, 2016.

Banerjea, Reverend Krishnamohan. *Dialogues on the Hindu Philosophy, Comprising the Nyaya, the Sankhya, the Vedant, to Which Is Added a Discussion of the Authority of the Vedas*. Calcutta: Williams and Norgate, 1861.

Barton Scott, J. *Spiritual Despots: Modern Hinduism and the Genealogies of Self-Rule*. Chicago: University of Chicago Press, 2016.

Basu, Amrita. *Violent Conjectures in Democratic India*. New York: Cambridge University Press, 2015.

Basu, Anustup. *Bollywood in the Age of New Media: The Geotelevisual Aesthetic*. Edinburgh: Edinburgh University Press, 2010.

Basu, Anustup. "Encounters in the City: Cops, Criminals, and Human Rights in Hindi Film." *Journal of Human Rights* 9, no. 2 (2010): 175–90.

Basu, Anustup. "The Eternal Return and Overcoming 'Cape Fear': Science, Sensation, Superman, and Hindu Nationalism in Recent Hindi Cinema." *South Asian History and Culture* 2, no. 4 (October 2011): 557–71.

Basu, Anustup. "The Passion of the Digital: The Ontology of the Photographic Image in the Age of New Media." *Recherches sémiotiques/Semiotic Inquiry* 31, nos. 1–3 (2011): 175–202.

Basu, Manisha. *The Rhetoric of Hindu India*. New Delhi: Cambridge University Press, 2017.

Basu, Tapan, Pradip Datta, Sumit Sarkar, Tanika Sarkar, and Sambuddha Sen. *Khaki Shorts and Saffron Flags: A Critique of Hindu Nationalists*. New Delhi: Orient Longman, 1993.

Baxi, Upendra. "The Constitutional Discourse on Secularism." In *Reconstructing the Republic*, edited by Upendra Baxi, Alice Jacob, and Tarlok Singh, 211–32. New Delhi: Har-anand Publications, 1999.

Baxi, Upendra. "The Gujarat Catastrophe: Notes on Reading Politics as Democidal Rape Culture." In *The Violence of the Normal Times*, edited by Kalpana Kannabiran, 332–83. New Delhi: Women Unlimited, 2005.

Belvalkar, S. K. "Introduction." In *The Mahabharata: Bhismaparvan*, vol. 7. Poona: Bhandarkar Oriental Research Institute, 1947.

Benjamin, Walter. "Capitalism as Religion." In *Walter Benjamin: Selected Writings*, vol. 1, edited by Marcus Bullock and Michael W. Jannings, 288–91. Cambridge, MA: Belknap, 2000.

Benjamin, Walter. "The Storyteller: Reflections on the Works of Nikolai Leskov." Translated by Harry Zohn. In *Illuminations*, 83–107. London: Fontana, 1973.

Berenschot, Ward. "Rioting as Maintaining Relations: Hindu-Muslim Violence and Political Mediation in Gujarat, India." *Civil Wars* 11, no. 4 (2009): 414–43.

Bhattacharya, Sibesh. "Methodology of the Critical Edition of the *Mahabharata*." In *Mahabharata Now: Narration, Aesthetics, Ethics*, edited by Sibaji Bandyopadhyay and Arindam Chakrabarti, 37–56. Delhi: Routledge, 2014.

Bhaumik, Kaushik. "The Emergence of the Bombay Film Industry, 1913–1936." PhD dissertation, Oxford University, 2001.

Biswas, Moinak. "Mourning and Blood Ties: Macbeth in Mumbai." *Journal of the Moving Image* 5 (2006). https://jmionline.org/article/mourning_and_blood_ties_macbeth_in_mumbai/.

Blavatsky, H. P. *Isis Unveiled*. Vol. 1. London: J. W. Bouton, 1877.

Blumenberg, Hans. *The Legitimacy of the Modern Age*. Translated by Robert Wallace. Cambridge, MA: MIT Press, 1983.

Bose, Subhash Chandra. *The Indian Struggle*. Bombay: Asia Publishing House, 1964.

Brass, Paul. *Language, Religion, and Politics in Northern India*. New York: Cambridge University Press, 1974.

Brass, Paul. *The Production of Hindu-Muslim Violence in Contemporary India*. Seattle: University of Washington Press, 2003.

Bryson, John. "The 'Second' Global Shift: The Offshoring or Global Sourcing of Corporate Services and the Rise of Distanced Emotional Labor." In *Geografiska Annaler: Series B, Human Geography* 89, supp. 1 (2007): 31–43.

Butcher, Melissa. *Transnational Television, Cultural Identity, and Change: When STAR Came to India*. London: SAGE, 2003.

Casolari, Marzia. "Hindutva's Foreign Tie-Ups in the 1930s." *Economic and Political Weekly* 35, no. 4 (January 22, 2000): 218–28.

Castells, Manuel. *The Information Age: Economy, Society and Culture*. Vol. 3, *End of Millennium*. Oxford: Blackwell, 2000.

Chakraborty, Chandrima. *Masculinity, Asceticism, Hinduism: Past and Present Imaginings of India*. New Delhi: Permanent Black, 2011.

Chakravarty, Swapan, ed. *Mudroner shongskriti o bangla boi*. Calcutta: Abobhaas, 2007.

Chandru, K. "Ad-hocism in the Decisions to Modify Labor Laws." *Economic and Political Weekly* 49, no. 30 (July 26, 2014): 15–18.

Chatterjee, Partha. *Nationalist Thought and the Colonial World: A Derivative Discourse?* New Delhi: Oxford University Press, 1986.

Chatterjee, Partha. *The Nation and Its Fragments*. Princeton, NJ: Princeton University Press, 1993.

Chattopadhyay, Bankimchandra. "Buddhism and Sankhya Philosophy." In *Bankim Rachanabali*, vol. 3, edited by Jogesh Chandra Bagal, 125–36. Calcutta: Sahitya Samsad, 1969.

Chattopadhyay, Bankimchandra. "Dharmatattva." In *Bankim Rachanabali*, vol. 2, edited by Jogesh Chandra Bagal, 512–615. Calcutta: Sahitya Samsadad, 1954.

Chattopadhyay, Bankimchandra. "Krishnacharitra." In *Bankim Rachanabali*, vol. 2, edited by Jogesh Chandra Bagal, 407–583. Calcutta: Sahitya Samsad, 1954.

Chattopadhyay, Bankimchandra. "Letters on Hinduism." In *Bankim Rachanabali*, vol. 3, edited by Jogesh Chandra Bagal, 227–69. Calcutta: Sahitya Samsad, 1969.

Chaudhuri, Sukanta, ed. *Calcutta: The Living City*. Vol. 1, *The Past*. Calcutta: Oxford University Press, 1990.

Cheah, Pheng. *Spectral Nationality: Passages of Freedom from Kant to Postcolonial Literatures of Liberation*. New York: Columbia University Press, 2013.

Clough, Patricia, and Jean Halley, eds. *The Affective Turn: Political Economy, Biomedia, and Bodies*. Durham, NC: Duke University Press, 2007.

Comte, Auguste. *The Positive Philosophy of Auguste Comte*. Translated by Harriet Marineau. Vol. 6, *Social Sciences*. New York: William Gowans, 1868.

Connolly, William. *Capitalism and Christianity, American Style*. Durham, NC: Duke University Press, 2008.

Dalmia, Vasudha. *The Nationalization of Indian Traditions: Bharatendu Harishchandra and Nineteenth-Century Banaras*. Delhi: Oxford University Press, 1997.

Das, Anirban. "Of Sleep and Violence: Reading the *Sauptikaparvan* in Times of Terror." In *Mahabharata Now: Narration, Aesthetics, Ethics*, edited by Arindam Chakrabarti and Sibaji Bandyopadhyay, 203–18. London: Routledge, 2014.

Das, Kalyan Kumar. "Encountering John Dewey's 'Pragmatism' in an Indian Context: Ambedkar's Critique of War, Violence, and Nationalism." *Dewey Studies* 2, no. 3 (2018): 125–42.

Das, Sisir Kumar. *A History of Indian Literature*. Vol. 8, 1800–1910. New Delhi: Sahitya Akademi, 1991.

Dasgupta, Shashibhushan. *Obscure Religious Cults*. Calcutta: Firma KLM, 1962.

Dasgupta, Sudeep. *Hindu Nationalism, Television, and the Avatars of Capital*. Veenendaal: Universal Press, 2001.

Dasgupta, Surendranath. *A History of Indian Philosophy*. 7 vols. Delhi: Motilal Banarasidass, 1975.

Debord, Guy. *The Society of the Spectacle*. Translated by Donald Nicholson-Smith. New York: Zone Books, 1995.

Deleuze, Gilles. *Cinema 2: The Time-Image*. Translated by Hugh Tomlinson and Robert Galeta. Minneapolis: University of Minnesota Press, 1989.

Deleuze, Gilles. *Foucault*. Translated by Sean Hand. Minneapolis: University of Minnesota Press, 1997.

Deleuze, Gilles. *Spinoza: Practical Philosophy*. Translated by Robert Hurley. San Francisco: City Lights, 2001.

Derne, Steve. *Globalization on the Ground: Media and the Transformation of Culture, Class, and Gender in India*. London: SAGE, 2008.

Derrida, Jacques. "Racism's Last Word." *Critical Inquiry* 12, no. 1 (autumn 1985): 290–99.

Derrida, Jacques, and Bernard Stiegler. *Echographies of Television*. Cambridge, MA: Polity Press, 2002.

Desai, Radhika. "A Latter-Day Fascism?" *Economic and Political Weekly* 49, no. 35 (August 30, 2014): 48–58.

Desai, Renu. "Governing the Urban Poor: Riverfront Development, Slum Resettlement, and the Politics of Inclusion in Ahmedabad." *Economic and Political Weekly* 47, no. 2 (January 14, 2012): 49–56.

Deshpande, Satish. *Contemporary India: A Sociological View*. New Delhi: Viking, 2003.

Devy, G. N. *After Amnesia: Tradition and Change in Indian Literary Criticism*. Hyderabad: Orient Blackswan, 2017.

Devy, G. N., ed. *People's Linguistic Survey of India*. Vol. 1, *The Being of Bhasha: A General Introduction*. Hyderabad: Orient Blackswan, 2014.

Doniger, Wendy. *The Hindus: An Alternative History*. New York: Penguin, 2009.

Doniger, Wendy, and Brian K. Smith, eds. *The Laws of Manu*. New Delhi: Penguin, 1991.

Dumont, Louis. *Homo Hierarchus: The Caste System and Its Implications*. Translated by Mark Sainsbury. Chicago: University of Chicago Press, 1980.
Eck, Diana. *India: A Sacred Geography*. New York: Random House, 2012.
Embree, Ainslie T., ed. *Sources of Indian Tradition*. Vol. 1. 2nd ed. New York: Columbia University Press, 1988.
Faruqi, Samsur Rahman. *Early Urdu Literary Culture and History*. Delhi: Oxford University Press, 2001.
Fazl, Abul. *The Ain-I-Akbari*. Vol. 3, translated by H. S. Jarrett. Calcutta: Asiatic Society, 1894.
Fernandes, Leela. *India's New Middle Class: Democratic Politics in an Era of Economic Reform*. Minneapolis: University of Minnesota Press, 2006.
Fichte, J. G. *Addresses to the German Nation*. Translated by R. F. Jones and G. H. Turnbull. Chicago: University of Chicago Press, 1922.
Foucault, Michel. *Language, Counter-memory, Practice: Selected Essays and Interviews*. Edited by Donald F. Bouchard. Ithaca, NY: Cornell University Press, 1977.
Foucault, Michel. *Society Must Be Defended: Lectures at the Collége de France, 1975–76*. Translated by David Macey. New York: Picador, 2003.
"The Fourth Estate That Vanished." *Economic and Political Weekly* 49, no. 21 (May 24, 2014). https://www.epw.in/journal/2014/21/editorials/fourth-estate-vanished.html.
Fukuyama, Francis. *The End of History and the Last Man*. New York: Avon, 1992.
Gandhi, M. K. *The Essential Writings of Mahatma Gandhi*. Edited by Raghavan Iyer. New Delhi: Oxford University Press, 1990.
Ghassem-Fachandi, Parvis. *Pogrom in Gujarat: Hindu Nationalism and Anti-Muslim Violence in India*. Princeton, NJ: Princeton University Press, 2012.
Golwalkar, M. S. *Bunch of Thoughts*. Bangalore: Vikrama Prakashan, 1966.
Golwalkar, M. S. "Students Are Not the Pillars of the Nation: They Are Its Servants." *Organizer*, January 2, 1961, 5.
Golwalkar, M. S. *Thoughts on Some Current Problems*. Bombay: Hindustan Sahitya, 1957.
Golwalkar, M. S. *We, or, Our Nationhood Defined*. Nagpur: Bharat, 1939.
Gordon, Leonard A. *Brothers against the Raj: A Biography of Indian Nationalists Sarat and Subhas Chandra Bose*. New York: Columbia University Press, 1990.
Goswami, Manu. *Producing India: From Colonial Economy to National Space*. Chicago: University of Chicago Press, 2004.
Gudavarthy, Ajay. *India after Modi: Populism and the Right*. London: Bloomsbury, 2018.
Guha, Ranajit. *Elementary Aspects of Peasant Insurgency in Colonial India*. Durham, NC: Duke University Press, 1999.
Guha, Ranajit. *An Indian Historiography of India: A Nineteenth-Century Agenda*. Calcutta: K. P. Bagchi, 1988.

Guichard, Sylvie. "How Autonomous Are the Branches? A Study of Narendra Modi's BJP." *Economic and Political Weekly* 48, no. 9 (March 2, 2013): 40–46.

Gupta, Dipankar. *Mistaken Modernity: India between Worlds*. New Delhi: HarperCollins, 2000.

Gupta, Suman. "On the Indian Readers of Hitler's *Mein Kampf*." *Economic and Political Weekly* 47, no. 46 (November 17, 2012): 51–58.

Hakala, Walter N. *Negotiating Languages: Urdu, Hindi, and the Definition of Modern South Asia*. New York: Columbia University Press, 2016.

Hall, Ian. "India's New Public Diplomacy." *Asian Survey* 52, no. 6 (November/December 2012): 1089–110.

Hansen, Thomas Blom. *The Saffron Wave: Democracy and Hindu Nationalism in Modern India*. Princeton, NJ: Princeton University Press, 1999.

Hardiman, David. "Power in the Forests: The Dangs, 1820–1940." In *Subaltern Studies VII: Essays in Honor of Ranajit Guha*, edited by David Arnold and David Hardiman, 89–147. Delhi: Oxford University Press, 1994.

Hassan, Robert. *The Information Society: Cyber Dreams and Digital Nightmares*. Cambridge: Polity, 2008.

Hayles, Katherine N. *How We Became Posthuman: Virtual Bodies in Cybernetics, Literature, and Informatics*. Chicago: Chicago University Press, 1999.

Hegel, G. W. F. *Introductory Lectures on Aesthetics*. Translated by Bernard Bosanquet. London: Penguin, 1993.

Hegel, G. W. F. *Lectures on the Philosophy of World History: Introduction*. Translated by H. B. Nisbet. Cambridge: Cambridge University Press, 1975.

Hegel, G. W. F. *On the Episode of the Mahabharata Known by the Name Bhagwad-Gita by Wilhelm von Humbolt*. Translated by Herbert Herring. New Delhi: Indian Council of Philosophical Research, 1995.

Hegel, G. W. F. *Phenomenology of Spirit*. Translated by A. V. Miller. London: Oxford University Press, 1977.

Hegel, G. W. F. *Philosophy of Right*. Translated by T. M. Knox. New York: Oxford University Press, 1967.

Hiriyanna, M. *Essentials of Indian Philosophy*. Delhi: Motilal Banarasidass, 2015.

Hirway, Indira, Amita Shah, and Ghanshyam Shah, eds. *Growth or Development: Which Way Is Gujarat Going?* New Delhi: Oxford University Press, 2014.

Hobbes, Thomas. *Leviathan*. New York: Oxford University Press, 1996.

Ilaiah, Kancha. "Towards the Dalitization of the Nation." In *Wages of Freedom: Fifty Years of the Indian Nation State*, edited by Partha Chatterjee, 267–91. New Delhi: Oxford University Press, 1998.

Ilaiah, Kancha. *Why I Am Not a Hindu: A Sudra Critique of Hindutva Philosophy, Culture, and Political Economy*. Calcutta: Samya, 1996.

International Institute for Population Sciences (IIPS) and ICF. *National Family Health Survey (NFHS-4), 2015–16: India*. Mumbai: IIPS, 2017. Accessed June 1, 2018. http://dhsprogram.com/pubs/pdf/FR339/FR339.pdf.

Iwanek, Krzystof. "'Love Jihad' and the Stereotypes of Muslims in Hindu Nationalism." *Journal of Alternative Perspectives in the Social Sciences* 7, no. 3 (2016): 355–99.

Jaffrelot, Christophe. *Dr. Ambedkar and Untouchability: Fighting the Indian Caste System*. New York: Columbia University Press, 2005.

Jaffrelot, Christophe. "Gujarat 2002: What Justice for the Victims? The Supreme Court, the SIT, the Police, and the State Judiciary." *Economic and Political Weekly* 47, no. 8 (February 25, 2012): 77–89.

Jaffrelot, Christophe. "Hindu Nationalism and Democracy." In *Transforming India: Social and Political Dimensions of Democracy*, edited by Francine R. Frankel, Zoya Hasan, Rajeev Bhargava, and Balveer Arora, 353–78. New Delhi: Oxford University Press, 2000.

Jaffrelot, Christophe. *The Hindu Nationalist Movement in India*. New Delhi: Viking, 1996.

Jaffrelot, Christophe. *The Hindu Phenomenon*. New Delhi: Viking, 1993.

Jaffrelot, Christophe. *India's Silent Revolution: The Rise of the Low Castes in North Indian Politics*. New Delhi: Permanent Black, 2003.

Jaffrelot, Christophe. "The Modi-centric BJP 2014 Election Campaign: New Techniques and Old Tactics." *Contemporary South Asia* 23, no. 2 (2015): 151–66.

Jaffrelot, Christophe. *Religion, Caste and Politics in India*. New Delhi: Primus, 2010.

Jaffrelot, Christophe. "The 2002 Pogrom in Gujarat: The Post-9/11 Face of Hindu Nationalist Anti-Muslim Violence." In *Religion and Violence in South Asia*, edited by J. Hinnels and R. King, 173–92. London: Routledge, 2006.

Jain, Anuja. "'Beaming It Live': 24-Hour Television News, the Spectator and the Spectacle of the 2002 Gujarat Carnage." In *Intermedia in South Asia: The Fourth Screen*, edited by Rajinder Dudrah, Sangita Gopal, Amit S. Rai, and Anustup Basu, 70–86. London: Routledge, 2012.

Jain, Kajri. "More Than Meets the Eye: The Circulation of Images and the Embodiment of Value." *Contributions to Indian Sociology* 36 (2002): 33–70.

Jalal, Ayesha. *Partisans of Allah: Jihad in South Asia*. Ranikhet: Permanent Black, 2008.

Janich, Peter. *What Is Information?* Translated by Eric Hayot and Lea Pao. Minneapolis: University of Minnesota Press, 2018.

Jeffrey, Robin. "The Mahatma Didn't Like the Movies and Why It Matters: Indian Broadcasting Policy, 1920s–1990s." In *The Indian Public Sphere*, edited by Arvind Rajagopal, 171–87. New Delhi: Oxford University Press, 2009.

Jeffrey, Robin, and Assa Doron. "Mobile-izing: Democracy, Organization and India's First 'Mass Mobile Phone' Elections." *The Journal of Asian Studies* 71, no. 1 (February 2012): 63–80.

Jenkins, Henry. *Convergence Culture: Where Old and New Media Collide*. New York: New York University Press, 2006.

John, Mary E. "Globalization, Sexuality, and the Visual Field: Issues and Non-issues for Cultural Critique." In *A Question of Silence: The Sexual Economies of Modern India*, edited by Mary E. John and Janaki Nair, 368–96. New Delhi: Kali for Women, 1998.

Jones, William. "On the Hindus." In *The British Discovery of Hinduism in the Eighteenth Century*, edited by P. J. Marshall, 246–61. Cambridge: Cambridge University Press, 1970.

Judy, Ronald A. T. "Democracy or Ideology." *boundary 2* 33, no. 3 (2006): 35–59.

Katju, Manjari. *Vishwa Hindu Parishad and Indian Politics*. New Delhi: Orient Blackswan, 2010.

Kautilya. *Arthasastra*. Translated by R. Shamasastry. Mysore: Mysore Publishing House, 1915.

Kaviraj, Sudipta. *The Unhappy Consciousness: Bankimchandra Chattopadhyay and the Formation of Nationalist Discourse in India*. London: School of Oriental and African Studies, 1998.

Keer, Dhananjay. *Dr. Ambedkar: Life and Mission*. Bombay: Popular Prakashan, 1954.

Khalidi, Omar. "Hinduising India: Secularism in Practice." *Third World Quarterly* 29, no. 8 (2008): 1545–62.

Khilnani, Sunil. *The Idea of India*. New York: Penguin, 1997.

Kohli, Atul. *Poverty amid Plenty in the New India*. Cambridge: Cambridge University Press, 2012.

Kohli-Kandhekar, Vanita. *Indian Media Business*. 3rd ed. London: SAGE, 2010.

Kothari, Rajni. "Caste and Modern Politics." In *Politics in India*, edited by Sudipta Kaviraj, 57–70. New Delhi: Oxford University Press, 1997.

Kothari, Rajni. *Politics in India*. Boston: Little, Brown, 1970.

Kumar, Shanti. *Gandhi Meets Primetime: Globalization and Nationalism in Indian Television*. Urbana: University of Illinois Press, 2006.

Lal, Chaman. *Hindu America*. Bombay: New Book Company, 1940.

Latour, Bruno. *Reassembling the Social: An Introduction to Actor-Network Theory*. Oxford: Oxford University Press, 2005.

Leopold, Joan. "The Aryan Theory of Race in India, 1870–1920." *Indian Economic and Social History Review* 7, no. 2 (1970): 271–97.

Lipner, Julius. *Brahmabandhab Upadhyay: The Life and Thought of a Revolutionary*. Delhi: Oxford University Press, 1999.

Lobo, Nancy, and Biswaroop Das. *Communal Violence and Minorities: Gujarat Society in Ferment*. New Delhi: Rawat, 2006.

Locke, John. *Political Writings of John Locke*. Edited by David Wootton. New York: Mentor, 1993.

Lorenzen, David N. "Who Invented Hinduism?" *Comparative Studies in Society and History* 41, no. 4 (October 1999): 630–59.

Loynd, Maxine. "Politics without Television: The Bahujan Samaj Party and the Dalit Counter-public Sphere." In *Television in India: Satellites, Politics, and Cultural Change*, edited by Nalin Mehta, 62–86. New York: Routledge, 2008.

Machiavelli, Niccolò. *The Prince and The Discourses*. New York: Modern Library, 1950.

Mallapragada, Madhavi. "Desktop Dieties: Hindu Temples, Online Cultures and the Politics of Remediation." In *Intermedia in South Asia: The Fourth Screen*, edited by Rajinder Dudrah, 6–18. London: Routledge, 2012.

Mallapragada, Madhavi. *Virtual Homelands: Indian Immigrants and Online Cultures in the United States*. Champaign: University of Illinois Press, 2014.

Mankekar, Purnima. *Screening Culture, Viewing Politics: An Ethnography of Television, Womanhood and Nation in Postcolonial India*. Durham, NC: Duke University Press, 1999.

Markandeya Puranam. Translated by Manmatha Nath Dutt. Calcutta: Elysium Press, 1896.

Marshall, P. J, ed. *The British Discovery of Hinduism in the Eighteenth Century*. Cambridge: Cambridge University Press, 2009.

Marx, Karl. *Grundrisse*. Translated by Martin Nicholaus. London: Penguin Books, 1973.

Matilal, Bimal Krishna. *Ethics and Epics: The Collected Essays of Bimal Krishna Matilal*. Edited by Jonardhan Ganeri. New Delhi: Oxford University Press, 2002.

Mazumdar, Ranjani. *Bombay Cinema: An Archive of the City*. Minneapolis: University of Minnesota Press, 2007.

Mazzarella, William. "Beautiful Balloon: The Digital Divide and the Charisma of New Media in India." *American Ethnologist* 37, no. 4 (November 2010): 783–804.

Mazzarella, William. "Close Distance: Constructing the 'Indian Consumer.'" In *The Indian Public Sphere: Readings in Media History*, edited by Arvind Rajagopal, 247–59. New Delhi: Oxford University Press, 2009.

Mazzarella, William. *Shoveling Smoke: Advertising and Globalization in Contemporary India*. Durham, NC: Duke University Press, 2003.

Mehta, Nalin. "Modi and the Camera: The Politics of Television in the 2002 Gujarat Riots." *South Asia* 29, no. 3 (2006): 395–414.

Mehta, Nalin, ed. *Television in India: Satellites, Politics, and Cultural Change*. New York: Routledge, 2008.

Mehta, Suketu. *Maximum City: Bombay Lost and Found*. New York: Vintage, 2005.

Mill, J. S. *Utilitarianism, On Liberty, and Considerations on Representative Government*. Edited by H. B. Acton. London: Everyman Library, 1972.

Mitta, Manoj. *Modi and Godhra: The Fiction of Fact-Finding*. New Delhi: HarperCollins, 2015.

Mohamed, Feisal G. "'I Alone Can Solve': Carl Schmitt on Sovereignty and Nationhood under Trump." In *Trump and Political Philosophy*, edited by A. Jaramillo Torres and M. B. Sable, 293–309. New York: Palgrave Macmillan, 2018.

Mohanty, J. N. *Classical Indian Philosophy*. New York: Rowman and Littlefield, 2000.

Mufti, Amir R. *Enlightenment in the Colony: The Jewish Question and the Crisis of Postcolonial Culture*. Princeton, NJ: Princeton University Press, 2007.

Mukul, Akshyaya. *Gita Press and the Making of Hindu India*. Noida: HarperCollins, 2015.

Murphie, Andrew. "The Fallen Present, Time in the Mix." In *24/7: Time and Temporality in the Network Society*, edited by Robert Hassan and Ronald E. Pursur, 122–40. Stanford, CA: Stanford University Press, 2007.

Nair, Janaki. *The Promise of Metropolis: Bangalore's Twentieth Century*. New Delhi: Oxford University Press, 2005.

Nandy, Ashis. *At the Edge of Psychology*. New Delhi: Oxford University Press, 1991.

Nandy, Ashis. "A Critique of Modern Secularism." In *Politics in India*, edited by Sudipta Kaviraj, 329–41. New York: Oxford University Press, 1997.

Nandy, Ashis, Shikha Trivedy, Shail Mayaram, and Achyut Yagnik. *Creating a Nationality: The Ramjanambhumi Movement and the Fear of the Self*. New Delhi: Oxford University Press, 1998.

Negroponte, Nicholas. *Being Digital*. New York: Vintage, 1996.

Nehru, Jawaharlal. *An Autobiography*. New Delhi: Oxford University Press, 1982.

Nehru, Jawaharlal. *Discovery of India*. Delhi: Oxford University Press, 1985.

Neyazi, Tabarez. "Politics after Vernacularisation: Hindi Media and Indian Democracy." *Economic and Political Weekly* 46, no. 10 (March 5–11, 2011): 75–82.

Nicholson, Andrew. *Unifying Hinduism: Philosophy and Identity in Indian Intellectual History*. New York: Columbia University Press, 2010.

Nietzsche, Fredrich. *The Birth of Tragedy; and The Genealogy of Morals*. Translated by Francis Golffing. New York: Anchor, 1956.

Nigam, Aditya. "Secularism, Modernity, Nation: Epistemology of the Dalit Critique." *Economic and Political Weekly* 35, no. 48 (November 25, 2000): 4256–68.

Oak, P. N. *The Taj Mahal Is a Temple Place*. New Delhi: Hindi Sahitya Sadan, 2003.

Oak, P. N. *World Vedic Heritage: A History of Histories*. 2 vols. New Delhi: Hindi Sahitya Sadan, 2003.

O'Connell, Joseph T. "Vaisnava Perceptions of Muslims." *The Muslim World* 107, no. 2 (April 2017): 170–90.

O'Hanlon, Rosalind. *Caste, Conflict and Ideology: Mahatma Jotirao Phule and Low Caste Protest in Nineteenth-Century Western India*. Cambridge: Cambridge University Press, 1985.

Olivelle, Patrick, ed. *Dharmasutras: The Law Codes of Apastamba, Gautama, Baudhayana, and Vasistha*. New Delhi: Oxford University Press, 1999.

Omvedt, Gail. *Ambedkar: Toward an Enlightened India*. New Delhi: Penguin, 2004.

Omvedt, Gail. *Dalit Visions: The Anti-caste Movement and the Construction of an Indian Identity*. New Delhi: Orient Longman, 1995.

Orsini, Francesca. *The Hindi Public Sphere, 1920–1940: Language and Literature in the Age of Nationalism*. Delhi: Oxford University Press, 2002.

Pandey, Gyanendra. "The Secular State and the Limits of Dialogue." In *The Crisis of Secularism in India*, edited by Anuradha Dingwaney Needham and Rajeshwari Sunder Rajan, 157–76. Durham, NC: Duke University Press, 2007.

Parekh, Bhikhu. *Gandhi's Political Philosophy: A Critical Examination*. Notre Dame, IN: University of Notre Dame Press, 1989.

Pinney, Christopher. "The Politics of Popular Images: From Cow Protection to M. K. Gandhi, 1890–1950." In *The Indian Public Sphere*, edited by Arvind Rajagopal, 65–87. New Delhi: Oxford University Press, 2009.

Pocock, David. *Kanbi and Patidar: A Study of the Patidar Community of Gujarat*. Oxford: Clarendon Press, 1972.

Pollock, Sheldon. "Deep Orientalism? Notes on Sanskrit and Power beyond the Raj." In *Orientalism and the Postcolonial Predicament: Perspectives on South Asia*, edited by Carol A. Breckenridge and Peter van der Veer, 76–133. Philadelphia: University of Pennsylvania Press, 1993.

Pollock, Sheldon. *The Language of the Gods in the World of Men: Sanskrit, Culture, and Power in Premodern India*. Berkeley: University of California Press, 2006.

Pollock, Sheldon, ed. *Literary Cultures in History: Reconstructions from South Asia*. Berkeley: University of California Press, 2001.

Pollock, Sheldon. "The Ramayana Text and the Critical Edition." In *The Ramayana of Valmiki*, edited by Robert Goldman, 82–93. Princeton, NJ: Princeton University Press, 1984.

Poster, Mark. *Information Please: Culture and Politics in the Age of Digital Machines*. Durham, NC: Duke University Press, 2006.

Prakash, Gyan. *Mumbai Fables: A History of an Enchanted City*. Princeton, NJ: Princeton University Press, 2011.

Prakash, Gyan. "Secular Nationalism, Hindutva, and the Minority." In *The Crisis of Secularism in India*, edited by Anuradha Dingwaney Needham and Rajeshwari Sunder Rajan, 177–88. Durham, NC: Duke University Press, 2007.

Prasad, M. Madhava. *The Ideology of the Hindi Film: A Historical Reconstruction*. New Delhi: Oxford University Press, 1998.

Price, Lance. *The Modi Effect: Inside Narendra Modi's Campaign to Transform India*. London: Hodder and Stoughton, 2015.

Punathambekar, Ashwin. *From Bombay to Bollywood: The Making of a Global Media Industry*. New York: New York University Press, 2013.

Punathambekar, Ashwin, and Anandam P. Kavoori, eds. *Global Bollywood*. New York: New York University Press, 2008.

Radhakrishnan, Sarvepalli. *The Hindu View of Life*. New York: Macmillan, 1973.

Radhakrishnan, Sarvepalli, ed. *History of Philosophy Eastern and Western*. Vol. 2. London: George Allen and Unwin, 1952.

Rai, Alok. *Hindi Nationalism*. Delhi: Orient Longman, 2000.

Rai, Amit. *Untimely Bollywood: Globalization and India's New Media Assemblage.* Durham, NC: Duke University Press, 2009.

Rajagopal, Arvind. "The Emergency as Prehistory of the New Indian Middle Class." *Modern Asian Studies* 45, no. 5 (September 2011): 1003–49.

Rajagopal, Arvind. "The Gujarat Experiment and Hindu National Realism: Lessons for Secularism." In *The Crisis of Secularism in India*, edited by Anuradha Dingwaney Needham and Rajeswari Sunder Rajan, 208–24. Durham, NC: Duke University Press, 2007.

Rajagopal, Arvind. *Politics after Television: Hindu Nationalism and the Reshaping of the Public in India.* Cambridge: Cambridge University Press, 2001.

Rajagopalchari, C. *Hinduism: Doctrine and Way of Life.* New Delhi: Hindustan Times, 1959.

Ram, N. "The Changing Role of the News Media in Contemporary India." *Proceedings of the Indian History Congress* 72, pt. 2 (2011): 1289–310.

Ramanujan, A. K. *The Collected Essays of A. K. Ramanujan.* Edited by Vinay Dharwadkar. Oxford: Oxford University Press, 1999.

Ramaswamy, Sumathi. *The Lost Land of Lemuria: Fabulous Geographies, Catastrophic Histories.* Berkeley: University of California Press, 2004.

Ramaswamy, Sumathi. "Remains of the Race: Archaeology, Nationalism, and the Yearning for Civilization in the Indus Valley." *Indian Economic and Social History Review* 38, no. 2 (2001): 105–45.

Rancière, Jacques. *The Future of the Image.* Translated by Gregory Elliot. London: Verso, 2009.

Rancière, Jacques. *The Politics of Aesthetics: The Distribution of the Sensible.* London: Continuum, 2004.

Rawls, John. *Political Liberalism.* New York: Columbia University Press, 1993.

Rawls, John. *A Theory of Justice.* Cambridge, MA: Harvard University Press, 1971.

Raychaudhuri, Tapan. *Europe Reconsidered: Perceptions of the West in Nineteenth-Century Bengal.* New Delhi: Oxford University Press, 1988.

Ricci, Ronit. *Islam Translated: Literature, Conversion, and the Arabic Cosmopolis of South and Southeast Asia.* Chicago: University of Chicago Press, 2011.

Robb, Peter, ed. *The Concept of Race in South Asia.* New Delhi: Oxford University Press, 1995.

Rousseau, Jean-Jacques. *The Social Contract and Discourses.* London: Everyman, 1993.

Roy, Rammohun. "A Defense of Hindu Theism, in Reply to the Attack of an Advocate for Idolatry, at Madras." In *The English Works of Rammohun Roy*, vol. 1, edited by Jogendra Chunder Ghose, 103–18. Calcutta: Oriental Press, 1885.

Roy, Rammohun. "A Letter to Rev. Henry Ware (of America) on the Prospects of Christianity and the Means of Promoting Its Reception in India." In *The English Works of Rammohun Roy*, vol. 1, edited by Jogendra Chunder Ghose, 247–62. Calcutta: Oriental Press, 1885.

Roy, Rammohun. "A Second Defence of the Monotheistical System of the Veds." In *The English Works of Rammohun Roy*, vol. 1, edited by Jogendra Chunder Ghose, 119–48. Calcutta: Oriental Press, 1885.

Saeed, Saima. "Negotiating Power: Community Media, Democracy, and the Public Sphere." *Development in Practice* 19, no. 4/5 (June 2009): 466-78.

Sarangi, Asha, ed. *Language and Politics in India*. Delhi: Oxford University Press, 2010.

Saraswati, Dayanand. *Satyartha Prakasha*. New Delhi: Sarvadeshik Arya Pratinidhi Sabha, 1975.

Sardesai, Rajdeep. *2014: The Election That Changed India*. New Delhi: Viking, 2014.

Sarkar, Sumit. "Calcutta and the Bengal Renaissance." In *Calcutta: The Living City*, vol. 1, *The Past*, edited by Sukanta Chaudhuri, 95–105. Calcutta: Oxford University Press, 1990.

Sarkar, Sumit. "Indian Nationalism and the Politics of Hindutva." In *Making India Hindu*, 2nd ed., edited by David Ludden, 270–94. New Delhi: Oxford University Press, 2007.

Sarkar, Sumit. *Modern India, 1885–1947*. New Delhi: Macmillan, 1983.

Sarkar, Susobhan. *Bengal Renaissance and Other Essays*. New Delhi: People's Publishing House, 1970.

Sarkar, Tanika. *Hindu Wife, Hindu Nation: Community, Religion, and Cultural Nationalism*. New Delhi: Permanent Black, 2001.

Sarkar, Tanika. "Jitu Santal's Movement in Malda, 1924–1932." In *Subaltern Studies IV: Writings on South Asian History and Society*, edited by Ranajit Guha, 136–64. Delhi: Oxford University Press, 1985.

Sassen, Saskia. *Globalization and the World System: Contemporary Conditions for the Representation of Identity*. Minneapolis: University of Minnesota Press, 1998.

Sastri, Sivanath. *History of the Brahmo Samaj*. Calcutta: Sadharan Brahmo Samaj, [1911–1912] 1974.

Sastri, Sivanath. *Ramtanu Lahiri o totkalin bongosamaj*. Edited by Baridboron Ghosh. Calcutta: New Age Publications, [1904] 1955.

Savarkar, V. D. *Hindutva: Who Is a Hindu?* Bombay: Veer Savarkar Prakashan, 1969.

Schmitt, Carl. *The Concept of the Political*. Translated by Charles Schwab. New Brunswick, NJ: Rutgers University Press, 1976.

Schmitt, Carl. *The Crisis of Parliamentary Democracy*. Translated by Ellen Kennedy. Cambridge, MA: MIT Press, 1988.

Schmitt, Carl. *Political Theology: Four Chapters on the Concept of Sovereignty*. Translated by George Schwab. Cambridge, MA: MIT Press, 1985.

Scott, David C., ed. *Keshub Chunder Sen*. Madras: Christian Literature Society, 1979.

Sen, Asok. *Iswar Chandra Vidyasagar and His Elusive Milestones*. Calcutta: Ridhi-India, 1977.

Sen, Ronojoy. "The Indian Supreme Court and the Quest for a 'Rational' Hinduism." *South Asian History and Culture* 1, no. 1 (2009): 86–104.

Sen, Sukumar. *History of Bengali Literature*. New Delhi: Sahitya Akademi, 1960.

Shah, Umakant P. "Ramayana in Jaina Tradition." In *Asian Variations in Ramayana*, edited by K. R. S. Iyengar, 57–76. New Delhi: Sahitya Akademi, 2005.

Shani, Ornit. *Communalism, Caste, and Hindu Nationalism: The Violence in Gujarat*. Cambridge: Cambridge University Press, 2007.

Shannon, Claude. "A Mathematical Theory of Communication." *The Bell System Technical Journal* 27, no. 3 (1948): 379–423.

Sharma, Arvind. "How to Read the Manusmriti?" *Studies in Humanities and Social Sciences* 9, no. 2 (winter 2002): 29–39.

Sharma, Jyotirmaya. *Hindutva: Exploring the Idea of Hindu Nationalism*. New Delhi: Penguin, 2003.

Shraddhanand, Swami. *Hindu Sangathan: Savior of the Dying Race*. Delhi: Arjun Press, 1926.

Singh, Sweta. "Citizen Journalism: Women Leaders Make Their Own News through Video and Blogging." *Agenda: Empowering Women for Gender Equity*. No. 77, Community Media (2008): 82–89.

Sloterdijk, Peter. *Rage and Time*. Translated by Mario Wenning. New York: Columbia University Press, 2010.

Sood, Atul. *Poverty amidst Prosperity: Essays on the Trajectory of Development in Gujarat*. New Delhi: Aakar Books, 2012.

Spivak, Gayatri C. *An Aesthetic Education in the Era of Globalization*. Cambridge, MA: Harvard University Press, 2012.

Spivak, Gayatri C. *A Critique of Postcolonial Reason: Toward a History of the Vanishing Present*. Cambridge, MA: Harvard University Press, 1999.

Spodek, Howard. "In the Hindutva Laboratory: Pogroms and Politics in Gujarat, 2002." *Modern Asian Studies* 4, no. 2 (2010): 349–99.

Srinivas, M. N. "A Note on Sanskritization and Westernization." *Far Eastern Quarterly* 15, no. 4 (1956): 481–96.

Srinivas, M. N. *Social Change in Modern India*. Berkeley: University of California Press, 1966.

Stiegler, Bernard. *Technics and Time 2: Disorientation*. Translated by Stephen Barker. Stanford, CA: Stanford University Press, 2009.

Stiglitz, Joseph. *Globalization and Its Discontents Revisited: Anti-globalization in the Era of Trump*. New York: W. W. Norton, 2017.

Stoler, Ann Laura. *Duress: Imperial Durabilities in Our Times*. Durham, NC: Duke University Press, 2016.

Stoler, Ann Laura. *Imperial Debris: On Ruins and Ruination*. Durham, NC: Duke University Press, 2013.

Sud, Nikita. *Liberalization, Hindu Nationalism and the State: A Biography of Gujarat*. New Delhi: Oxford University Press, 2012.

Sukthankar, V. S. "Prolegomena." In *The Critical Edition of the Mahabharata: The Adiparvan*, vol. 1 of 19, part 1. Edited by V. S. Sukthankar, i–cx. Poona: Bhandarkar Research Institute, 1933.

Suleri, Sara. *The Rhetoric of English India*. Chicago: University of Chicago Press, 2013.

Sundaram, Ravi. "Beyond the Nationalist Panopticon: The Experience of Cyberpublics in India." In *Electronic Media and Technoculture*, edited by John Caldwell, 270–94. New Brunswick, NJ: Rutgers University Press, 2000.

Sundaram, Ravi. *Pirate Modernity: Delhi's Media Urbanism*. London: Routledge, 2009.

Tagore, Rabindranath. "Kalantar." In *Rabindra Rachnabali*, vol. 24: 241–384. Calcutta: Vishwa Bharati, 1947.

Tagore, Rabindranath. *Nationalism*. London: Macmillan, 1918.

Taylor, Charles. *A Secular Age*. Cambridge, MA: Belknap, 2007.

Tejani, Shabnum. *Indian Secularism: A Social and Intellectual History, 1890–1950*. Ranikhet: Permanent Black, 2007.

Tejani, Shabnum. "Reflections on the Category of Secularism in India: Gandhi, Ambedkar, and the Ethics of Communal Representation, c. 1931." In *The Crisis of Secularism in India*, edited by Anuradha Dingwaney Needham and Rajeshwari Sunder Rajan, 45–65. Durham, NC: Duke University Press, 2007.

Thapar, Romila. *Interpreting Early India*. New Delhi. Oxford University Press, 1999.

Thapar, Romila. "Secularism, History, and Contemporary Politics in India." In *The Crisis of Secularism in India*, edited by Anuradha Dingwaney Needham and Rajeshwari Sunder Rajan, 191–207. Durham, NC: Duke University Press, 2007.

Thapar, Romila. *Time as a Metaphor of History: Early India*. New Delhi: Oxford University Press, 1996.

Thussu, Daya Kishan. *Communicating India's Soft Power: Buddha to Bollywood*. New York: Palgrave, 2013.

Thussu, Daya Kishan. *News as Entertainment: The Rise of Global Infotainment*. London: SAGE, 2007.

Tilak, B. G. *The Arctic Home in the Vedas*. Poona: Tilak Brothers, 1903.

Tilak, B. G. *Bal Gangadhar Tilak: His Writings and Speeches*. Madras: Ganesh, 1919.

Trautmann, Thomas. *Aryans and British India*. Berkeley: University of California Press, 1997.

Turrow, Joseph, and Lokman Tsui, eds. *The Hyperlinked Society: Questioning Connections in the Digital Age*. Ann Arbor: University of Michigan Press, 2008.

Udayakumar, S. P. *Presenting the Past: Anxious History and Ancient Future in Hindutva India*. London: Praeger, 2005.

Upadhyay, D. D. *Integral Humanism*. New Delhi: Jagriti Prakashan, [1962] 1992.

Urban, Hugh B. *Zorba the Buddha: Sex, Spirituality, and Capitalism in the Global Osho Movement*. Oakland: University of California Press, 2015.

Valmiki. *The Ramayana of Valmiki*. Vol. 1, *Bal Kandya, Ayodhya Kanda*. Translated by Hari Prasad Shastri. London: Santi Sadan, 1952.

Vanaik, Achin. *Situating the Threat of Hindu Nationalism: Problems with the Fascist Paradigm*. New Delhi: Center for Contemporary Studies, 1994.

van der Veer, Peter. "Hindu Nationalism and the Discourse of Modernity: The Vishwa Hindu Parishad." In *Accounting for Fundamentalisms*, edited by M. Marty and S. Appleby, 653–58. Chicago: University of Chicago Press, 1994.

van der Veer, Peter. *Imperial Encounters: Religion and Modernity in India and Britain*. Princeton, NJ: Princeton University Press, 2001.

van der Veer, Peter. *Religious Nationalism: Hindus and Muslims in India*. Berkeley: University of California Press, 1994.

van der Veer, Peter. "Virtual India: Indian IT Labor and the Nation State." In *Sovereign Bodies: Citizens, Migrants, and States in the Postcolonial World*, edited by Thomas Blom Hansen and Finn Stepputat, 276–90. Princeton, NJ: Princeton University Press, 2005.

Vatsayana. *The Kamasutra of Vatsayana*. Translated by Sir Richard Burton. New York: Modern Library, 2002.

Vivekananda, Swami. *The Complete Works of Swami Vivekananda*. Vol. 5. Calcutta: Advaita Ashrama, 1999.

von Stietencron, Heinrich. *Hindu Myth, Hindu History: Religion, Art, and Politics*. New Delhi: Permanent Black, 2005.

Vyasa. *The Bhagwad Gita*. Translated by Juan Mascaro. London: Penguin, 2003.

Vyasa. *The Mahabharata*. Translated by Kisari Mohan Ganguly. Delhi: Munshiram Manoharlal, 2004.

Weber, Max. *Economy and Society: An Outline of Interpretive Sociology*. Edited by Guenther Roth and Claus Wittich. Berkeley: University of California Press, 1978.

Weber, Max. *Religion of India: The Sociology of Hinduism and Buddhism*. Translated by Hans H. Gerth and Don Martindale. New York: The Free Press, 1958.

Weiner, Norbert. *The Human Use of Human Beings: Cybernetics and Society*. Boston: Houghton Mifflin, 1954.

Yajnavalkya. *The Brihadaranyaka Upanishad, with the Commentary of Sankaracharya*. Translated by Swami Madhavananda. Almora: Advaita Ashrama, 1950.

Zachariah, Benjamin. "Rethinking (the Absence of) Fascism in India, c. 1922–45." In *Cosmopolitan Thought Zones: South Asia and the Global Circulation of Ideas*, edited by Sugato Bose and Kris Manjapra, 178–209. New York: Palgrave, 2010.

Zielinski, Siegfried. *Deep Time of the Media: Towards an Archaeology of Hearing and Seeing by Technical Means*. Cambridge, MA: MIT Press, 2006.

INDEX

Aam Aadmi Party (AAP), 168
Aastha TV, 188
Aatish (film), 191
Abhinavagupta, 38
Abhinav Bharat, 159
Ab Tak Chhappan (film), 196
Abu Hamid al-Ghazali, 212n11
ABVP, 210n8
Achaemenis Empire, 54
Acts, book of, 108. *See also* Bible, the
Adani, Gautam, 168
Adityanath, Yogi, 199
Adorno, Theodore, 178
Advaita, 94, 126–27, 131, 134, 146, 223n55
Advani, L. K., 157, 165, 173, 176
advertised modernization, 8–9, 85, 158, 165–66, 174–99, 207, 246n48. *See also* Hindutva 2.0; informational world; media; modernization; techno-financial modernity
Aeneid (Virgil), 94
Afghanistan, 71–72
AFSPA, 199
Aga Khan III, Sultan Mohammed Shah, 98
Agamben, Giorgio, 84, 200
Agastya, 66
Age of Consent Bill, 110, 227n85. *See also* gender
Agni, 35, 115–16
agrarian conservatism, 24, 81, 148, 202
ahimsa. *See* nonviolence
Ahmad, Imtiaz, 15
Ain-I Akbari (Fazl), 90–91
Ajatsatru, 218n12
Ajivika, 42, 46, 220n35, 225n75

Akbar, Jalaluddin Muhammad, 15, 90, 236n3, 238n36
Akhand Bharat, 6, 70–76, 161, 231n122. *See also* Sangh Parivaar
Akhil Bharatiya Vidyarthy Parishad (ABVP), 210n8
al-Farabi, 236n3
Ali, Syed Qasim, 154
Aligarh Muslim University, 95
Al Jazeera, 64, 72
All-India Muslim League, 97
Ambani, Lukesh, 168
Ambedkar, Bhimrao Ramji: critique of Hinduism and caste by, 7, 135–49, 232n140, 235n159, 242n93; and Indian monotheism, 26, 65, 177, 203, 241n89
Anandamath (Chattopadhyay), 121
Anandavardhana, 38
Anderson, Benedict, 212n16
Anglophone culture, 80, 85, 157, 170–73, 185, 188, 236n163, 247n68
Anglophone revolution, Indian, 26, 171
Angre, Ravinda, 249n104
animism, 78, 92, 97–99
Annihilation of Caste (Ambedkar), 135–44
Anthropological Survey, 211n10
anthropology, Hindu, 122, 125, 147
anthropology, religious, 17, 35, 47, 78, 92–95, 98, 105, 126–27, 150
anticolonialism, 9, 121, 224n67. *See also* colonialism
Antigone, 101
antimodernism, 144, 148
Anti-Sedition Act, 199
anti-Semitism, 29–30, 160, 217n7, 231n118. *See also* Jewish people; Nazism

Anushilan, 113–14, 119–21
Apastamba, 38
APCO, 168
Apte, Hari Narayan, 239n53
Aquinas, Thomas, 39, 97
Arabic language, 84–85, 115, 234n155
Aravamudan, Srinivas, 236n163
Archaeological Survey of India, 224n63
Arendt, Hannah, 18, 160–64, 178, 198, 242n10
Aristotle, 104, 131, 225n75
Arjuna, 40, 43–44, 50, 81, 94, 99–100, 115–16, 119, 222n42, 238n29
Armed Forces Special Powers Act (AFSPA), 199
Arnold, Edwin, 81
Arthasastra (Kautilya), 31–32, 66, 218nn11–12, 229n100
Article 15 (Indian Constitution), 19
Article 370 (Indian Constitution), 161
Arundale, Rukmini Devi, 152
Arya Kirti (Gupta), 240n54
Aryan Invasion Theory, 49, 67–68, 71, 231n123
Aryanism: fascism and, 25, 30, 217n7; and Hindu monotheism, 112, 122, 125, 129–31, 135, 151, 240n54; and the organismic Hindu nation, 49–50, 57–71, 74–78, 83, 86, 224n63, 227n92. *See also* race
Arya Samaj: about Hindu monotheism and, 5, 49, 109–10, 123, 235n158; about the, 97, 135, 155, 209n7, 237n19; practices of the, 142, 232n130.
See also nationalism, Hindu
Asad, Talal, 47
asceticism, 44, 101, 113, 217n49, 233n145, 235n158
Ashoka the Great, 48
Asiatick Researches, 90
Asiatic Society of Bengal, 89, 103
Asoka, 54
Assam, 19, 185, 205, 213n25
Astika, 90–92
Asvaghosa, 229n104
Ataturk, Mustafa Kemal, 24
Atman, 35–36
Atmiya Sabha, 104, 108
Augustine of Hippo, 225n75
Augustus, 48
Aurangzeb, 226n83

Aurobindo, Sri, 93, 124, 241n74
authoritarianism. *See* despotism, oriental; dictators; fascism; Modi, Narendra
the Avesta, 71, 81–83, 231n123
Azhar Moin, A., 15

Baapaanoollu. *See* Brahmins
Babri Masjid demolition, 3, 157, 165–67, 226n83. *See also* Islamophobia
Bachchan, Harivansh Rai, 154
Badarayana, 242n93
Bahujan Samaj Party (BSP), 135n159, 245n37
Bajirao Mastani (film), 193
Bandyopadhyay, Sibaji, 93–94, 116, 121, 233n146
Banerjea, Krishnamohan, 95, 103, 122
Bangadarshan (journal), 111
Bangladesh, 72, 84
Baniyas, 1–2, 153, 246n42
BARC, 248n77
Bareilly ki Barfi (film), 195
Basu, Girindrasekhar, 94
Basu, Manisha, 157, 236n163
Basu, Rajnarayan, 111
Battle of Haldighati, 54, 225n80
Baudhayana, 65–66, 89, 238n36
Baxi, Upendra, 88
Bengali Bible, 90
Bengal Social Science Association, 111
Bengal Swadeshi Movement, 24
Benjamin, Walter, 178, 204
Bentnick, William, 103, 110
Bergson, Henri, 56, 126
Bhagat, Chetan, 157
Bhagwad Gita: influence on political thinkers of the, 81, 237n23, 242n93; Matilal and the, 36–38, 42–46; and the search for Indian monotheism, 7, 89, 93–95, 98–103, 113, 116, 121–24, 128, 153. *See also* Hinduism
Bhagwata Puranas, 118
Bhakti tradition: about the, 56, 120, 212n11, 220n27, 221n40; Hindu monotheism and the, 4, 67, 92, 95, 112, 124, 153; Matilal and the,
36–40, 44
Bhandarkar Research Institute, 67, 230n112
Bharatiya Janata Party (BJP). *See* BJP
Bharatiya Mazdoor Sangh, 210n8

270 Index

Bhasha Research and Publication Centre, 190
Bhatkhande, V. N., 152
Bhatt, Sanjiv, 244n31
Bhaumik, Kaushik, 152
Bhishma Parvan, 66, 89, 222n41
Bhonsala Military School, 29
Bhonsle, Praful, 249n104
Bible, the, 33, 39, 57, 81, 84, 90, 104–5, 213n26, 214n28. *See also* Christianity; *specific books*
Bible Society, 153
Bimbisara, 218n13
Biswas, Moinak, 196
BJP: and Hindutva 2.0, 161, 164–73, 176–77, 188, 209n6, 243n22, 244n33; and identity politics, 19, 246n42; rise of the, 3, 85, 158. *See also* Modi, Narendra
Blake, William, 94
Blanchot, Maurice, 10
Blavatsky, Helena, 49, 70, 122
Bollywood, 8, 178, 189–95, 200–201, 246n48. *See also* advertised modernization; media
Bolsonaro, Jair, 3
Bose, Subhash Chandra, 25, 215n42
Bourdieu, Pierre, 231n122
Brahma, 57, 77, 107, 116, 146
Brahmaism, 146–48
Brahman, 7, 35–36, 42, 51, 105, 146, 220n35, 223n55
Brahmanas, 35, 67, 219n23, 220n35
Brahmasutras, 120, 223n55, 242n93
Brahmavarta, 65–66, 71–72, 86
Brahminical tradition: about Hindu nationalism and the, 9, 15, 27, 32, 73, 78–88, 235nn158–59, 241n89; about the, 216n48, 220n27, 221n36, 228n98, 241n81; and critiques of Hindu monotheism, 5–6, 41–46, 60–63, 67–70; exclusivity of the, 61–63, 106, 120; and Hindutva 2.0, 161, 182, 192; and the search for Indian monotheism, 90–92, 96, 106, 110, 113, 117, 143–45, 153–54
Brahmins: about, 54, 210n8, 223n50, 228n97, 229n100, 237n19, 238n36; about Hindu monotheism and, 1–2, 90, 106, 130–32, 135–42; and Hindutva 2.0, 151, 161, 246n42; social hierarchy and, 44–46, 241n81, 241n89; and twentieth century Hindutva, 60–63, 68, 209n7, 230n117. *See also* caste

Brahmo Samaj, 5, 95–96, 104, 108–9. *See also* nationalism, Hindu
Brhatsamhita (Varahamihira), 229n104
Brihadaranyaka Upanishad, 228n98
Britain, 12, 15
Broadcast Audience Research Council (BARC), 248n77
Brown, Dan, 25
BSP, 135n159, 245n37
Buddha, 7, 115, 119, 122, 127, 141–43, 225n81
Buddhism: influence of, 48, 54–55, 66–67, 73, 76, 83, 225n81, 230n117; and the search for Hindu monotheism, 90–94, 98, 118, 133, 145–47, 156, 226n83; theism and beliefs of, 36, 42–46, 220n35, 225n75
Burke, Edmund, 154

Caesar, Julius, 129
Caldwell, Robert, 230n115
Calvinism, 7, 114, 211n9, 214n28, 220n27, 231n118. *See also* Christianity; Protestantism
capitalism: about Hindu nationalism and, 23–25, 42–43, 83–87, 103, 111, 114, 122–24, 133; in an electronic and informational world, 8–10, 151–54, 158, 164–67, 170–89, 199–207; Calvinism and, 7, 214n28; colonialism and, 42, 222n45; electronic, 8–10, 83, 87, 151, 189; inequality and, 129, 153, 164, 192; print, 10, 83–84, 87, 103, 111, 151–53, 189; right-wing politics and, 11–12. *See also* globalization; neoliberalism
Carlyle, Thomas, 81
Carvakas, 36, 42, 90–91
caste: about, 209n3, 210n8, 216n48, 222n49, 228n94, 229n100, 234n154, 235n159, 241n81; about Hindu nationalism and, 1–10, 15, 26–27, 222n48, 227n92; Ambedkar and, 135–49, 203, 241n89; and the Gita Press, 153–56; and Hindu fascism, 159–66; and Hindutva 2.0, 151, 167–76, 182–203, 246n42; and the search for Indian monotheism, 88, 92–93, 96–98, 101–3, 113, 120–21, 125, 128–49; and twentieth century Hindutva, 30–33, 39, 43–48, 52–70, 77–84. *See also* class; race; *specific castes*
Castells, Manuel, 183
Catholicism, 21, 74, 96–97, 113, 211n9. *See also* Christianity

Index 271

CBI, 163
cell phones, 167–70, 185–86, 189, 245n37.
    See also techno-financial modernity
Central Bureau of Investigation (CBI), 163
Chal Mere Bhai (film), 192
Chamberlain, Houston Stewart, 30
Chandalas, 30, 61–62, 229n100
Chandalika (Tagore), 148
Chandidas, 120
Chandni Bar (film), 196
Chandogya Upanishad, 43–45, 220n35
Chandragupta, 143
Chatterjee, Partha, 110, 212n16, 233n145, 237n17, 240n63
Chatterjee, Suniti Kumar, 154
Chattopadhyay, Bankimchandra, 7, 93, 103, 109–22, 147
Chaturanga (Tagore), 148
chauvinisms, 3, 13, 50, 64–66, 85, 134, 159, 241n74. See also Hindutva 2.0; masculinity; patriarchies
Cheah, Pheng, 30–31
Chennai Express (film), 195
child marriage, 121, 140, 155
Child Marriage Restraint Act, 155
China, 71–72, 161, 174
Chitrangada (Tagore), 148
Chopra, Aditya, 191
Chopra, Yash, 192
Christ, Jesus, 7, 107, 119, 122, 126, 213n26, 214n28, 237n17
Christianity: about, 213n26, 214n28, 220n33, 225n75, 233n143; about Hindu nationalism and, 1, 7, 14–16, 141, 202; discrimination and violence against, 154, 163; the history of India and, 54, 79; Matilal and, 36–39, 46; and the search for Indian monotheism, 90, 93–98, 104–8, 113–15, 122–28; and twentieth century Hindutva, 73–76, 79, 84. See also Bible, the; *specific denominations*
Churchill, Winston, 215n42
Cicero, 224n59
Cincinnatus, Quintius, 215n37
Citizenship Amendment Bill (2016), 19
class: about Hindu nationalism and, 1–2; Ambedkar and, 140–45; authoritarianism and, 160, 181, 245n40; Hindutva 2.0 and, 152–53, 164–75, 184, 189–97, 202, 205; Radhakrishnan and, 133–35. See also caste; gender; race

climate change, 12, 207
Clive, Robert, 238n32
A Code of Gentoo Laws (Halhed), 89
Colbert, Stephen, 168
Colebrook, Henry Thomas, 89–91
colonialism: about Hindu nationalism and, 17, 33–35; Islamic, 7, 14, 48, 55, 83, 122, 131; and the organismic Hindu nation, 48–54, 58, 67–68, 78–83, 87, 222n45; race and caste and, 64, 228n94, 235n159; and the search for Indian monotheism, 3–4, 90–92, 95–98, 101–3, 110, 122, 171. See also anticolonialism
communism, 50, 73–76, 80, 155–56, 174, 215n42, 233n145. See also Marxism; socialism
Comparative Grammar of the Dravidian or South-Indian Family of Languages (Caldwell), 230n115
Comte, August, 109, 114
Concerned Citizens Tribunal, 243n26, 244n31
Confessions (Augustine), 225n75
Congress Party, 82
Connolly, William, 5
Constitution, Indian, 19, 22, 26–28, 59, 63, 135, 144, 161
constructivism, 13, 91, 131, 212n16
consumerism, 8, 178, 182, 186, 189–91, 194, 202. See also advertised modernization
Contract Labor Act, 175
Coomaraswamy, Ananda, 152
Corinthians, 214n28
cosmopolitanism, 85, 127, 152, 186, 234n155
craniology, 50, 58. See also scientific racism
Creative Evolution (Bergson), 56
Crey, William, 90
Cunningham, Joseph, 111

Dalits: about, 1–2, 235n159, 250n109; about Hindu nationalism and, 1–2, 84–88, 134–35, 144, 152; activism and, 110, 135, 144, 205, 209n7, 232n140, 245n37, 245n39; discrimination and violence against, 137, 156, 163, 167–68, 197, 216n48, 250n112; Hindutva 2.0 and, 163–69, 176, 190, 194, 197–99. See also caste; untouchables
Dandekar, R. N., 221n36, 241n84
Dandin, 234n155
Dangal (film), 194

272 Index

Dante Alighieri, 94, 236n162
Darr (film), 192
Darwin, Charles, 58, 131
Das, Bhagwan, 51
Dasaratha Jataka, 41
Dasgupta, Surendranath, 35
Dasyus, 61, 227n91
Da Vinci Code (Brown), 25
Deb, Biplab, 183
Debi Chaudhurani (Chattopadhyay), 121
Debord, Guy, 52
"A Defense of Hindoo Theism, in Reply to the Attack of an Advocate of Idolatry, at Madras" (Roy), 105–6
Dehats, 172–74, 182, 185, 194, 246n42. *See also* caste
Deleuze, Gilles, 162, 178–80
Delhi Asian Games, 186
della Tomba, Marco, 91
democracy: about Indian, 28, 129, 216n43; about Hindu nationalism and, 24–37; and Hindutva 2.0, 176–83, 189, 198, 207; reactions to liberalism and modern, 11–12; Schmitt and, 11–14, 20, 213n23; and the search for Indian monotheism, 128–32, 135, 141–48; and twentieth-century Hindutva, 30, 57, 69
Democratic National Committee (DNC), 12
demonetization, 185, 247n70
Deng Xiaoping, 174
de Nobili, Roberto, 91
Depressed Classes resolution, 142
Derne, Steve, 202–3
Derozio, Henry Louis Vivian, 103
Derrida, Jacques, 70, 178, 231n118
despotism, oriental, 14, 22–23, 99. *See also* dictators
development, 133, 155, 164–71, 174–76, 186, 191, 195–98, 205–7. *See also* industrialism; modernization
De Vries, Hugo, 131
De vulgari eloquentia (Dante), 236n162
Devy, G. N., 34, 134, 190
Dewey, John, 142–44, 233n146
Dey, Lal Behari, 95, 239n53
Dhamaal (film), 196
Dharma: about, 220n35, 223n50, 229n103, 241n84; about Hindu nationalism and, 34–35, 38–40, 43–46, 57–63, 71–75, 146, 156; Bankim and, 113–14, 119–22; Radhakrishnan and, 126, 130; Sanatan, 34, 73, 96, 155, 237n19
Dharma Samsad, 217n49
Dharmasastras, 31, 38–39, 51, 64, 89, 220–21nn35–36, 229nn104–5
Dharmasutras, 65, 228n97, 238n36
"Dharmatattva" (Chattopadhyay), 112–13, 120
Dhawan, David, 191–92
Dial 100 (television show), 198
dictators, 18–23, 26, 160–61, 181, 215n37. *See also* despotism, oriental
Diderot, Denis, 179
Discorsi (Machiavelli), 211n5, 215n37
"Discourse on Political Economy" (Rousseau), 214n32
Discovery (Nehru), 57, 238n36
DNC, 12
Doniger, Wendy, 61, 224n72
Doordarshan, 186
double consciousness, 34, 127
Dravidians, 6, 25, 58, 65–70, 82, 125, 129, 135, 230n115
DreamWorks SKG, 187
Drona, 117–19, 222n42
Dubashi, Jay, 157
DuBois, W. E. B., 60
Duff, Alexander, 111
Dumont, Louis, 46, 131
Durbasa, 116
Durga, 2, 77–78
Durgeshnandini (Chattopadhyay), 112
Durkheim, Émile, 202
Durvasa, 37
Duryodhana, 37, 40, 117–19, 222n41
Dutt, Michael Madhusudan, 111
Dutt, Romesh Chunder, 111

Eaton, Richard, 226n83
Economy and Society (Weber), 221n40
Eknath, 91
Election Commission, India, 163
elections of 2009, Indian, 169
elections of 2014, Indian, 3, 168–70
elections of 2019, Indian, 246n48
electronic capitalism, 8–10, 83, 87, 151, 189. *See also* advertised modernization; capitalism
Elphinstone, Mountstuart, 111

emasculation, Hindu, 49, 55, 124, 162, 227n85. *See also* gender; masculinity
encounter killings, 168, 196–201, 249nn103–4
Encounter Squad, 197
Encyclopedia (Diderot), 179
Encyclopedia of the Physical Sciences (Hegel), 237n23
endogamy, 60–62, 139–40, 149, 222n48. *See also* caste; miscegenation
English. *See* Anglophone culture; Anglophone revolution, Indian
English Bengal Peasant Life (Dey), 239n53
Enlightenment, 12, 17, 39, 94–95, 98, 113
Epic of Tradition, 41, 76–78, 83, 194
Erdoğan, Recep Tayyip, 3
Essays on the Life of Mohammed (Khan), 240n54
Essel, 187
Euclid, 104
eugenics, 25, 59, 131, 136, 217n7. *See also* race; scientific racism
Eurocentrism, 17–18, 102. *See also* orientalism
Eusebius of Cesarea, 105
Evola, Julius, 30
Existentiells, 96, 110, 142, 186, 195
exogamy. *See* miscegenation

Factories Act, 175
Faiz, Faiz Ahmad, 147
Faizi, 236n3
Fanon, Frantz, 103
Farquhar, John Nicol, 93–94
fascism, 5, 17, 23–25, 28–30, 48, 72, 158–62, 174, 206, 215n42
fatalism, 52, 79, 107, 128, 144
Fazl, Abu, 90–91, 154, 236n3
federalism, 4, 8
Federalist Papers (Jay, Hamilton, Madison), 26
femininity, 55, 59, 120, 234n153. *See also* gender
feudalism, 129, 172
Fichte, Johann Gottlieb, 33, 114, 122
finance capital, 8, 12, 173, 185–88, 192, 195, 204–5. *See also* advertised modernization; neoliberalism; techno-financial modernity
financial crisis of 2008, 11–12
Fire (film), 189

Foreign Investment Promotion Board, 175
Foucault, Michel, 54–56, 62, 95, 98, 178
Fox, 187
France, 28, 55
Francis (King), 55
Franco, Francisco, 160
Freud, Sigmund, 94
Fukuyama, Francis, 11, 210n1

Galton, Francis, 131
Gana Sanghas, 54, 225n81
Gandhi, Mohandas Karamchand: Ambedkar and Tagore and, 140–48; assassination of, 152–54, 234n153; authoritarianism and, 24–25, 215n42; the Bhagwad Gita and, 93–94, 242n93; caste and, 135, 140, 143–44; nationalism and, 7, 55, 80–82, 142, 224n67; Nehru and, 82, 233n145
Gandhi, Rahul, 168
Gandhian ideology, 80–82, 143–45, 148, 152–54, 171, 176, 188
Garibaldi, Giuseppe, 24
Gateway of India attack, 198
GATT, 248n83
Gaudiya Vaishnavism, 92, 115, 147, 240n63. *See also* Vaishnavism
Gautama, 38, 89, 223n50
Geeta Seva Dal, 153
Geet Govinda (Jaidev), 117, 120
Gellner, Ernest, 212n16
gender: about Hindu nationalism and, 4, 56, 64, 84, 120–21, 143–45, 155–56, 216n48, 218n11; caste and, 39, 132; education and, 103, 143, 155; Gandhi and, 81; and Hindutva 2.0, 9–10, 163–66, 204; and violence and discrimination against women, 56, 120, 163–64, 227n92, 235n159. *See also* class; race; sexuality; sexual politics
The Genealogy of Morals (Nietzsche), 207
General Agreement on Tariffs and Trade (GATT), 248n83
genocide, 3, 161, 166–67, 175
Gentoos, 83, 171–75, 182, 185, 188–90, 195, 205, 246n41. *See also* caste; class
gentrification, 175, 186. *See also* race
George III (King), 23
geotelevisual, 190–94, 203. *See also* advertised modernization
Germany, 3, 24, 29, 160

274 Index

Ghare Baire (Tagore), 148
Ghosh, Aurobindo, 92, 123
Ghosh, Girish Chandra, 111
Ghulamgiri (Phule), 232n140
Girlfriend (film), 192
Gita Press, 152–56, 165, 182
Gita Rahasya (Tilak), 94
globalization, 2–7, 12, 85, 168, 171, 184–95, 199, 202–6. *See also* capitalism; modernization
Global Vision Conference, 248n83
Gobineau, Arthur de, 30
Godhra incident, 167, 244n27. *See also* Islamophobia
Godse, Nathuram, 82, 234n153
Gokhale, Gopal Krishna, 109, 224n67
Golwalkar, Madhav Sadashiv: about the work of, 6, 60, 87, 151, 224n61; authoritarianism and, 29–32, 81, 216n44; Hindutva 2.0 and, 201–2; the literary-cultural work of, 47–49, 54–57, 68–76, 154, 230n117, 231–32nn128–29; organicity and, 32, 47–48, 212n16; Radhakrishnan and Ambedkar and, 128, 131, 145
Google, 187
Gora (Tagore), 148
Gospels, the, 108, 213n26
Goswami, Manu, 66, 227n92, 231n122
Govindadas, 120
Goyandka, Jaydayal, 153
Gramsci, Antonio, 121
Great War, 37, 40, 49
Grotius, Hugo, 21, 213n19
Grundrisse (Marx), 184
Guantanamo Bay, 197
Guha, Ranajit, 212n16
Gujarat, 166–68
Gupt, Maithilisharan, 154
Gupta, Dipankar, 171, 245n40
Gupta, Rajani Kanta, 240n54
Gupta, Sanjay, 191
Gupta Empire, 54–55, 76
Guru English, 236n163

Halhead, Nathaniel Brassey, 89
hard Hinduness, 8–9, 86, 134, 150, 158, 169, 174. *See also* Hindutva
Harishchandra, Bharatendu, 84, 111
Harivamsha (text), 117
Harun al-Rashid, 48, 76

Hastie, William, 122
Hastings, Warren, 83, 89
Hauer, Jakob Wilhelm, 30
Hayles, Katherine, 178
Hegel, Georg Wilhelm Friedrich: about the political philosophy of, 63, 94, 114, 148, 238nn28–29, 238n32; the Bhagwad Gita and, 7, 99–103, 122; and the Indian state, 32, 41, 229n103, 237n23; Schmitt and, 11–13, 20
Heidegger, Martin, 24, 148
Herder, Johann Gottfried, 30, 48
Hewitt, James Francis, 49
Himmler, Heinrich, 30, 160
Hindi, 83–85, 111, 152–57, 190, 235n156
Hindi Vardhini Sabha, 84
Hindu America (Lal), 49–51
Hindu code bills of 1955–56
Hindu College, 103
Hinduism: about, 3, 220n33, 221n40, 228n97; about political monotheism and, 1–10, 150–51; and Hindutva 2.0, 8–10, 157–207; print capitalism and, 151–56; Puranic, 36, 51–52, 78–80, 107, 112, 118, 193, 228n97, 232n140; Schmitt and political, 4–5, 11–27; and the search for Indian monotheism, 7–8, 89–151; and twentieth-century Hindutva, 5–6, 28–88. *See also* nationalism, Hindu; *specific sects*
Hinduism (Monier-Williams), 91
Hindu Mahasabha party, 6, 29, 155, 209n7
Hindus (Doniger), 224n72
The Hindu Superiority (Sarda), 49
Hindutva: 2.0, 4, 8–9, 85, 158, 165–207, 246n48; about political monotheism and, 1–5, 16–17, 23–26, 151, 209n6, 226n83; and an organismic Hindu nation, 47, 58–59, 64–87; fascism and, 24–25, 28–47, 157–66; and the Gita Press, 152–56; Golwalkar and, 47–55, 68–72, 75–76; Schmitt and, 5, 16, 19–26; and the search for Indian monotheism, 92–93, 125, 133–34, 240n74; twentieth-century, 5–6, 25–87. *See also* nationalism, Hindu
Hindutva (Savarkar), 73
Hindutva 2.0, 4, 8, 85, 151, 157–207, 246n48. *See also* advertised modernization; Modi, Narendra
The Hindu View of Life (Radhakrishnan), 125–33

Index 275

Hinduvta (Savarkar), 29
"The Hindu Way of Life" (Dandekar, Raghavan), 241n84
Hiriyanna, M., 219n24
History of India (Mill), 35, 111
The History of India (Elphinstone), 111
Hitler, Adolf, 24–25, 154, 161–62, 215n42, 215n44. *See also* Nazism
Hobbes, Thomas, 16–18, 30, 56, 211n5, 213n17
Hobsbawm, Eric, 212n16
Hollande, François, 174
Human Development Indices, 167
humanism, 11, 98, 113, 120, 147, 180, 210n1
Humboldt, Wilhelm von, 28, 237n23
Hume, A. O., 231n128
Hussain, M. F., 189

Ibn Arabi, 15
Ibn Miskawayh, 212n11
Ibn-Rushd, 236n3
Ibrahim, Dawood, 196
Ilaiah, Kancha, 1–2, 235n159
Ilyin, Ivan, 11
imaginative geography, 64–76
IMF, 11
imperialism. *See* colonialism
India. *See* nationalism, Hindu; *specific leaders*
India Everywhere campaign, 189
India in Greece (Pococke), 49
Indian Civil Services, 241n89
Indian Emergency, 25, 152, 171, 199
Indian National Army, 215n42
Indian National Congress, 25, 80, 110, 142, 163–64, 231n128
India Today, 244n29
Indic traditions, 4–6, 15, 36, 41–42, 54–56, 90, 113, 228n98
Indology, 58, 217n7, 220n33, 237n23
Indra, 50, 116, 231n123
Industrial Disputes Act, 175
industrialism, 80, 109, 133, 144, 155, 186, 204, 235n159. *See also* development; modernization
informational world, 7–8, 12, 157, 165–73, 177–90, 198–206, 246n41, 247n68. *See also* advertised modernization; Hindutva 2.0
Information Technology Act, 199
INSAT satellites, 186
International Monetary Fund, 11

Inter-Services Intelligence (ISI), 164
Iran, 15, 71–72
Irani, Smriti, 77
Irenaeus, 105
Isa Upanishad, 220n35
ISI, 164
Isis Unveiled (Blavatsky), 70
Islam: about, 15–16, 212n11; about Hindu nationalism and, 5–9, 14–16, 81, 151–52, 209n7, 226n83, 240n54; and Hindutva 2.0, 161–62, 174, 196, 199–201; India and discrimination against, 9, 18–19, 199–201, 227n92, 243–44nn26–27, 250n109, 250n112; the *Kalyan* and, 154–56; and the search for Indian monotheism, 92, 95, 98, 107, 110, 121–24, 138, 148; twentieth-century Hindu nationalism and, 34–36, 43, 48–49, 54–57, 72–75, 83–85. *See also* Muslims
Islamophobia, 3, 9, 18–19, 174, 189, 199–201, 209n7, 226n83, 243–44nn26–27, 250n109, 250n112. *See also* Babri Masjid demolition; Muslims
Israel, 48, 60
Italy, 24, 28–29, 160
Itihas Timirnashak (Sharma), 227n92
Iyer, V. R. Krishna, 244n27

Jacobins, 28
Jaffrelot, Christophe, 217n49, 244n33
Jaidev, 117, 120
Jaimini, 36, 44
Jainism: beliefs of, 36, 41–42, 220n35, 225n75; Hindu nationalism and, 66–67, 81; history of India and, 54, 225n81, 226n83, 230n117; Indian monotheism and, 90–92, 156; Karma and, 42, 45–46
Jalal, Ayesha, 212n11
Jalal-e-Ahmad, 245n40
James, William, 126
Jan Sangh, 6, 152
Jatis, 43–46, 56, 64, 123, 128, 135–38, 143–44, 222nn48–49. *See also* caste
Jat-pat, 140–41
Jat Pat Todak Mandal, 136, 139
Jats, 169, 175, 246n42, 246n45. *See also* caste
Jefferson, Thomas, 108
Jeffrey, Robin, 190
Jewish people, 13, 18, 30, 54, 60, 75, 113, 160, 163–64, 231n118. *See also* anti-Semitism

Job, book of, 220n33. *See also* Bible, the
Johar, Karan, 191
Jones, William, 50, 89–90
Judaism. *See* anti-Semitism; Jewish people
Judges, book of, 57. *See also* Bible, the
Justice Party, 230n115

Kaagar (film), 197
Kabhi Khushi Kabhi Gham (film), 191
Kabir, 44, 91, 147, 223n52
Kala, 37–38, 43, 51
Kalam, A. P. J. Abdul, 200
Kalantar (Tagore), 148
Kali, 51–53, 80
Kalidasa, 66
Kali Yuga, 51–53, 62
Kalyan (journal), 153–56
Kalyana-Kalpataru (journal), 153
Kalyan Ashram, 154
Kamasutra (Vatsayana), 39
Kambar, 40, 67
Kanbi and Patidar (Pocock), 212n12
Kant, Immanuel, 94, 114, 122, 147
Kapoor, Rajiv, 191
Karma, 36, 41–46, 60–62, 75, 113, 120, 124, 128, 223n55
Karmayoga, 36, 43, 114–16, 120, 123, 128
Karna, 40, 43, 119
Karni Sena, 165
Kashmir, 3, 25, 72, 161, 175, 199
Katha Upanishad, 220n35
Katju, Manjari, 27, 217n49
Kautilya, 31–32, 66, 218nn11–13
Kavyadarsha (Dandin), 234n155
Kejriwal, Arvind, 168
Kelsen, Hans, 213n23
Kena Upanishad, 220n35
Kesari (newspaper), 29
Keskar, B. V., 151
Khan, Sayed Ahman, 110, 240n54
Khetan, Ashish, 244n31
Khilafat Movement, 209n7
Khilnani, Sunil, 14, 211n8
Khomeini, Ruhollah, 245n40
Kierkegaard, Søren, 21
King James Bible, 108
Kishore, Giriraj, 169
Kohn, Hans, 212n16
Koran, the, 33, 104. *See also* Islam
Kothari, Rajni, 87, 158, 245n39

Krishna, 4, 7, 36–37, 40–44, 80–82, 93–95, 99–101, 107, 113–20, 223n52, 238n29
"Krishnacharitra" (Chattopadhyay), 112–18
Krrish (film), 193
Krrish 3 (film), 193
Krta Yuga, 51–53
Krttivasa, 40, 67
Kshatriya honor code, 30, 43–44
Kshatriyas, 45, 60–63, 69, 81, 130–32, 210n8, 229n100, 246n42. *See also* caste
Kumar, Shanti, 189
Kurukshetra War, 49, 117

Labour, Blairite, 12
Lal, Chaman, 49–51
language. *See* Anglophone culture; Arabic language; Hindi; Sanskrit; Sanskritization; Tamil language; Urdu
Latour, Bruno, 202
Laws of Manu, 106
Laxmana, 37, 41
League of Nations, 20
Lectures on the Philosophy of History (Hegel), 99, 237n23
Lee Kuan Yew, 174
Leibniz, Gottfried Wilhelm, 21, 100, 179, 220n33
"Letters on Hinduism" (Chattopadhyay), 115
Leviathan (Hobbes), 211n5, 213n17
liberalism, 11–14, 20–21, 24, 28, 130–32, 204–6, 212n16, 214n28
liberalization, 151, 163, 171, 187, 190, 202
The Life and Morals of Jesus of Nazareth (Jefferson), 108
Life of Mohamet (Muir), 240n54
Likud Party, 189
Locke, John, 11, 14, 18, 130, 211n9, 214n28, 217n9
Lokayata, 42, 56
Lorenzen, David N., 91–92
Lorinser, Franz, 94
The Lost Lemuria (Scott-Eliot), 70
love jihad, 163, 199
Luther, Martin, 143
Lutheranism, 38, 220n33, 221n40. *See also* Christianity

Machiavelli, Nicolò, 16, 22, 87, 211n5
Madhav, Ram, 72
Madhava, 46, 220n27

Madhvacharya, 94
Mahabharat (television series), 187
Mahabharata: about the, 89, 104, 223n54, 227n91, 229n104, 233n146; Bankim and the, 115–20; Hindutva 2.0 and the, 165, 183; Matilal and the, 36, 40, 43–44, 220n32, 222nn41–42; the organismic Hindu nation and the, 49–53, 57, 66–67, 80; television and the, 151, 157. *See also* Hinduism
Mahapurana, 223n55
Maharaj, Karpatri, 154
Mahavira, 225n81
Mahisasura, 77–82
Mahmud, Syed, 24
Mahmud of Ghazni, 226n83
Mahratta (newspaper), 29
Malamaal Weekly (film), 195
Malaviya, Madan Mohan, 51, 144
Malebranche, Nicholas, 21
Mallaya, Korra, 79
Man Singh, 225n80
Manto, Saadat Hasan, 147
Manu, 38–39, 51–53, 58–65, 69, 86, 120, 128–30, 141, 229n104
Manu, 220–21nn35–36, 228n97
Manusmriti, 7, 45–46, 60–64, 89, 100, 141, 232n140
Manuvaad, 63–64, 156, 166
Maoism, 199
Mao Zedong, 94
Marathi language, 84, 111, 239n52
Marathi madhali sthiti (Apte), 239n53
Marathis, 196, 209n7
Marg Darshak Mandal, 27
Markandeya Purana, 77
Marx, Karl, 103, 164, 184
Marxism, 140, 145, 205. *See also* communism
Mascaró, Juan, 94
masculinity: about Hindu nationalism and, 17, 23–25, 41, 52, 55, 59, 81, 86; Hindutva 2.0 and, 157, 162–63, 206. *See also* emasculation, Hindu; gender
materialism, 36, 42, 133, 154. *See also* advertised modernization
Matilal, Bimal Krishna, 6, 36–47, 117, 219n26, 220n32, 220n35, 222n41, 223n55
Maya, 36, 128, 146
Mayan people, 50, 225n75
Mayavati, Kumari, 245n37
Mazumdar, Ranjani, 190

Mazzarella, William, 184
Mazzini, Giuseppe, 24, 212n16
media, 8, 151–53, 163–97, 244n29, 244n31, 244n33, 245n37, 248n77, 249n88. *See also* advertised modernization; techno-financial modernity
Medical College of Bengal, 103
Meghduta (Kalidasa), 66
Mein Kampf (Hitler), 25
Menander, 54
Mill, James, 35, 53, 111
Mill, John Stuart, 114, 122, 214n28
Mimamsa, 90–91
Mimansa, Jaimani Purva, 242n93
Mimansasutra (Jaimini), 44, 242n93
Ministry of Health and Family Welfare, 209n3
Minto, Gilbert Elliot-Murray-Kynynmound, Lord, 98
Minto-Morley Reforms, 209n7
miscegenation, 59–63, 68–70, 130–32, 135–39, 155. *See also* caste; endogamy
Mitra, Dinabandhu, 111
Mlecchas, 52, 58, 65, 92, 227n91, 230n117
mobile phones, 167–70, 185–86, 189, 245n37. *See also* techno-financial modernity
modernization, 8–9, 85–87, 103, 108–14, 133, 158, 165–66, 174–99, 203, 207. *See also* advertised modernization; development; globalization; industrialism
Modi, Narendra: about Hindu nationalism and, 72, 213n25; Hindutva 2.0 and, 162–77, 181–82, 185, 188, 199, 205, 246n48; rise of, 3, 158, 166–77, 244n29, 244n31, 244n33. *See also* BJP; Hindutva 2.0
Mohabbatein (film), 191
Mohamed, Feisal, 23
Mohammad, 107, 119, 122, 143
Mohenjo Daro (film), 193
Moksha, 42, 95, 220n27, 220–21nn35–36
Monier-Williams, Monier, 91
monism, 3, 7, 11, 38, 94, 100, 108, 126, 219n24, 223n55
Moonje, Balakrishna Shivram, 29
Moplah revolt, 209n7
moral economy, 80, 139, 190, 200
Morant Bay uprising, 55
Mufti, Aamir, 33–34, 134, 235n156
Mughal regime, 14–15, 110, 225n80
Muhammad (prophet), 15
Muir, William, 240n54

Mukhopadhyay, Bhudeb, 111, 240n54
Mukul, Akshaya, 152–54
Mulayam, Yadavs, 172
Müller, Friedrich Max, 35, 122, 231n123
Mumbai, 191–92, 195–98
Munda, Birsa, 79
Munshi, K. M., 151
Murphie, Andrew, 166
Murthy, Narayana, 246n41
Musion, 169
Muslims: about, 15, 212nn11–12, 246n42; about Hindu monotheism and, 1, 34–35, 60, 73–76, 209n7, 225n80; discrimination and violence against, 18–19, 155, 163–69, 175–76, 194, 197, 200–201, 243–44nn26–27, 250n112; and Hindutva 2.0, 161–69, 175–76, 194, 197, 200–201; othering and, 73–76, 121, 134, 200–201; and the search for Indian monotheism, 95–98, 110, 121, 134. *See also* Islam; Islamophobia
Mussolini, Benito, 24–25, 48, 160, 215n42
Muzaffarnagar riots, 169, 245n35. *See also* Islamophobia
mysticism, 15–17, 30, 118, 127, 212n11, 223n52

Nabobidhan philosophy, 96, 122
Nachiketa, 220n35
Nagari Pracharini Sabha, 84
Nagarjuna, 223n55
Nahusa, 43, 223n50
Naidu, Chandra Babu, 173
Naidu, Sarojini, 51
Namboodri Brahmans, 69, 239n53
NAMO TV, 246n48
Nanak, 141, 147, 223n52
Nandy, Ashis, 211n8, 233n143, 234n153
Nastika, 61, 90–92
Nationalism (Tagore), 148
nationalism, Hindu: about political monotheism and, 1–5, 16–17, 23–26, 151, 209n6, 226n83; Ambedkar and, 142–43, 149; and an organismic Hindu nation, 47, 58–59, 64–87; fascism and, 24–25, 28–47, 157–66; Gandhi and, 55, 80–82, 142–44, 224n67, 233n145; and the Gita Press, 152–56; Golwalkar and, 47–55, 68–72, 75–76; and Hindutva 2.0, 4, 8–9, 85, 158, 165–207, 246n48; Schmitt and, 5, 16, 19–26; and the search for Indian monotheism, 92–93, 125, 133–34, 240n74; Tagore and, 147–49; and twentieth-century Hindutva, 5–6, 25–87. *See also* Hinduism
National Register of Citizens (NRC), 19, 161, 185, 205, 213n25
nativism, 3, 12, 25, 148, 181, 205–6. *See also* nationalism, Hindu
NATO, 28
Nayak the Real Hero (film), 191
Nazi Final Solution, 18
Nazism, 17–18, 29–30, 75, 159–61, 215n42. *See also* anti-Semitism; Hitler, Adolf
NDTV, 198
Negroponte, Nicholas, 183
Nehru, Jawaharlal, 25, 56–57, 76, 82, 88, 103, 215n42, 224n67, 233n145, 238n36, 245n39
Nehruvianism, 25–28, 124, 155
neoliberalism, 11–12, 23, 158, 164–66, 171–75, 188–89, 199, 204–7. *See also* capitalism; techno-financial modernity
Netflix, 187
Network 18, 168, 187
Newton (film), 194
Nicholson, Andrew, 91–92
Nietzsche, Friedrich, 21, 30, 49, 128, 207
Nirguna, 44, 106, 127, 147, 223n52
Nishadhas, 58–64, 227n91
Niyoti, 42, 46
Non-Aligned Movement, 28
nonviolence, 17, 42, 52, 80–82, 94, 233n146
North Atlantic Treaty Organization (NATO), 28
North Indian Movement, 109
nova effect, 206–7
NRC, 19, 161, 185, 205, 213n25
Nyak, Daya, 249n104
Nyaya school, 90–91, 219n26, 220n32

Oak, P. N., 55, 227n86
OBCS, 2, 175, 209n3, 235n159, 246n42. *See also* caste
O'Connell, Joseph T., 92
Ogilvy, David, 181
Olcott, Henry Steel, 122
organic nationhood: about Indian monotheism and, 4, 21, 26, 31–35, 43, 46, 150, 212n16; and the organismic Hindu nation, 47–48, 70, 86; Schmitt and, 3, 16–18, 31; and the search for Indian monotheism, 129, 133, 140–42, 206. *See also* nationalism, Hindu

Index 279

Organiser (newspaper), 152–54
organismic nation, 4–5, 20, 28–88, 218n15
Oriental Institute, 67
orientalism, 5, 17, 39, 49, 58, 76, 79, 91, 98–99, 109, 217n7. *See also* race
Origen Adamantius, 105
Other Backward Castes (OBCs), 2, 175, 209n3, 235n159, 246n42. *See also* caste
Otto, Rudolph, 126

Padmavat (film), 189, 193
Padmavati (Queen), 35
Pakistan, 3, 71–73, 84, 155, 161
Pal, Bipin Chandra, 123
Paluskar, V. D., 152
Pandavas, 37, 100, 227n91
Pandya, Haren, 244n31
parabasis, 9–10, 85, 88, 145, 151, 204. *See also* Hindutva 2.0
Paramanu (film), 246n48
Parampara, 34–35
parliamentarianism, 20, 24–26, 161–62, 165
partition, 6, 25, 71–72, 213n25
Patanjala, 90–91
Patanjali, 36
Patel, Sardar Vallabhbhai, 82
paternalism, 8, 26, 68, 129, 133, 143–46, 165, 192, 215n42. *See also* caste
patriarchies, 112, 121, 129, 163, 192, 234n153. *See also* gender
Paul, Saint, 214n28
Peepli Live (film), 195
People of India (study), 211n10
Pericles, 48
Periyar E. V. Ramasway, 147, 232n140
Persian language, 83–85
Phas Gaye Re Obama (film), 195
The Phenomenology of Spirit (Hegel), 238n28
The Philosophy of Jesus of Nazareth (Jefferson), 108
Philosophy of Right (Hegel), 102
Phule, Mahatma Jyotirao, 95, 232n140, 235n159
Pillai, Samuel Vedanayagam, 111, 239n53
Pindar, 94
Pinney, Christopher, 193
Plato, 70, 94, 130, 210n1
pluralism: about Hindu nationalism and, 4–5, 15–17, 21, 28, 32–34, 46–47, 159, 228n94; and an organismic Hindu nation,

46–47, 66, 87; and Hindutva 2.0, 170–72, 190, 199, 205; political theory and, 11, 21, 28; Radhakrishnan and, 129, 132, 135; Schmitt and, 14–17, 21–22, 28, 31; and the search for Indian monotheism, 129, 132, 135, 151; and twentieth-century Hindutva, 5, 46–47. *See also* Hinduism
Pocock, David, 212n12
Pococke, Edward, 49
Poddar, Hanuman Prasad, 153–56
political monotheism: about, 14–18, 59–60, 211n5; about Indian, 1–10, 24–27, 150–51, 209n6; and Hindutva 2.0, 8–10, 157–207; print capitalism and, 151–56; Schmitt and, 4–5, 11–27; and the search for Indian, 7–8, 89–151, 241n74; and twentieth-century Hindutva, 5–6, 28–88, 226n83, 234n154. *See also* nationalism, Hindu
The Politics of Aesthetics (Rancière), 247n64
Pollock, Sheldon, 45, 217n7, 224n72, 230n116, 234n155
polytheism, 4, 7, 15, 109, 126–27, 211n5. *See also* pluralism
Poona Pact, 144, 152
Poona revivalists, 123
positive ignorance, 38, 126–27
positivism, 34, 53, 95, 109, 112–14, 119, 159, 184, 206
POTA, 197
POTO, 197
Prakash, Gyan, 209n6
Prarthana Samaj, 110
Prasad, M. Madhava, 190
Prasad, Raja Shiva, 240n54
Prasad, Rajendra, 50, 154
Prathapamudaliar charitram (Pillai), 239n53
The Precepts of Christ (Roy), 108
Premchand, Munshi, 154
Prem Granth (film), 191
Premji, Azim, 200
Prevention of Insults to National Honor Act, 199
Prevention of Terrorism Ordinance (POTO), 197
Prevention of Terrorist Activities (POTA), 197
Priam, 55
Primitive Tradition History (Hewitt), 49
print capitalism, 10, 83–84, 87, 103, 111, 151–53, 189. *See also* capitalism

Progressive Writers Association, 154
Protestantism, 42, 84, 211n9, 222n45, 235n158. *See also* Calvinism; Christianity
Proudhon, Pierre-Joseph, 21
Punyani, Ram, 226n83
Puranic Hinduism, 36, 51–52, 78–80, 107, 112, 118, 193, 228n97, 232n140. *See also* Hinduism
Purusa Sukta, 45
Purva Mimansa (Jaimini), 44, 242n93

race: about Hindu nationalism and, 5–7; and Hindutva 2.0, 179–81; Schmitt and Savarkar and, 16, 22, 29–30; and scientific racism, 50, 58–59, 109, 131, 228n94, 238n37; and the search for Indian monotheism, 125, 129–32, 135–41; and twentieth-century Hindu nationalism, 47–49, 56–75. *See also* Aryanism; caste; class; gender
Radha, 80, 118
Radhakrishnan, Sarvepalli, 7, 50–51, 92–93, 125–36, 139–41, 144, 149–51, 154, 241n74, 242n93
Raees (film), 196
Raghavan, V., 221n36, 241n84
Rai, Amit, 178, 182
Rajagopal, Arvind, 157, 171–72, 188, 198
Rajagopalchari, C., 65, 124, 151, 154, 241n74
Raje, Vasundhara, 225n80
Rajogopalchari, Chakravarty, 93
Rajputs, 50, 75, 137
Rajsingha (Chattopadhyay), 112, 121
Ram, Kanshi, 235n159
Rama, 4–7, 37–41, 49, 68–70, 81, 114–15, 127, 232n140
Rama Dandu uprising, 79
Ramanuja, 94, 220n27
Ramanujan, A. K., 41, 53, 63, 77, 134, 222n44
Ramaswamy, Sumathi, 70
Ramayan (television series), 187
the Ramayana, 37–44, 67–68, 77, 115, 151, 157, 227n91
Ramcharitmanas (Tulsidas), 40, 153
Ram Janmabhoomi movement, 151
Ramkrishna Mission in Calcutta, 110
Ram Rajya, 47, 81
Ram Rajya Parishad, 152
Ramsay, Gordon, 144
Ram Temple, 161, 224n63

Ram Temple movement, 157
Ranade, Mahadev Govind, 239n52
Rana Pratap, 54, 225n80
Rancière, Jacques, 182, 247n64
Ra.One (film), 193
Rashtriya Swayamsevak Sangh (RSS), 6, 29, 47, 51, 152–54, 158, 165, 171, 176, 209n7. *See also* Hindutva; Vishwa Hindu Parishad (VHP)
Ravana, 40–41, 68–70, 232n140
Rawls, John, 11
Razdan, Karan, 192
Reagan, Ronald, 12, 174
Red Alert (television show), 198
refugees, 12, 18–19
Reliance Entertainment, 187
religion. *See specific religions*
Republic (Plato), 210n1
republicanism, 20–22, 28, 56–57
Republic TV, 246n48
Reserve Bank of India, 163
revisionism, 53–54, 62, 82, 225n80, 246n48
Rg Veda, 35, 45, 53, 82, 93, 219n24, 231n123
Rhetoric of Hindu India (Basu), 236n163
Ria, Amit, 178
Ritambhara, Sadhvi, 157
Rizvi, Anusha, 195
Rolland, Romain, 215n42
Roshan, Rakesh, 193
Rousseau, Jean-Jacques, 18, 21, 87, 130, 211n5, 212n16, 213n19, 213n27, 214n32
Roy, Rammohun, 7, 95–96, 103–12, 122, 146
RSS, 6, 29, 47, 51, 152–54, 158, 165, 171, 176, 209n7. *See also* Hindutva; Vishwa Hindu Parishad (VHP)
Rta, 45, 220n35
Rumi, Jallaluddin, 212n11
Ruskin, John, 81

Sabarmati Express, 167, 244n27
Sachar, Rajinder, 250n112
Saint Paul, 104
Saint Peter of Alcántara, 94
Salaskar, Vijay, 249n104
Salazar, António de Oliveira, 159
Salt March of 1930, 80
Sambhudan, 79
Samkhya, 36, 53, 90–91, 95, 113, 220n32
Sanatan Dharma, 34, 73, 96, 155, 237n19
Sanatan Panthis, 235n158

Sanatan Sanstha, 159
Sangh Parivaar: about Hindu monotheism and, 8, 22, 26–27, 210n8; fascism and, 161–63; Hindutva 2.0 and, 166, 171, 174–76, 188; and the organismic Hindu nation, 64, 69, 80, 225n80, 226n83; print capitalism and media and, 151–52. *See also* Akhand Bharat; BJP; Hindutva; Rashtriya Swayamsevak Sangh (RSS)
Sankara, Adi, 36, 46, 66, 94, 128, 220n27, 223n55
Sanskar TV, 188
Sanskrit, 33, 64–67, 70–71, 106, 152, 227n91, 234n155
Sanskritization, 6, 33, 82–85, 98, 114–15, 151–52, 157, 234n154, 235n159
Santi Parvan, 53, 57
Sanyasi rebellion, 121
Saraswati, Dayanand, 43, 49, 58, 93–97, 222n48
Sarda, Har Bilas, 49
Sardesi, Rajdeep, 169
Sarkar, Benoy Kumar, 24
Sarkar, Sumit, 78–79, 230n115, 239n52
Sarkar, Tanika, 119
Sastri, Haraprasad, 111
Satapatha Brahmana, 35
Sati, 103, 110, 113, 156
Satya (film), 196
Satyarth Prakash (Saraswati), 43, 49, 58, 93
Savarkar, Vinayak Damodar, 6, 24, 29, 73–76, 87, 92, 133, 145, 155, 188
Savarna groups: about, 2, 209n3, 210n8; about Hindu nationalism and, 2, 8, 41, 51, 59, 64, 68; dominance of, 156, 209n3; Hindutva 2.0 and, 157, 171, 174, 191, 198; print capitalism and, 151–52; and the search for Indian monotheism, 144–45, 149. *See also* caste; Varna system
Schedule 5, Indian Constitution, 59, 175
Schedule 6, Indian Constitution, 59
Scheduled Castes (SCs), 2, 77, 209n3, 235n159. *See also* caste
Scheduled Tribes (STs), 2, 77, 209n3, 235n159. *See also* caste
Schelling, Friedrich Wilhelm Joseph von, 237n23
Schlegel, Karl Wilhelm Friedrich, 237n23
Schmitt, Carl: about the work of, 3–5, 48, 86, 211n5, 213n23, 242n10; and Hindu political monotheism, 11–23, 131, 134, 150; twentieth-century Hindutva and, 28–31, 34, 74
School Book Society, 103
Schopenhauer, Arthur, 30, 94, 237n23
scientific racism, 50, 58–59, 109, 131, 228n94, 238n37. *See also* race
Scott-Eliot, W., 70
SCs, 2, 77, 209n3, 235n159. *See also* caste
"A Second Defence of the Monotheistical System of the Veds; in Reply to an Apology for the Present State of Hindoo Worship" (Roy), 106
The Secret Doctrine (Blavatsky), 70
secularism: critiques of, 145, 233n143; fascism and, 24–25; Hegel and, 7, 238n29; Hindutva 2.0 and, 164–66, 174–78, 199–201, 204; Schmitt and, 4, 12–14, 18–23, 78, 150; and the search for Indian monotheism, 5–8, 27, 47, 52, 87–88, 124, 132, 145–47, 209n6
Seleucid Empire, 54
Sen, Kaliprasanna, 123
Sen, Keshub Chandra, 95–96, 122, 237n17
Sen, Kshitimohan, 154
Sepoy Mutiny, 55, 95, 109–10
September 11 terrorist attacks, 3
sexuality, 19, 163, 190. *See also* gender
sexual politics, 39, 62, 121, 132, 138–41, 221n40. *See also* gender
Shah, Amit, 19
Shah, Wajid Ali, 110
Shaivas, 41–44, 94, 117, 188, 226n83, 228n97
Shakeel, Chota, 196
Shakespeare, William, 94
Shaktas, 34, 42, 44, 77, 107, 115, 228n97
Shankar, S., 191
Shannon, Claude, 183
Sharif, Nawaz, 72–73
Sharma, Pradeep, 249n104
Sharma, Raja Shiva Prasad, 227n92, 241n74
Shastras, 141, 156, 241n89
Shaw, George Bernard, 154, 215n42
Shia Islam, 15, 236n3. *See also* Islam
Shiksha Bachao Andolan Samiti, 224n72
Shiva, 39, 43, 107, 115, 223n52
Shivaji, 54–55, 142–43
Shootout at Wadala (film), 196
Shuddhi movement, 97, 142
Sikander Lodhi, 226n83

Sikhism, 15, 92, 142, 147, 156, 223n52
Singh, Chaudhary Charan, 172
Singh, Kumar Suresh, 211n10
Singh, Manmohan, 250n112
Sinha, Anubhav, 193
SIT, 244n31
Sita, 40–41
Sitaram (Chattopadhyay), 121
slavery, 75, 102, 125, 137, 144, 214n28. *See also* caste; race
Sloterdijk, Peter, 210n1
Smith, Brian, 61
The Social Contract (Rousseau), 211n5
social contracts, 13, 17–20, 30, 57, 130, 213n19, 213n27, 217n9
Social Darwinism, 58, 109
socialism, 24–25, 81, 124, 171, 188. *See also* communism
social media, 165, 169–70, 202
Socrates, 94
soft Hinduness, 9, 124, 134, 150–51, 158, 241n74. *See also* Hindutva
The Song Celestial (Arnold), 81
Sony, 187
Sophocles, 101
Spain, 16, 159
Spear, Perceval, 14
Special Investigative Team (SIT), 244n31
Spencer, Herbert, 109, 114
Spinoza, Baruch, 114, 147, 180
Spivak, Gayatri Chakravorty, 9, 138
Sramana tradition, 41–45, 49, 56, 80, 91, 220n35
Srinivas, M. N., 234n154
Star News, 198
Stiegler, Bernard, 178
Strauss, Leo, 11
Strauss, Otto, 154
STS, 2, 77, 209n3, 235n159. *See also* caste
Sudras: about caste and, 44–46, 60–62, 65, 69, 132, 135–36, 235n159, 238n36; Gandhi and Tagore and, 144–45, 149; Hindu nationalism and, 1–2, 113, 130. *See also* caste
Sufism, 15, 76, 91, 212n11, 223n52, 240n54. *See also* Islam
Suleri, Sara, 34
Sunderam, Ravi, 184
Sunga Empire, 54, 228n97
Sunni Islam, 15, 236n3. *See also* Islam
Sutras, 38

Swadharma, 43–44, 75, 82, 95, 119, 129, 137, 149
Swamy, Subramanian, 169
Swapnalabdha bharatbarsher itihash (Mukhopadhyay), 240n54
Swaraj, 80, 143–44, 155
Swaraj, Sushma, 173
Syed, Muhammad Hafiz, 154

Tacitus, 49
TADA, 197
Tagore, Debendranath, 108
Tagore, Rabindranath, 108, 111, 147–49
Tamil language, 40, 66–67, 70, 84, 111, 239n53
Tandon, Purushottam Das, 154
Tantra, 42–44, 92, 107, 115, 118, 212n11, 223n52, 228n97
Tarde, Gabriel, 202
Tarkachudamani, Sasadhar, 123
Tata, Ratan, 167
Taylor, Charles, 206, 210n1, 225n75
technocracy, 16, 85–86, 165–66, 185–86, 189. *See also* advertised modernization
techno-financial modernity, 2–3, 8–12, 85–86, 109, 123–24, 165–79, 184–95, 202–4. *See also* advertised modernization; finance capital
television, 83, 151–52, 157, 177–81, 187–90, 198, 201–3, 246n48, 248n77. *See also* advertised modernization
Templin, Ralph T., 154
Terrorist and Disruptive Activities Act (TADA), 197
Tertullian, 105
Thackeray, Bal, 216n44
Thapar, Romila, 220n27, 222n45, 222n49, 224n72, 226n83, 227n91, 228n97, 231n123
Thatcher, Margaret, 12, 174
theodicy, 7, 32, 43–46, 62–63, 100, 123, 138, 200, 220n33, 223n55
Theosophical Society in Madras, 110
Thiong'o, Ngũgĩ wa, 103
Third Anglo-Maratha War of 1817–18, 95
Saint Thomas, 54
"Three Hundred Ramayanas" (Ramanujan), 222n44
Thussu, Daya Kishan, 198
Tibet, 71–72

Tilak, Bal Gangadhar, 49, 93–94, 123, 224n67, 227n85, 230n112, 242n93
Time magazine, 197
"Tintern Abbey" (Wordsworth), 94
Tirukkural, 68, 83
Tod, James, 111
Togadia, Pravin, 72, 173
Tolstoy, Leo, 81
Torah, the, 33
Treaty of Versailles, 160
Treta Yuga, 51, 68
Tripathi, Govardhanran, 111
Trump, Donald, 3, 19, 181
Trumpian lie, 181–83
Truschke, Audrey, 226n83
Tufat-ul-Muahiddin (Roy), 104
Tulsidas, 40–41, 67
Turkey, 3, 72
Twelve-Door Thesis (Nagarjuna), 223n55
"26/11" Mumbai Attacks, 198
Twitter, 8, 169

UIDAI, 185
Ulgulan uprising, 79
UN, 28
UNESCO, 78
Unifying Hinduism (Nicholson), 91
Unique Identification Authority of India (UIDAI), 185
Unitarianism, 108, 122
United Nations (UN), 28
United Progressive Alliance (UPA), 163, 175
United States, 3, 12–14, 19
untouchables: about, 45, 61–63, 79, 98, 120; about Hindu nationalism and, 4, 82, 92, 135–39, 143–47, 155; Muslim rule and blame for, 43, 131. See also caste; Dalits
UPA, 163, 175
Upadhyay, Brahmabandhab, 96–97
Upadhyay, Deen Dayal, 32, 218n15
Upanishads: about Hindu nationalism and the, 67, 91; about the, 219nn23–24, 219n26, 220n35, 223n50; and the search for Indian monotheism, 103, 106, 120, 127, 147; theism and morality and the, 35–38, 45
Upton Lectures, 125
urbanization, 3, 8, 164, 175–76, 190, 204, 228n97, 235n159
Urdu, 83–85, 111, 147, 152, 200, 235n156
Uri (film), 246n48

utilitarianism, 95, 109, 114, 123
Uttanka, 37

Vaisesika school, 90–91, 219n26, 220n32
Vaishnavism, 34, 41–44, 54, 90–96, 107, 115, 118, 147, 188, 228n97, 240n63
Vaishyas, 45, 60, 69, 130, 210n8, 229n100. See also caste
Vajpayee, Atal Bihari, 176, 224n63, 246n48
Vajrasuci (Asvaghosa), 229n104
Valin (monkey king), 40–41, 232n140
Valmiki, 37, 40, 44, 62, 115
Valmiki Ramayana, 37–40
Vanaik, Achin, 176
Vana Parvan, 51
van der Veer, Peter, 224n67, 230n115
Varahamihira, 229n104
Varma, Mahadevi, 154
Varna system: about the, 32, 222nn48–49, 228n97, 229n100; and the Gita Press, 155–56; and the search for Hindu monotheism, 102, 128–31, 135–36, 140, 143–48; and twentieth-century Hindutva, 43–50, 53, 56–64, 68, 73, 86. See also caste
Varuna, 35
Vashishtha, 38
Vatsayana, 39
Vedanta, 36, 42, 90–97, 104, 114, 123–24, 128, 132–35, 219n23
Vedantic philosophy, 7, 36, 94, 97, 123, 127, 131, 136, 146
Vedas: about the, 219n23, 220n35, 224n63, 227n91, 229n103; and the search for Indian monotheism, 90–93, 97–98, 103–6, 113, 118–20, 123–26, 141, 146; and twentieth-century Hindu nationalism, 6, 37–38, 49, 53, 57–58, 62–65, 68, 74
Vedism: about, 225n75, 227n91, 228n97; about Hindu monotheism and, 4, 15, 219n24, 220n35; and Hindutva 2.0, 158, 165, 183, 188, 193; and the search for Indian monotheism, 92–97, 104–8, 112–13, 120–25, 131, 147–48, 153; and twentieth-century Hindu nationalism, 35–38, 42–48, 56–60, 66–68, 72–74, 78–80, 83
Veeresalingam, Kandukuri, 111
Vena, 57–58
VHP, 27, 158, 173, 210n8, 217n49, 232n130, 248n83. See also Hindutva; Rashtriya Swayamsevak Sangh (RSS)

Vidyakalpadhrum of Encyclopedia Bengalensis (Banerjea), 103
Vidyapati, 91, 120
Vidyasagar, Ishwar Chandra, 95
Vijay, Tarun, 64
Vijnanabhikshu, 91
Vimalsuri, 81
violence. *See* Babri Masjid demolition; encounter killings; genocide; Godhra incident; Islamophobia
Virajas, 57
Virgil, 94
Vishnu, 2, 37, 40, 57–58, 77, 80–82, 107, 114–15, 118–19, 232n140
Vishnu Puran, 50–51
Vishnu Purana, 66, 239n42
Vishva Hindu Parishad, 6
Vishwa Hindu Parishad (VHP), 27, 158, 173, 210n8, 217n49, 232n130, 248n83. *See also* Hindutva; Rashtriya Swayamsevak Sangh (RSS)
Visvesvaraya, M., 24
Vivekananda, Swami, 92–93, 123–25, 134, 241n74
Völkischer Beobachter (newspaper), 29
Vrindavana, 80, 118–20
Vyasa, 44, 77, 104–5, 118, 239n42

Wagner, Richard, 30
Waliullah Dehlavi, 111, 212n11
Ware, Henry, 108
Warner, 187
War of the Roses, 1412
We, or Our Nationhood Defined (Golwalkar), 29, 47–49

Weber, Max, 39, 42, 46, 221n40, 223n55
Weimar Republic, 13, 160
Weiner, Norbert, 183
Weismann, August, 131
welfare state, 9, 12, 218n11
What Congress and Gandhi Have Done to the Untouchables (Ambedkar), 144
WhatsApp, 8, 199
Why I Am Not a Hindu (Ilaiah), 1
widowhood, 103, 110, 113, 138–40, 155–56, 218n11
Wilde, Oscar, 154
Wilkins, Charles, 89, 93, 237n23
William the Conqueror, 56
Wisner, Frank, 173
Wittfogel, Karl August, 14
Wordsworth, William, 94
World Bank, 11
World Parliament of Religions, 123
Wüst, Walther, 30

Yaarana (film), 191
Yadava clan, 37, 120
Yajnavalkya, 89, 221n36, 228n98
yoga, 8, 42, 99, 118, 187
Yogasutra (Patanjali), 36
Young Bengal Movement, 103
YouTube, 187
Yudhisthira, 57, 223n50

Zachariah, Benjamin, 24–25, 162
Zafar, Bahadur Shah, 110
Zaveri Bazaar attack, 198
Zee News, 246n48
Zionism, 48, 189

www.ingramcontent.com/pod-product-compliance
Lightning Source LLC
Chambersburg PA
CBHW070755230426
43665CB00017B/2365